Hopkins2

Colin Davies with essays
by Charles Jencks and
Patrick Hodgkinson
Interview by Paul Finch

The work of
Michael Hopkins
and Partners

Hopkins 2

Phaidon Press Limited
Regent's Wharf
All Saints Street
London N1 9PA

Phaidon Press Inc.
180 Varick Street
New York
NY 10014

www.phaidon.com

First published 2001
© Phaidon Press 2001

ISBN 0 7148 3925 6

A CIP catalogue record
for this book is available
from the British Library

All rights reserved. No part
of this publication may be
reproduced, stored in
a retrieval system or
transmitted, in any form
or by any means,
electronic, mechanical,
photocopying, recording
or otherwise, without the
prior permission of
Phaidon Press Limited

Designed by
Esterson Lackersteen

Printed in Hong Kong

Introduction	Colin Davies	6
Buildings: 1989–2000	Glyndebourne Opera House, 1989–1994	22
	Inland Revenue Centre, 1992–1995	36
	Queen's Building, Emmanuel College, 1993–1995	52
	Buckingham Palace Ticket Office, 1994–1995	60
	Jewish Care, 1993–1996	66
	Saga Group Headquarters, 1996–1998	72
	Dynamic Earth, 1990–1999	82
	Jubilee Campus, University of Nottingham, 1996–1999	90
	The Pilkington Laboratories, Sherborne School, 1995–2000	108
	Wildscreen at Bristol, 1995–2000	114
	Sheltered Housing, Charterhouse, 1994–2000	124
	Westminster Underground Station, 1990–1999	130
	New Parliamentary Building, 1989–2000	136
Open House at Westminster	Patrick Hodgkinson	156
Interview	Sir Michael Hopkins talks to Paul Finch	164
Projects: 1994–	Hampshire County Cricket Club, 1994–	170
	Manchester City Art Gallery, 1994–	174
	Royal Academy of Arts, 1995–	178
	Norwich Cathedral Education and Visitors' Centre, 1995–	182
	Norfolk and Norwich Millennium Project, 1996–	186
	Haberdashers' Hall, 1996–	190
	Goodwood Racecourse, 1997–	194
	The Cakehouse, St James' Park, 1998–	198
	King Fahad National Library, Saudi Arabia, 1999–	202
	The Wellcome Trust, 1999–	206
	Evelina Children's Hospital, 1999–	210
	National College of School Leadership, 2000–	214
	University College Suffolk, 1998–	218
Hopkins Gravitas	Charles Jencks	222
	Chronology and credits	232
	Select bibliography and index	236
	Photography credits and acknowledgements	240

Introduction

In 1975 Michael and Patty Hopkins decided to build themselves a house in Hampstead, big enough to accommodate the office of their newly established practice. That house has become a classic. Two storeys high, steel-framed and metal-decked, with walls of profiled steel and glass, it is High-Tech applied in the domestic sphere. Many people would find it hard to live in, but the Hopkinses love it and there is no doubt that as a public relations vehicle and a demonstration piece for potential clients it has worked beautifully. For almost ten years following the completion of the house, Hopkins continued to develop the High-Tech idiom with ever-increasing skill and refinement in buildings like the Green King Brewery at Bury St Edmonds, the Patera standard industrial units and the Schlumberger research building outside Cambridge – the first British building to make convincing use of a Teflon-coated, glassfibre membrane structure. The practice grew rapidly and decamped to a new building in Marylebone, based on the Patera building system. Hopkins was now firmly established as one of British High-Tech's big four – the others being Norman Foster, Richard Rogers and Nicholas Grimshaw – and the architecture of industrialized metal and glass components seemed well placed to conquer new territories and new building types.

But that is not what happened. It turned out that there was, and always had been, much more to Hopkins than High-Tech. His work was changing, or rather he had gained the confidence to reveal other aspects of his architectural character. The buildings and projects illustrated in this book represent the fruits of this gradual flowering. The extent of the development can be judged if we compare the prototype Patera industrial unit of 1982 with the Pilkington Laboratories at Sherborne School completed in 1999. They are roughly the same size and were designed to house similar functions but architecturally they are utterly different. How, one might ask, could they possibly have been designed by the same architect? One answer might be that the industrial unit and the school science block are really brothers under the skin; brought up to respect the family traditions but adapting their behaviour politely to different social and physical settings. A brief for a standard factory/office building is best answered by a simple, flexible enclosure, assembled from a closed

Colin Davies

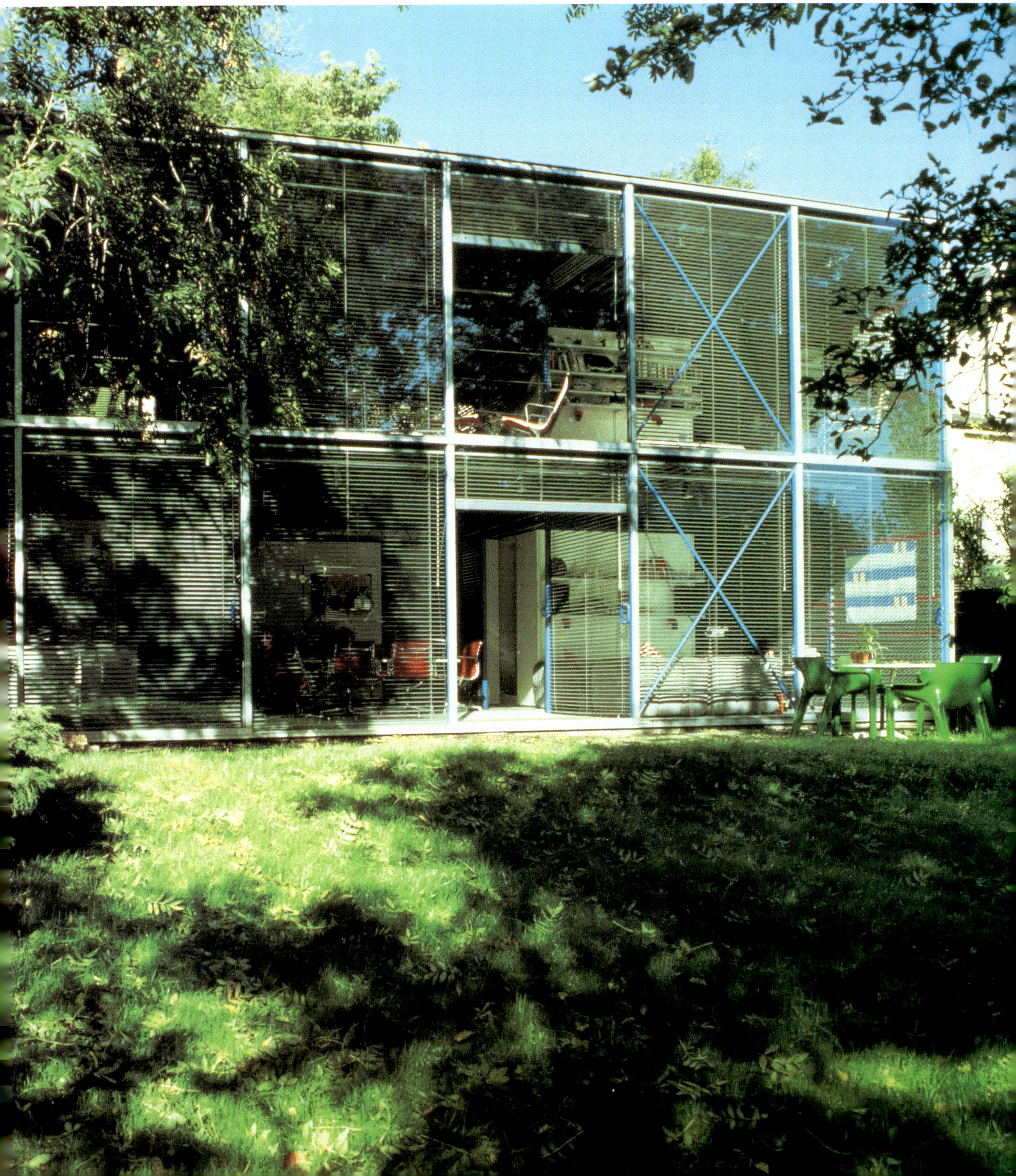

system of factory-made metal and glass components. An addition to a public school in a small Dorset town, on the other hand, demands something more solid, more specific and more neighbourly – a one-off, hand-crafted building in local stone with mullioned windows and a slate roof. The common factors are truth to materials, honesty of expression, and a logical progression from brief to building. Different circumstances call for different materials, which in turn give rise to different forms.

And yet somehow this answer fails to satisfy and the question remains: how could these buildings possibly be the product of the same design intelligence? The visible and tangible differences between them seem to be more fundamental than the abstract qualities they share. Asked how and when the apparent change in his architecture occurred, Michael Hopkins will cite the Mound Stand at Lord's Cricket Ground as the pivotal project. The street-level arcade of the existing stand, designed by Frank Verity in the 1890s, introduced him to a new form, the curved facade, and a new material – old-fashioned brickwork. He decided not just to rebuild the arcade, but to extend it to form the base of the new building. Sticking to the principles that had always guided his work, he insisted that the new brickwork should be loadbearing, with real arches, not just the cladding of a hidden frame. Having taken this first step away from rectilinear metal and glass, he was free to expand his palette of materials, and consequently his repertoire of forms. Stone, wood, concrete, bronze, lead – a feast of 'new' materials was laid out before him and he relished every opportunity to explore their potential, at first tentatively in transitional projects like the two buildings for David Mellor at Hathersage and Shad Thames, then with growing confidence in major commissions like Bracken House, Glyndebourne, the Inland Revenue Centre in Nottingham and the New Parliamentary Building.

But still the explanation seems to leave out something essential. For one thing, it says nothing about the sacrifice that was made. During the High-Tech years it was taken for granted that the new metal and glass architecture meant more than just a series of one-off solutions to specific briefs and sites. It represented a whole new approach to building. High-Tech was more than just a style or a fashion, it was a movement, and though it gave itself no name ('High-Tech' was merely a critic's label) and published no manifesto, nevertheless it was something to subscribe to, something to believe in. The essentially nineteenth-century ideas of truth to materials and honesty of expression were only part of its creed. Lightness, flexibility, indeterminacy, what Buckminster Fuller called 'ephemeralization', and above all the gleaming image of industrial technology triumphant were equally important. In setting out to explore territories beyond the boundaries of High-Tech, Hopkins was not just responding to different clients and different contexts, he was questioning a whole belief system. High-Tech was essentially a reductive style. Its approved range of materials was limited, and it ignored architectural virtues like solidity, permanence and the making of places. It was also uniform and monothematic. It only had one story to tell, and it left too many architectural possibilities unexamined. Why, for example, should the pleasures of carpentry and masonry, the sensuality of wood and stone, be excluded from the professional practice of architecture? And was it really appropriate to build the same tin shed in the differing landscapes and cultural contexts of, say, a historic Dorset town and a suburban science park?

Expanding his architectural repertoire answered a need in Hopkins that was as much personal and emotional as practical and professional. Ever since his school days at Sherborne, he has been a great tourer of the English countryside and an architectural sightseer. As well as the usual churches, castles and stately homes of the National Trust and English Heritage trails, the industrial buildings of the nineteenth century – factories, mills, maltings, breweries and boathouses – have always held a special fascination for him. They represent a pure and practical architecture, unencumbered by the stylistic preoccupations of conventional architectural history. In the early twentieth century, these brick, timber and cast-iron buildings were largely ignored by modernist historians who were more interested in steel-framed skyscrapers and concrete grain silos. But then in 1959, a book of black and white photographs by Eric de Mare was published under the title of *The Functional Tradition*, with an introduction by the distinguished critic, J M Richards. De Mare had toured the country with his camera, ignoring the urban monuments designed by well-known architects, and venturing instead into the anonymous industrial back streets, the wharves and dockyards. The book quickly became a classic and the buildings that housed the Industrial Revolution were suddenly legitimized as a source of inspiration for modern architects. Ask Michael Hopkins about the influences on his work and he is sure to mention this little book. Leaf through its pages and you will see the formal and structural prototypes of many Hopkins buildings. With these images of oast houses, pottery kilns, viaducts, windmills and warehouses in mind, the development of his architecture suddenly makes more sense. The Woollen Mill at Stonehouse in the Stroud Valley has stone piers infilled with brickwork and shallow-arched windows – it could be Glyndebourne in a hundred years time.

The Functional Tradition was supposed to be a contribution to the theoretical debate about functionalism in modern architecture. But it was the quality of the photographs, as much as the strength of the argument, that appealed to Hopkins. Eric de Mare was a true artist and he captured more than just the forms and textures of his sublime, impassive subjects. His photographs are as much about time and memory as about function, and they are touched by romantic melancholy. Hopkins is not much interested in architectural theory. The principles to which his architecture conforms are for guidance only. For him, the starting point of the design process is never an intellectual idea, always an instinctive response to brief and context – context in the widest sense, including memories, associations, traditions and cultural continuities. In De Mare's photographs he found an architecture that was functional and honest, that arose out of practical problem solving and technical invention, but that also participated in an older tradition of simple buildings built to last, buildings like the barns, manor houses and parish churches, buildings with which individuals and communities identify.

It has been suggested that Englishness is the defining characteristic of Hopkins' architecture. The practice rarely ventures overseas and its clients include some of the most ancient and venerable English institutions: Charterhouse, Emmanuel College,

Previous page:
Hopkins House,
Hampstead,
London, 1976.
Far left: Mound Stand,
Lord's Cricket Ground,
London, 1987.
Left: Masterplan for Lord's
Cricket Ground, 1990.

Top: Patera Building
System prototype unit,
Canary Wharf, 1985.
Bottom: Pilkington
Laboratories, Sherborne
School, 1999–2000.

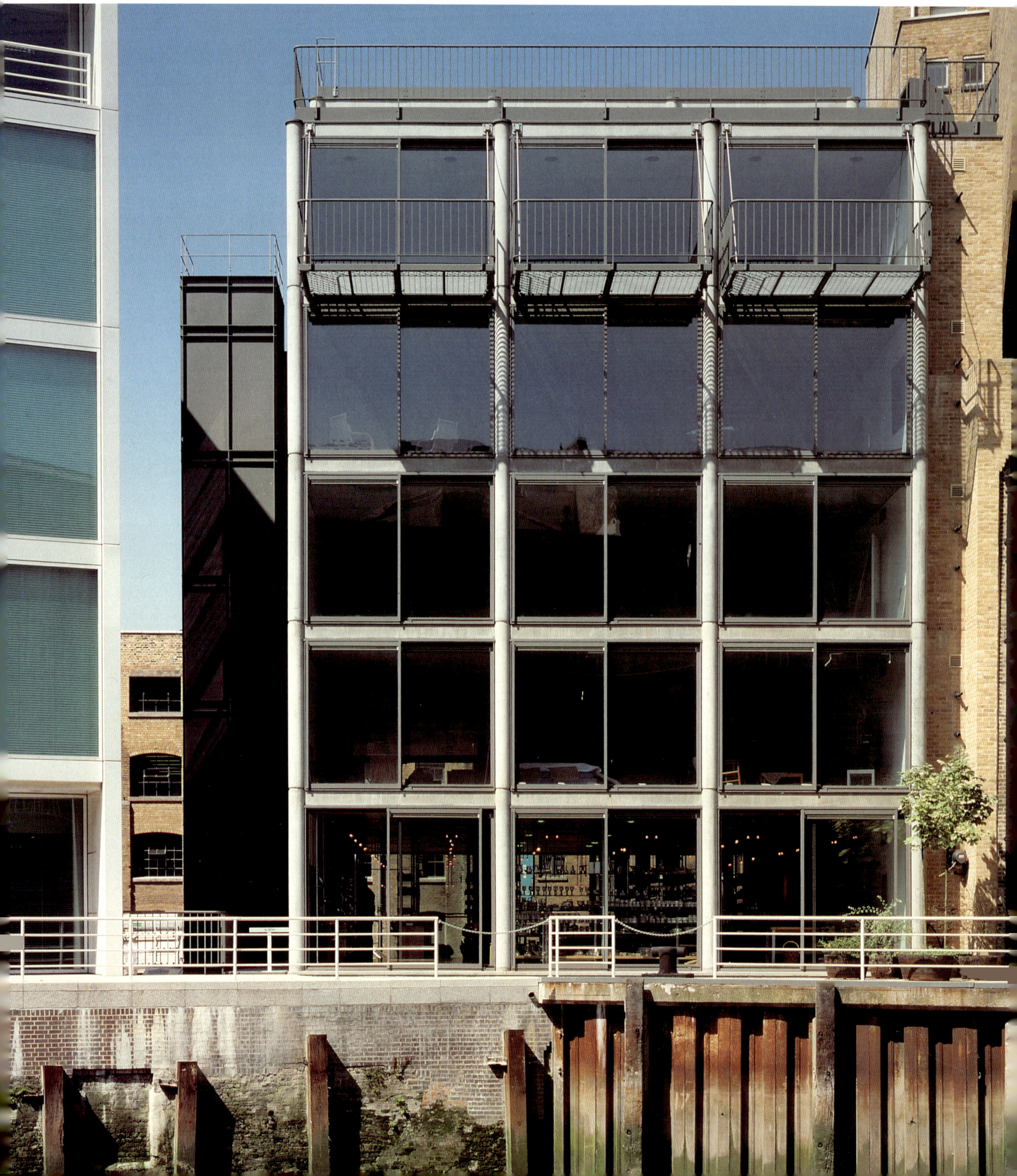

Cambridge, Haberdashers, Norwich Cathedral, Hampshire Cricket Club, Lord's, Glyndebourne, Goodwood, The Royal Academy, not to mention Parliament and Buckingham Palace. All the buildings in this book, bar one, are in England, and the exception is in Scotland. From the critic's point of view it would be neat if Hopkins himself could be characterized as the traditional English gentleman architect – an Edwin Lutyens, say, or an Albert Richardson. But the stereotype doesn't really fit. Although Hopkins admires certain Lutyens country houses (not the classical ones and not New Delhi) they can't really be adduced as a key influence on his own buildings, which are strict and orderly, rather than relaxed and picturesque. The point of his architecture is not to paint nostalgic pictures but to continue a living tradition of practical building.

It is in retrospect that barns and watermills are perceived as pretty. They were not built to be pretty, they were built to do a job, and Hopkins' buildings are conceived in the same spirit. Often they are large, unified forms that are not afraid to assert themselves in their settings, whether rural or urban; Glyndebourne is a good example. Hopkins' main rival in the design competition was James Stirling, who produced one of the best schemes of his later years, converting the old opera house into a restaurant and spreading the new accommodation over a wide area in an array of relatively small forms. It was the obvious response to a Picturesque setting – the garden of a neo-Elizabethan country house nestling in the Sussex downs. Hopkins' design, on the other hand, was not picturesque – a big, oval form, dug into the ground at the back of the house and using a matching red brick, but otherwise making few formal concessions to its rambling host. It won the competition because Hopkins realized that the client wanted the new opera house to occupy the same site as the old one. It was the kind of irrational, sentimental desire that architects often misunderstand and underestimate. But what he also realized was that there was no need to be apologetic about the massive form of the new opera house. It was a big building and it was more important than the house, so it was right that it should alter the formal balance of the whole ensemble. When Hopkins lectures about his work, he illustrates the point with a slide showing a reconstruction of a Cistercian Abbey, dominated by the simple, barn-like form of the chapel. Abbeys, barns, nineteenth-century warehouses – all share this direct attitude to building form, untroubled by aesthetic anxieties. We see the same kind of big, unified form in the Norwich Millennium Centre, an important public building imposing itself on its urban square like a Roman amphitheatre. Even the smart suited Queen's Building at Emmanuel College Cambridge – a miniature Glyndebourne Opera House – is a self-contained and self-possessed presence, refusing to be intimidated by its ancient setting.

There are, of course, many other influences on Hopkins' recent architecture apart from nineteenth-century industrial buildings and their medieval forebears. He well remembers the lecture courses he attended as a relatively mature student at the Architectural Association, some of them given by the most important historians and theorists of the day: Graham Shankland on the Functional Tradition; Peter Reyner Banham on Theory and Design in the First Machine Age (the book version of which set the agenda for the High-Tech style); Robert Furneaux Jordan on Gothic; John Summerson on Georgian London. But the architect Hopkins' teachers talked about most was Le Corbusier. For design tutors like Neave Brown and Alan Colquhoun, Corb was God and the *Oeuvres Complet* was the bible. And yet Corb, though respected and admired by Hopkins, has never been a strong influence on him.

This resistance to the influence of Corb highlights something essential in all Hopkins' work. Architects can be divided into two main types – those for whom architecture is essentially a visual art, not too different from painting or sculpture, and those for whom it is essentially a constructional art, not too different from engineering or boat building. It is a crude but useful distinction. For the visual architects the most important thing is what the building looks like. For the constructive architects the important thing is what the building is. In philosophical terms, the distinction is between the epistemological and the ontological – how things are known, and what things are. Le Corbusier, a painter as well as an architect, falls into the former category. 'The masterful, correct and magnificent play of masses brought together in light' was his definition of architecture. He admired engineering structures like concrete grain

Opposite: David Mellor
Offices and Showroom,
London, 1988–91.
Above: David Mellor
Cutlery Factory,
Hathersage,
Derbyshire, 1988–89.

Right: Queen's Building,
Cambridge, 1993–95.

12

silos not for their ingenuity or their usefulness, but for their beauty. Hopkins definitely falls into the latter category. He is not a painter, he is a builder. It would be a gross oversimplification to say that he doesn't care what his buildings look like – he does care, and passionately – but for him form and space are constructional rather than painterly. It is not surprising then that, apart from Prouvé and Eames, it was Mies van der Rohe with whom he felt the strongest affinity. Mies, too, was a builder. We associate him mainly with the architectural expression of steel-frame construction – think of the Seagram Building in New York or the Illinois Institute of Technology campus in Chicago. The High-Tech style owed a great debt to Mies, who was the first architect to expose steel roof beams on the outside of a building. (Crown Hall at IIT and the Mannheim Theatre project are examples.) The Patera industrial units and the side blocks at Schlumberger are Hopkins' High-Tech versions. But the Miesian strand in Hopkins' work continues beyond the High-Tech phase, most obviously in the steel-framed IBM office block at Bedfont Lakes of 1992, a building directly inspired by Crown Hall. At IBM we see Hopkins consciously trying to improve on Mies, using new technologies like intumescent coatings to achieve the reality of an exposed steel frame, where Mies was forced to fake it by attaching steel pilasters to concrete fireproofing. Another 'improvement' at Bedfont is the way the columns get smaller as they rise, storey by storey, in proportion to the diminishing load they bear. This is made possible by a typically neat detail – a tapered cast-steel block to effect the transition from one size to another. The detail was reused in the office block of the Saga headquarters in Folkestone of 1999.

It is arguable that, at heart, Mies was really a classicist in the tradition of Karl Friedrich Schinkel rather than a structural rationalist. But influences work in oblique ways, and are never just a question of straight copying. Hopkins is a structural rationalist and he reinterprets Mies in his own terms, which highlights another important general characteristic of his architecture, albeit a negative one. It is in his admiration for Mies that he comes closest to the classical tradition. But classicism, which values order, proportion and propriety more than constructional realities, is too abstract a discipline to exert much influence on his buildings, which are celebrations of concreteness, of the intrinsic nature of building materials, their structural characteristics and their sensual qualities.

Structural rationalism is the ground on which the Miesian influence meets the heavyweight masonry structures that are more characteristic of the recent Hopkins buildings. Bedfont Lakes and Glyndebourne were actually designed at the same time, and though superficially they are completely different, there are structural similarities. The loadbearing brick piers of Glyndebourne also taper as they rise and have their equivalent of Bedfont's cast-steel blocks in the haunches from which the flat arches spring. We can see the same detail executed in precast concrete in the Inland Revenue Centre, the Queen's Building and the New Parliamentary Building. The material varies, but same structural principle applies because they all use columns designed to resist mainly compressive forces. And there is another way in which Miesian characteristics translate into masonry buildings. There are two basic modes of construction in brick and stone. One is to build plain, solid walls, punctured by isolated and unconnected openings for windows and doors as the plan dictates. In this mode, the wall is primary, and the openings secondary. The other mode is to make the openings primary and reduce the wall to a frame, which is what Hopkins does. Ever since his first essay in brickwork at the base of the Mound Stand at Lord's, his masonry structures have always been regular, repetitive arcades of one kind or another. This regularity has classical overtones – Roman more than Greek – but it arises from a constructional rather than a visual logic. More accurately, it is the visual expression of an orderly and economical design and construction process.

A designer in the Hopkins office can spend weeks perfecting a constructional detail, like the junction between an arch and a pier, or a beam and a column. In a regular, modular structure the detail can repeated, with variations, throughout the building. And it can be applied not just to one, but to a whole family of buildings. Recent Hopkins buildings are remarkably diverse in form, structure and material, but the variation results from the reuse of similar elements in different combinations. Here are just a few examples of standard Hopkins elements and their applications: tapered

Opposite: New Square, Bedfont Lakes, 1989–92.
Above: Glyndebourne Opera House, Sussex, 1989–94.

masonry piers (Glyndebourne Opera House, Queen's Building, Inland Revenue Centre, New Parliamentary Building, Haberdashers' Hall); flat arches (Glyndebourne, Queen's Building, Charterhouse); circular towers clad in glass blocks (Queen's Building, Inland Revenue, Saga offices); curved precast concrete floor panels (Inland Revenue, NPB); lead roofs (Glyndebourne, Inland Revenue, Norwich Cathedral Education and Visitors Centre); wood-panelled external walls (Queen's Building, Charterhouse, Sherborne, Jewish Care); stone-mullioned windows (Sherborne, Dynamic Earth). And there are many more, as a careful analysis of the projects in this book will reveal. This recycling of design energy is not laziness but common sense. Every time a detail is repeated it is further refined as part of a continuous, practice-wide programme of research and development. The details become 'traditional', like the traditional details of vernacular building, or like the super-refined steel details of Mies van der Rohe.

Apart from Eames, Prouvé and Mies, the most important modernist influence on Hopkins is Louis Kahn. Hopkins has studied many Kahn buildings, both in the flesh and in books. The obvious example is the library of Phillips Exeter Academy in New Hampshire of 1972, which has arcaded external walls with tapered brick piers and flat arches, just like Glyndebourne and its siblings. Kahn's use of massive brickwork in this and other buildings (the Institute of Public Administration in Ahmedabad and the government complex in Dacca, for example) undoubtedly encouraged Hopkins in his search for more rugged alternatives to steel and glass. But Kahn's plans exert as much influence as his structures. Often, as at the Phillips Exeter Academy library, they are symmetrically disposed, the result of a process of reduction and refinement, a search for archetypal form summed up in the famous phrase 'what the building wants to be'. Many, in fact the great majority, of Hopkins buildings also have symmetrical plans. Partly this is a natural outcome of the desire to produce unified forms: the accommodation required for an opera house, for example, falls naturally into a symmetrical arrangement radiating out from the centre-stage performer. Equally, it makes practical sense for an office block on a rectangular urban site to be arranged symmetrically around a courtyard, as at the

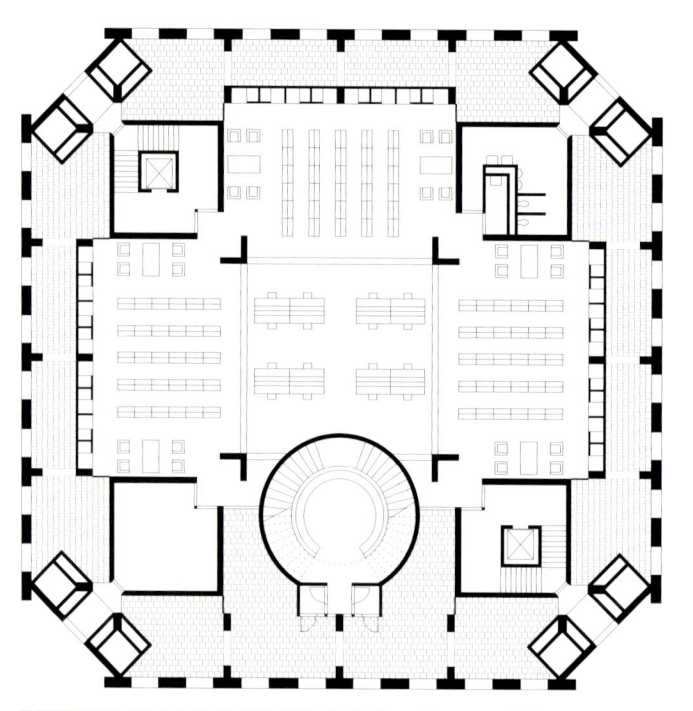

Above and left: Louis Kahn, Phillips Exeter Academy, New Hampshire, 1965–72. Opposite: New Parliamentary Building, Westminster, London, 1989–2000.

New Parliamentary Building – it would be perverse to force an artificial asymmetry on these traditional institutional forms. But Hopkins is prepared to admit that symmetry can sometimes be merely a compositional habit. He worries about symmetry, and he regularly goes back to Kahn to try to fathom the mysteries of archetypal form.

In a Hopkins plan, clarity and legibility are the watchwords. Internal spaces, like the external volumes they occupy, tend to be simple, unified and discrete. Small rooms, such as the cellular offices of the New Parliamentary Building, are regular and repetitive, like the structural elements that define them, and they relate to one another in logical groupings along well-defined circulation routes. There is no attempt to introduce variety for its own sake. In a Hopkins building, you always know where you are, which way you are supposed to go and when you have arrived. The legibility of the plan is often enhanced by the legibility of the structure, which is always and everywhere visible. The straight corridors of NPB for example, which could easily have been airless, artificially lit tunnels, are spatially transformed by frameless glass panels above door head height. It is not just that these panels borrow daylight from the offices on either side, but they show the curved soffits of the precast concrete floor units spanning right across the building. Corridor and offices are revealed as the subdivisions of a larger space. You see the wavy ceiling, you see the daylight, you know where you are. Larger public or social spaces are well-proportioned volumes, each with a distinctive character. The covered courtyard of NPB is typical. Its central position and glazed diagrid roof, through which the rest of the building is visible, distinguish it as a space of special importance. Quasi-external social spaces, such as this, have been a common feature of Hopkins buildings ever since the planning breakthrough of the Schlumberger building in Cambridge, with its low side blocks and high tented centre. Sometimes the social space is subsumed within the building form, like the NPB courtyard or the atria of the faculty buildings on the Jubilee Campus at Nottingham, but sometimes it breaks free and becomes a separate building. Often that building, following the precedent of Schlumberger, is a tent.

Hopkins is known for his tents even more than for his rediscovery of loadbearing masonry. There is a whole family of them: Inland Revenue; Saga; Dynamic Earth; Wildscreen; Hampshire Cricket Club; Goodwood racecourse – not to mention dozens of secondary applications as canopies and sunshades. Usually they denote social space, space in which to gather, eat, play and party. But how can these light, flamboyant structures be reconciled architecturally with the heavy seriousness of Hopkins' other buildings? Like the High-Tech style with which they were first associated, they seem to represent a completely different sensibility. They look like alien invaders, huge albino bats come to settle, wings folded, among the earthbound indigenous population. The reason they have adapted so well, thrived and evolved, is that their playful forms and light materials are well suited to their function. For these large volumes, it would be clumsy and wasteful to provide solid, fully insulated enclosures. The activities they house do not require a constant air temperature of 20 degrees Celsius. Intermittent radiant heating, cheap to install and run, is perfectly adequate and the enclosure can therefore be reduced to a thin, translucent membrane. The lightness of the tents emphasizes the solidity of the 'host' buildings. At Dynamic Earth, for example, the tent sits on its stone base like a piece of sculpture on a plinth – the one part would make no sense without the other. Contrast heightens perception. At the Inland Revenue Centre, the tent provides the necessary focus, both visual and social, for the repetitive surrounding buildings and the community they house. At Saga, tent and office building complement one another and give architectural expression to the client's socially responsible policies. Another way to look at these relationships is in terms of the ever-present theme of structural rationalism. If the masonry structures, with their tapered piers and real arches, represent the architecture of compression, then by the same logic the tents, with their double-curved membranes and suspension cables, represent the architecture of tension. These are balanced opposites and they belong together.

Though the tents are obviously members of the same family, they nevertheless have strong individual characters. The High-Tech habit of exposing structural members, in this case masts and cables, on the outside of the building is carried over from Schlumberger to the Inland Revenue sports centre, even though the adjacent office buildings have begun to speak a different architectural language. Dynamic Earth also allows its eight masts to dominate the scene. But, in the Saga tent, the species has mutated. The masts have disappeared, their place taken by tubular steel bows, stretching the membranes like the bones of pterodactyl wings. And whereas its predecessors are inward looking and doubly symmetrical, this particular animal responds to the sunlight, turning its gaze towards the marine horizon. Its weird forms might be taken for mere constructed doodles, the playful products of a fertile visual imagination, but this is a false impression. Membranes curve and bones bend no more than is necessary to contain the forces within the structure. And though Hopkins' tents may have some affinity with the technology of wind power, they are not designed to look like sailing ships.

The combination of light and heavy construction has implications for environmental performance. Energy-saving by passive means, using the static form and structure of the building, has in recent years become an office tradition. Hopkins admits that he was not the originator of this tradition. It was the next generation of designers in the office – a generation trained to think green – that introduced him to the possibilities of low-energy architecture. The New Parliamentary Building, the first designs for which date back to 1989, though it was not finished until 2000, was the practice's first major low-energy exercise. European Union research funds were applied for and it became a 'demonstration project'. Almost every major element of the building has a part to play in the tempering of the internal climate: the shallow plan makes maximum use of the daylight; the 'light shelves' reduce solar heat gain while reflecting light up onto the ceiling; the heavy structural elements, in particular the precast concrete floor units, help to even out internal temperature fluctuations; and, most visibly, the fourteen bronze chimneys are the exhaust terminals of a comprehensive fan-assisted natural ventilation system. The building demonstrates the two fundamental principles of low-energy architecture: first, natural ventilation using ambient heat energy to move air by the 'stack effect'; and second the judicious combination of lightweight, energy-receiving elements with heavyweight, energy-storing elements. The research carried out on NPB has informed almost all of the practice's buildings ever since. Structural rationalism has always been a major theme in Hopkins' work and now it is accompanied by what might be called 'environmental rationalism'. The effect on building form has been profound, from the glass block stair turrets-cum-chimneys of the Inland Revenue Centre and the 'oast houses' of the Jubilee Campus, to the ETFE-tented greenhouse of Wildscreen and the aerodynamic curved roofs of the Evelina Hospital. Hopkins has seized upon the passive energy theme as an opportunity to extend his architectural vocabulary. It offers a functional justification for the use of heavyweight, traditional materials, the materials that were anathema to High-Tech.

Hopkins and his colleagues love building materials. They hunt for them, play with them, enjoy their sensual qualities, test them to destruction, research their histories, discover their origins, and, of course, make things with them. A profound knowledge and appreciation of materials is fundamental to Hopkins' architecture. Perhaps it always was. It was always important to know, for example, exactly how a pressed steel panel was made, how big it could be, what profiles and finishes were possible and how long it would last. Components were never just chosen out of catalogues. The factory would have to be visited and the specialists interrogated. Now that the High-Tech restrictions have been lifted, the materials game has become something like a collective office obsession. The task of choosing a type of stone, for example, will involve a grand tour of quarries at home and abroad. Rock beds will be scrutinized, colours and textures compared, samples gathered and mock-ups made. The same is true when it comes to bricks. First the right clay will have to be found. Nottingham's clay beds were worked out years ago, but a geologically identical source was found in Cumbria to make the bricks for the Inland Revenue Centre. Then there is the method of manufacture to be decided – in this case the bricks were fired in coal-fuelled kilns to achieve the right colour and texture. At Glyndebourne, the bricks were made in old-fashioned imperial sizes to match the house.

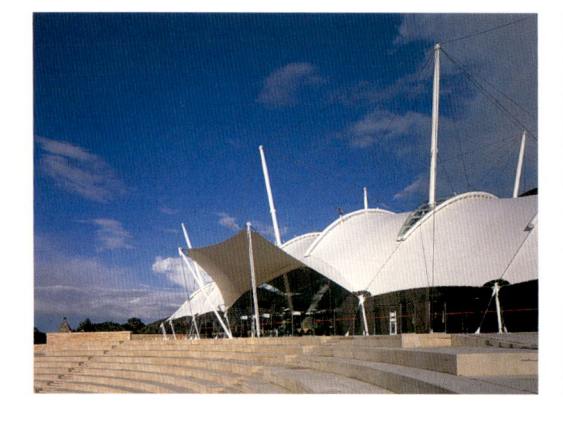

Far left: Dynamic Earth, Edinburgh, 1990–1999.
Left: Saga Headquarters, Folkestone, 1996–1998.

Above: Schlumberger Cambridge Research Centre, Cambridge, 1982–1992.

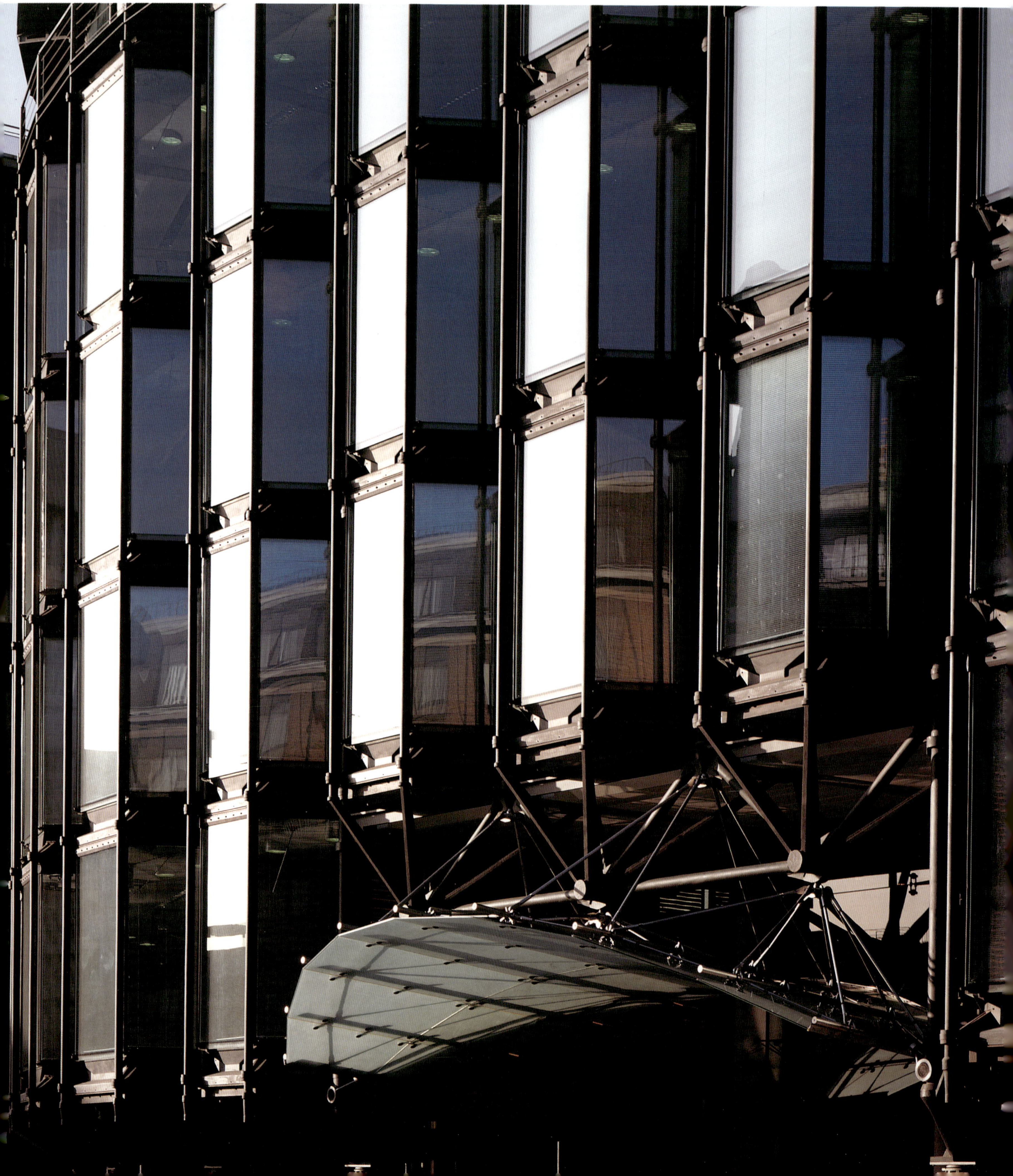

Piers and arches of brick or stone almost always function as true loadbearing elements in the finished building, but they are not necessarily built in the traditional way. Craftmanship is important but prefabrication saves time and improves quality. The piers of the Inland Revenue Centre were built by trained bricklayers, who were working in a clean, dry factory, not on a wet, muddy site. The bricks were laid around stainless-steel rods so that they could be lifted onto a lorry. A similar technique was used at NPB and the Queen's Building, where the piers were prestressed and post-tensioned. And just as a typical High-Tech building makes an architectural display of its method of assembly, so the prefabricated nature of the piers is signalled by the precast concrete pads at each floor level and the circular metal eyes that allow access to the tensioning nuts.

Similarly obsessive is the care taken in the sourcing and working of all the other materials that make up the new, expanded palette: in situ and precast concrete, cast steel, oak, cedar, plywood, lead and, most interestingly and daringly, bronze. The practice discovered aluminium bronze in Albert Richardson's Financial Times building, which became Bracken House in 1992. Stronger than steel, and highly resistant to corrosion, aluminium bronze is commonly used to make gun mountings (it is sometimes called 'gunmetal'), propellers, pump casings, binnacles and other marine fittings. It can be cast, extruded or rolled into sheets. Richardson used it for window frames and spandrel panels and Hopkins used it in all three forms for the brackets, columns and cladding panels of Bracken House's new bay-windowed facades. It is easy to see why the material should have appealed to Hopkins at that stage in his career; self-finished, richly coloured and long lasting, it is High-Tech but without the industrial associations. One thinks of antique sculpture rather than tin sheds. From the start the New Parliamentary Building was conceived in terms of stone and bronze. The steeply pitched roof with its fourteen chimneys is machine-like but also heraldic. It can be seen as a purely functional element, but when burnished and weathered it will be a shining crown.

We have seen how the passive energy strand in Hopkins' work was initiated by the younger generation in the practice.

How much, then, does the enrichment of his architecture owe to his fellow directors? The most senior of these is Bill Taylor, who has worked with Michael and Patty for more than twenty years. This triumvirate has now been joined by Andy Barnett, Jim Greaves and David Selby, with Pam Bate taking responsibility for interior design work. In addition there is a group of ten project directors, most of whom have been with the practice for ten years or more. And we must not forget former directors who left to set up their own practices – John Pringle, Ian Sharratt, Bill Dunster and Peter Romaniuk. In talking to these people, it is clear that they were, and are, allowed a large measure of design freedom. They can reasonably claim at least partial authorship of many of the practice's buildings. But it is also clear that design always proceeds according to office standards and traditions. Important design decisions, including those at the level of constructional detail, are never taken without Hopkins' personal scrutiny and approval. He works like a newspaper editor, deciding policy, supervizing production, guiding innovation and regularly contributing his own creative work. A Hopkins building is still a Hopkins building.

When asked where his architecture goes from here, Michael Hopkins chooses the Jubilee Campus for Nottingham University to represent a hopeful future. A relaxed arrangement of relatively simple buildings, juxtaposing ordinary in situ concrete with lightweight, prefabricated steel and timber components, it is hardly typical of the practice's recent work for grander and wealthier clients. Perhaps the economical simplicity of those early essays in High-Tech, never far below the surface, is beginning to reassert itself. In the end, however, the gradual sea change apparent in Hopkins and Partners' work over the last fifteen years cannot really be explained in conventional critical terms. Influences and circumstances, continuities and discontinuities, consistencies and contradictions all intersect in a complex weave rather than a simple linear progression. A new style has emerged and is now firmly established. It is not part of any movement, it bears no label and it has no imitators. Hopkins' architecture is on the move again.

Opposite: Bracken House, City of London, 1987–92.
Above: Prefabricated piers of Inland Revenue, Nottingham, 1992–95.

Right and overleaf: Jubilee Campus, University of Nottingham, 1996–99.

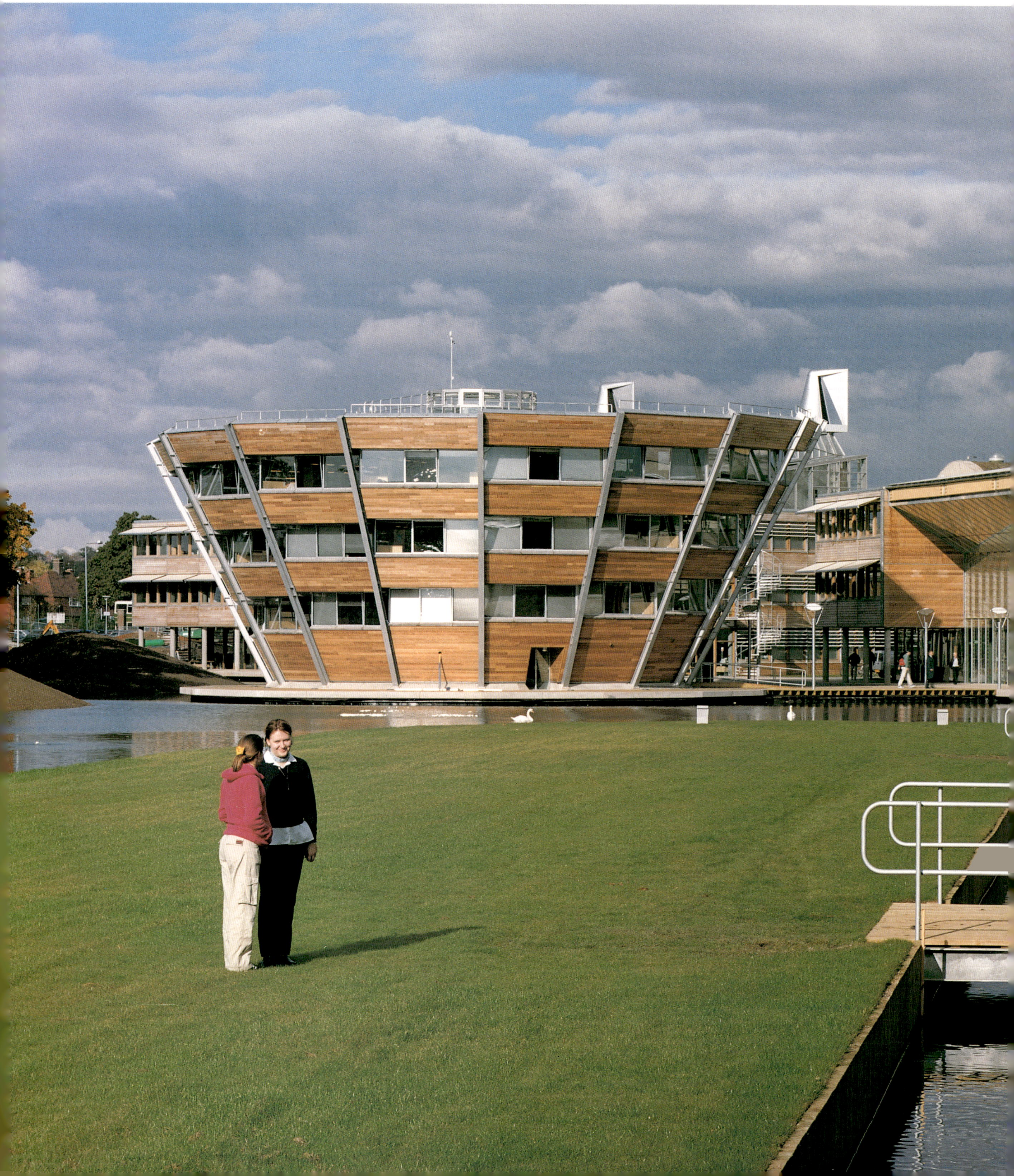

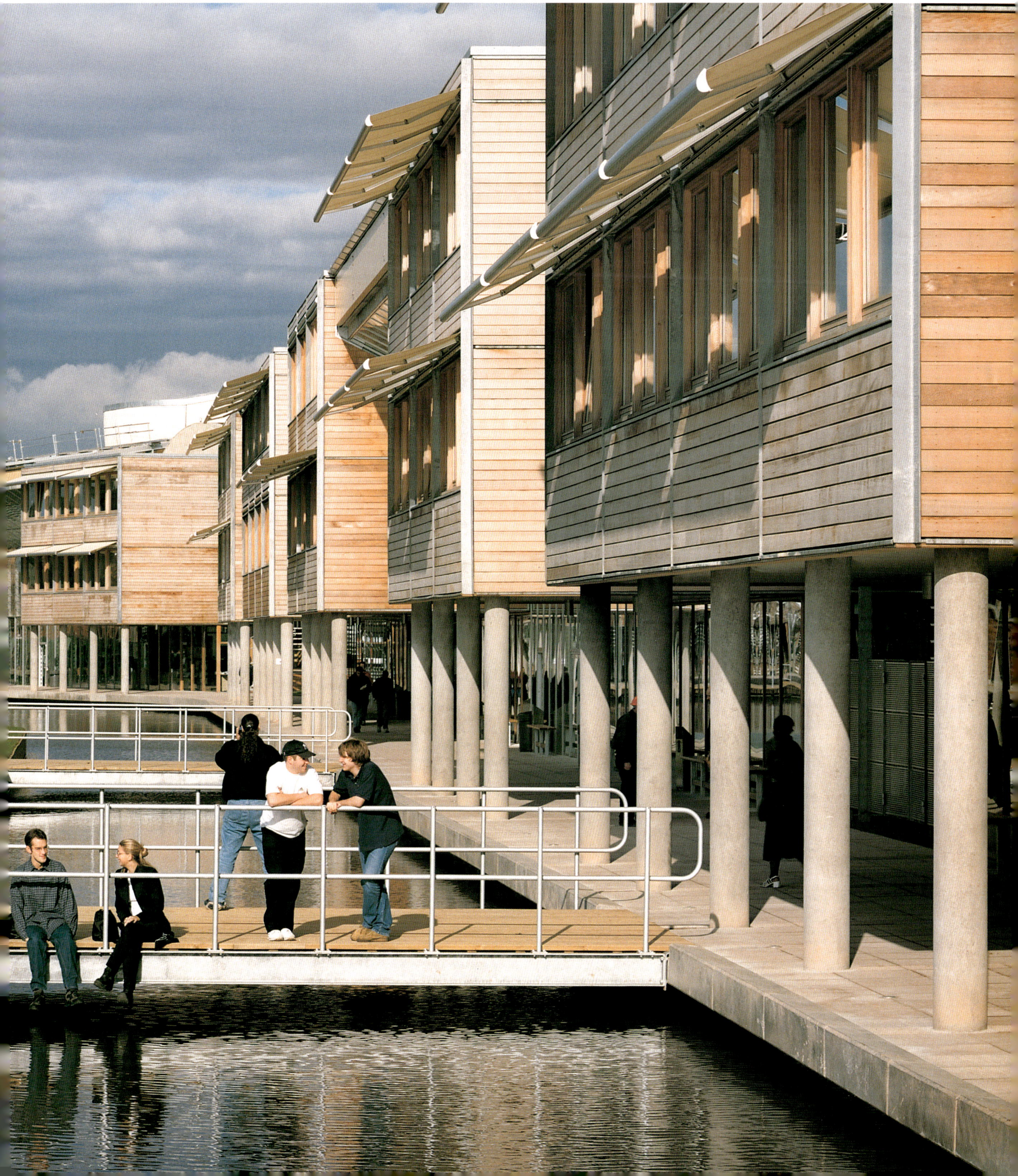

Glyndebourne Opera House 1989–1994

Almost every summer since the 1930s, a six-week season of opera has been staged at a country house near the Sussex village of Glyndebourne. The old auditorium seated 800 people in far from ideal conditions, but any discomfort suffered was balanced by the quality of the performance and the pleasure of picnicking in the garden during the interval. The new opera house, which seats 1,200 people, is designed to banish the discomfort without destroying the country house party atmosphere. It takes the form of a unified, freestanding building, sited close to the back of the picturesque, neo-Elizabethan house. It is oval in plan, with shallow pitched roofs and a prominent central fly tower. Only the rehearsal stages, dug into rising ground at the north end of the site and linked to the backstage area by a short umbilical corridor, are excluded from the enveloping oval. A yard between the house and the new building serves as a turning circle and drop-off point. From here, opera-goers filter into an open arcade surrounding the auditorium end of the oval. Since this is a building for summer use only, there is no need for a large enclosed foyer. There is no portico or front door, only a modest fabric canopy, with frameless glass end walls, stretched between the main bulk of the new building and a single-storey existing building converted into a bar. Space flows out freely into the adjacent gardens that are such an important part of the Glyndebourne tradition.

Auditorium, stage, fly tower, wings and backstage area are disposed axially within the oval perimeter. Smaller spaces, such as dressing rooms, green room, studios, offices, staircases and WCs, are stacked up to three storeys and wrapped around the building. This simple arrangement, with a continuous 'racetrack' corridor on each level, makes the plan easily legible for performers and audience alike. It also insulates the auditorium and stage from the noise of passing aeroplanes. The windows of the smaller spaces, and the open galleries at the auditorium end, give views out and scale and proportion to the exterior of the building. The auditorium takes the traditional European opera house form, with a gently raked bank of stalls and three horseshoe-shaped balconies; all housed in a double-skinned circular drum with a shallow conical roof. Although the form is traditional, it was arrived at by a logical analysis of sightlines and acoustic qualities. The effect is relatively small-scale and intimate. At the furthest point, the back wall is actually 2 metres closer to the proscenium arch than that of the original auditorium. Wood, mainly reclaimed pitch pine, is the dominant material inside the auditorium. Walls are mostly panelled, floors are boarded and balconies have wooden fronts with special curved profiles to reflect the sound from the stage. All of the wood has a natural waxed finish, and is without plaster or paint throughout. The ceiling and the balcony soffits are precast concrete, slightly coffered, with an exceptionally smooth self-finish.

The auditorium has a composite structure of concrete and steel, contained

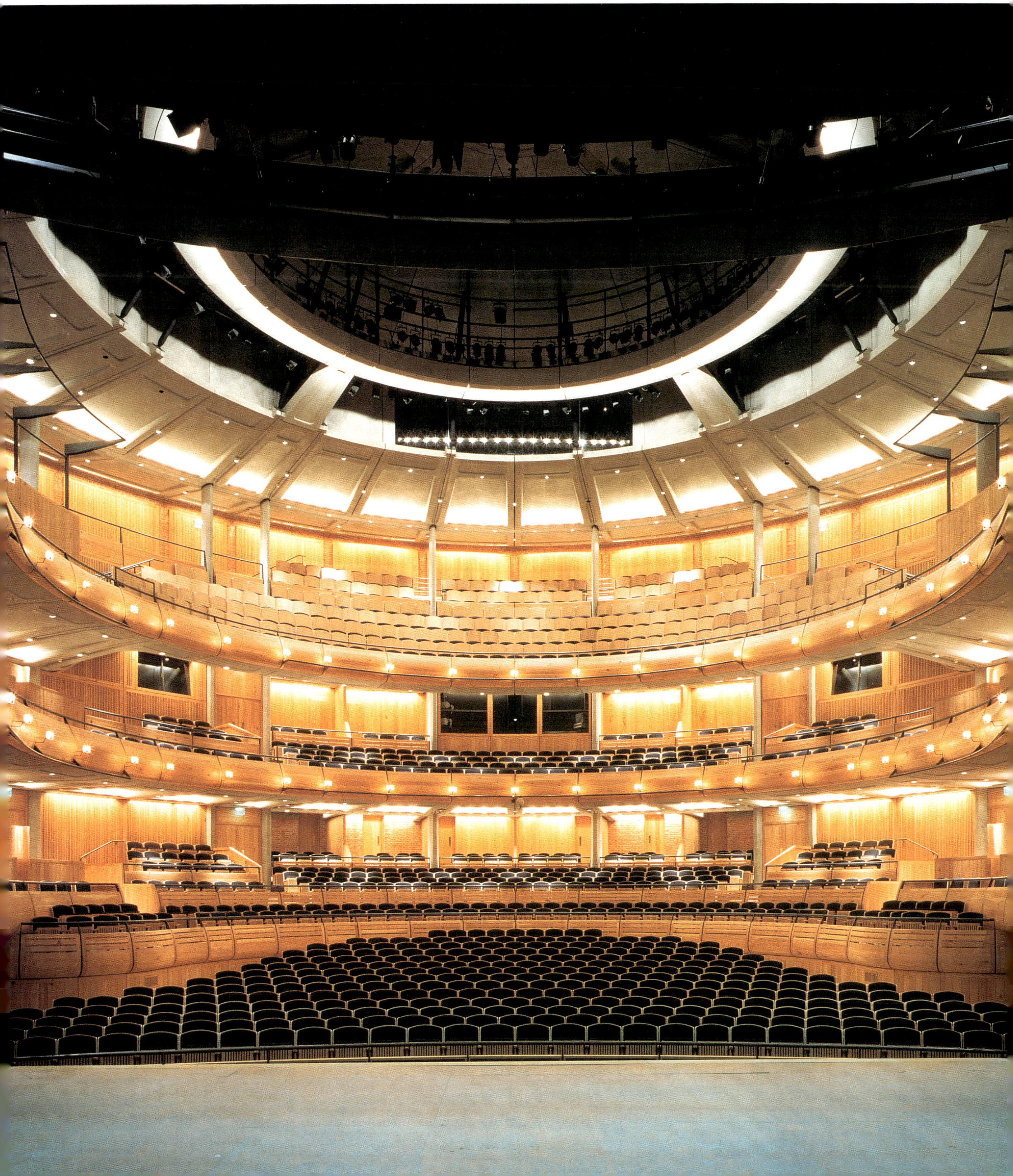

Previous page: the 1,200-seat auditorium takes on the form of the traditional European opera house, with a gently raked bank of stalls and three horseshoe-shaped balconies.

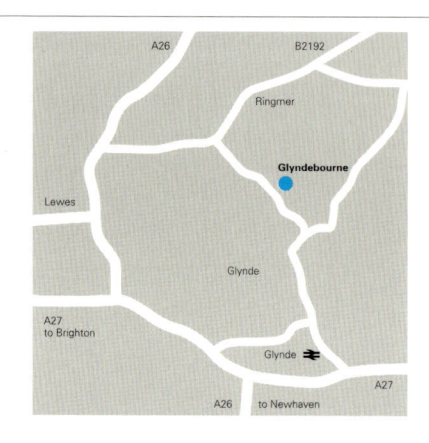

within a loadbearing brick drum of two 220-millimetre thick skins with a 50-millimetre cavity. Steel roof trusses are supported by the upward extensions of the slender concrete columns supporting the balconies. Tied back to the brick drums, they cantilever radially towards the centre, where they are joined by a 3-metre diameter ring beam. The precast ceiling units are suspended from these trusses. At the proscenium arch, the auditorium drum and its conical roof are interrupted by the fly tower, which adopts a completely different structural principle. Four corner columns, half concrete and half steel, support heavy steel trusses exposed externally at the top of the tower. The lead-clad, precast concrete walls of the tower are suspended from this frame in steel grids that also support the surrounding roof. The two columns furthest from the auditorium are, therefore, the only physical obstructions in the whole stage, backstage and wings area. All roofs, with the exception of the flat roof of the fly tower, are made from prefabricated, lead-covered plywood panels, laid in a stepped configuration.

Brick is the dominant material in the three-storey band of ancillary spaces that surrounds the whole building. A Hampshire red brick, handmade in old imperial sizes and laid in English bond, was chosen to match the old house. All brickwork is fair face, inside and out, and expansion joints are avoided by the use of old-fashioned, lime putty mortar. This is a true loadbearing structure, not the cladding of a hidden frame. A two-storey arcade of massive brick piers and flat arches is sometimes infilled by windows, and sometimes left open. Floors are of precast concrete, with the ends of the main beams showing through on the outer face of the piers. The soffits of the floor panels between the beams are exposed, with a finish similar to those in the auditorium. On the top storey, where there is only a relatively light roof to support, the structural system changes. Floor beams project from the facade to support slender, round steel columns that, in turn, support tapered timber 'flitch' roof beams. The galleries and ground-floor arcades at the auditorium end of the building serve as additional foyer spaces, open to the fresh air but sheltered from the rain.

Quiet mechanical services are mainly hidden away in the extensive basement, while noise-generating plant is housed in a separate neighbouring building. Ventilation plant, housed at the backstage end of the building, draws fresh air down from the roof level and sends it through horizontal sound-proof concrete ducts to risers in the perimeter wall of the auditorium. From here, it travels into the floor plenums and is discharged through the perforated metal pedestals of the seats. Stale warm air rises by convection and is extracted at roof level. Acoustically, the reverberation characteristics of the auditorium are carefully and deliberately tuned to resolve the conflicting requirements inherent in opera: the richness and sonority appropriate to the orchestral sound, and the dryness and clarity that suits the human voice.

Left: site plan showing roof. The new opera house occupies the same site as the old one, although backstage and front-of-house areas have been reversed, bringing the foyers down to the garden.

Below: the building is dug into the ground to reduce its apparent bulk, but it is still a large presence in the Sussex landscape.

1 main entrance
2 car park entrance
3 foyer
4 auditorium
5 stage
6 rehearsal stages
7 loading bay
8 restaurant
9 house
10 Mildmay Hall
11 car park

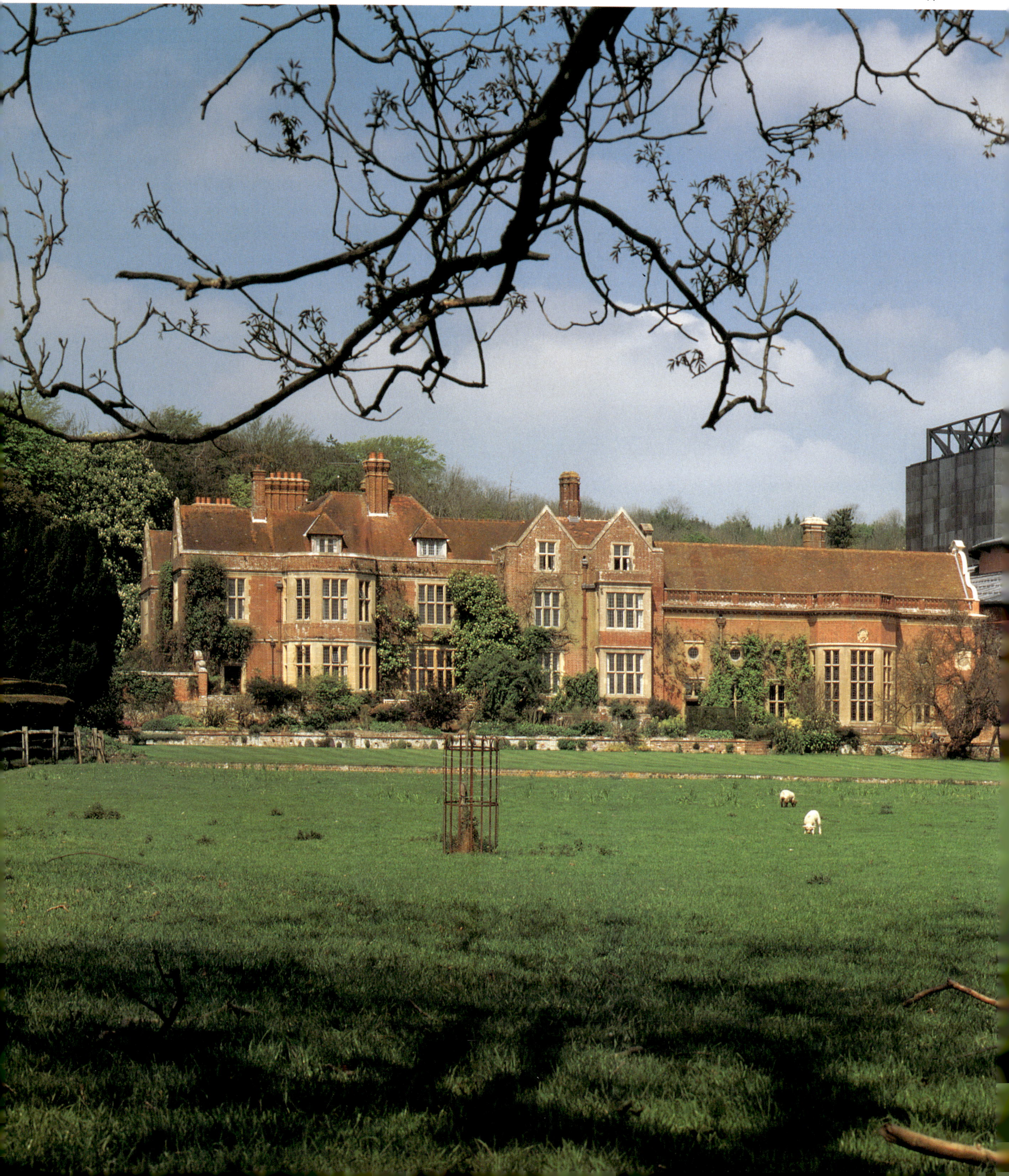

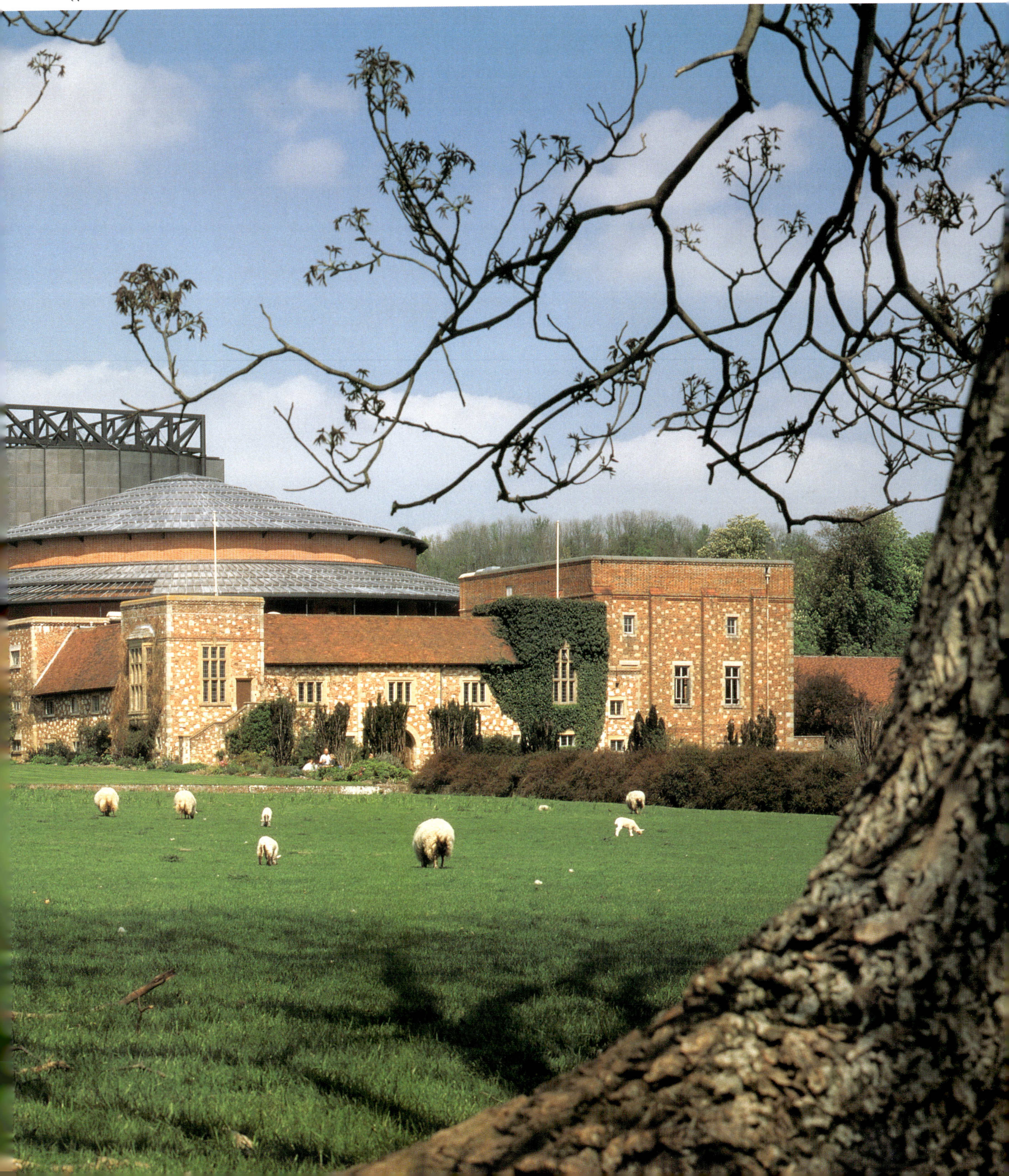

Previous page: with its lead-clad fly tower and conical auditorium roof, the new opera house has become the dominant member of the family of buildings, including the house on the left and the old backstage building on the right.

Below: longitudinal section and view from the east. The foyer and auditorium are on the left, the fly tower is in the centre and the semicircular backstage area is to the right.

Opposite: the handmade, red Hampshire bricks of the new building were specially made in imperial sizes and almost perfectly match those of the old house.

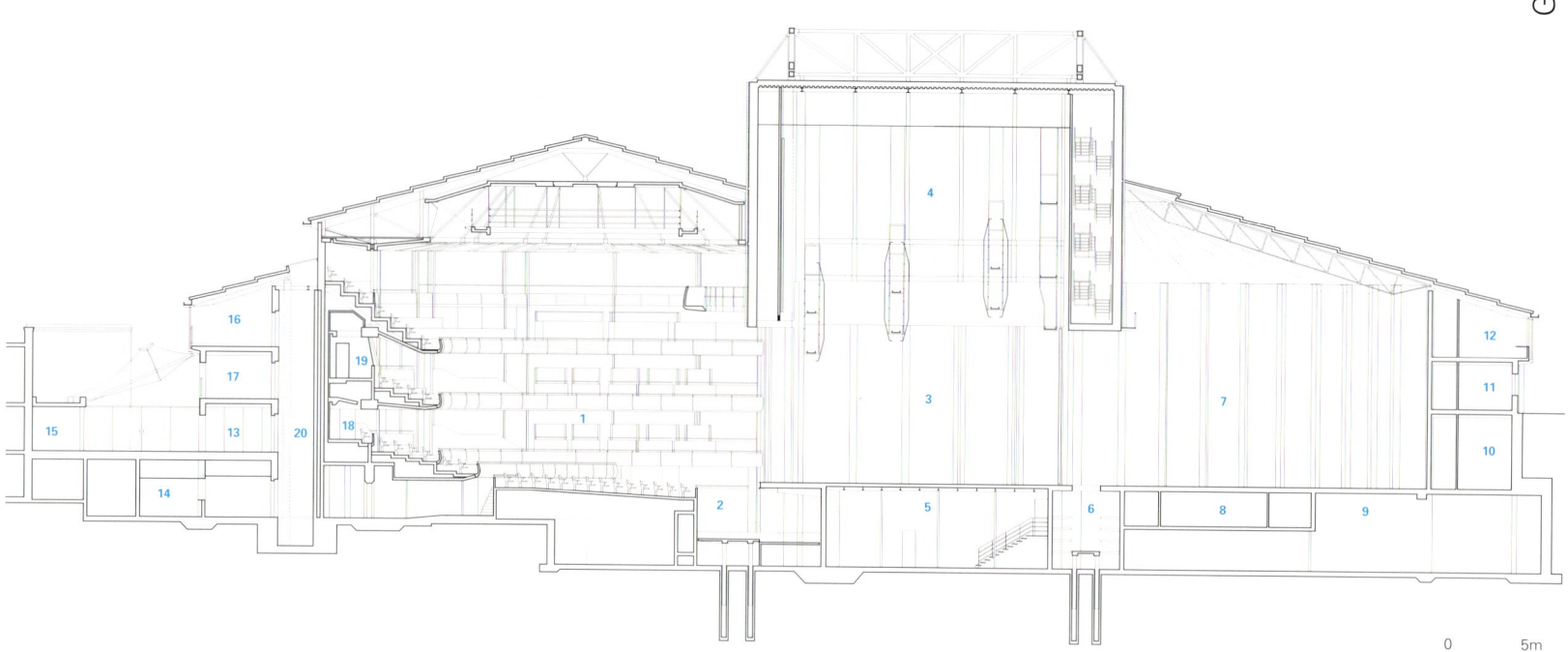

Glyndebourne Opera House

Longitudinal section

1 auditorium
2 orchestra pit
3 stage
4 flytower
5 understage
6 cloth store
7 backstage
8 storage
9 plant
10 warm-up
11 offices
12 workrooms
13 foyer
14 cloakroom
15 bar
16 upper circle balcony
17 circle balcony
18 box
19 control suite
20 lift

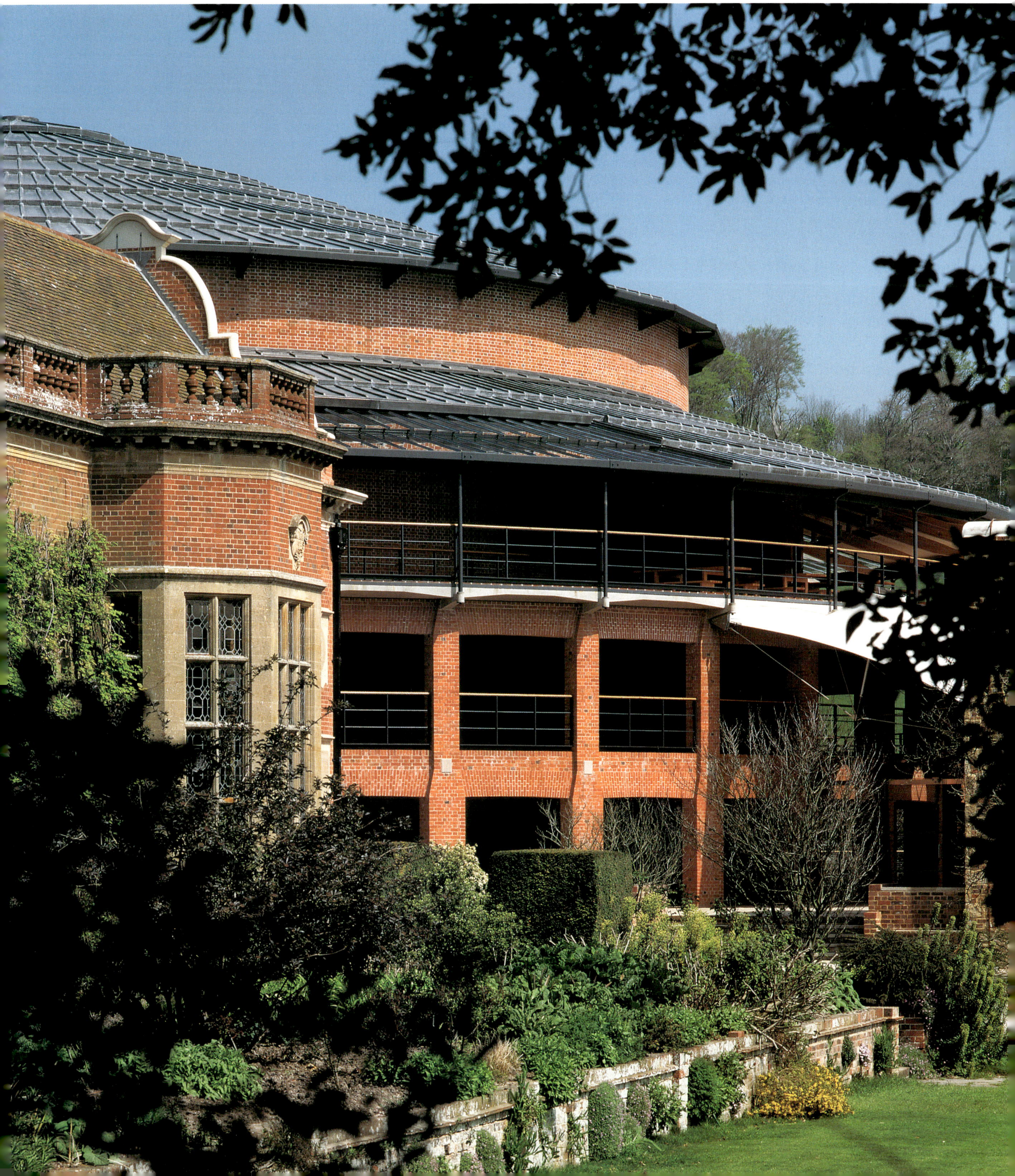

30

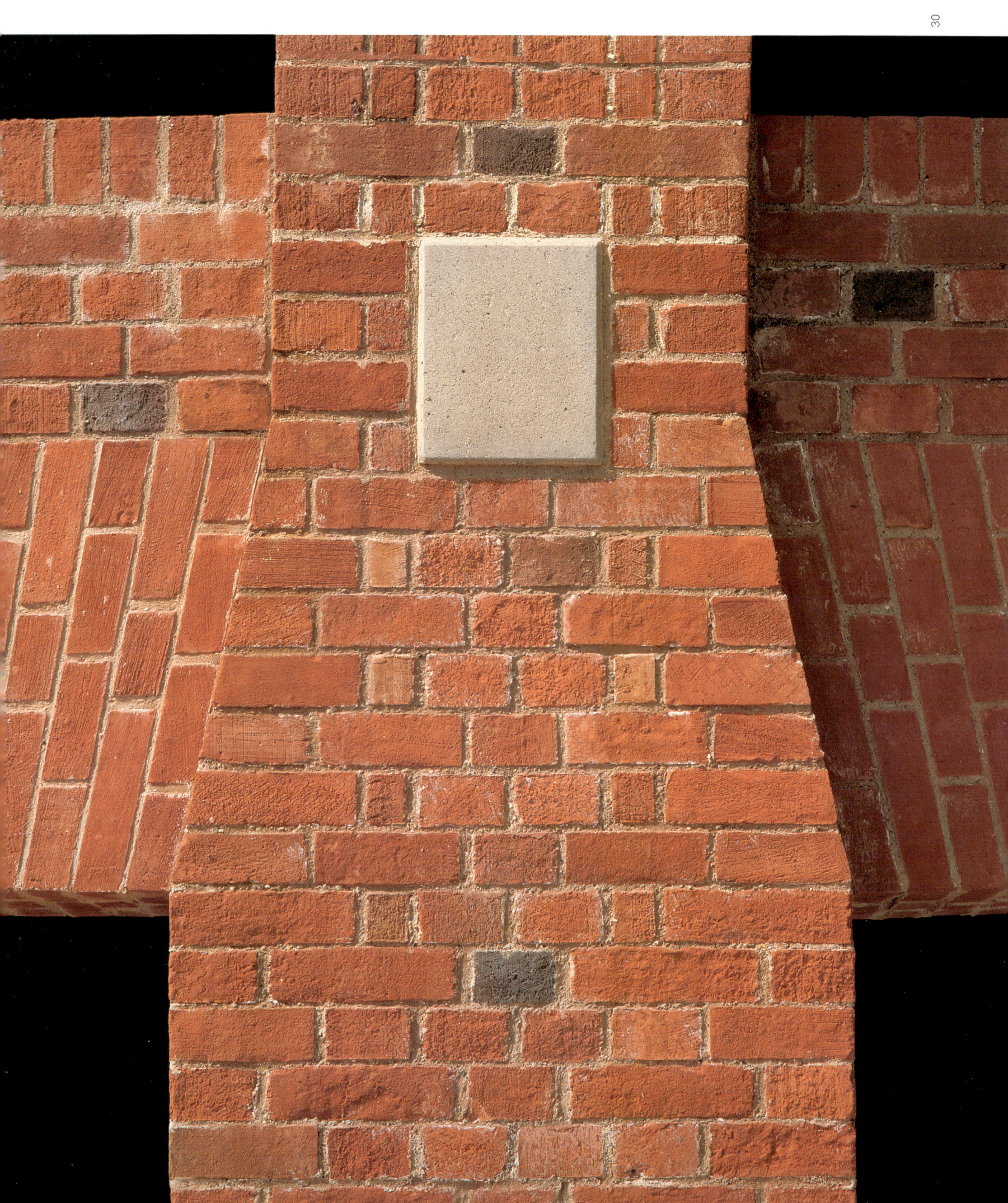

Opposite: brick piers taper as they rise, forming haunched springings for the flat arches. The ends of the precast concrete floor beams are visible on the exterior.

Right: the flat brick arches were laid on temporary centering. All arches are structural and without hidden frame or lintel.

Glyndebourne Opera House

Left: the foyer is enclosed by two glass walls and a fabric canopy spanning between the main building and the old backstage block, part of which has been converted into a bar, shop and box office.

Below: isometric projection of an arch and pier junction, showing the bond of the brickwork and a precast concrete floor beam penetrating the pier.

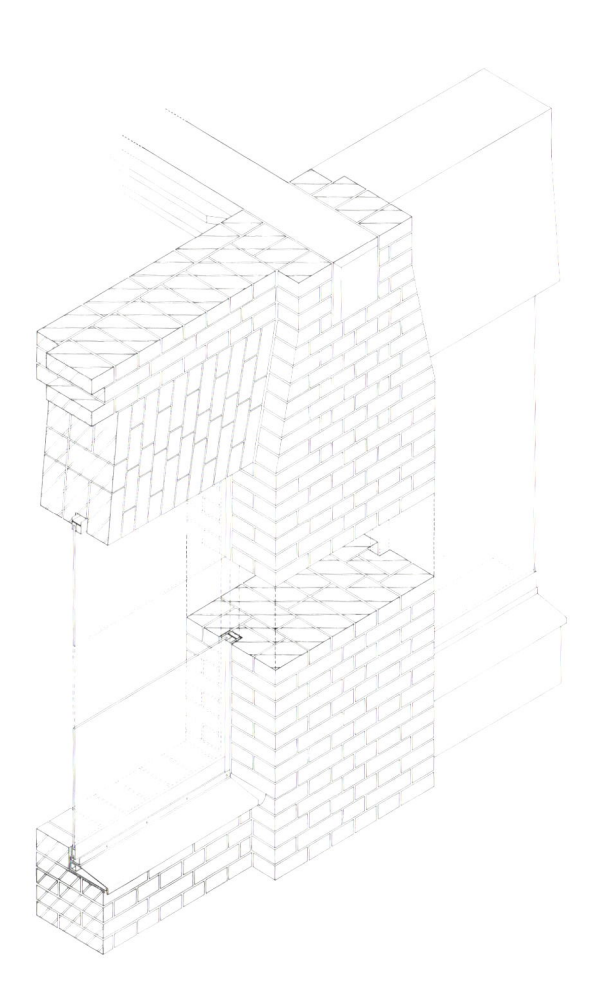

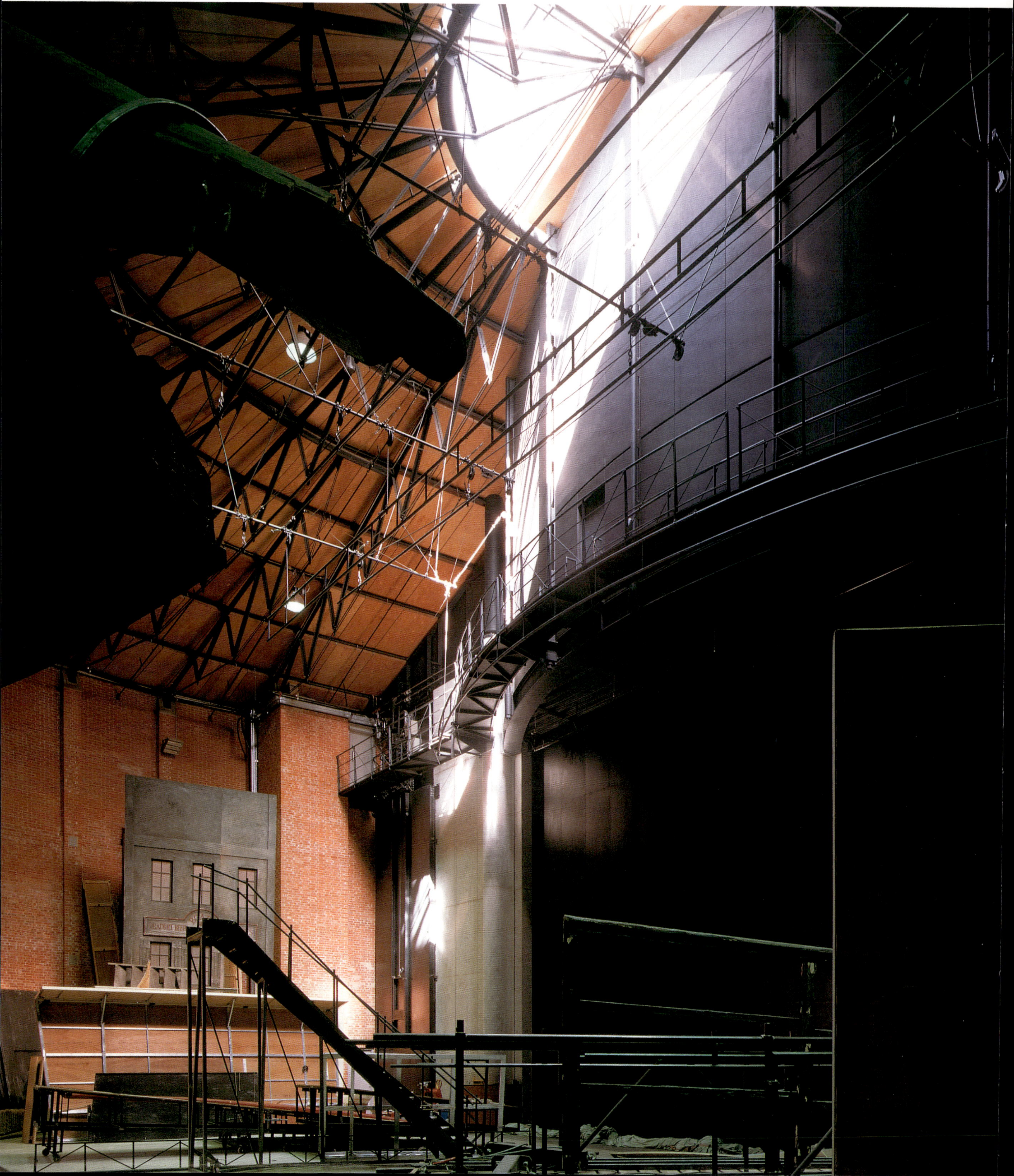

Opposite: the semicircular backstage area, with the stage and fly tower to the right. The lattice steel roof trusses rest on loadbearing brick walls.
Right: floor plans.

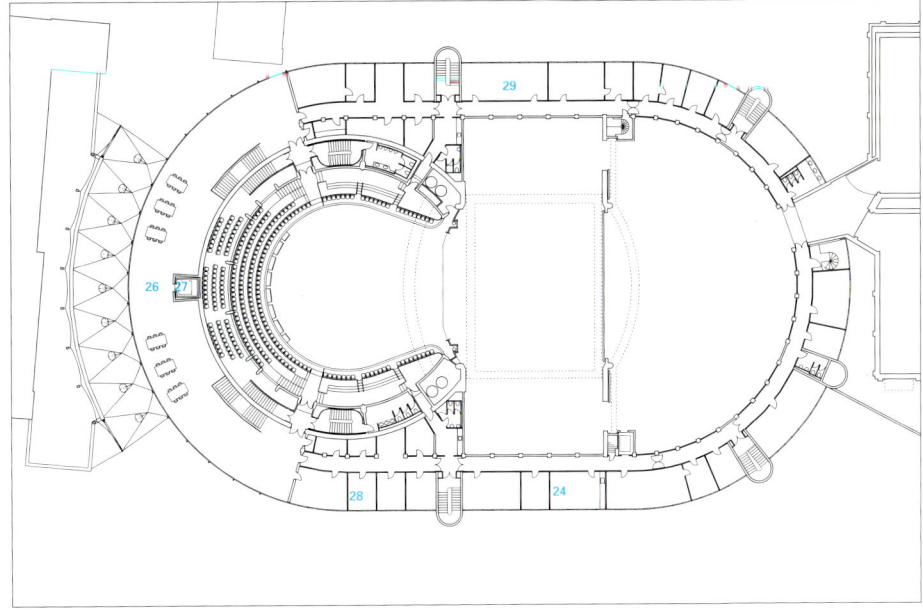

1 stalls
2 cloakroom
3 orchestra pit
4 understage
5 costume store
6 chorus changing
7 plant
8 prop store
9 plenum
10 cloth store
11 storage
12 foyer
13 auditorium
14 stage
15 backstage
16 sidestage
17 box office
18 bar
19 shop
20 existing organ room
21 rehearsal stages
22 director's recess
23 loading bay
24 dressing rooms
25 conductor's dressing room
26 circle balcony
27 control suites
28 green room
29 offices

Circle level

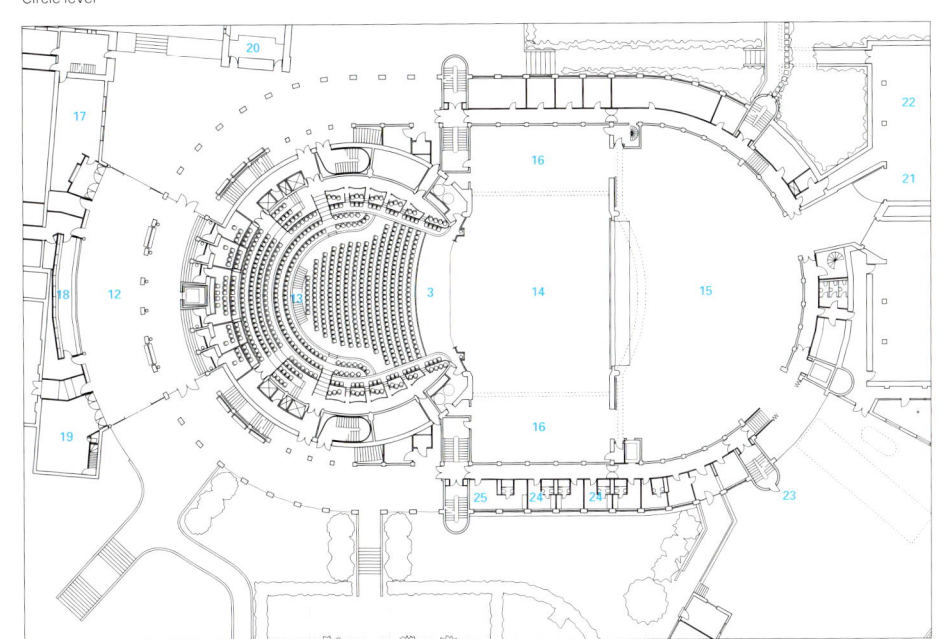

Foyer level

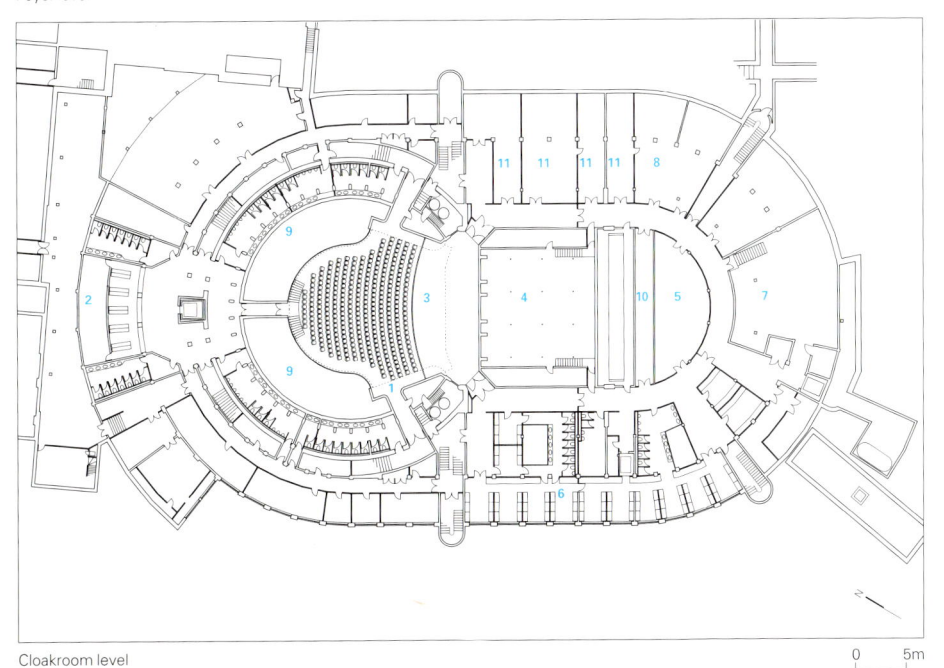

Cloakroom level

Glyndebourne Opera House

Left: production on the main stage: Alban Berg's *Lulu*, 1996.
Below: the foyer at night. Since the building is only used in the summer, the space is allowed to expand freely out onto the adjacent terrace.

Opposite: audience members return to their seats. Although the dress code is formal, the auditorium finishes are simple, with none of the traditional opera house trappings.

Glyndebourne Opera House

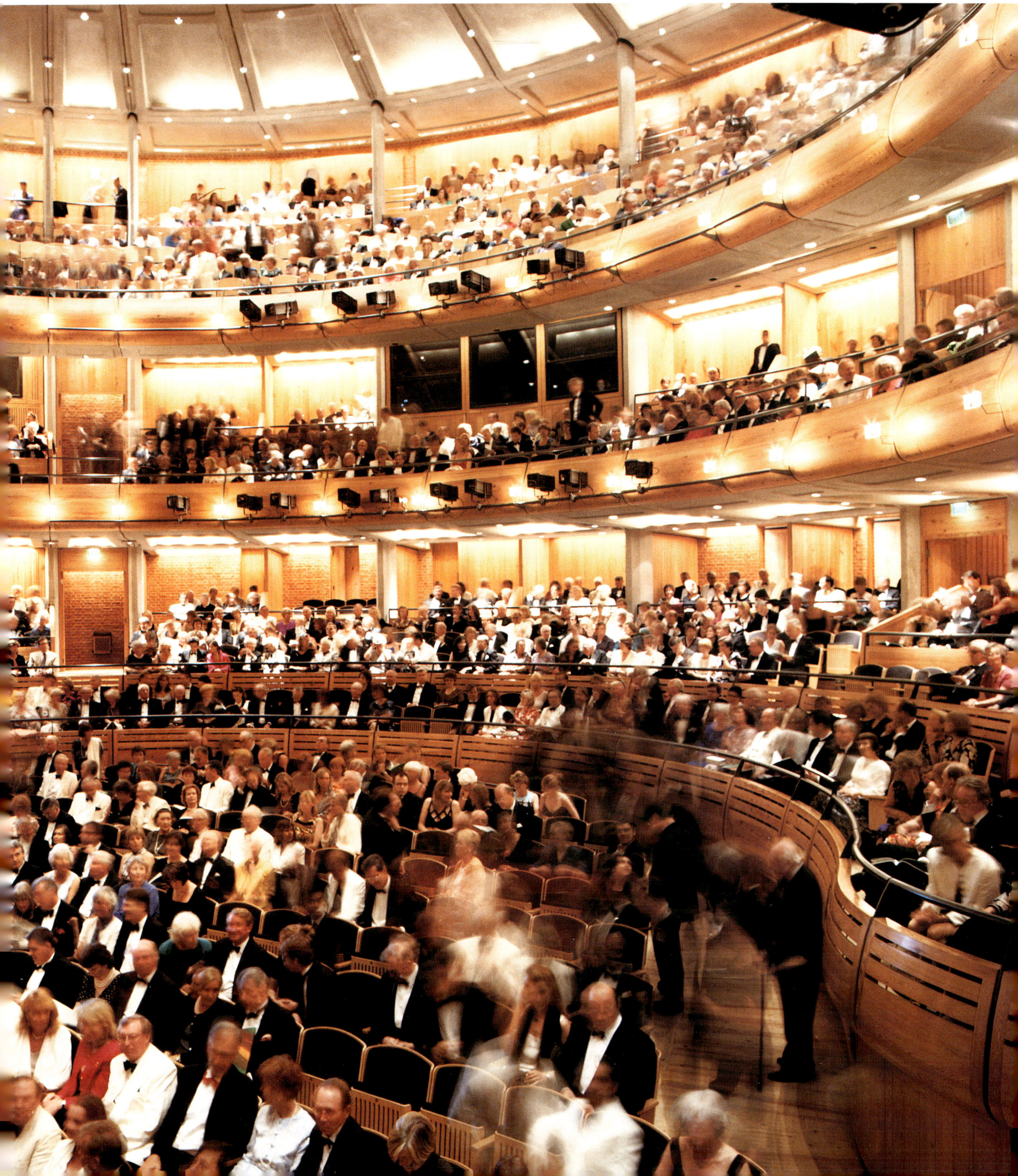

Inland Revenue Centre 1992–1995

The Inland Revenue Centre in Nottingham has created its own urban quarter on what was semi-derelict land between a railway line and a canal near the city centre. The Castle, on a steep bluff to the north, is the focal point of three radiating streets which cross a curving east–west spine. The office buildings themselves are linear, repetitive structures, three- and four-storeys high, forming a courtyard and L-shaped blocks. The streets are lined with trees and parking spaces. A fabric-roofed reception and amenity building occupies the central block between the public spine road and the canal towpath. Accommodation was divided between seven separate buildings so that the managing of the estate could be flexible, in response to unpredictable changes in technology and staffing levels.

The canal used to be lined with functional but handsome nineteenth-century industrial buildings of red brick with grey roofs. This tradition is consciously revived in the materials and forms of the new buildings. Piers of semi-engineering brick alternate with full-height glazing to form the external walls of the lower storeys. The traditional Nottingham brick, which is slightly larger than average, was carefully recreated using Cumbrian clay fired in coal-fuelled kilns. The top storeys are projecting attics, clad in lead-covered panels. Circular towers of glass brick house spiral staircases at the corners of the blocks, with ground-floor entrances on either side. Service cores, containing lifts and WCs, flank short entrance corridors, but floors are otherwise free of obstructions and designed to be laid out as either open-plan or cellular offices. The brick piers are placed at 3.2-metre centres – a comfortable width for a cellular office.

Energy conservation was a high priority for the client, who expressed a strong preference for natural light and ventilation. For this reason, the buildings are relatively narrow – 13.6 metres for the lower floors and 15 metres for the attic storey. In office buildings, heat gain – from windows, people and equipment – is more difficult and expensive to control than heat loss. External shading is therefore provided by horizontal, projecting, glass 'light shelves' at door-head height, which reflect daylight up onto the ceiling, and by the deep reveals of the brick piers. Windows are triple-glazed, with a venetian blind in the outer cavity. A continuous, metal, combined *brise-soleil* and rainwater gutter shades the top storey. Ventilation is mostly natural, using the form of the building to encourage air flow and to keep down the internal temperature. The full-height sliding glass windows, fitted with metal external balustrades, can be opened by the occupants in hot weather, but fresh air is normally introduced through perimeter grilles and fan/heater units beneath the raised floor. From here, it is drawn through the space using the power of the sun. The glass-block walls of the corner staircase towers are deliberately designed to encourage solar heat gain. Warm air rises in the towers and is exhausted around the edges of their fabric-covered roofs, which can be lifted hydraulically. This 'stack effect'

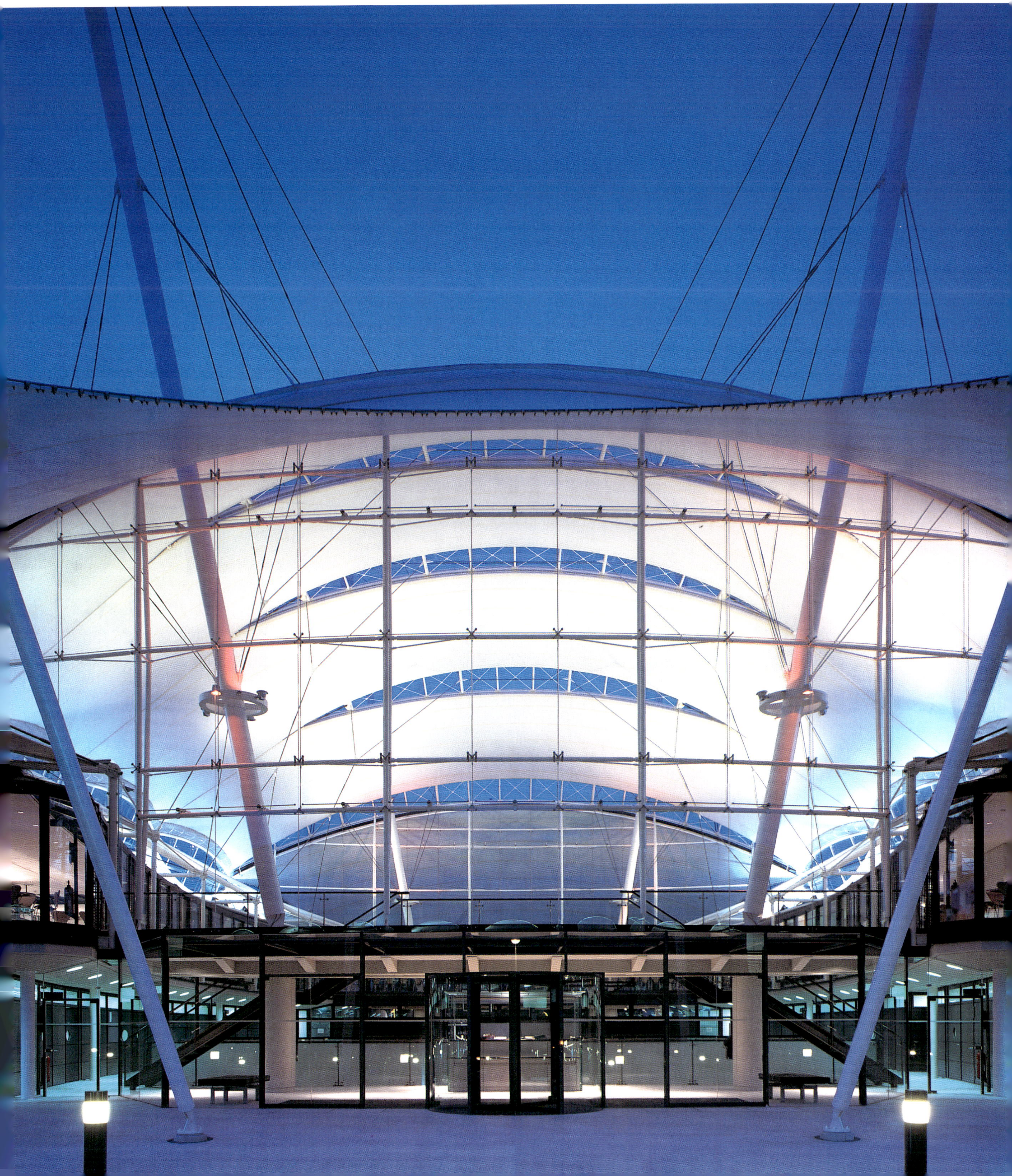

Previous page: the fabric-roofed reception and amenity building is both the visual and the social focus of the whole complex.

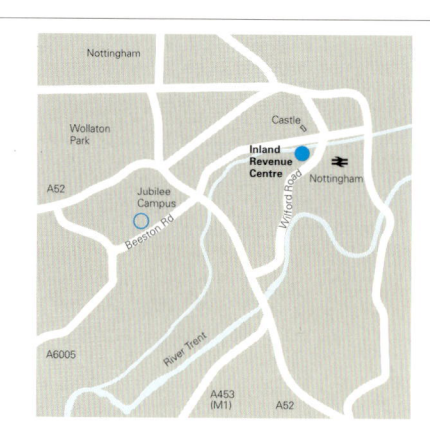

draws air from the adjacent offices through doors held open by magnetic catches, which release automatically in case of fire. In order to work effectively, the towers have to be at least 7 metres higher than the space ventilated. The ventilation of the top storey, therefore, works on a different principle, with a continuous vent along the ridge of the shallow pitched roof. The temperature inside the building is further moderated by the relatively massive brick and concrete structure which acts as a thermal 'flywheel'. At night in summer, the air flow is increased to cool the structure, in particular the exposed concrete ceilings, which then become 'cool radiators' during the day.

The building was extensively prefabricated in order to meet a tight construction timetable, even though loadbearing brickwork is a major element of its structure. The brick piers, which taper as they rise, were built in a factory and delivered to the site in storey-height units, complete with precast concrete caps. A steel rod was built into the middle of each pier so that it could be lifted safely by crane. The caps form the bearings for precast concrete floor units in the shape of shallow barrel vaults, one bay wide, spanning the whole width of the building. In open-plan areas, the exposed concrete soffits form a wavy ceiling with cast-in downlighters. All mechanical and electrical services are accommodated beneath a modular raised floor, standing on the stepped tops of the floor units. For the attic storey, the structure, like the ventilation, works on a different principle. Slender, round steel columns, attached to the cantilevered ends of the floor units, support steel trusses made of doubled angles tensioned by thin rods. The trusses support round purlins onto which lead-covered, plywood roof panels are hooked, like large overlapping tiles. The steel structure and plywood panels are exposed internally, giving the large open-plan offices a quasi-industrial character.

Architecturally, the reception and amenity building at the heart of the new quarter is in complete contrast to the office buildings. A rectangular, multipurpose sports court is bracketed by a pair of slightly curved, two-storey, concrete-framed buildings containing changing rooms at court level with restaurants and bars above. A reception area facing the road, and a crêche facing the canal, complete the plan. The sports court is covered by an uninsulated tent of teflon-coated, glass fibre panels, stretched between curved steel ladders which are infilled with glass and suspended from four raking steel masts. Full-height glass end walls are attached to the main steel ladders so that the outer fabric panels become simple external canopies. Eye-shaped ladders form clerestorey lights over the side blocks, which also have fabric roofs, but are this time double-skinned and insulated. The building represents an intermediate stage in the development of Hopkins' tent structures; between the original version at Schlumberger in Cambridge, and the latest incarnations at Saga in Folkestone and Wildscreen at Bristol.

Above: the canal defines the northern boundary of the site. Nottingham Castle, on a steep bluff to the north, is the focal point of the radiating street pattern.

Overleaf: the complex forms a whole urban quarter. Cars park next to the buildings, between the trees. The huge canopy of the amenity building reaches out to embrace the street.

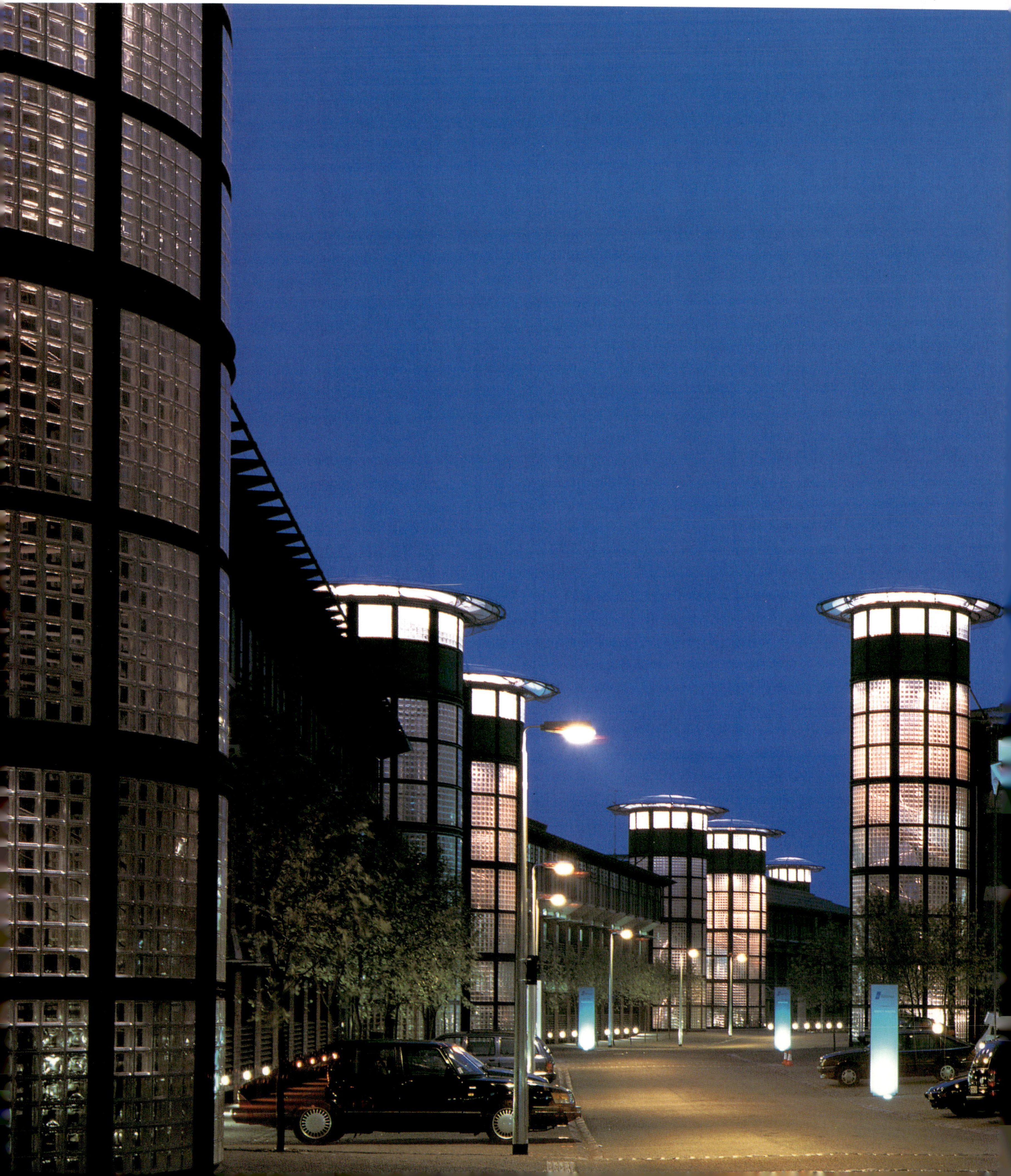

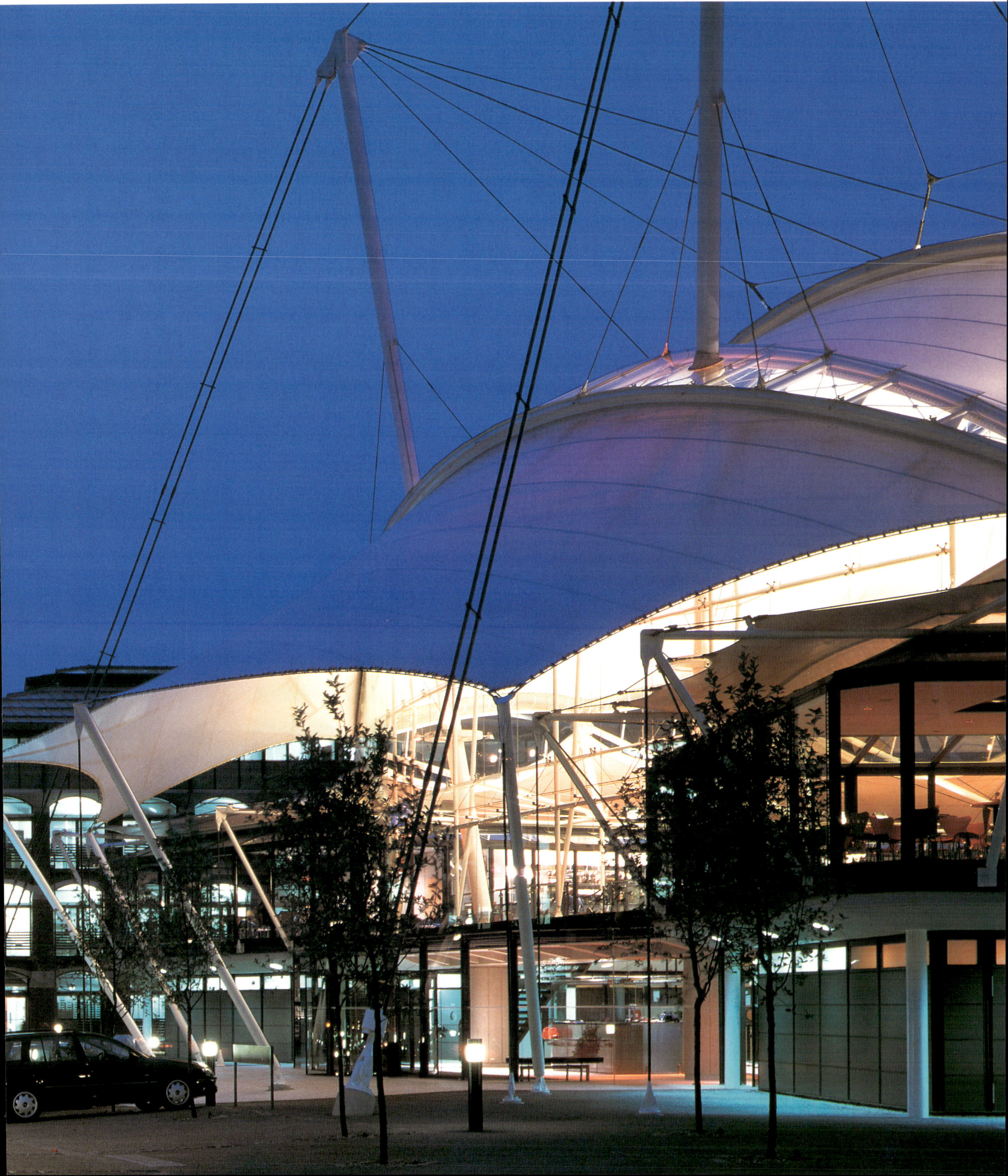

42

Opposite and left: cylindrical corner towers house spiral staircases, but also function as exhaust air 'chimneys' when their fabric-covered lids are raised.

Below left: cross section.
Below right: axonometric showing air flow.

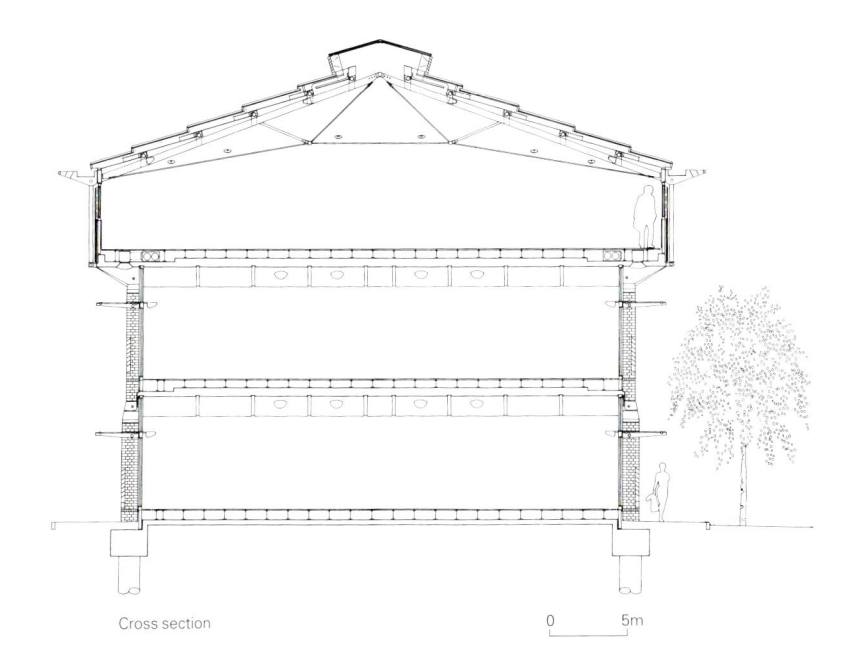

Cross section   0   5m

1. individual fan-assisted air intake under floor
2. air intake through floor grilles
3. air intake through windows
4. exhaust air drawn towards tower
5. tower acts as solar chimney
6. tower lid rises to allow escape of exhaust air

Inland Revenue Centre

Axonometric showing air flows

Left: precast concrete ceiling units take the form of shallow vaults spanning right across the building. The loadbearing brick piers were built in a factory around steel lifting rods.

Opposite: the ends of the precast concrete ceiling vaults, with their steel tensioning rods, are visible on the facade. The top floor has a lighter, steel-framed structure.

1. pre-built brick pier (lime/cement mortar)
2. triple glass, argon-filled sealed inner units, Venetian blinds between them and outer pane
3. concrete padstone
4. nib of precast concrete vault
5. steel tie
6. precast concrete vault
7. glass light shelf on brackets
8. uplighter
9. steel balustrade
10. intake air fan unit
11. floor grille
12. raised floor

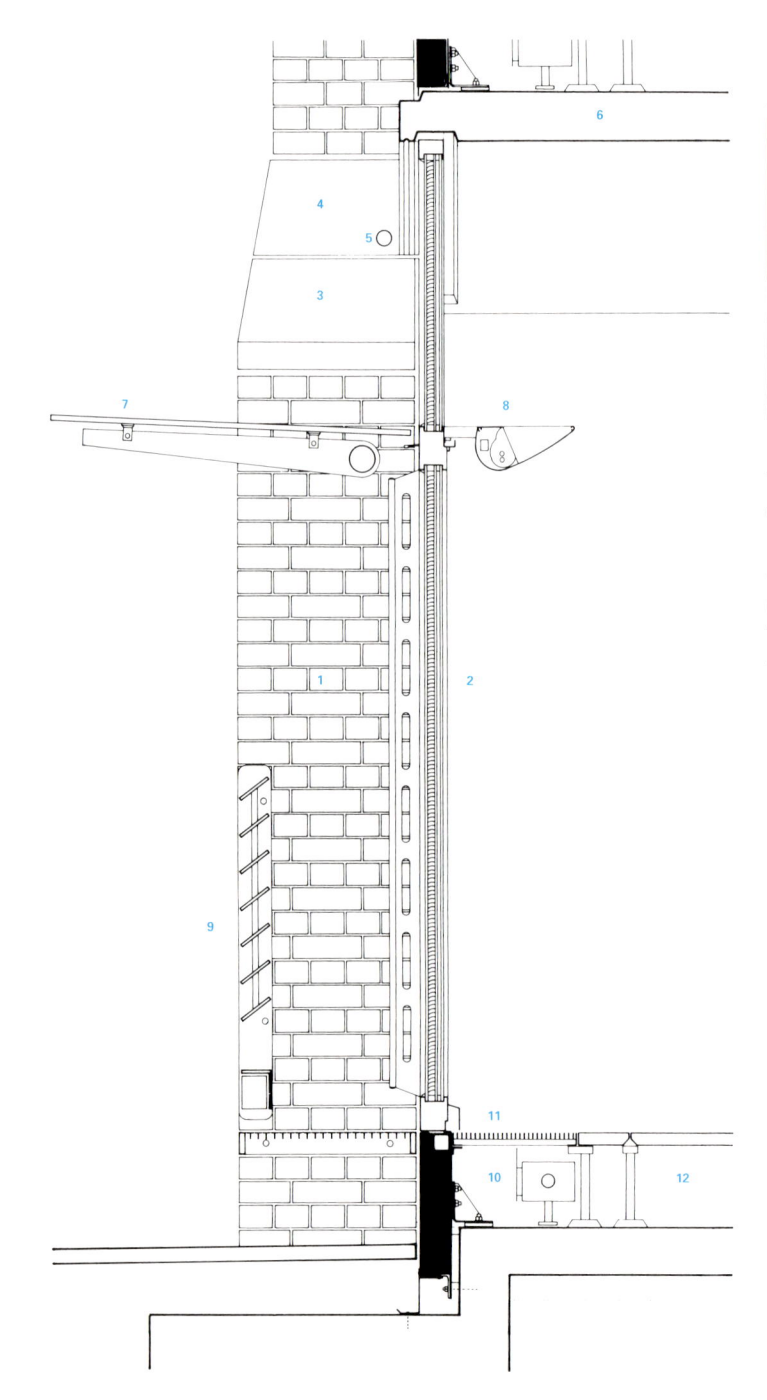

Left and above: section through the external wall and the open-plan office in use. Projecting 'light shelves' shade the perimeter of the building, while reflecting light up onto the undulating ceiling.

Inland Revenue Centre

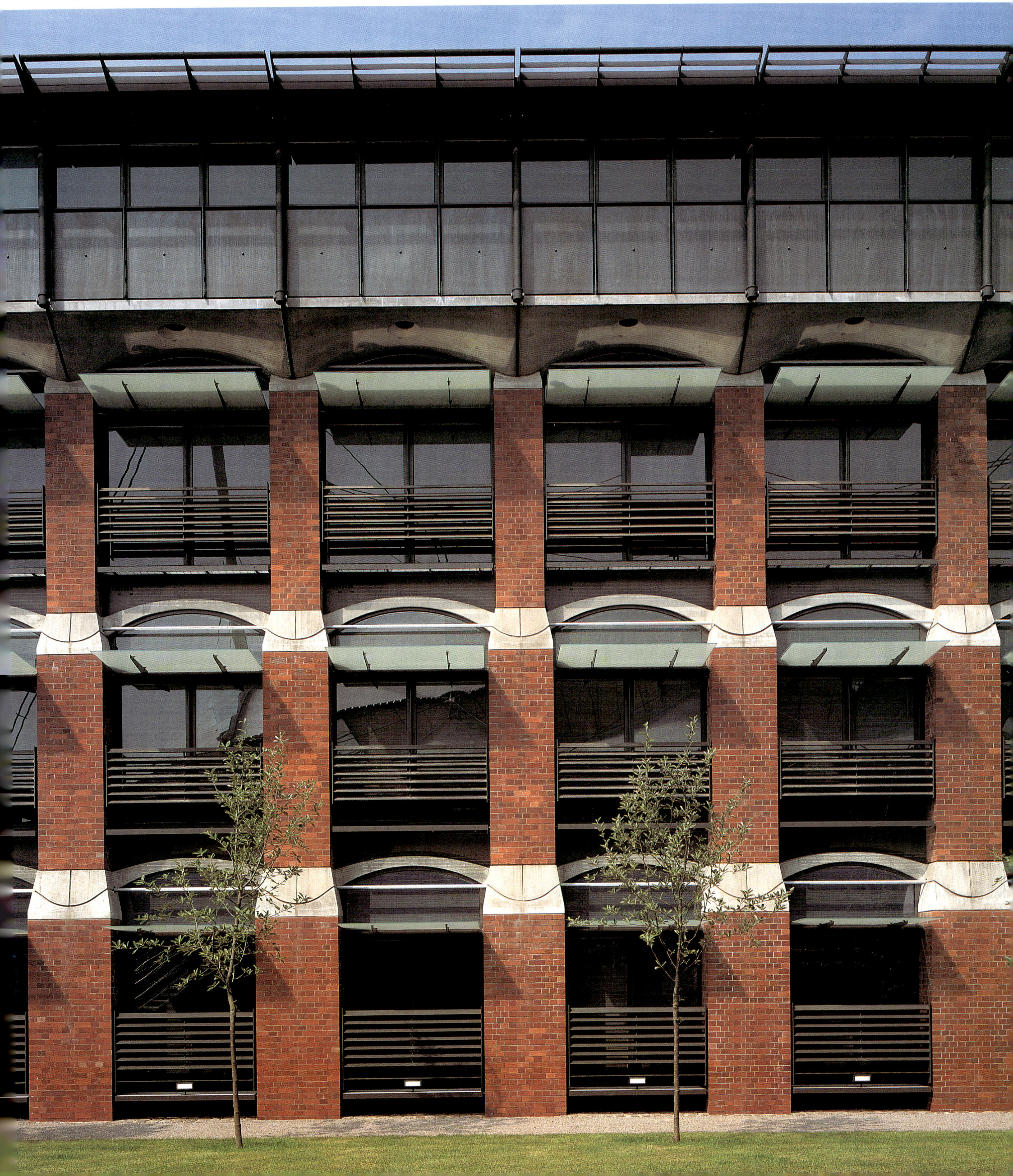

Left and below: suspended from four raking steel masts, the fabric roof of the amenity building is symmetrical on two axes. Side blocks are roofed with insulated, double-skinned fabric.

Opposite: the west side of the amenity building, with Nottingham Castle beyond. The side blocks are concrete-framed and slightly curved in plan.

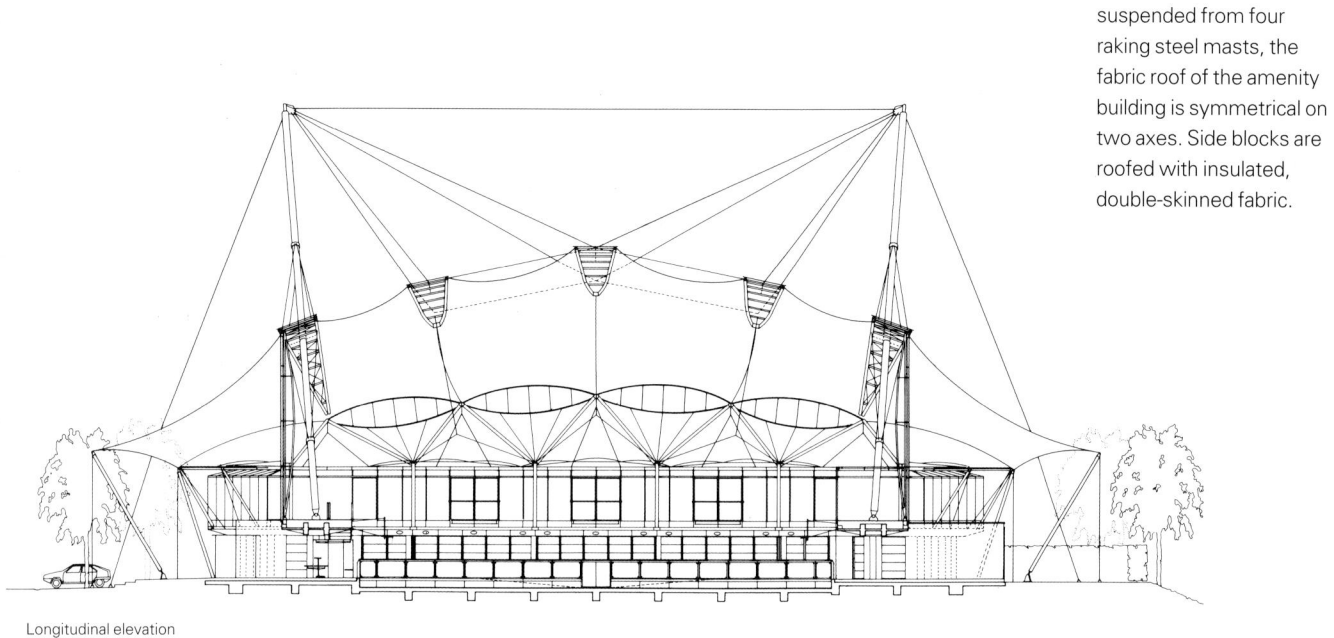

Longitudinal elevation

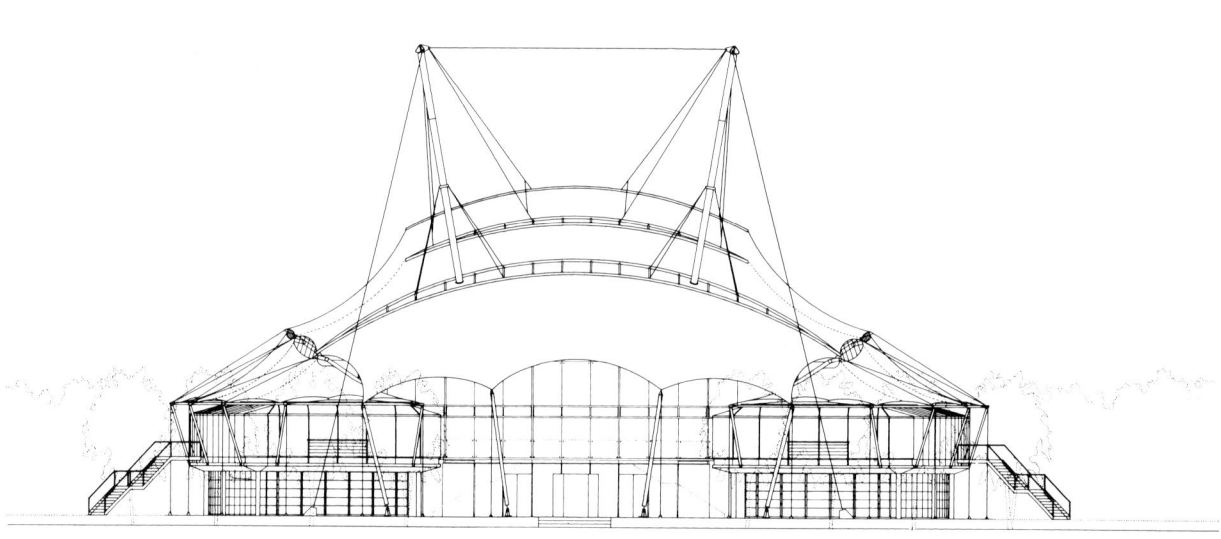

Inland Revenue Centre

Entrance elevation

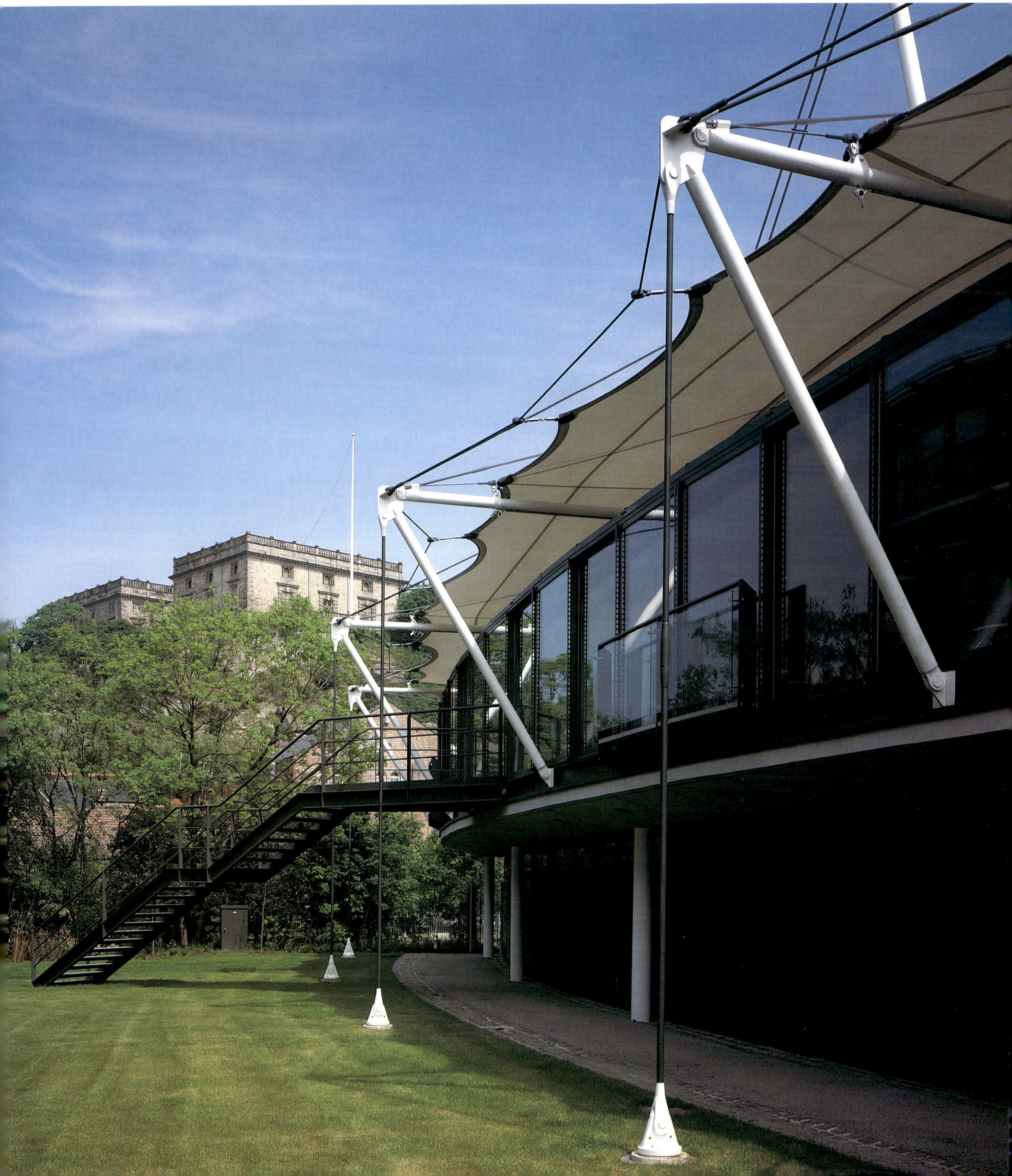

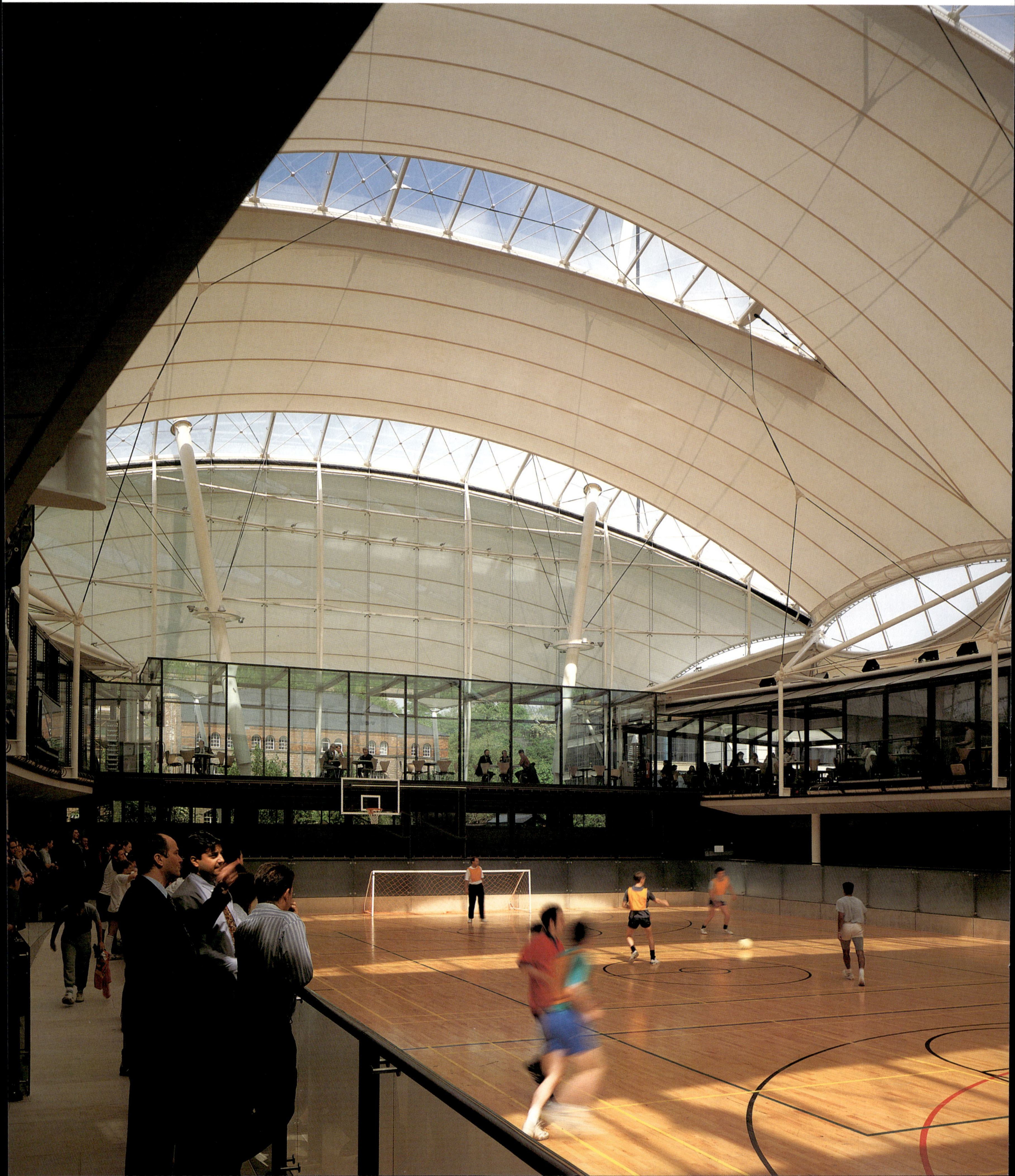

Opposite: the multi-purpose sports court in the amenity building is overlooked on either side by bars and restaurants. The changing rooms are on the ground floor. Also on this level, a crêche faces the canal and the reception area is opposite the road.

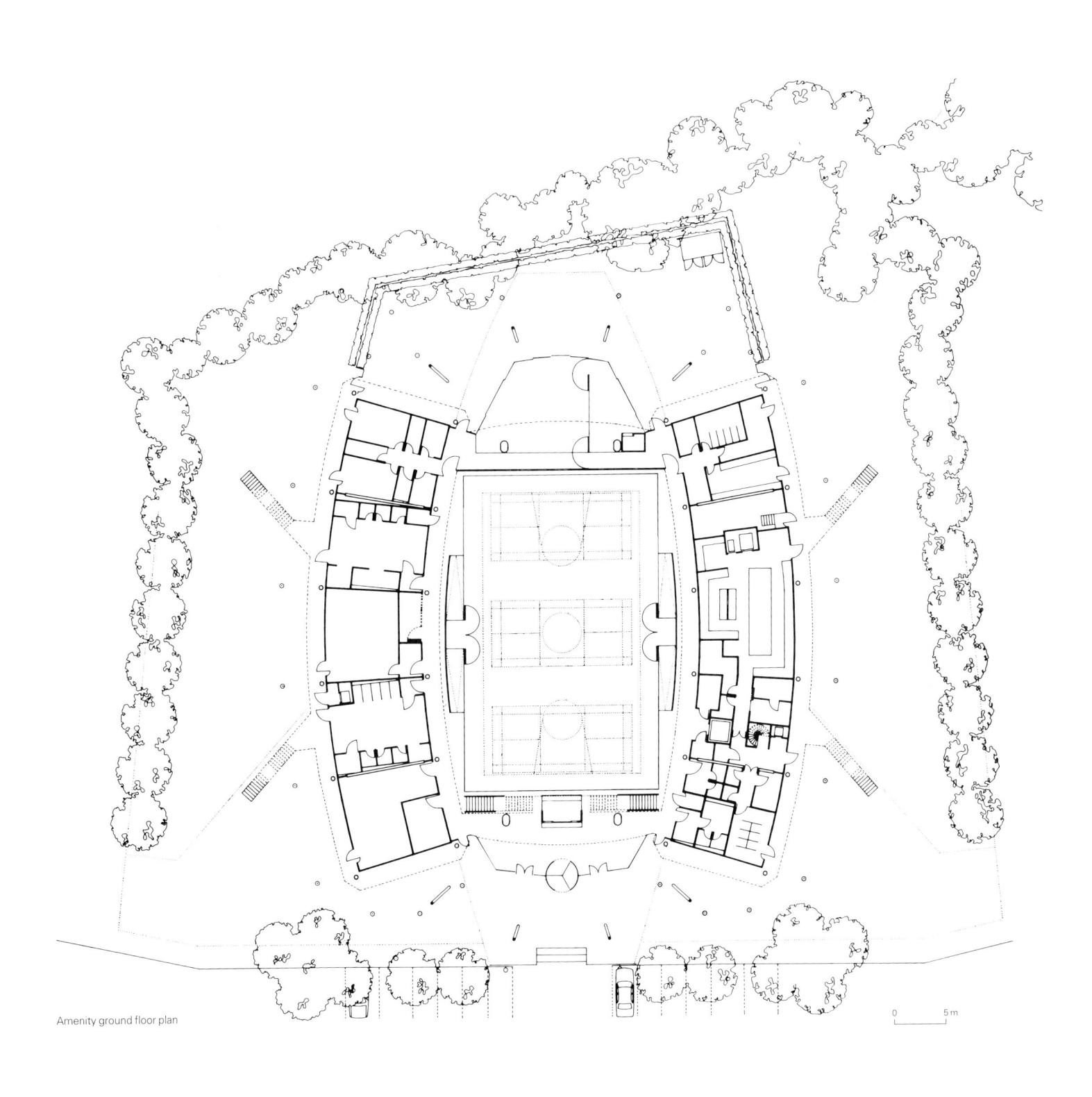

Inland Revenue Centre

Amenity ground floor plan

0   5m

Left and below: the fabric roof of the amenity building is tensioned by curved, steel-framed ladders, suspended from four steel masts. In the finished building, the ladders are clear glazed to add sparkle to the daylight inside.

Opposite: the fabric roof seen through the all-glass end wall. Eye-shaped ladders tension the edges of the fabric membrane and form clerestorey lights.

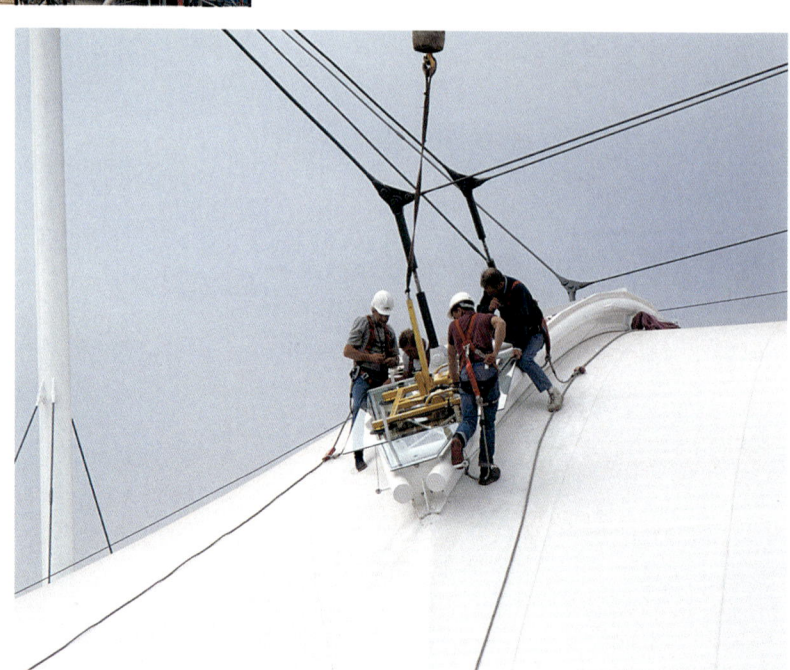

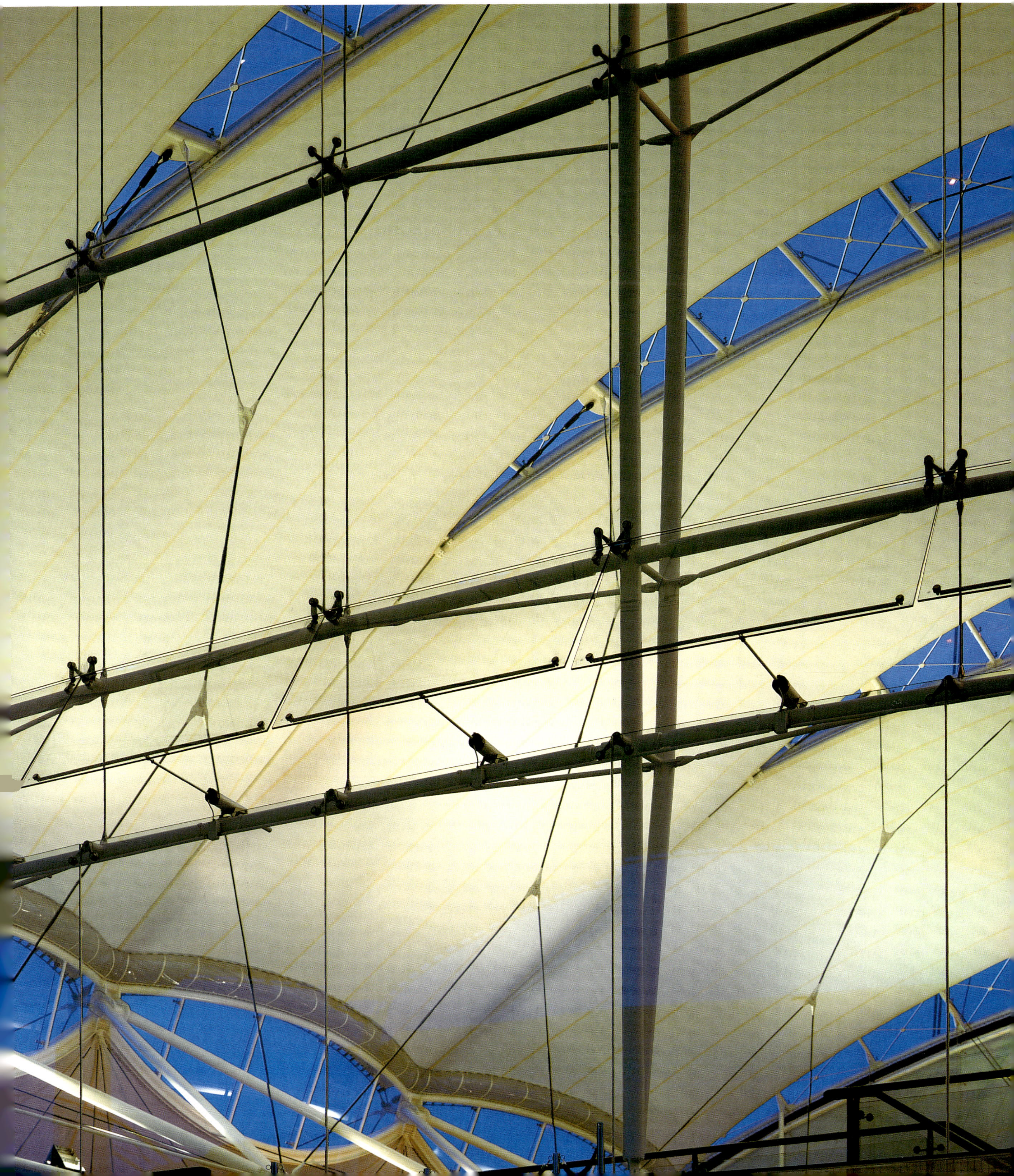

Queen's Building, Emmanuel College 1993–1995

Three-storey, freestanding, oval in plan and with a performance space at its heart, the Queen's Building at Emmanuel College, Cambridge, is like a miniature Glyndebourne Opera House. Designed for lectures, college ceremonies and chamber music recitals, its auditorium is a double-height, D-shaped room with a steeply raked block of 140 seats facing into the curve. A narrow gallery, or ambulatory, overlooks the performance space from the upper level. Four more apsidal rooms, like single-storey, flat-floored versions of the auditorium, occupy most of the rest of the building. They are used for receptions and seminars, as well as common rooms. The ground floor of the building is completely surrounded by a colonnade, and a passageway cuts right through it, linking a restored arcade in the corner of New Court with a gate in the wall of the Fellows' Garden opposite. The main entrance is buried in the middle of the plan, where the passageway crosses the longitudinal axis of the building. There are two staircases, both spirals: one carved out of the interior beside the entrance lobby; the other housed in an almost freestanding satellite drum of glass blocks in a steel frame, with a frameless glass link to the parent building.

The external facade of Ketton limestone (the stone used by Christopher Wren for the nearby college chapel) looks, at first, like a monolithic, loadbearing wall, smooth and flush with no projections of any kind, other than the suggestion of a cornice at the top. On closer inspection, however, it turns out to be a kind of frame structure of piers and flat arches, infilled by big windows and non-loadbearing stone panels. In fact, the piers are prestressed and post-tensioned by hidden steel rods. Precast concrete 'kneeling blocks' – heavily reinforced, but almost indistinguishable from the surrounding stone – are introduced into the piers at the springing points of the arches to receive thrust. Slightly tapered, so the piers diminish as they rise, the blocks are pierced by stainless steel tubes, to allow access to the tensioning nuts of the steel rods. The rods generate vertical compressive forces to resist the outward thrust of the floors and roof. Structurally, therefore, they are the equivalent of the buttresses and pinnacles of a medieval church.

The lead-covered, shallow-pitched roof is hardly visible from the outside, but in the auditorium and the top-floor reception room, its timber-boarded underside and supporting structure of composite steel and timber trusses are exposed to view. As far as materials are concerned, the interior and exterior of this building are treated in the same way. The stone walls continue through to the interior, the non-loadbearing external wall of the ground floor, within the colonnade, is oak-panelled inside and out, and all soffits, whether internal or external, are plastered and painted white. All colours and textures are natural and integral. The effect somehow manages to be austere and sumptuous at the same time; more like a fine piece of furniture than a building.

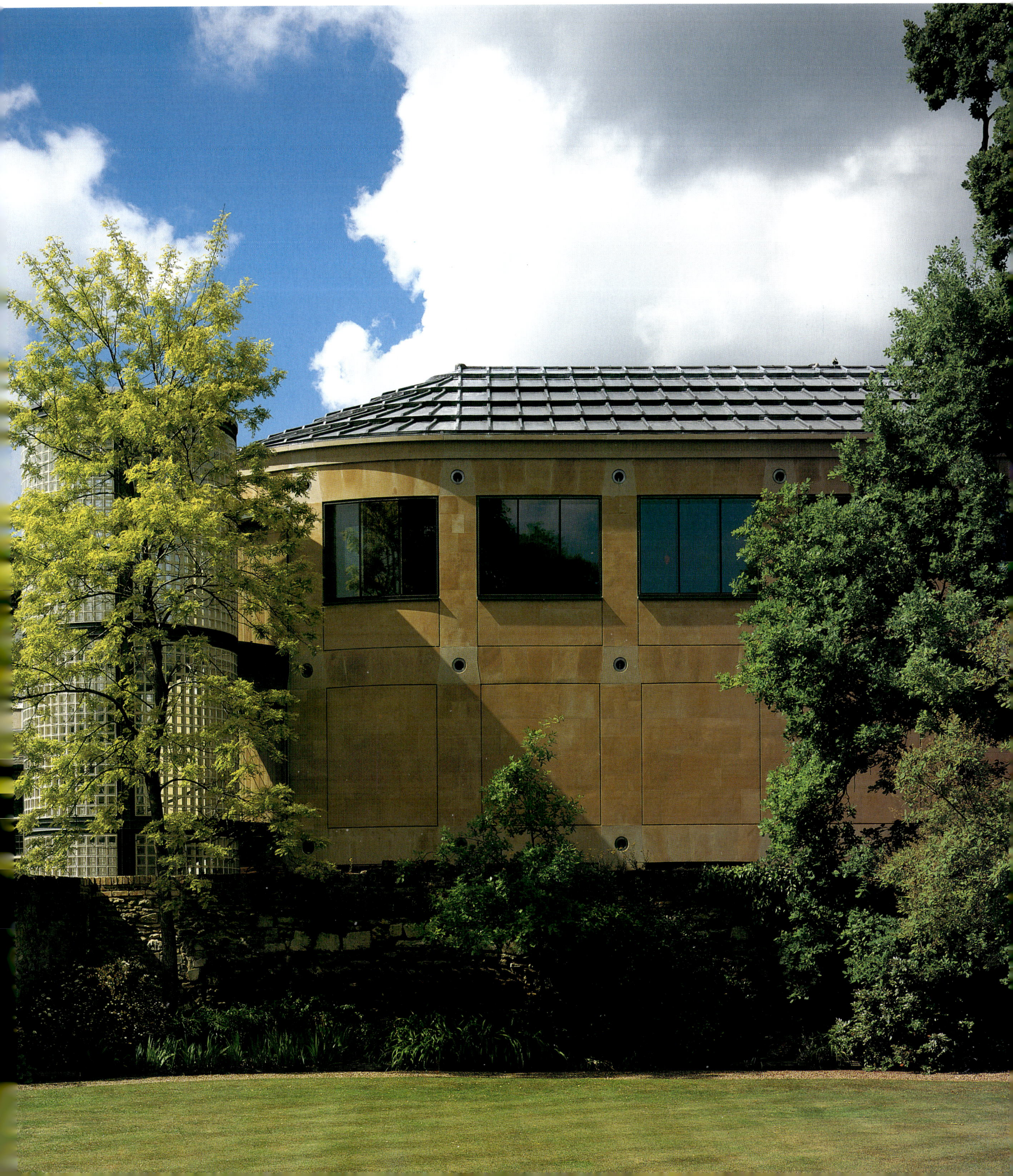

Previous page: the handsome smooth stone facade viewed from the Fellows' Garden. Circular holes allow access to the bolts that tension the stone piers. The roof is covered in lead.

Below: the performance space for events such as lectures and chamber music recitals, is double height with a single, steeply raked tier of seating.

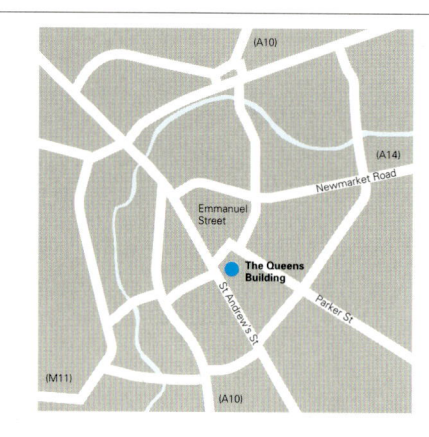

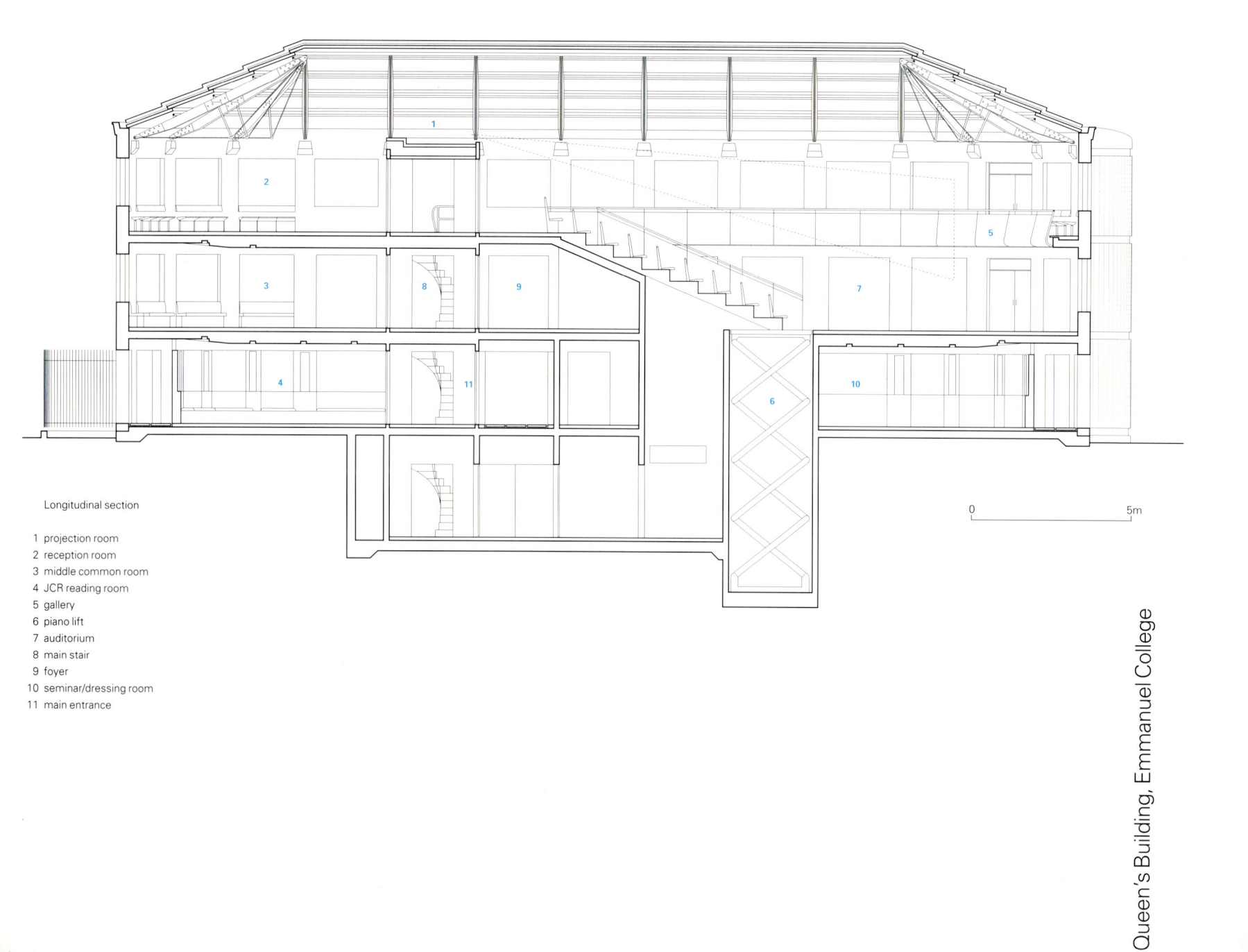

Longitudinal section

1. projection room
2. reception room
3. middle common room
4. JCR reading room
5. gallery
6. piano lift
7. auditorium
8. main stair
9. foyer
10. seminar/dressing room
11. main entrance

Queen's Building, Emmanuel College

Below: the yard between the Queen's Building and the corner of New Court. The arcade on the left links New Court with the subway to North Court under Emmanuel Street.

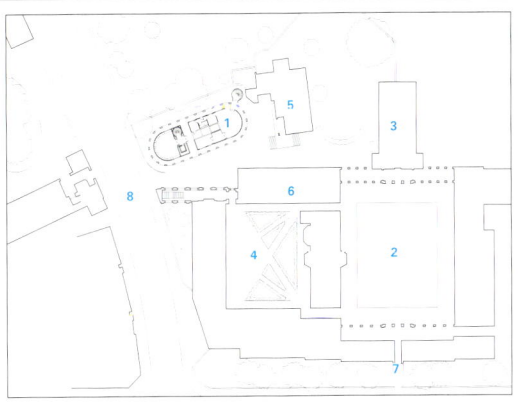

Site plan

1 Queen's Building
2 front court
3 Wren Chapel
4 New Court
5 Master's Lodge
6 The Old Library
7 main entrance off St Andrew's Street
8 subway under Emmanuel Street

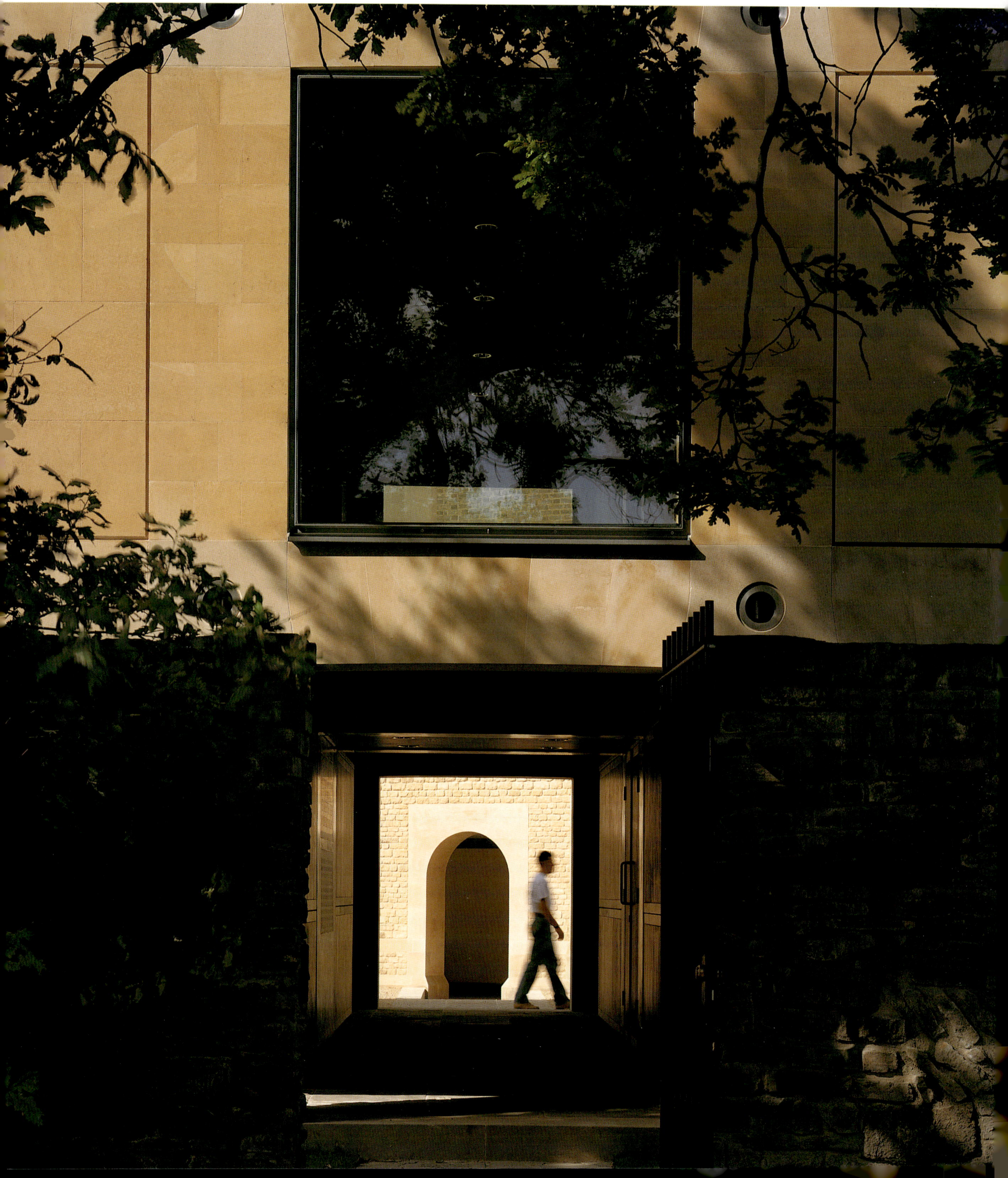

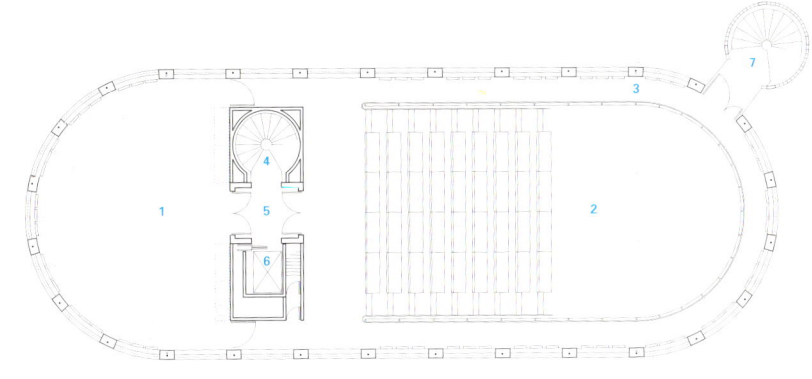

Second floor plan

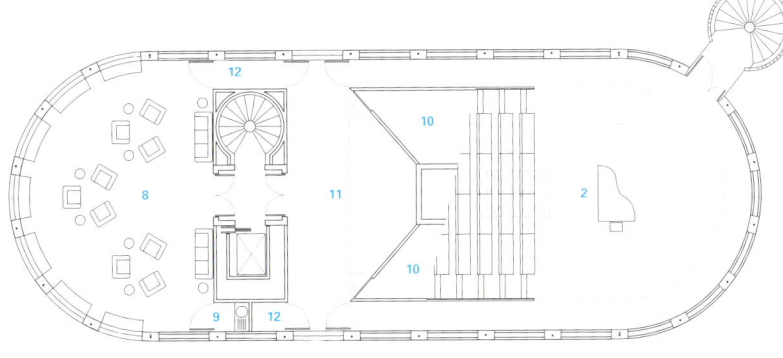

First floor plan

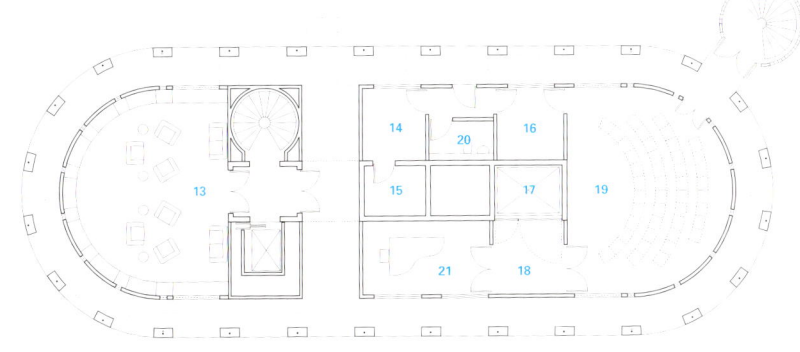

Ground floor plan

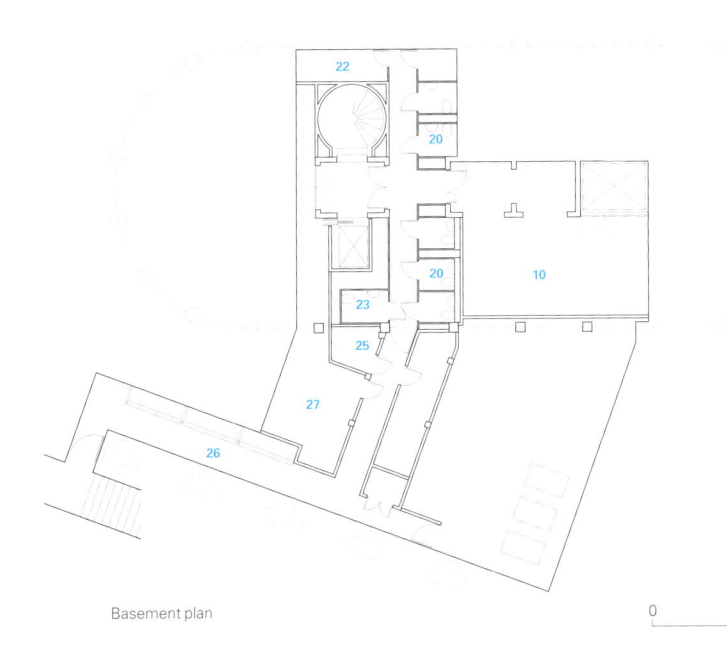

Basement plan

0   5m

1 reception room
2 auditorium
3 gallery
4 main stair
5 lobby
6 disabled lift
7 stair tower
8 middle common room
9 kitchen
10 store room
11 foyer
12 acoustic drape store
13 JCR reading room
14 music practice room
15 music store
16 meeting/supervision room
17 piano lift
18 piano lift lobby
19 seminar/dressing room
20 WC
21 keyboard practice room
22 cloakroom
23 disabled WC
25 lift motor room
26 link to subway under Emmanuel Street
27 plant room

Opposite: an entrance passageway cuts through the ground floor of the building, linking the Fellows' Garden with the restored arcade at the corner of New Court.

Above: the building has a simple, oval form. The cylindrical tower on the right is built of glass blocks in a steel frame and houses a spiral escape staircase.

Queen's Building, Emmanuel College

Left: the performance space viewed from the top of the tiered seating. A narrow gallery surrounds and overlooks the apse-like, double-height space.

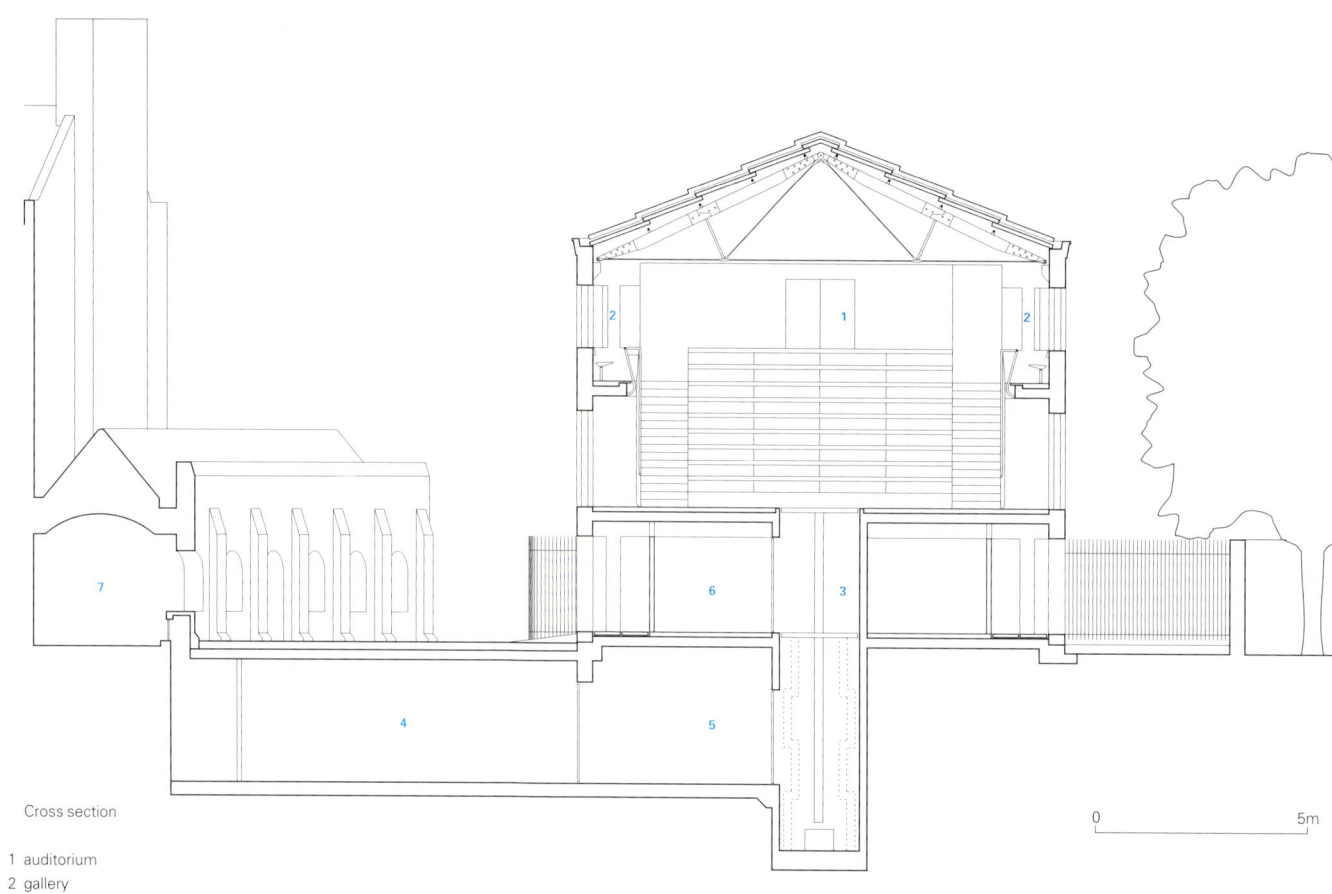

Cross section

1 auditorium
2 gallery
3 piano lift
4 plant room
5 store
6 piano lift lobby
7 arcade

Queen's Building, Emmanuel College

Below: the lead-covered roof is supported by composite steel and timber roof trusses which are exposed to view above the performance space and the top-floor reception room.

Buckingham Palace Ticket Office 1994–1995

Every summer, while the Royal Family is away on holiday, about 250,000 people visit Buckingham Palace. They buy their tickets from a little building that appears overnight at the beginning of August, and disappears at the end of September. It has three main components: a timber deck to protect the ground, a long narrow cabin to house the ticket sellers, and a fabric canopy for shade and shelter. Although this is a moveable building, it is nevertheless designed for a specific site; on the edge of Green Park, facing the Queen Victoria Memorial in the middle of its traffic roundabout and, beyond that, the Palace itself. The whole structure – deck, cabin and tent – is very slightly curved to follow the balustraded perimeter of the gardens and road in front of the palace.

But this is only one of many refinements that distinguish this building from the tents, trailers and Portakabins that usually serve this kind of function. The 15-metre long cabin is a wooden structure, built like a boat, with birch-faced plywood ribs and a skin of horizontal cedar boarding. The boarding is exposed internally and finished with yacht varnish to preserve the rich, reddish brown colour. Corners are rounded, with carved quadrant spheres top and bottom to create a completely smooth, continuous envelope. Built in two halves on a steel chassis with small wheels, the cabin can be easily transported on an ordinary lorry. Six ticket-sellers can be accommodated in the main space, sharing a long rectangular window at the front. In addition, there are hinged roof lights, taken straight from the chandler's catalogue, which light the small offices at each end and improve the ventilation.

The sheltering tent – the sail of the boat – is a clear formal expression of compressive and tensile forces. The compression part of the structure is a kind of double tree of laminated spruce masts and struts, connected by stainless steel plates. A horizontal 'keel' attached to the front eaves of the cabin provides lateral stability. The structure is tensioned by the balanced forces of the fabric membrane and the steel cables that guy the ends of the masts and struts to the ground. The fabric is acrylic canvas, which is not as strong as PVC or PTFE, but was preferred for its more natural texture. Curved timber bars gather the canvas at four points and are hitched, like coathangers, to a long cable stretched between the two main masts. Vertical cables anchor the ends of the struts to concrete blocks in the ground just outside the balustrade of the timber deck.

Since this is a building for summer use only, it is unheated. Solar heat gain is reduced by the shading of the canopy, and the heat generated by several computers in the small space is counteracted by adjustable fans in the floor, drawing in cool air from under the building. Built in only eight weeks from freehand working drawings, the ticket office was designed to last for five years. In August 2000, it was brought out for the sixth time, looking as good as new.

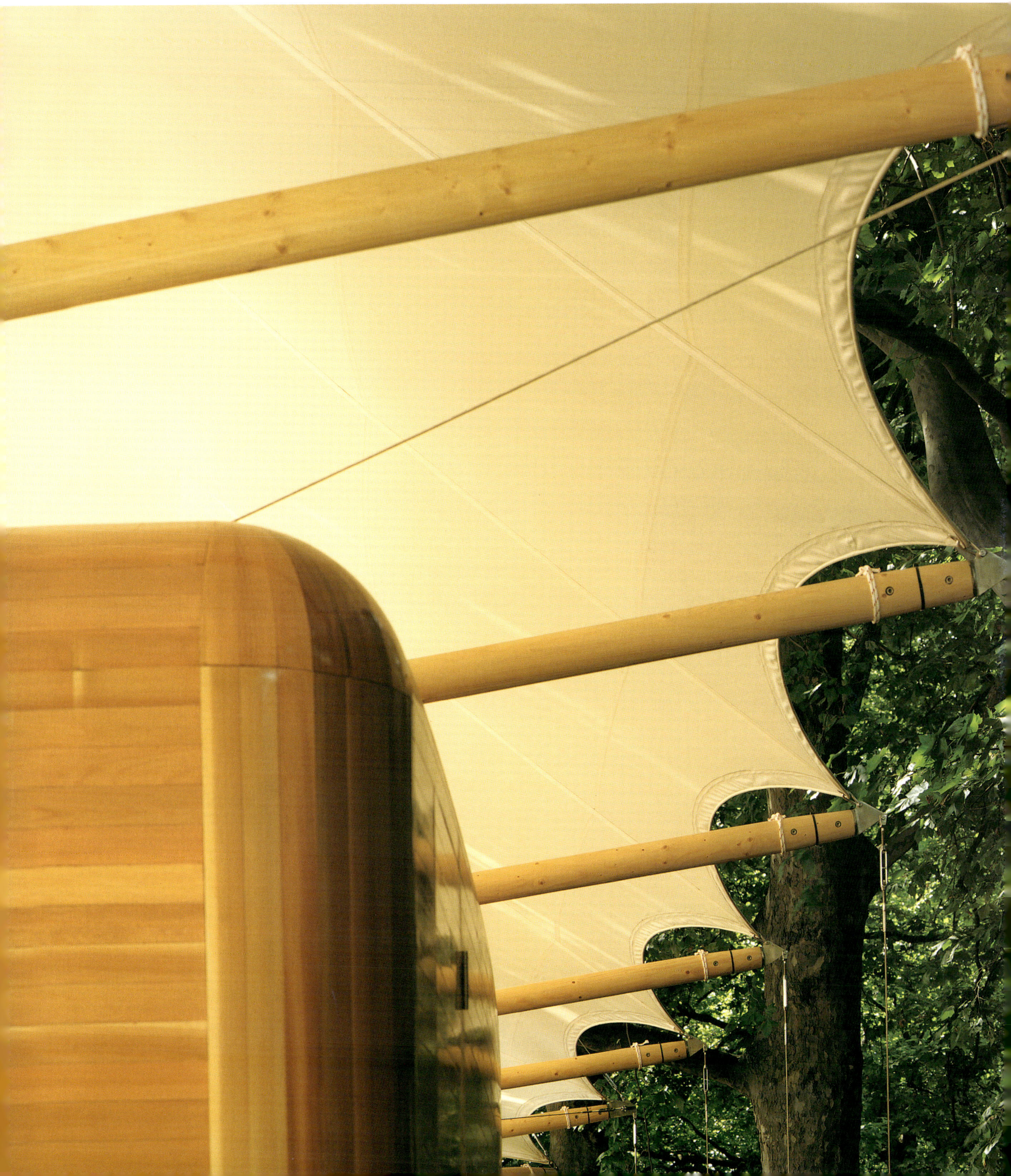

Previous page: the kiosk is clad in varnished cedar boarding with rounded corners and carved quadrant spheres, top and bottom. The struts that tension the fabric canopy are of laminated spruce.

Below: the temporary building is carefully sited at the edge of Green Park, facing the Queen Victoria Memorial and the front of Buckingham Palace.

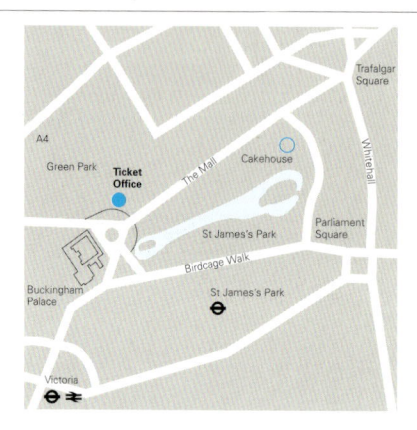

Cross section

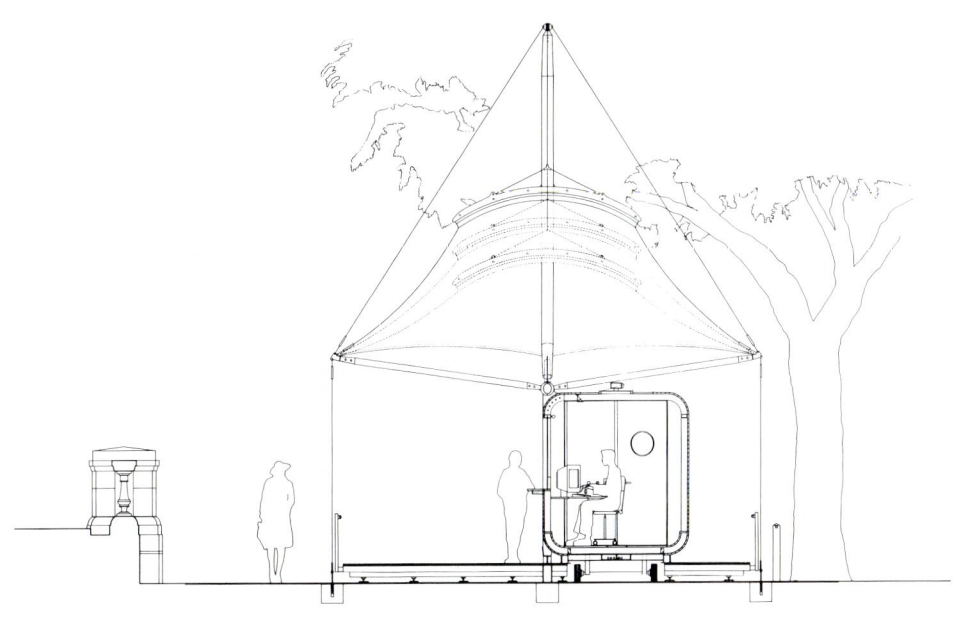

Overleaf: the fabric canopy nestling under the trees effectively and elegantly advertises the building's presence, while perfectly complementing the stone balustrade.

The building consists of three main elements: a wooden platform; a box-like kiosk, also of wood, with rounded corners; and a sheltering fabric canopy.

The whole building is slightly curved in plan to follow the line of the stone balustrade at the edge of the road. Although a mobile structure, the building is nevertheless designed for a specific site.

Buckingham Palace Ticket Office

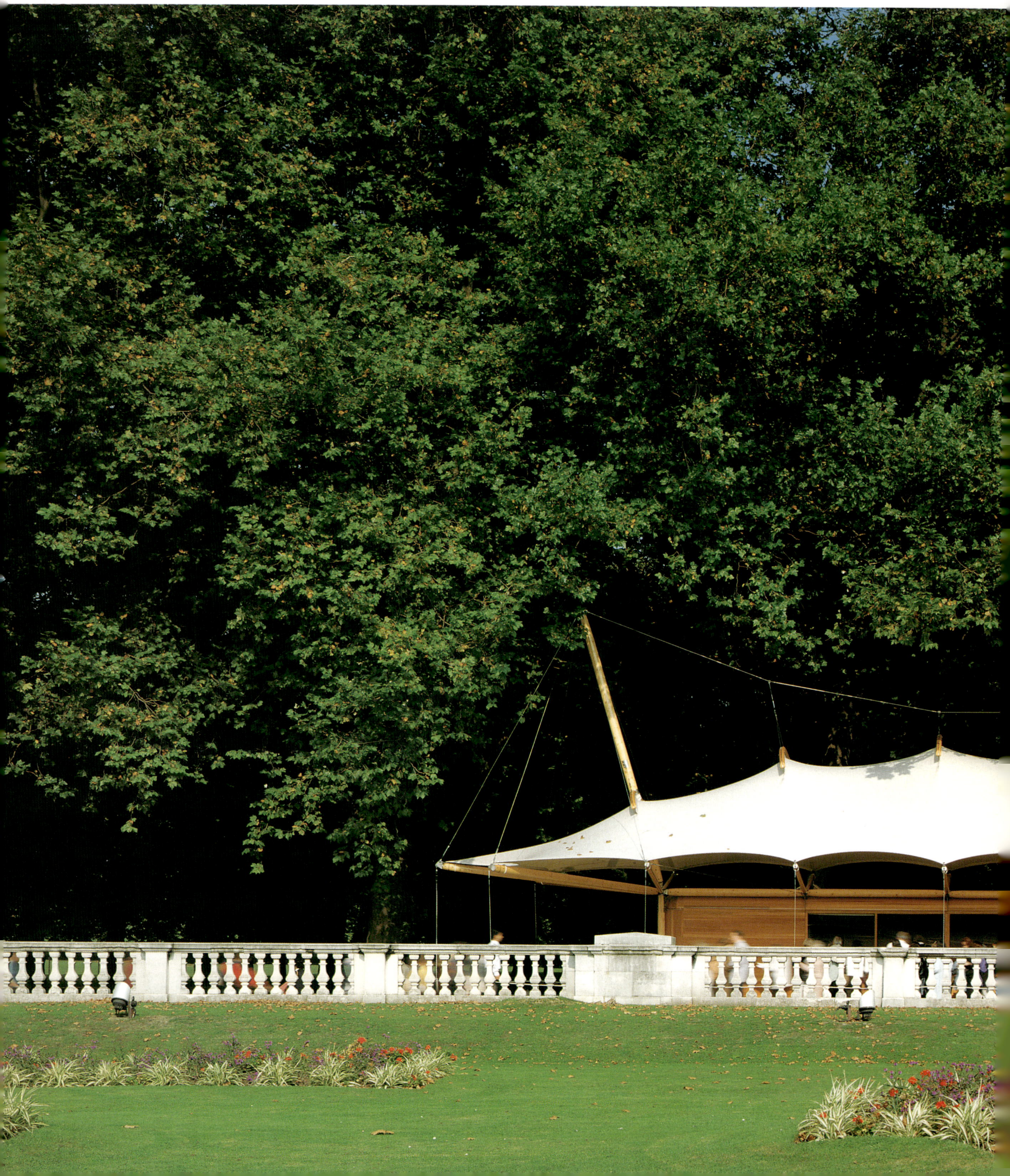

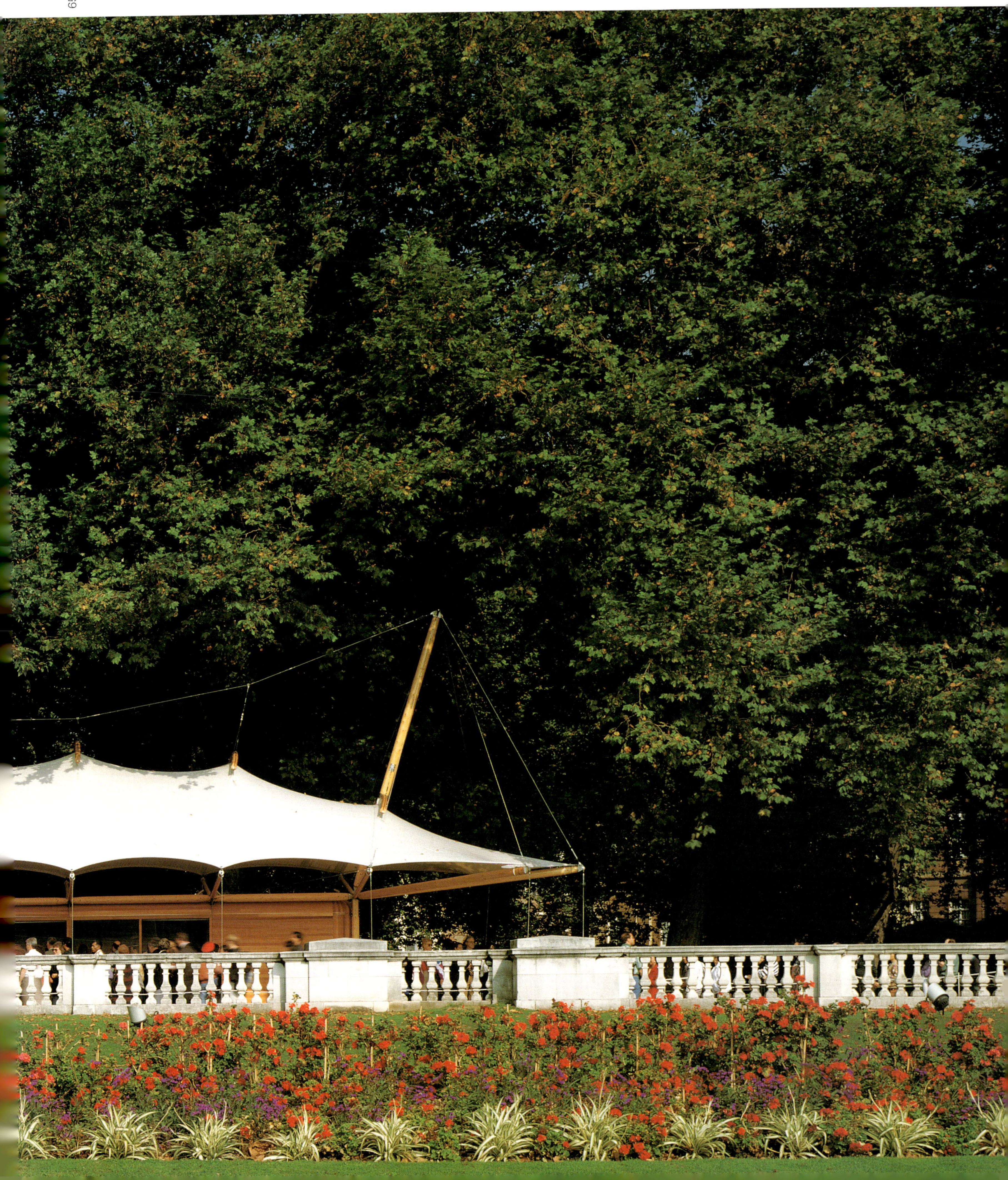

Jewish Care 1993–1996

Like country hotels, residential homes for the elderly are often conversions of large houses in extensive grounds. The country hotel therefore suggested itself as a possible model for this new residential home on an open site in a leafy part of north London, not far from the North Circular Road. After early studies exploring the potential of a dispersed plan with single-storey pavilions, it soon became clear that a unified, four-storey, rectangular building with a central courtyard offered a greater sense of community, as well as greater economy and operational efficiency. The three upper floors are almost identical; each has forty bed/sitting rooms, double banked along a continuous corridor with lifts and stairs at the corners. The ground floor accommodates a variety of shared facilities, including physiotherapy, hydrotherapy, recreational therapy, kitchen, laundry, café, library, offices and a synagogue.

The layout is formal, rational and symmetrical, but various subtle spatial devices ensure that it is not institutional or hospital-like. For example, corridors widen at intervals to form lobby spaces serving sub-groups of four rooms, and are aligned with windows in the re-entrant, diagonal corners so that daylight is visible, even in the heart of the building. Open dining and sitting areas on the south side of the building increase communal interaction. Individual rooms have an en-suite shower room and a projecting bay window which deals with all the heating, ventilating and daylighting for the room and doubles as a window seat.

What gives the building poise, on its plateau at the top of the sloping site, is the differentiation of the ground-floor level. Lightweight external walls of timber and glass are set back from the line of the red-brick walls above to form a recessed walkway. The main corridor is pushed inwards to the courtyard, where it becomes a fully-glazed cloister, while leaving room for the deeper spaces required by the various treatment and service rooms. Many of these rooms are private and must be screened from passers-by, but a sense of openness is maintained with high-level windows.

The effect of a brick box hovering, apparently unsupported, above the ground is achieved by means of a very unusual composite brick, concrete and steel structure. Aligned pairs of loadbearing brick fins at 8-metre centres are set back from the external walls at ground-floor level. Each pair supports a precast concrete beam which cantilevers out to the perimeter of the building. The slightly upturned ends of the cantilevers are connected by exposed steel members, like shallow king-post trusses turned upside down. The first floor is made of special precast concrete units spanning between the beams with an exposed soffit. On the upper levels, the structure becomes a straightforward, loadbearing, cross wall system.

The courtyard, with its raised planters and large areas of wheelchair-friendly paving, provides a secure and sheltered space, a perfect setting for outdoor festivals and activities.

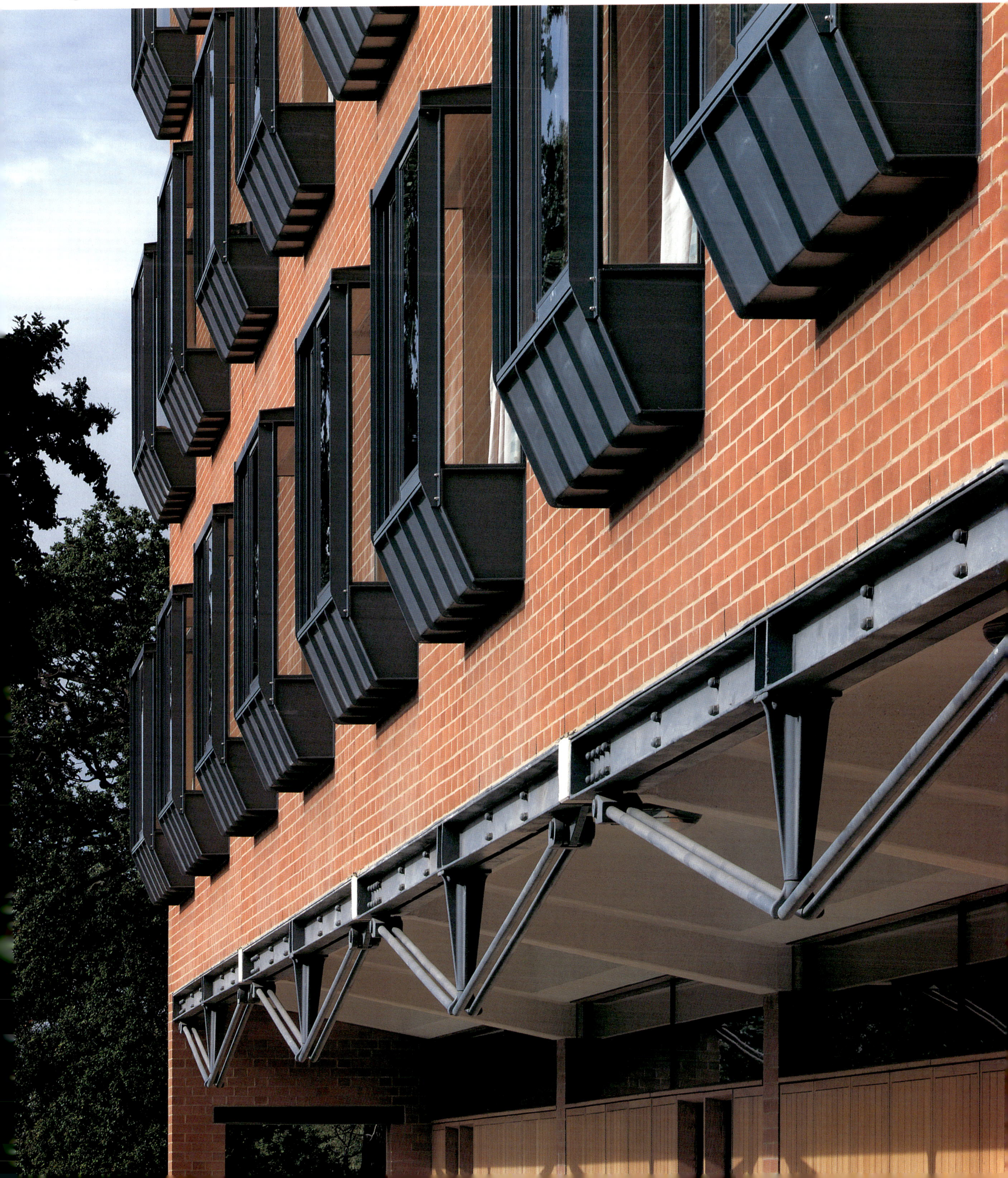

Previous page: each bed/sitting room has a projecting bay window incorporating a seat. The loadbearing brick wall is supported by ingeniously designed, braced steel beams.

Below: the building is a single, unified form, poised near the top of the sloping site. The ground floor is recessed with the main entrance in the diagonal south-west corner.

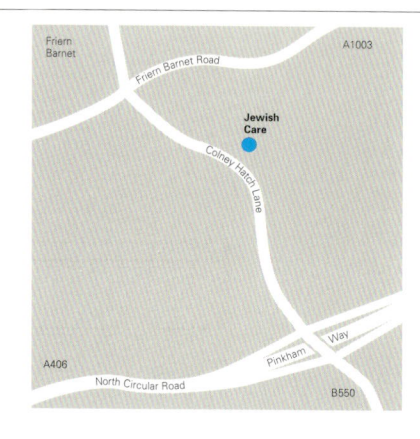

1 synagogue
2 courtyard
3 hydrotherapy pool
4 sitting area
5 dining area
6 bed/sitting room

Section

0 5m

On the ground floor, the corridor is moved inwards and becomes a glazed cloister around the open-air 'room' of the landscaped courtyard.

Jewish Care

Below: the ground-floor corridor widens into an open sitting area with a view of the courtyard.

Right: interior of the synagogue, showing the specially commissioned, illuminated stained-glass mural. The space can be opened to the corridor (or enclosed) by sliding folding doors.

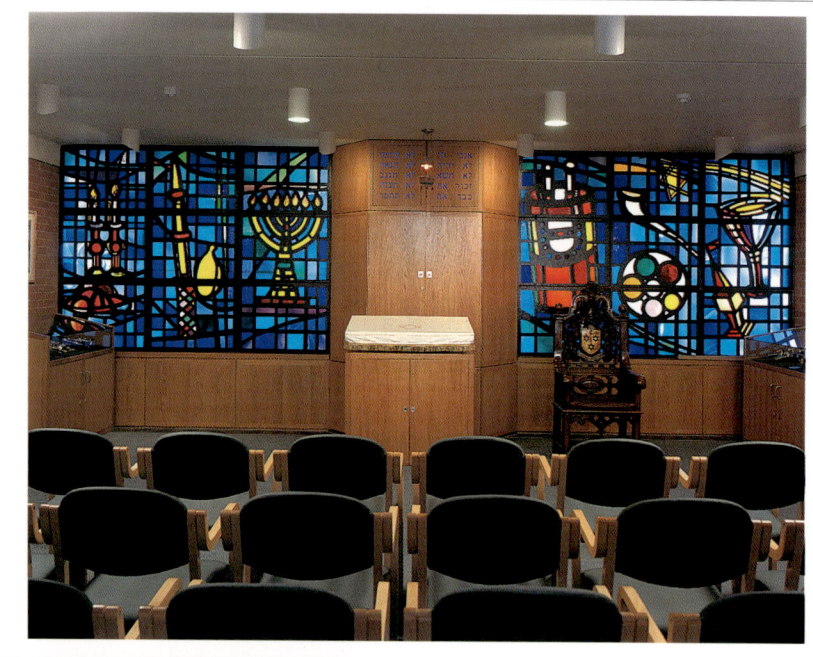

Jewish Care

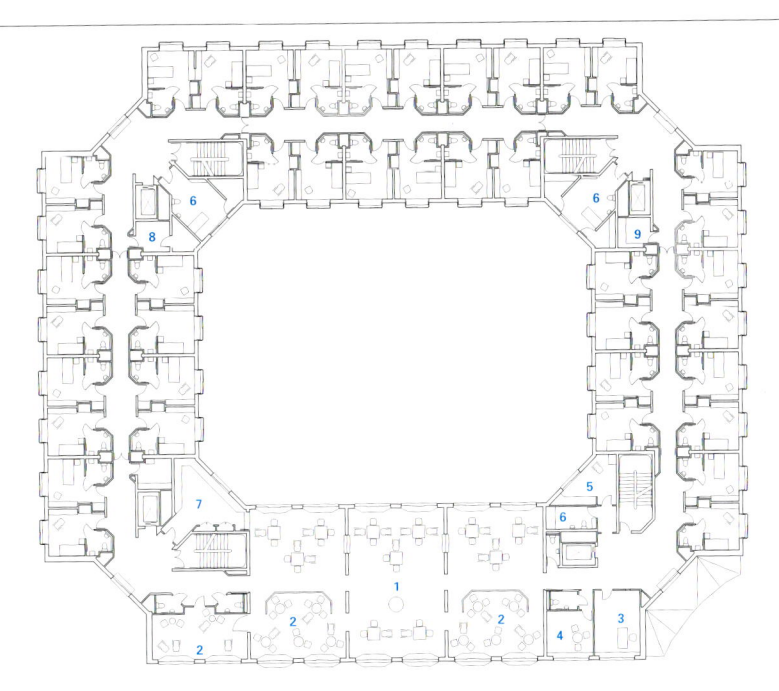

First floor plan

1 dining area	16 office
2 sitting area	17 doctor
3 sisters' office	18 kitchen
4 staff room	19 kitchen plant
5 treatment room	20 storage
6 assisted bathroom	21 staff washrooms/lockers
7 servery/utility room	22 laundry/sewing
8 sluice room	23 hydrotherapy pool
9 linen store	24 plant
10 main entrance	25 physiotherapy
11 security/reception	26 physiotherapy room
12 waiting	27 recreational therapy
13 café	28 hairdresser
14 synagogue	29 courtyard
15 library	30 car parking

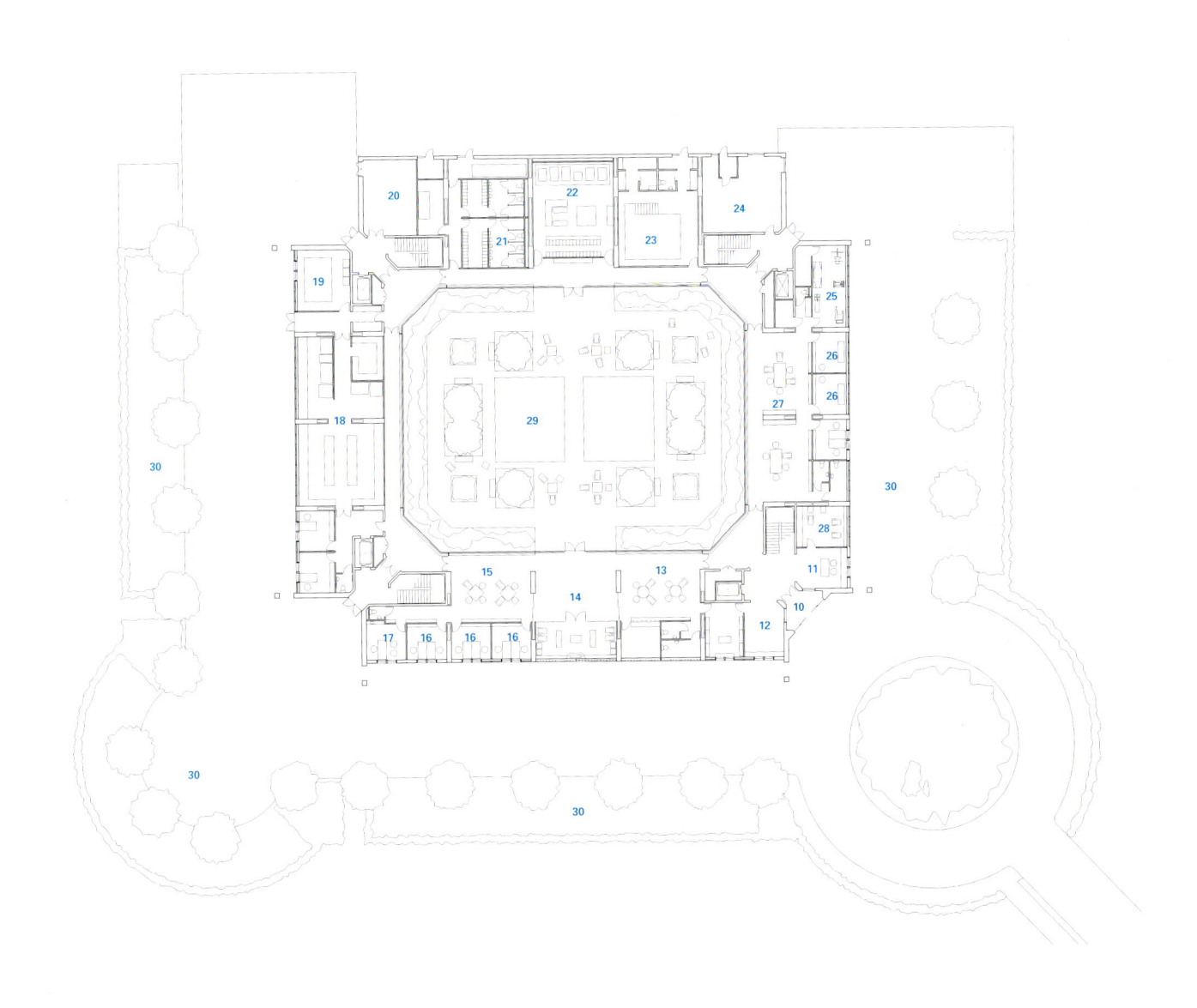

Ground floor plan

Saga Group Headquarters 1996–1998

The Saga Group sells holidays and financial services to the over-fifties. The company has been based in Folkestone since it was founded in 1951, and takes an unusually responsible attitude to its employees and the local community. This is reflected in the form of its new headquarters, built on a sloping site overlooking the sea – formerly the grounds of a country house by the nineteenth-century Gothic Revival architect, SS Teulon. The house was listed Grade II, but the authorities were persuaded to allow its demolition on the grounds that it had been much altered from its original state, and that it would be replaced by modern buildings of the highest architectural quality. The accommodation is divided between two separate and contrasting buildings: a serious-looking, steel- and concrete-framed office block, and a playful, fabric-roofed training and recreation building. Work and relaxation are thus differentiated architecturally, and the recreation building, known as the Pavilion, is made available for use by the local community. The two buildings are only loosely related to one another, with no formal architectural links, so that something of a relaxed, country house character is preserved, despite the fact that 900 people work on the site. A shuttle bus for employees limits the need for car parking and only 350 spaces are provided, hidden away in paddocks behind the Pavilion.

The Pavilion is one of a family of Hopkins tents, including the Inland Revenue amenity building in Nottingham, the Dynamic Earth museum in Edinburgh and, father of them all, the Schlumberger research building in Cambridge. But whereas its relations are all symmetrical about two axes and, like marquees, are largely uninfluenced by orientation or specific site conditions, the Pavilion is asymmetrical on its long axis, responding to the slope of the site and the pull of the sea view. Four separate glassfibre membranes are stretched between pairs of steel arches, tensioned like bows. Each pair is tilted up towards the south, with curved and tapered 'eyebrows' of vertical glazing filling the gaps in between. This segmented form gives the interior a directional quality. Standing at the south end facing north, one sees only the undersides of the membranes, washed with daylight, but at the north end facing south, the sky, in all its seaside variety, is revealed.

The big central space is used mainly as a restaurant, and occasionally for meetings of the whole workforce. In an emergency, however, it can be wired up to provide 400 workstations. It is naturally ventilated through doors in the end walls and vents in the high-level glazing. Underfloor heating provides background warmth, topped up in cold weather by high-level electric radiant heaters. Single-storey, flat-roofed secondary structures, housing kitchens, WCs, offices and training rooms, are threaded through the vertical supports of the tent structure along the east and west sides. At the south end,

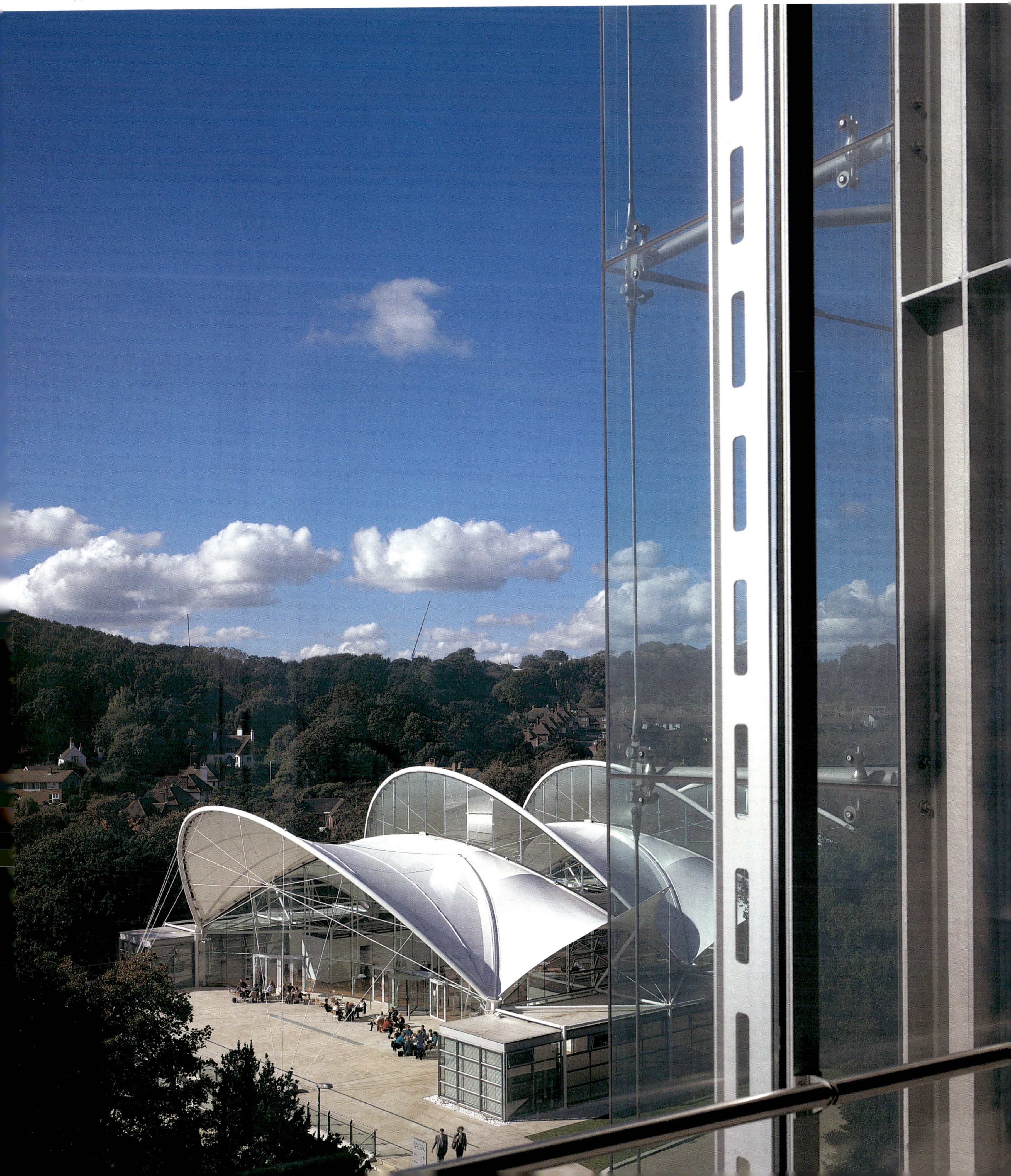

Previous page: the terrace of the Pavilion, viewed from the bridge between the office block and one of its stair turrets. The glass wall in the right foreground encloses a wall-climber lift.

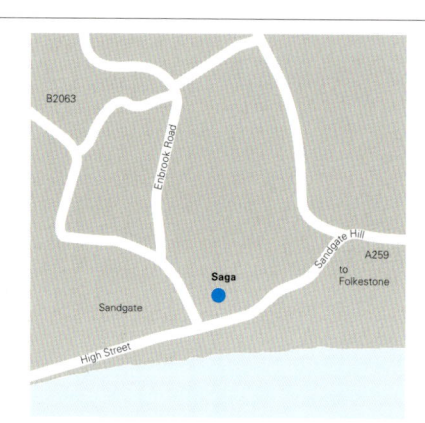

the central space continues out through a curved, full-height, glass curtain wall onto a generous open terrace, overlooking the sea and overarched by the last bay of the fabric roof. A day nursery for employees' children is tucked into the podium of the building, under the terrace, taking advantage of the sloping site.

The office block could hardly be more different, though it too responds to the pull of the sea view. A vertical, five-storey slab stands on the northern edge of a horizontal, two-storey podium, cut into the slope of the site. The podium has a courtyard carved out of its upper storey and a terrace on its roof, so that it forms a kind of garden apron in front of the vertical slab. The overall form of the building accommodates a variety of space plans, from open telesales areas in the podium to luxury executive offices on the top floor. Cellular offices are at the back of the building, so as not to obstruct the sea view. The structure is an unusual combination of round concrete columns, steel transverse beams and precast concrete slabs with exposed, vaulted soffits. There are no suspended ceilings and all services, including the fresh air supply, are distributed via raised floors.

The main entrance to the building is on the west side at basement level, signalling that, unlike the Pavilion, this is essentially a private building. A subterranean hall, with bare concrete walls, is entered through an opening like the mouth of a cave or the lifted edge of a concrete carpet.

From here, a grand flight of steps leads up through an opening in the ceiling to a daylit internal street. Above, a slightly leaning glass wall, bedecked with planting, rises from the roof of the podium almost to the full height of the building. This forms an atrium or, more accurately, an environmental buffer zone on the south side of the office slab. In summer, it is ventilated by the 'stack effect' of warm air rising, assisted by the wind; and in winter, it acts as a passive solar pre-heater. In short, it is a conservatory, which allows the office windows to be opened even on windy days. A timber deck on the roof of the atrium forms a terrace in front of the executive offices, with spectacular sea views. Two 'servant' towers, containing WCs, lift lobbies and plant rooms, stand outside the main footprint of the building at either end of the vertical slab. One of them is equipped with a bank of wall-climber lifts behind a protective screen of frameless glass. The most prominent external features, however, are the two circular stair turrets, thrust forward towards the sea at the ends of the glazed walkways. Like their counterparts at the Inland Revenue building, they are clad in glass blocks, but here the blocks are larger and more transparent, so that sea views can be enjoyed while descending the gentle spirals. The turrets are crowned by swivelling metal cowls, which assist the ventilation of the building by harnessing the suction power of the land and sea breezes.

Below: computer generated image. The mature, wooded site was once the garden of a large country house. Siting and orientation of both the office block and the Pavilion are strongly influenced by the proximity of the sea.

Right: the marine horizon viewed from the roof terrace of the office block, with one of the projecting staircase turrets in the foreground.

Overleaf: the two buildings, one for work and one for relaxation, are quite different in character and only loosely related to one another, though both face out to sea.

Saga Group Headquarters

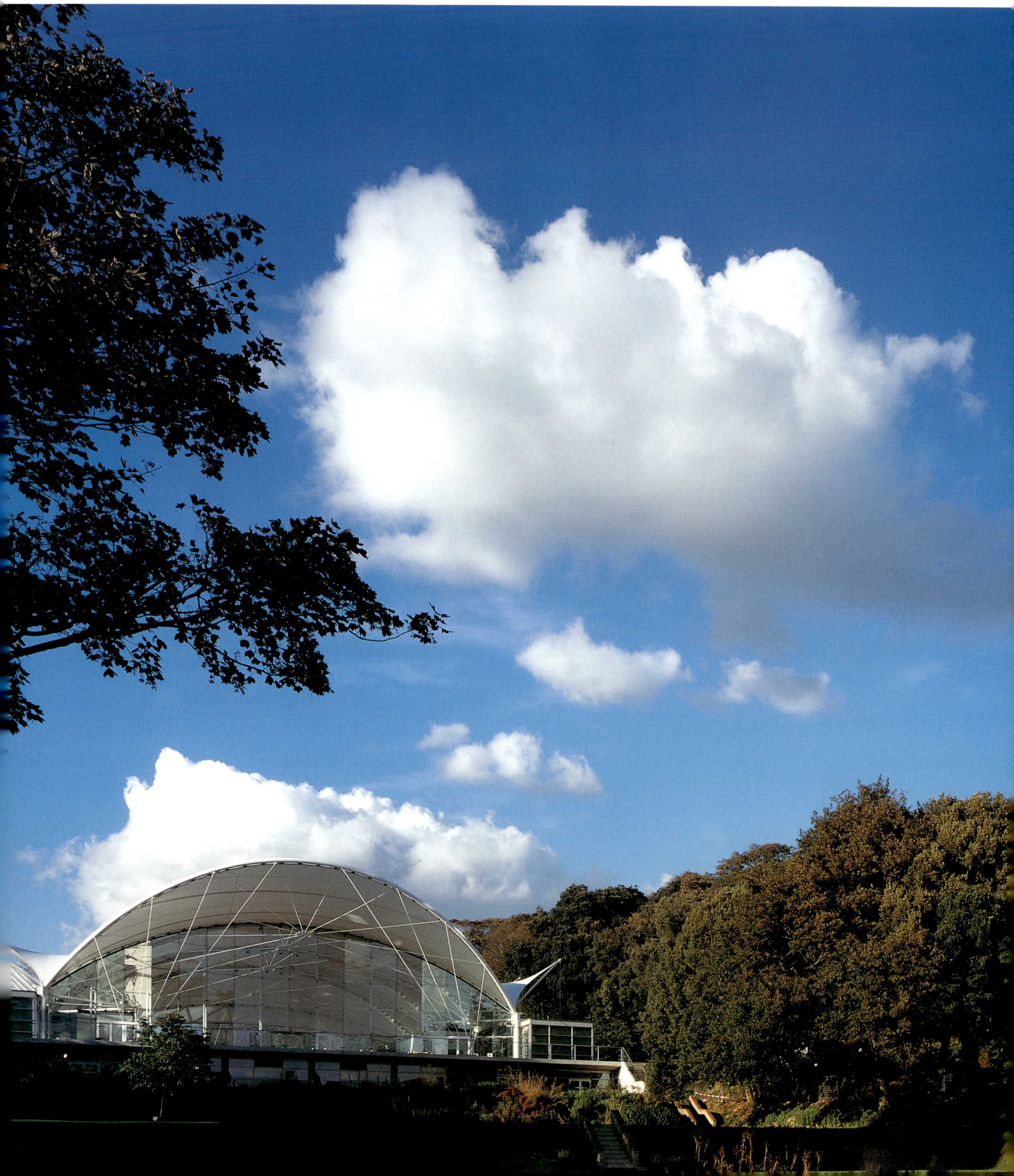

77

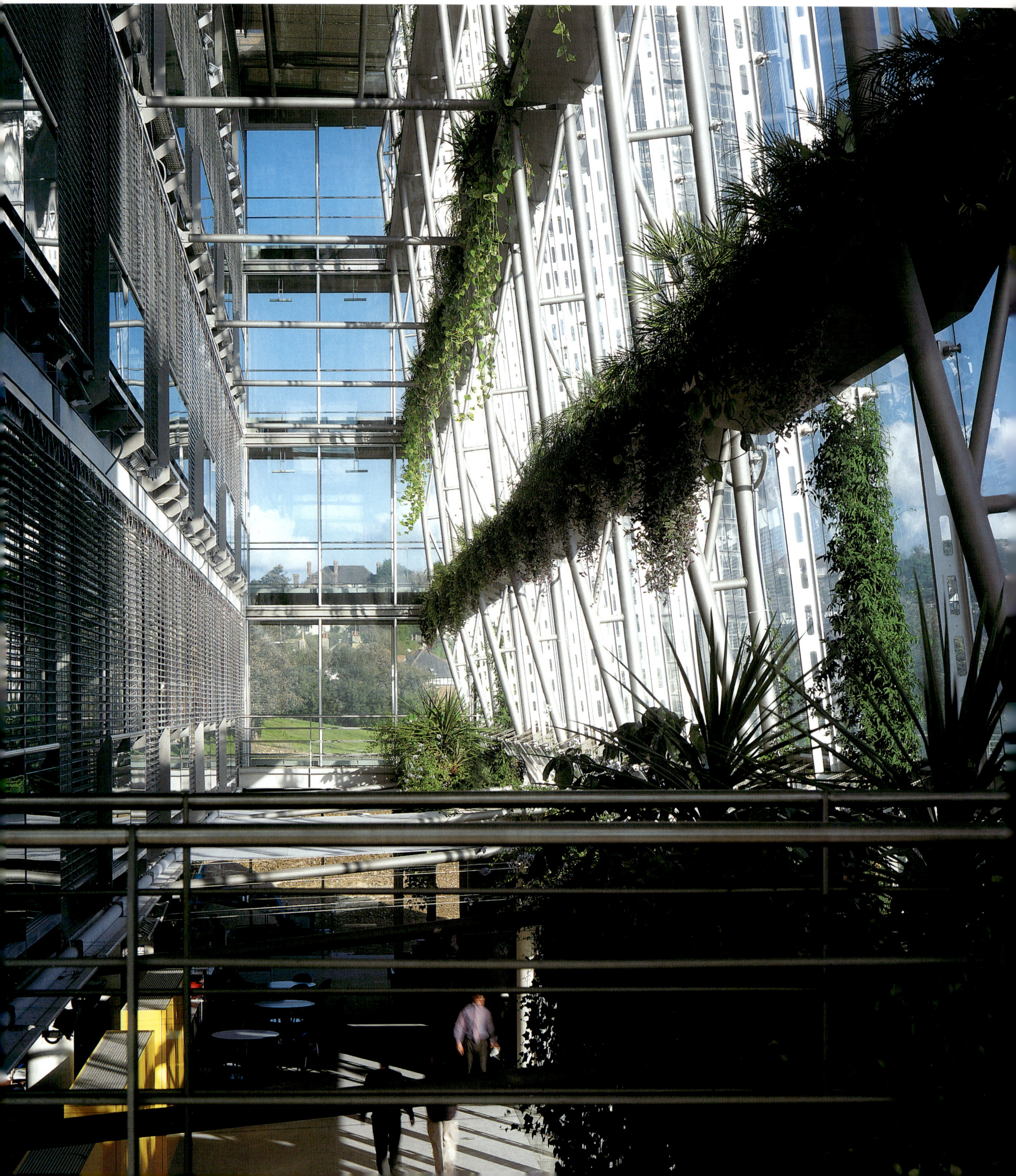

Opposite: the atrium of the office block forms an environmental buffer zone or conservatory. The windows of the offices on the left can be opened even in windy weather.

Left and below: office block section and plans. The upper level of the podium is occupied mainly by an open telesales area around a landscaped central courtyard.

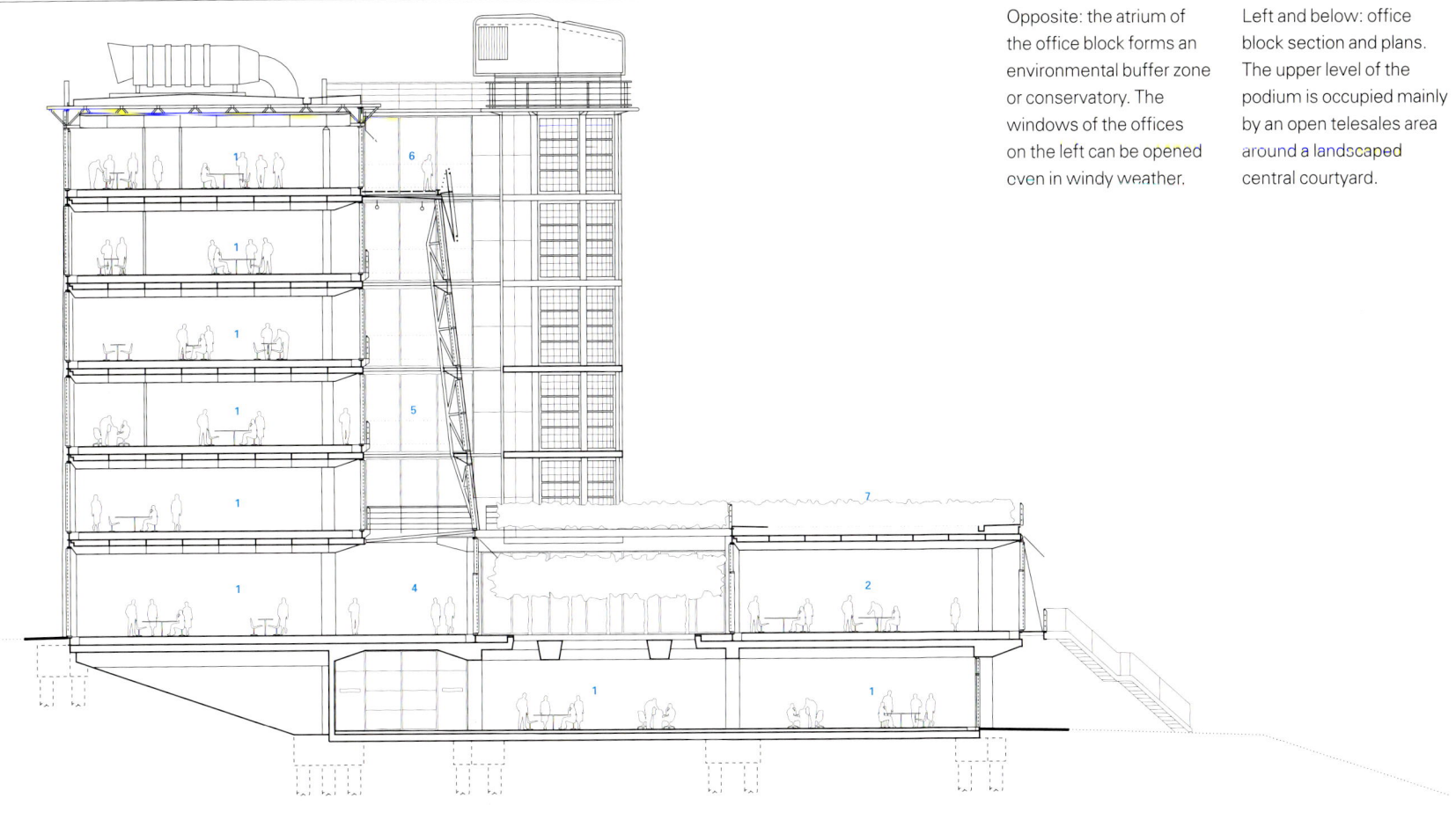

Transverse section

1 office
2 telesales
3 courtyard
4 street
5 atrium
6 terrace
7 roof garden
8 link bridge

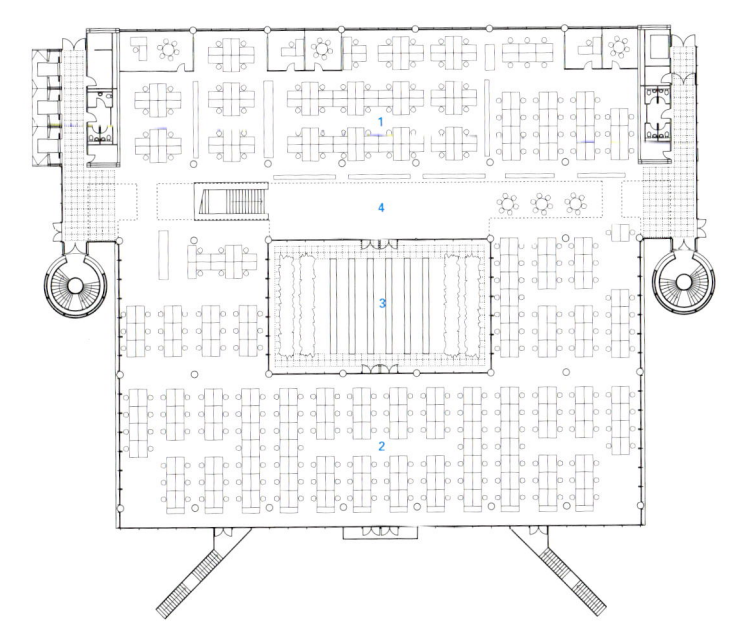

Ground floor plan

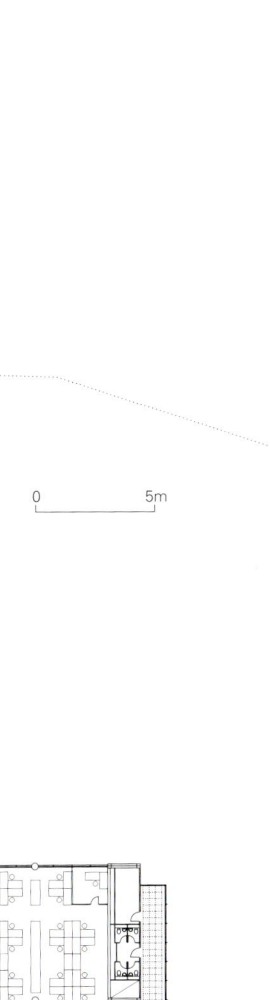

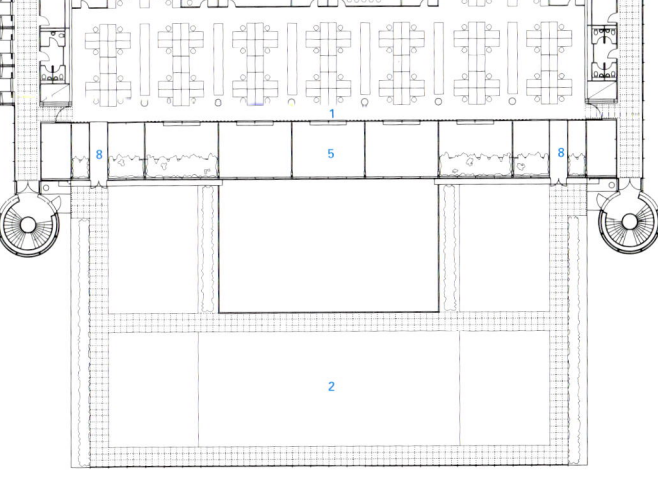

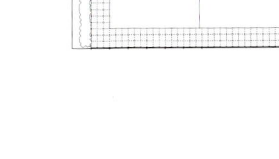

First floor plan

Saga Group Headquarters

Opposite: unlike other Hopkins tent structures, the Pavilion is a directional form, turning its 'eyebrows' of vertical glazing to the south and revealing large expanses of sky.

Right: the Pavilion is entered from a south-facing terrace sheltered by a vast fabric canopy. A concave wall of glass separates the terrace from the interior of the building.

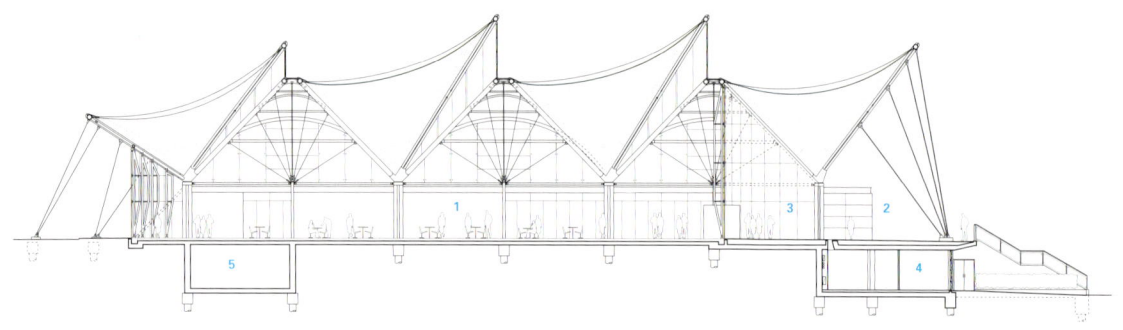

Section

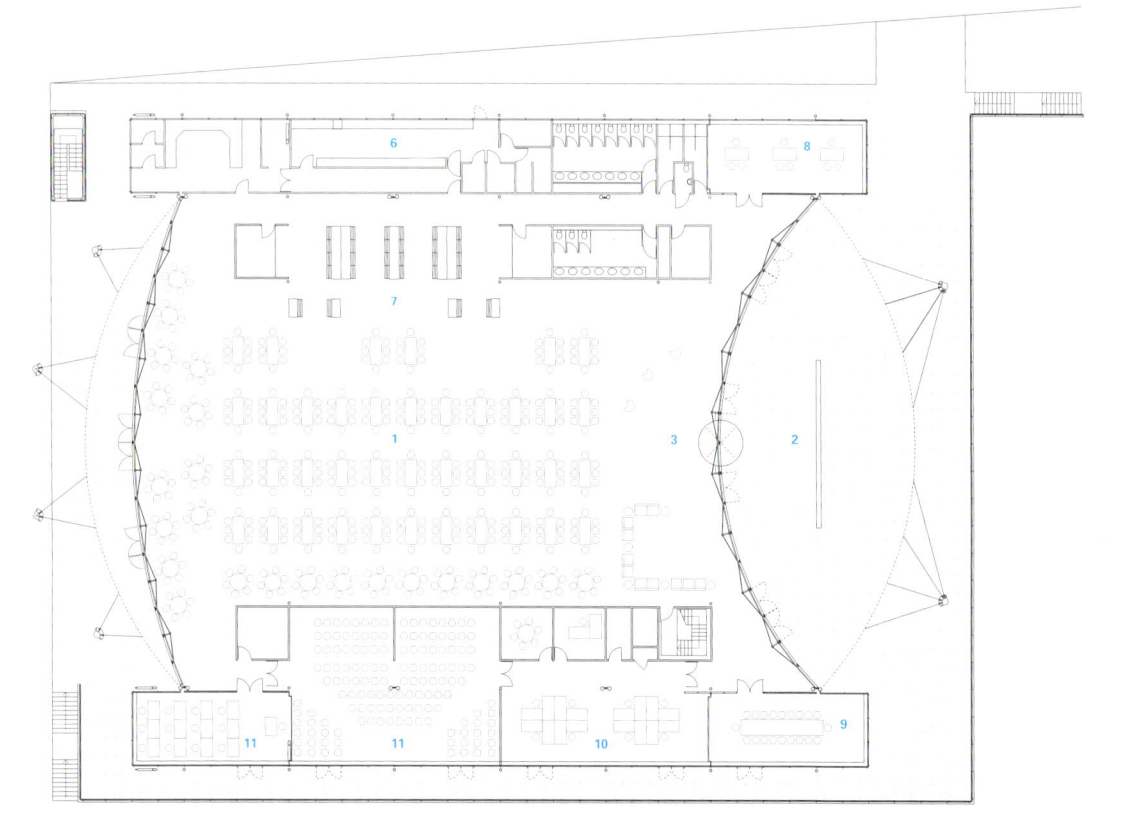

1 main hall
2 terrace
3 main entrance
4 crèche
5 plant
6 kitchen
7 servery
8 Saga shop
9 executive dining/meeting
10 office
11 training

Ground floor

Saga Group Headquarters

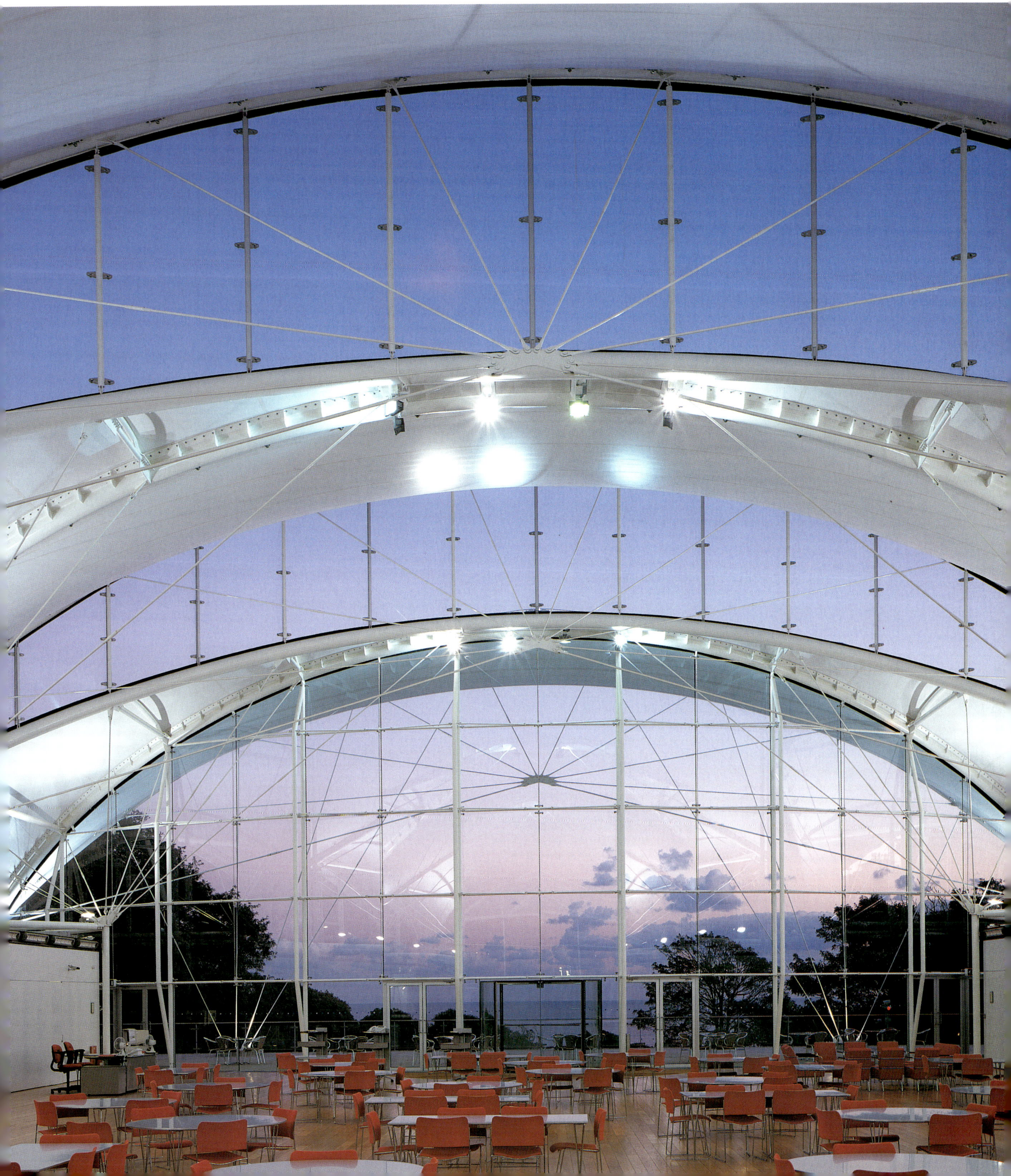

Dynamic Earth
1990–1999

Salisbury Crags in Edinburgh is the place where the eighteenth-century geologist, James Hutton, developed his folded plate theory of land formation. When the old Scottish and Newcastle Brewery vacated its site at the foot of the Crags, near Holyroodhouse, and bequeathed it to the city on condition that it be developed for public use, a decision was taken to build a visitor attraction with a geological theme. The result is Dynamic Earth, partially financed by the Millennium Commission. The brief simply called for a 'black box' to contain a variety of multimedia exhibits, including a planetarium; but if the architectural potential of the brief was limited, that of the site was enormous. Hopkins quickly arrived at a simple but dramatic solution. The black box would be accommodated within the existing walls of the old nineteenth-century brewery and a new entrance foyer created on the roof, accessed via a stepped amphitheatre and covered by a flamboyant tent structure set against the dark backdrop of the Crags.

The building consists of three main elements: box, theatre forecourt and tent. The box is two storeys high, over a basement car park. Some of the exhibition spaces are double height and the dome of the planetarium projects through the roof of the box into the tent. Administrative offices and a double-height function room are accommodated between the exhibition spaces and the old brewery walls. The old west side wall has been rebuilt in local sandstone with new stone-mullioned windows; the south and east sides have been renovated and a neo-Tudor castle turret on the south-east corner has been preserved. These loadbearing stone walls are stabilized by the new internal structure of flat or coffered concrete slabs supported by round columns on an 8 by 8 metre grid. The steps of the theatre forecourt are of York stone with granite paving for the stage area – which doubles as a turning circle for tourist coaches. The theatre forecourt is a public building in its own right and is used for a variety of performance events, especially during the Edinburgh Festival.

All this earthbound stone construction forms a solid base for the main architectural event, the light and airy tent. PTFE-coated, glass fibre membranes are stretched between elliptical, glazed, steel ladder trusses suspended from four pairs of steel masts. An all-glass perimeter wall, supported by structural glass fins, follows the contours of the underside of the tent to form an oval enclosure. The area enclosed is designed for use as a restaurant and viewing platform, as well as a gathering space for parties of visitors. Two big spiral staircases descend into the black box – one the entrance and the other the exit point of the controlled circulation route through the exhibition. Since the building opened, the management have used the tent for special events, such as conferences and banquets, but one of its main functions is to proclaim the presence of the building to tourists on the nearby Royal Mile.

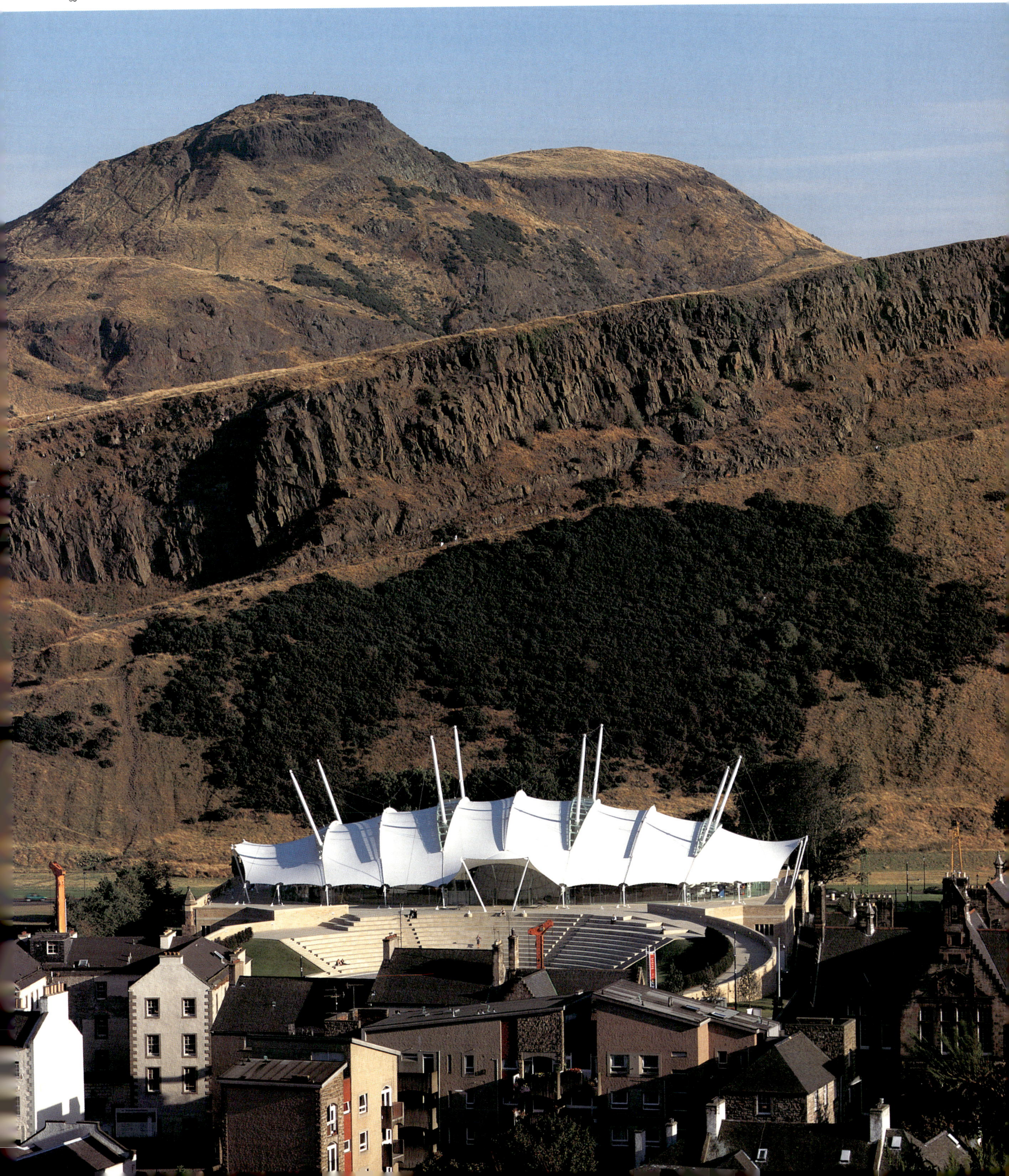

Previous page: the tented superstructure of the building squats like a strange animal at the foot of Salisbury Crags. The stepped theatre forecourt is just visible over the roofs of the houses.

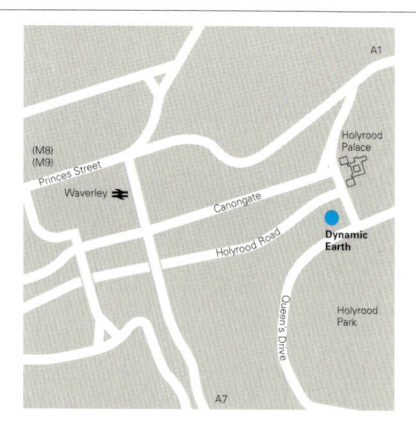

Left: a glass wall surrounds the tented superstructure and follows the contour of the underside of the fabric membrane. The wall is supported by structural glass fins.

Exploded axonometric

1 fabric roof
2 visitor concourse level
3 amphitheatre
4 bar
5 showdome
6 café
7 mezzanine level
8 shop
9 offices
10 education
11 ground floor level
12 function room
13 exhibition
14 kitchen
15 car park level

Below: the multimedia exhibition, including a domed planetarium (top), is housed in a 'black box' inside the stone plinth with no visual connection to the outside world.

Overleaf: at night the tent becomes a shining beacon, standing out against the dark silhouette of the Crags. The theatre forecourt doubles as a turning circle for coaches.

Dynamic Earth

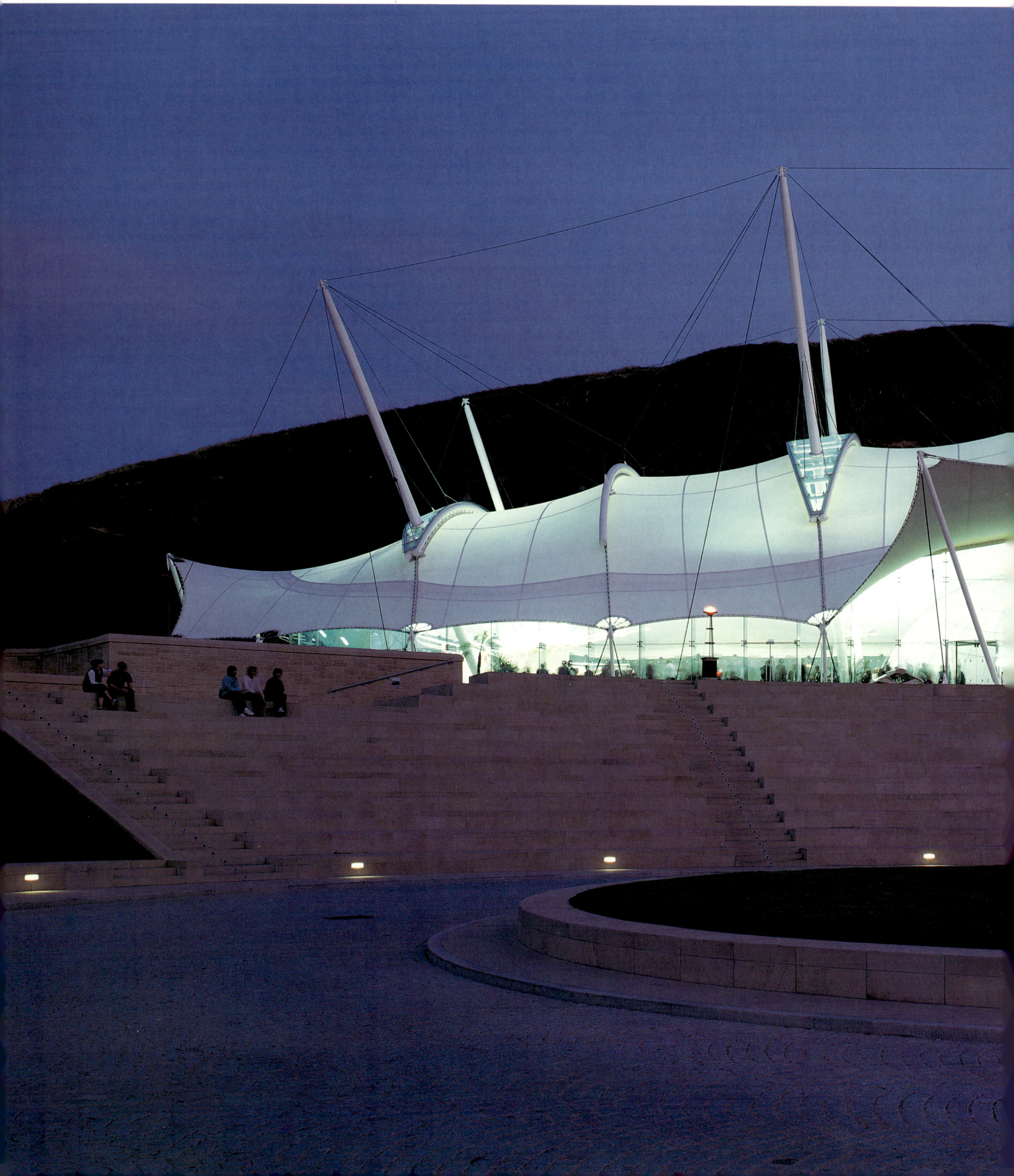

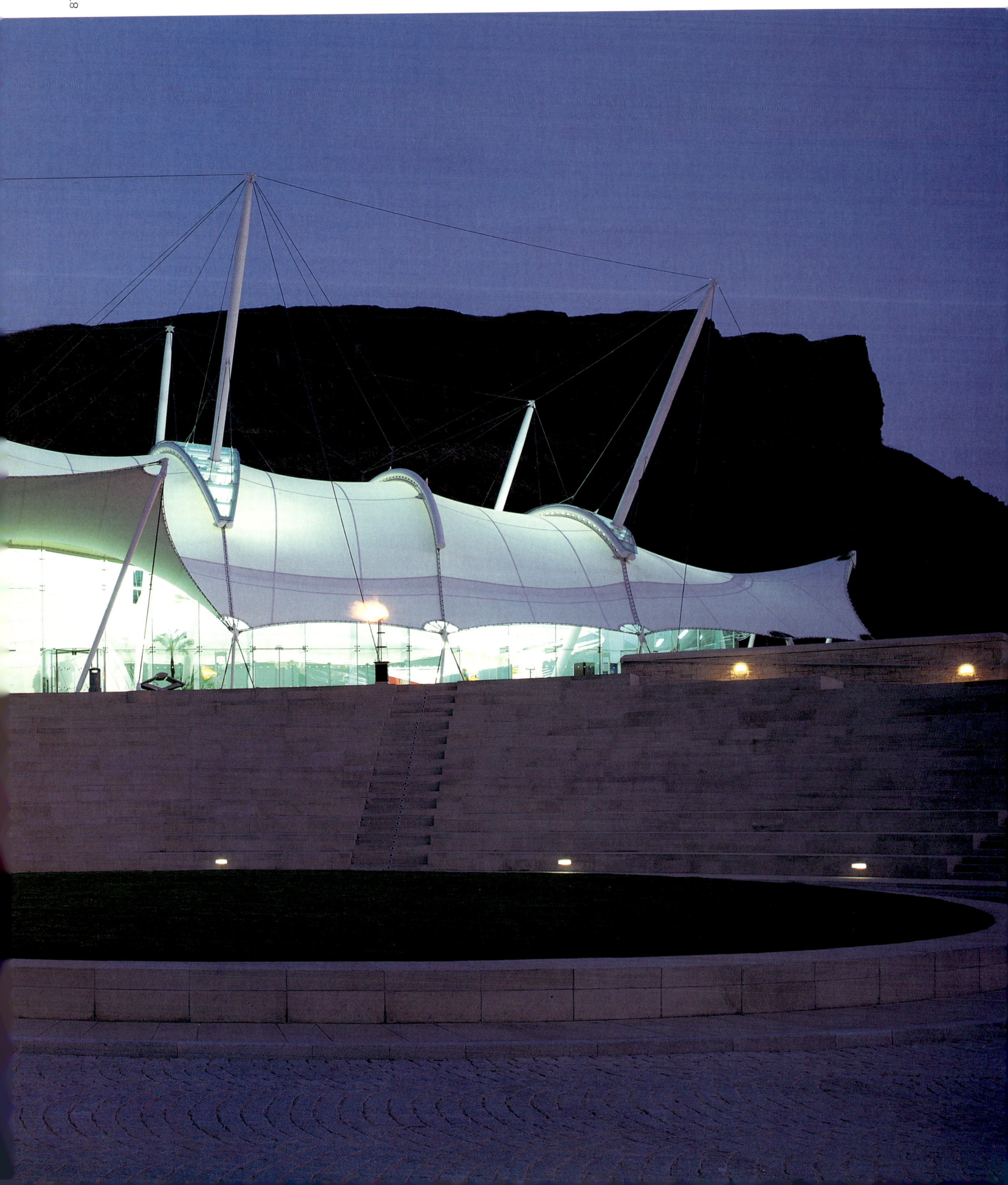

1 amphitheatre
2 visitor concourse
3 showdome
4 café
5 bar
6 auditorium
7 exhibition
8 administration
9 car parking
10 Holyrood Road

Left and below: section and site plan showing the relationships between the three main elements of the building: the stone plinth; the tented superstructure; and the open-air theatre of the forecourt.

Opposite: the dome of the planetarium projects through the roof of the plinth into the tent and becomes a symbolic representation of the Earth.

Longitudinal section

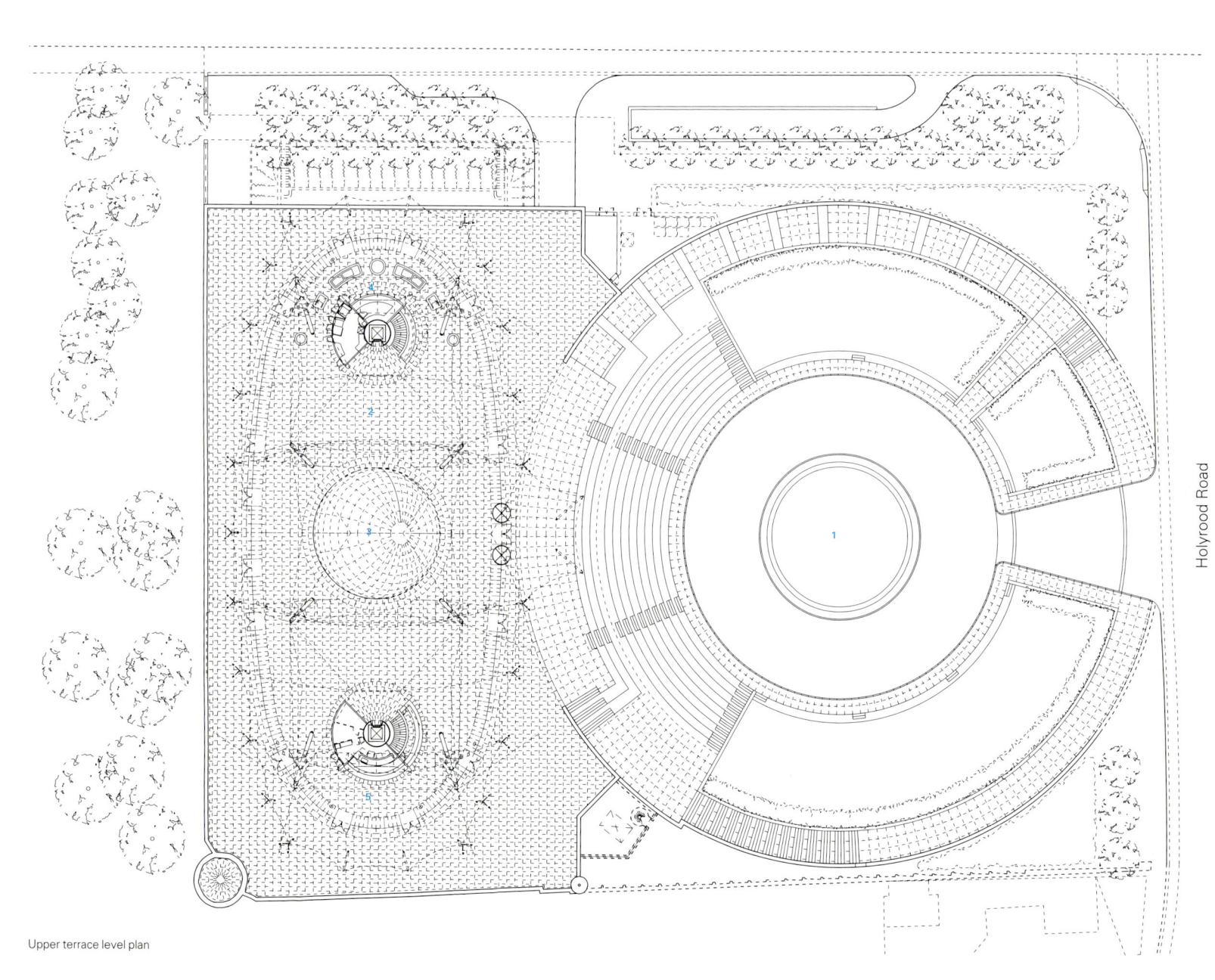

Upper terrace level plan

Dynamic Earth

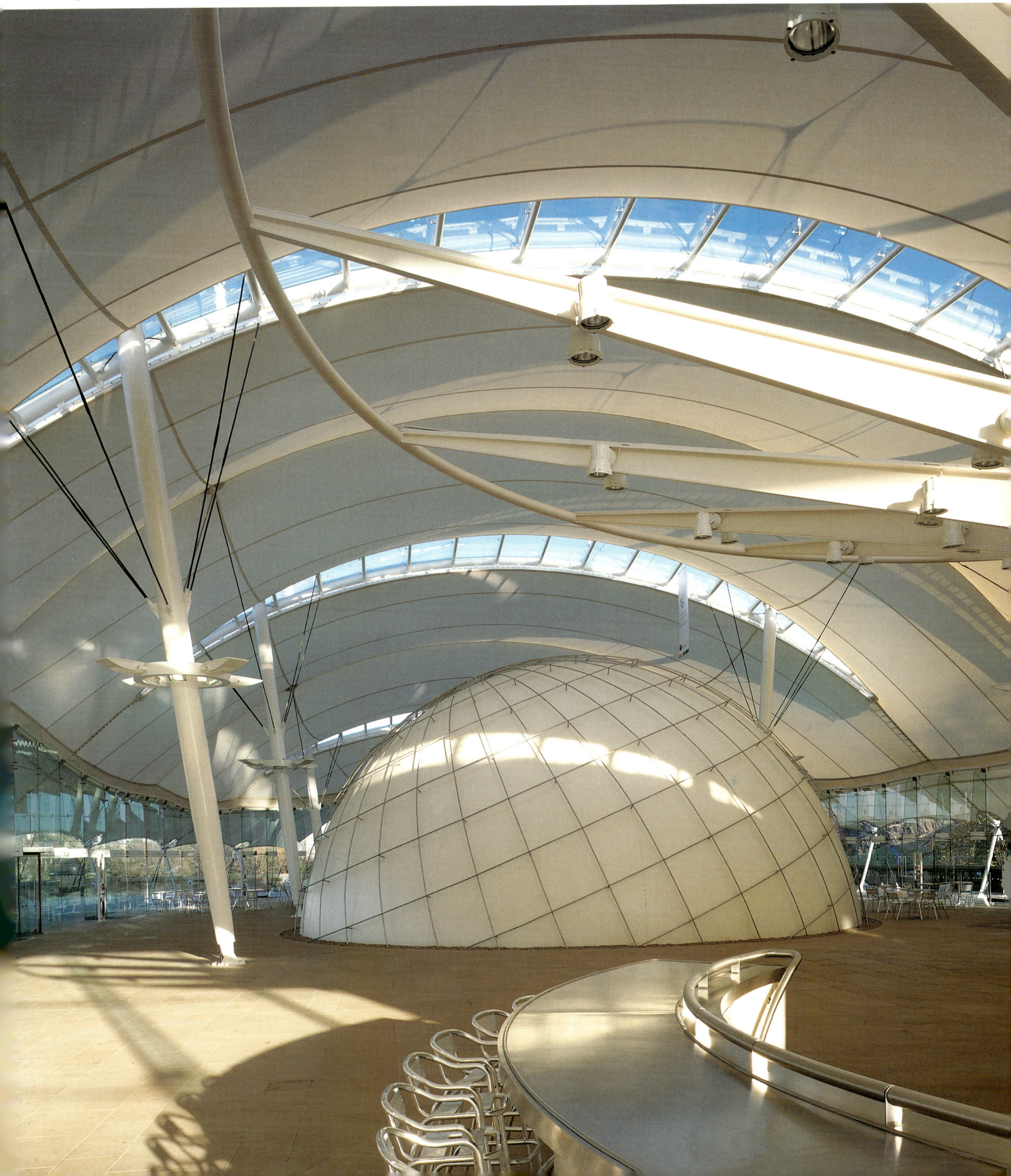

Jubilee Campus, University of Nottingham 1996–1999

Nottingham University's new Jubilee Campus for 2,500 students occupies the site of the old Raleigh bicycle factory, on the border between industrial and residential zones of the city. A central teaching facility, known as The Exchange, is flanked by faculty buildings housing the Schools of Business, Computer Science, Education and Continuing Education, ranged along the eastern shore of an artificial lake. Tree planting and landscaped mounds on the opposite side of the lake screen the development from suburban housing to the west. The visual focus of the campus is the Learning Resource Centre, on an island in the lake accessed by a short causeway, opposite The Exchange. Courtyard-planned, undergraduate halls of residence occupy the south-east corner of the site, and a crescent-shaped terrace of postgraduate halls overlooks an extension of the lake to the north.

The faculty buildings are simple, economical structures, using a repertoire of standard forms in different combinations. Three-storey, rectangular office and classroom blocks – set at right angles to, and bridging over, a lakeside promenade to create a discontinuous colonnade – alternate with either gardens or glazed atria. The blocks have simple 'domino', in-situ concrete structures of flat slabs supported by round columns on a 6 by 6 metre grid, reduced to 4 metres for the lakeside colonnade. External walls, including those facing the atria, are made from prefabricated panels clad in Western Red Cedar from a sustainable Canadian source with timber-framed windows. Designed on the 'breathing wall' principle, the panels are insulated by a thick core of 'Warmcell', which is made from recycled newspaper. The standard atrium is a relatively narrow, quasi-external space, paved, planted and furnished for casual communal use. Its glass curtain wall faces the lake, the top section of which is canted out over the promenade. From the top of this wall, a shallow-pitched glass roof – supported by laminated timber beams on galvanized steel stub columns – rises towards the back of the building. A stack of glazed-in footbridges links the blocks on either side of the atrium to a spiral staircase housed in a timber-clad tower with an oast house-like cowl on top.

The whole arrangement is designed to take advantage of passive solar and wind energy for the heating, cooling and ventilation of the building. The atria, which are single-glazed and unheated, act as conservatories in the winter, reducing the energy required to heat the building. In summer, their canted glass walls catch the cool breeze from the lake and funnel it through banks of openable glass louvers to reduce heat gain. The choice of heavy, in-situ concrete for the structure, with exposed soffits, is another internal climate-moderating measure, absorbing and storing heat to even out temperature fluctuations in the building. The roofs are grass-covered, which also increases thermal mass and prevents overheating in the top storey. The building is not, however, naturally

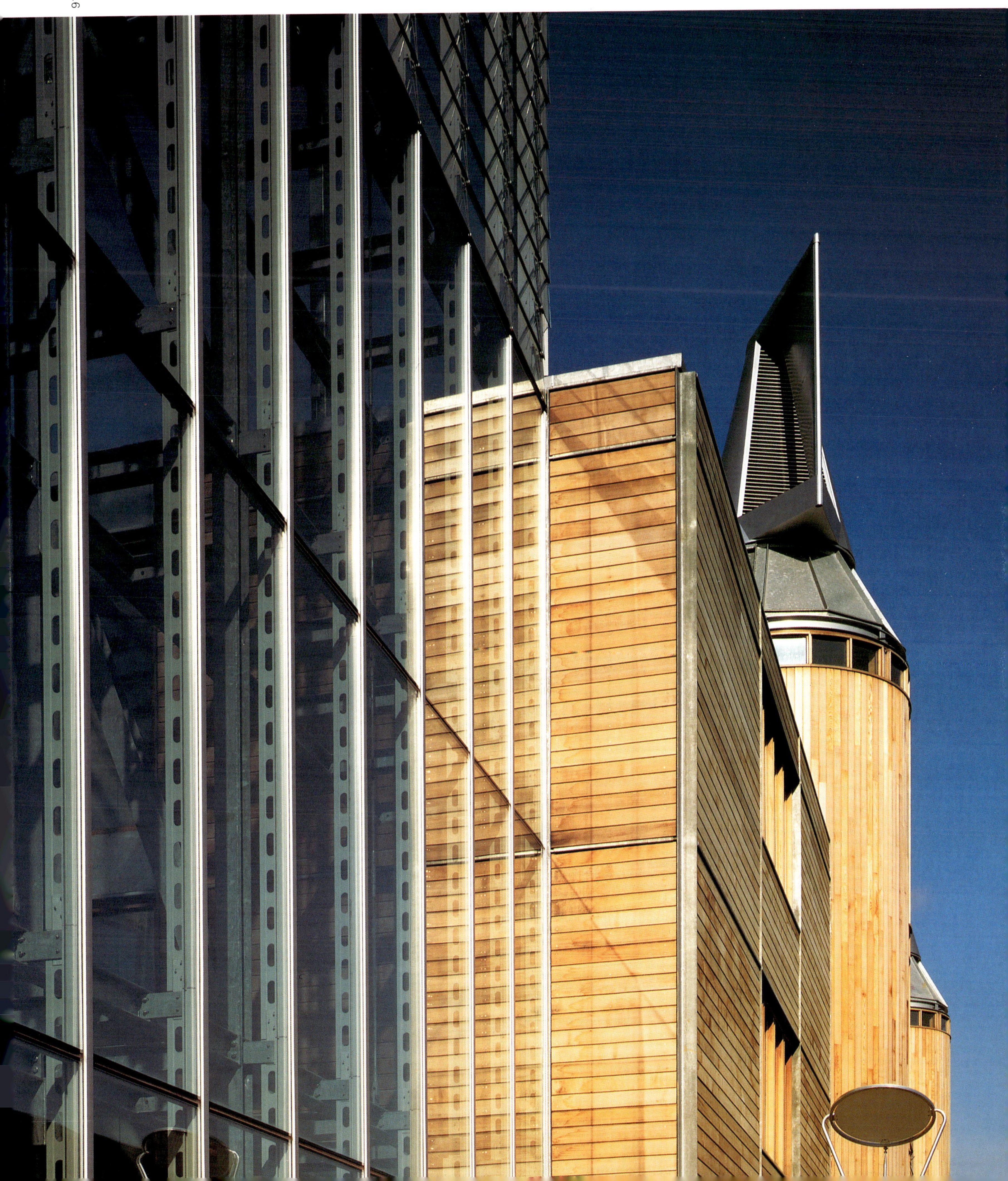

Previous page: glass and wood are the dominant external materials. The backs of the buildings facing the access road, are punctuated by round stair towers topped by oast house-like cowls.

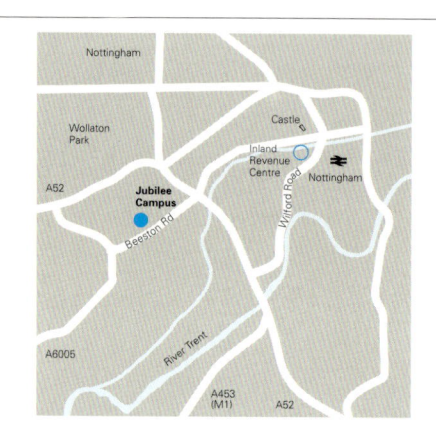

ventilated. Studies showed that a low-pressure mechanical system, incorporating heat recovery, would be more efficient. Fresh air is drawn into a modular air-handling unit housed in the top of the staircase tower. From here, it is blown down through vertical ducts into floor plenums and out through diffusers into the offices and classrooms. Exhaust air passes into the corridors through high-level, acoustically-baffled diffusers and finds its way to the spiral staircase where it is sucked out through the rotating oast-house cowl. The air-handling unit includes a thermal wheel to recover heat from exhaust air in winter. Electrical energy for the fans is generated by photovoltaic cells sandwiched between the glass panels of the atria roofs.

A typical ensemble – the Business School at the north end of the campus, for example – consists of three blocks, two atria and two staircase towers, but there are important variations on this standard pattern. Two of the atria are wider and have more complex programmes. In the atrium of The Exchange stands a massive, sculptural concrete structure, tapering towards its base. This building contains three lecture theatres, nested one above the other, with two staircase towers to cope with the circulation. Between the School of Computer Science and School of Education, the space that would normally be an open garden, twice the width of a standard atrium, has been glazed in to serve as a food court, with kitchens in the ground floor of the adjacent block.

In contrast with the rectilinear, repetitive nature of the faculty buildings, the Learning Resource Centre, on its lake isle, is a unique freestanding form – an inverted cone containing a continuous spiral ramp, not unlike a miniature version of the New York Guggenheim Museum. The building is entered across a short causeway in front of The Exchange. Users have a choice of two circulation routes: either the anti-clockwise ramp around the perimeter of the building, past segmental, book-lined reading alcoves, or the top-lit central core, which contains a helical stair and lifts. The spiral plan, unprecedented in a building of this kind, was developed to solve a particular planning problem. The building houses the computer centre as well as the library, and it is likely that the balance of space allocation to these two uses will alter in the near future. By providing what is, in effect, a single continuous strip of usable floor, the balance can be adjusted in small increments without the necessity for a major reorganization.

In drawing up the brief for the new campus, the client was anxious that it should not be a monumental megastructure, but that it should have a relaxed, park-like setting, similar to that of the existing University Park Campus. This has been achieved by the repetition of standardized building forms, combined with a few unique structures to create a picturesque variety of spaces. The environmentally-friendly nature of the scheme makes it a model for future industrial regeneration projects.

Left: the Raleigh factory occupying the whole site before development.

Below: faculty buildings are linked by a promenade along the edge of the lake. The Learning Resource Centre, on its lake isle, is the focal point of the whole plan.

Site plan

1 lake
2 grassed island
3 postgraduate hall
4 Business School
5 Central teaching facility
6 Learning Resource Centre
7 Department of Computer Science
8 central catering facility
9 Departments of Education and Continuing Education
10 undergraduate hall A
11 undergraduate hall B
12 entrance
13 main entrance

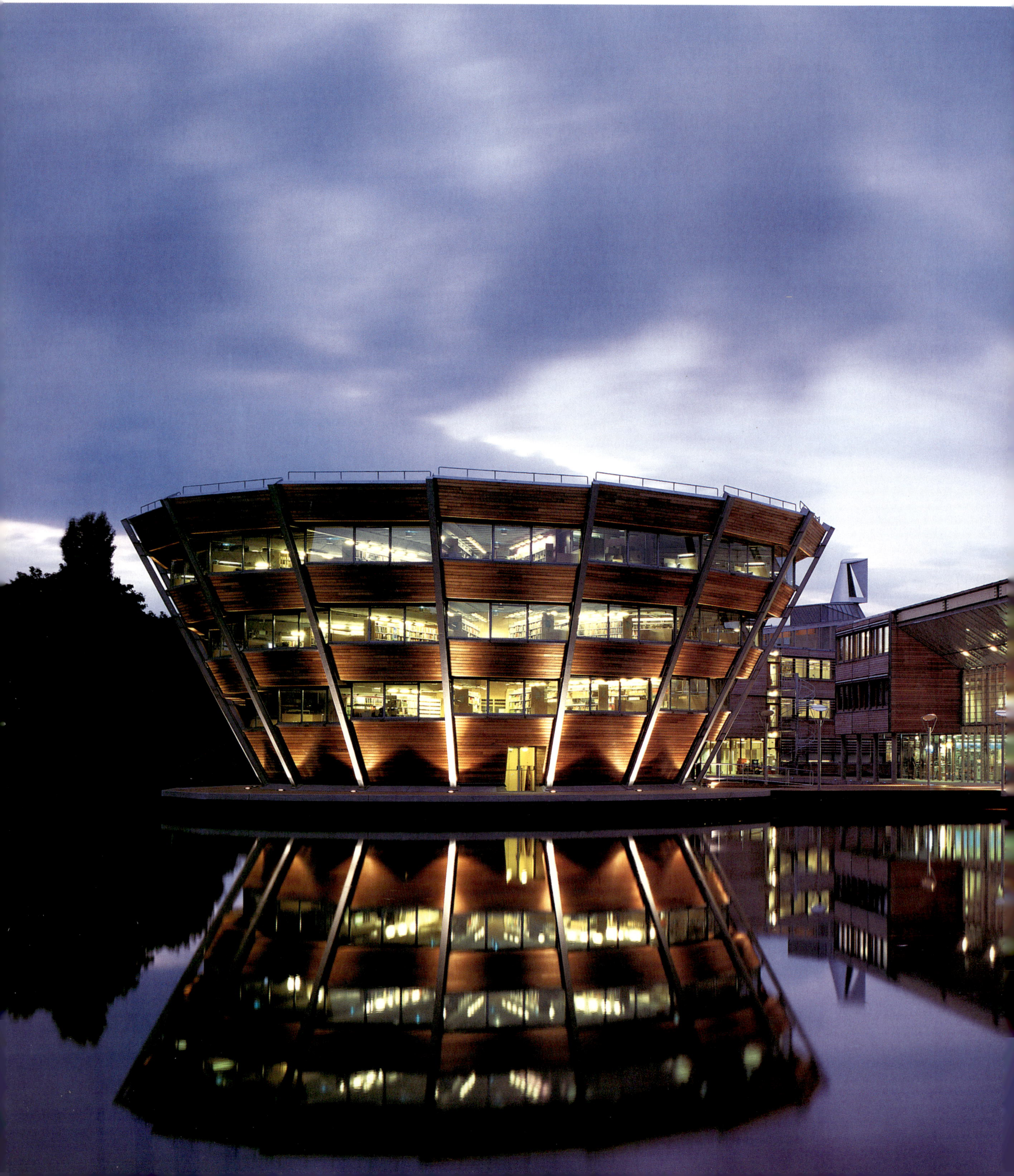

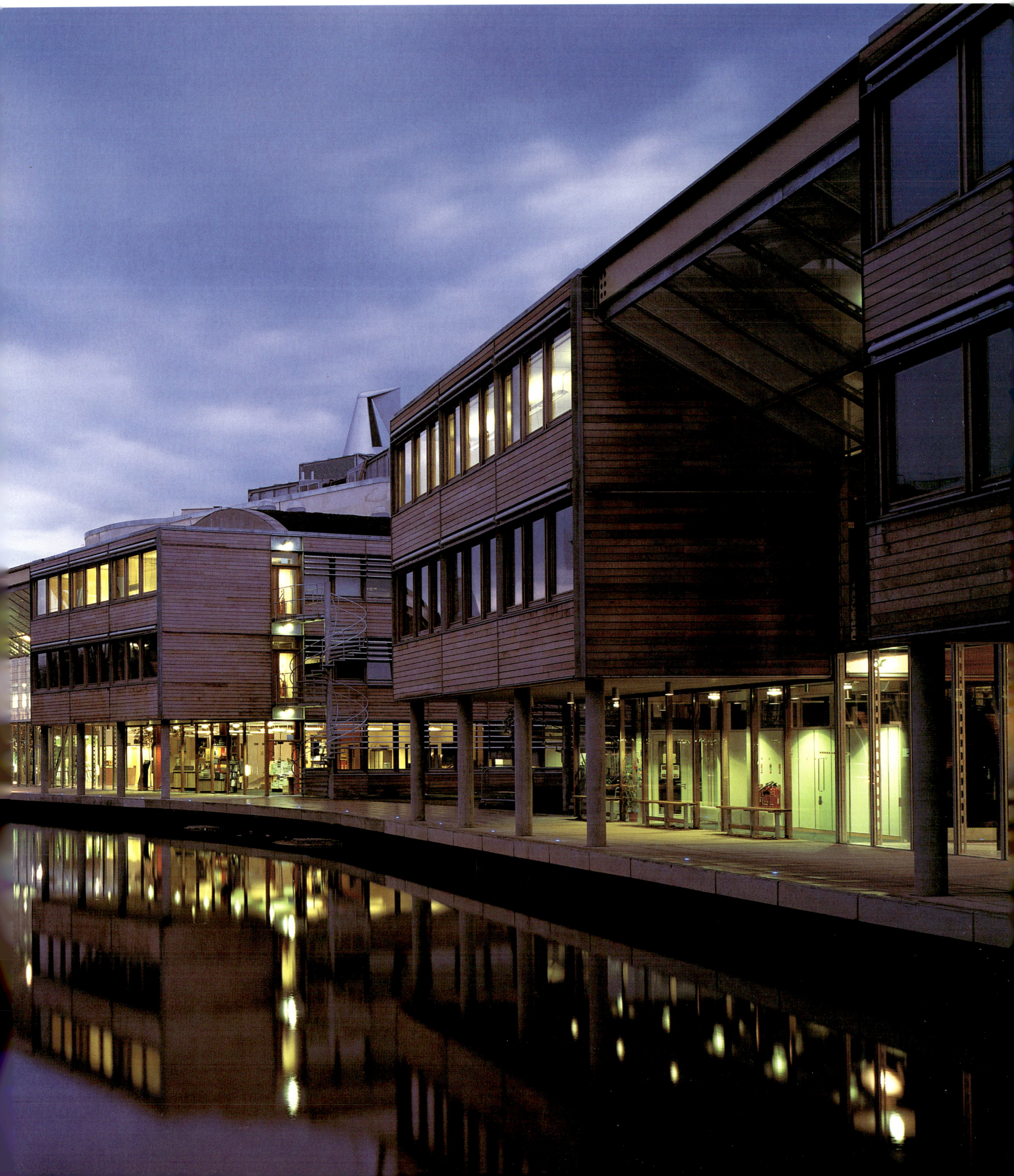

Previous page: the tapered form and spiral plan of the Learning Resource Centre are reminiscent of Frank Lloyd Wright's Guggenheim Museum in New York. The materials, however, are very different.

Below: exploded isometric showing the axial arrangement of The Exchange, with its stacked lecture theatres, and the Learning Resource Centre, accessible via a causeway.

Opposite: faculty buildings stand right on the edge of the lake, straddling the pedestrian promenade. Gangplanks connect the promenade to a grassy island at the south end of the lake.

Exploded isometric

1 new lake
2 Learning Resource Centre
3 Central Teaching Facility
4 100-seat theatre
5 200-seat theatre
6 300-seat theatre
7 roof plant

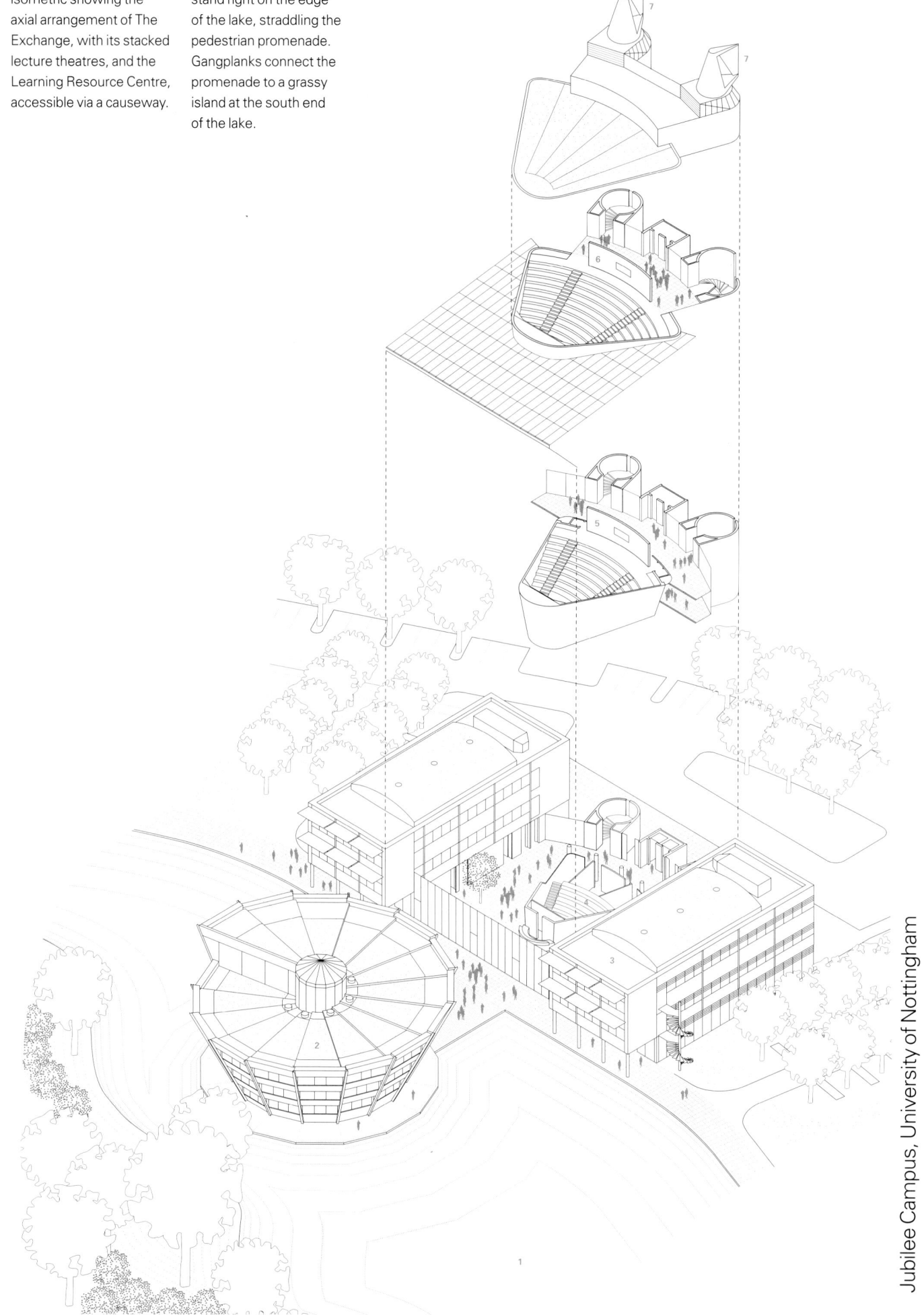

Jubilee Campus, University of Nottingham

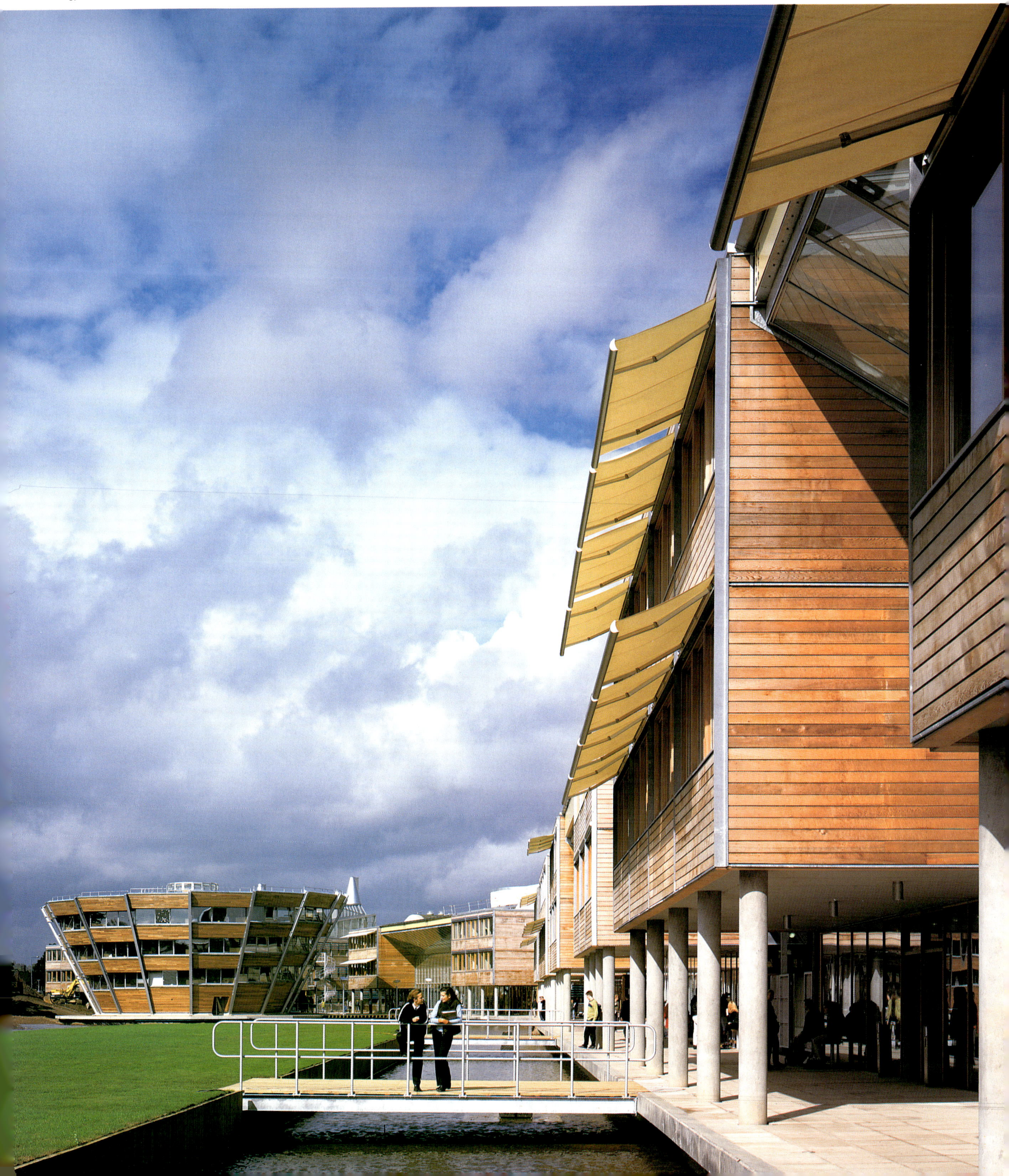

Below: longitudinal section through the Learning Resource Centre and the lecture theatres.

Opposite: looking into the atrium of The Exchange from the island in the lake. The exposed steel frame of the Learning Resource Centre is visible on the right.

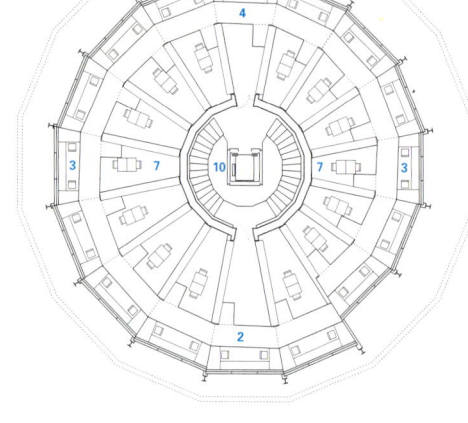

Learning Resource Centre
Ground floor plan

First floor plan

Longitudinal section

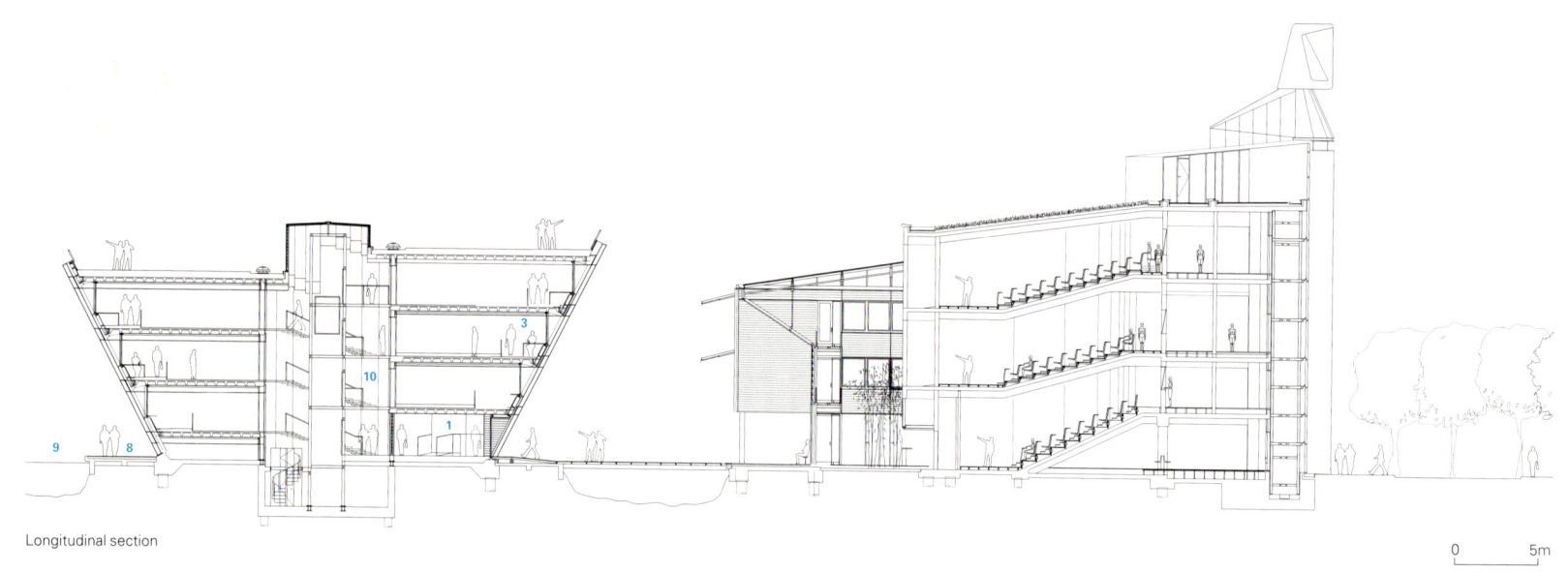

1 entrance lobby
2 ramp
3 perimeter study desks
4 book return
5 office
6 IT room
7 book stacks
8 timber decking
9 lake
10 stairwell

Jubilee Campus, University of Nottingham

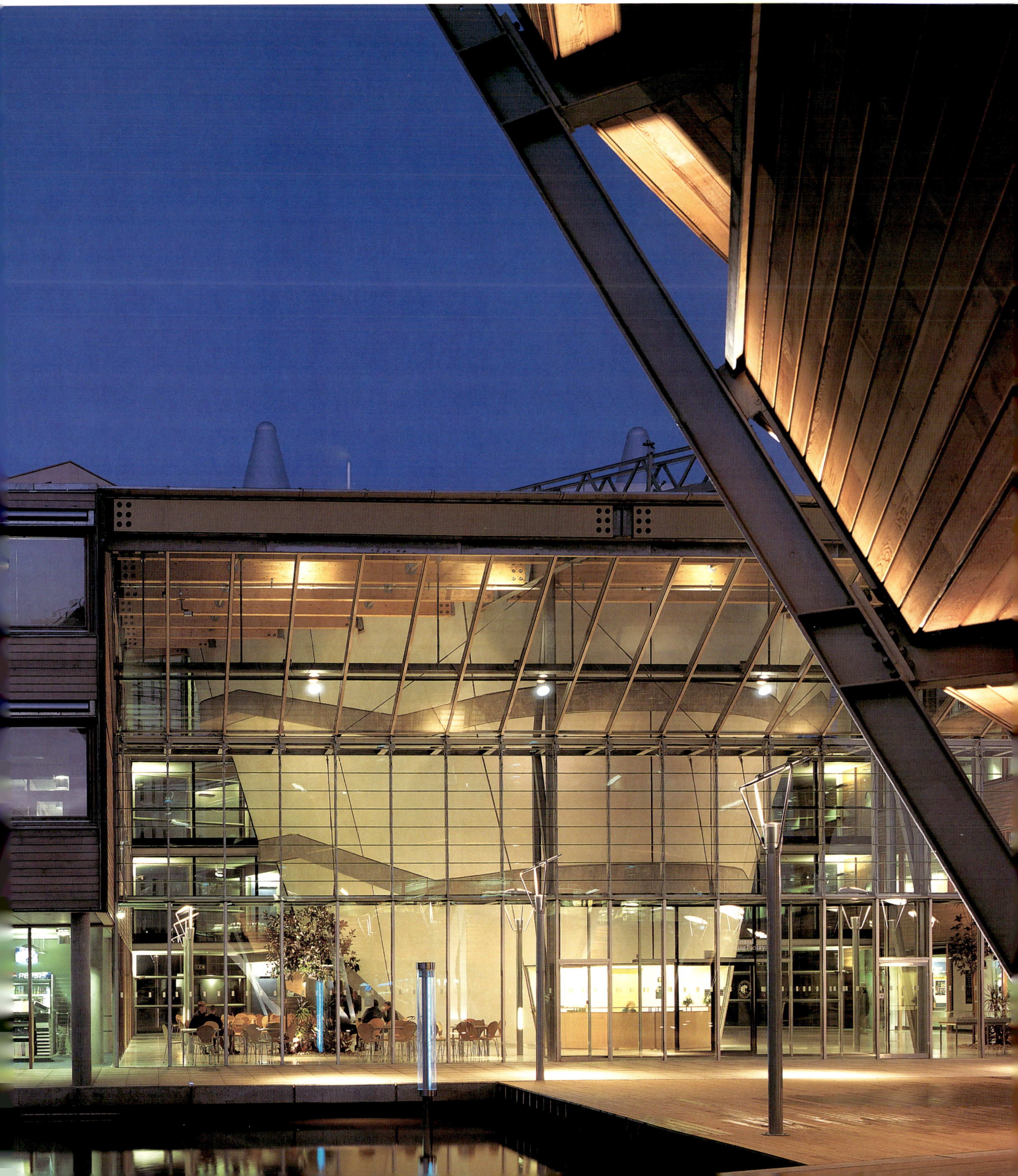

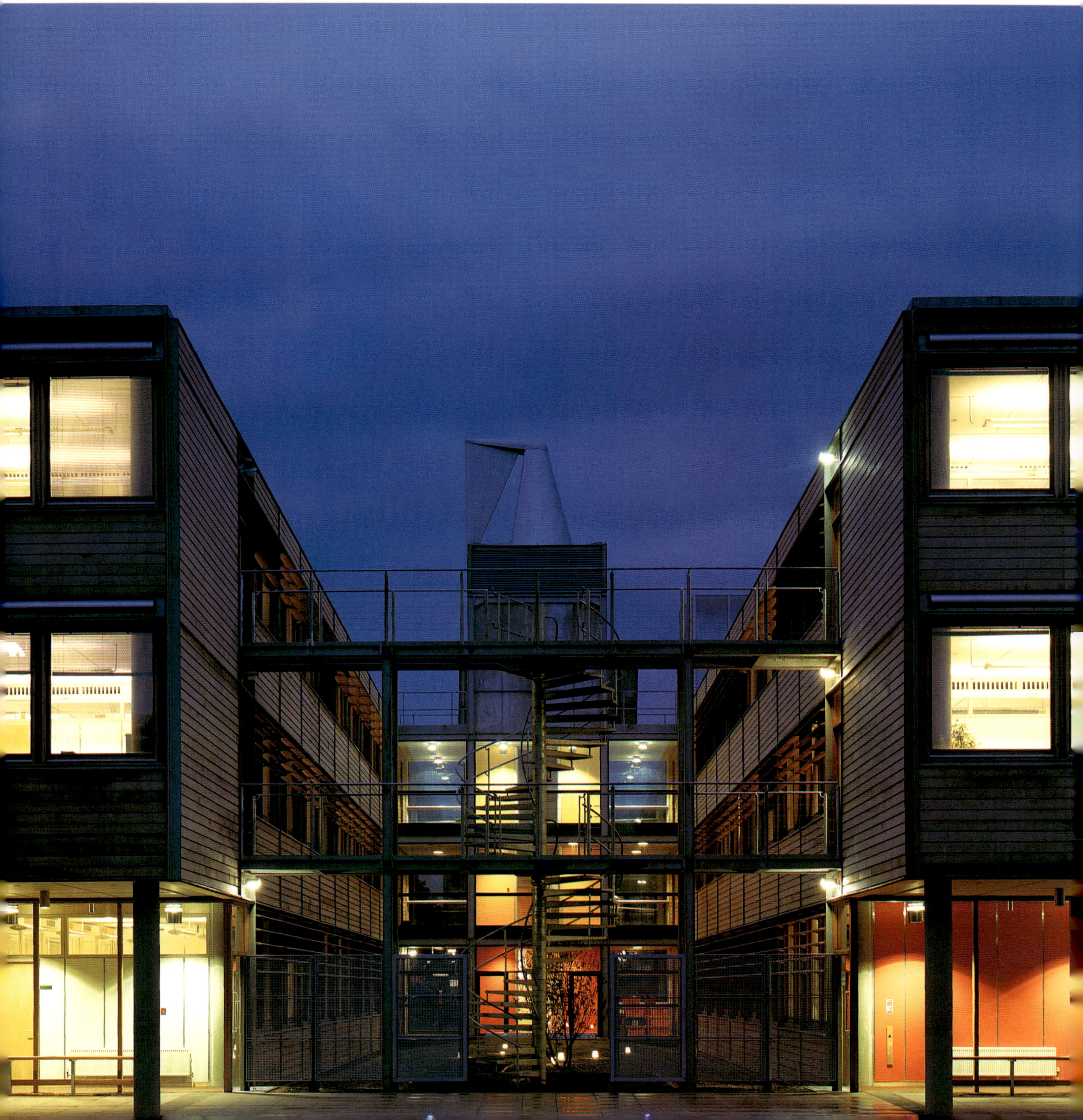

Opposite: the open courtyard between the teaching blocks, crossed by pedestrian bridges. The oast house cowl, over the circular stair tower, is visible at the far end of the courtyard.

Right: a modular air-handling unit is housed at the top of the stair tower. The tower itself doubles as an exhaust air duct with the assistance of the oast house cowl.

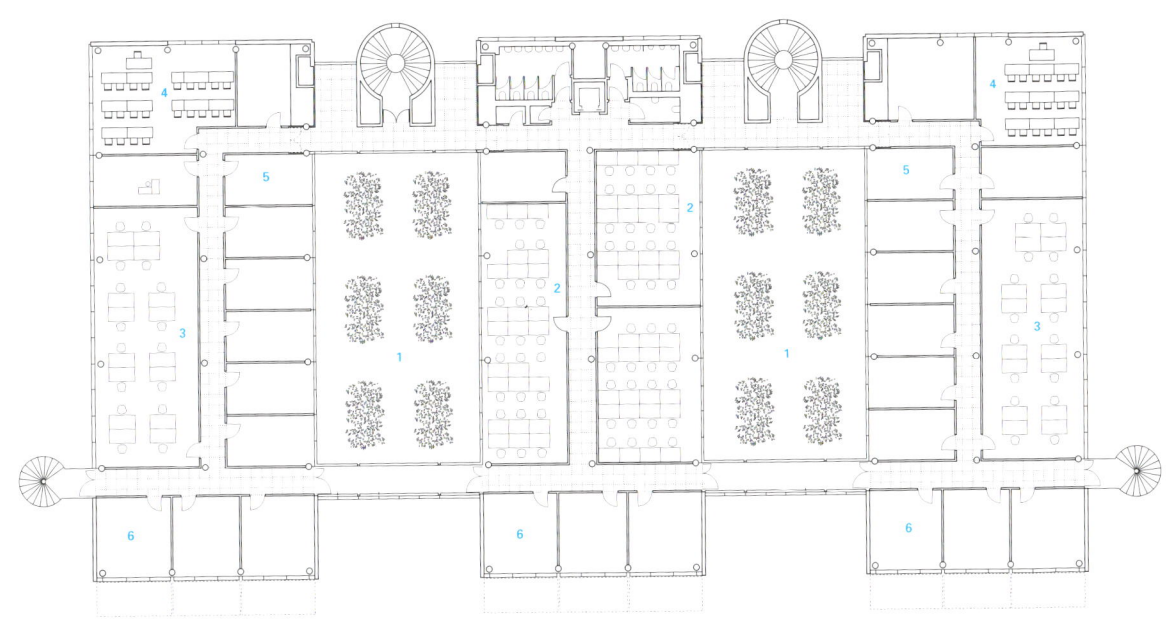

1 atrium void
2 computer room
3 postgraduate students
4 classroom
5 academic staff
6 professors' offices
7 promenade
8 main entrance
9 atrium
10 student common room
11 staff common room
12 reception office

First floor plan

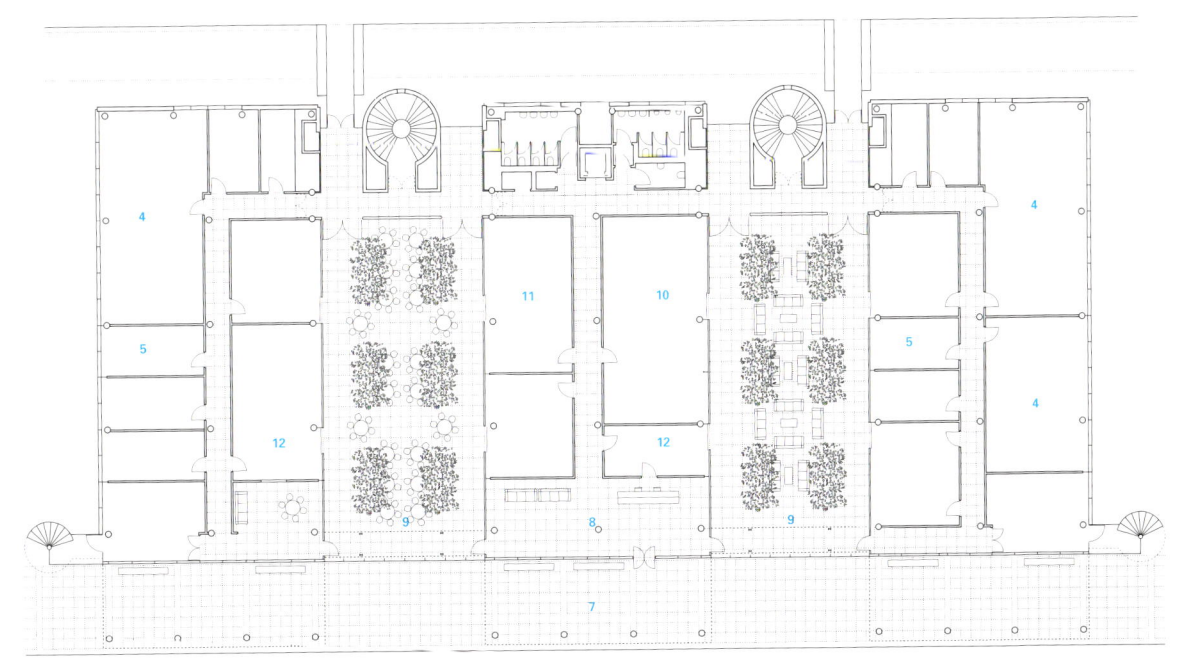

Business School ground floor plan

0 5m

Jubilee Campus, University of Nottingham

102

Opposite: a vertical stack of three lecture theatres is enclosed in a curved and tapered concrete form standing in the middle of The Exchange atrium. Access is via a pair of spiral staircases.

Below right: the lecture theatres viewed through the glass wall of the atrium from the causeway.

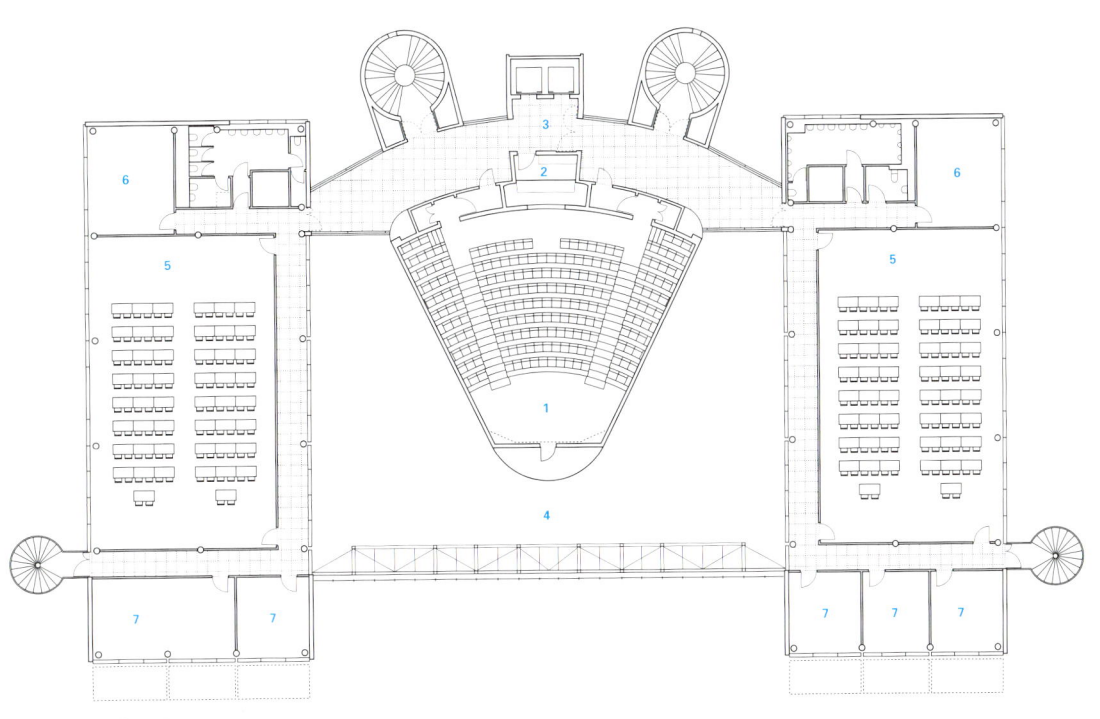

First floor plan

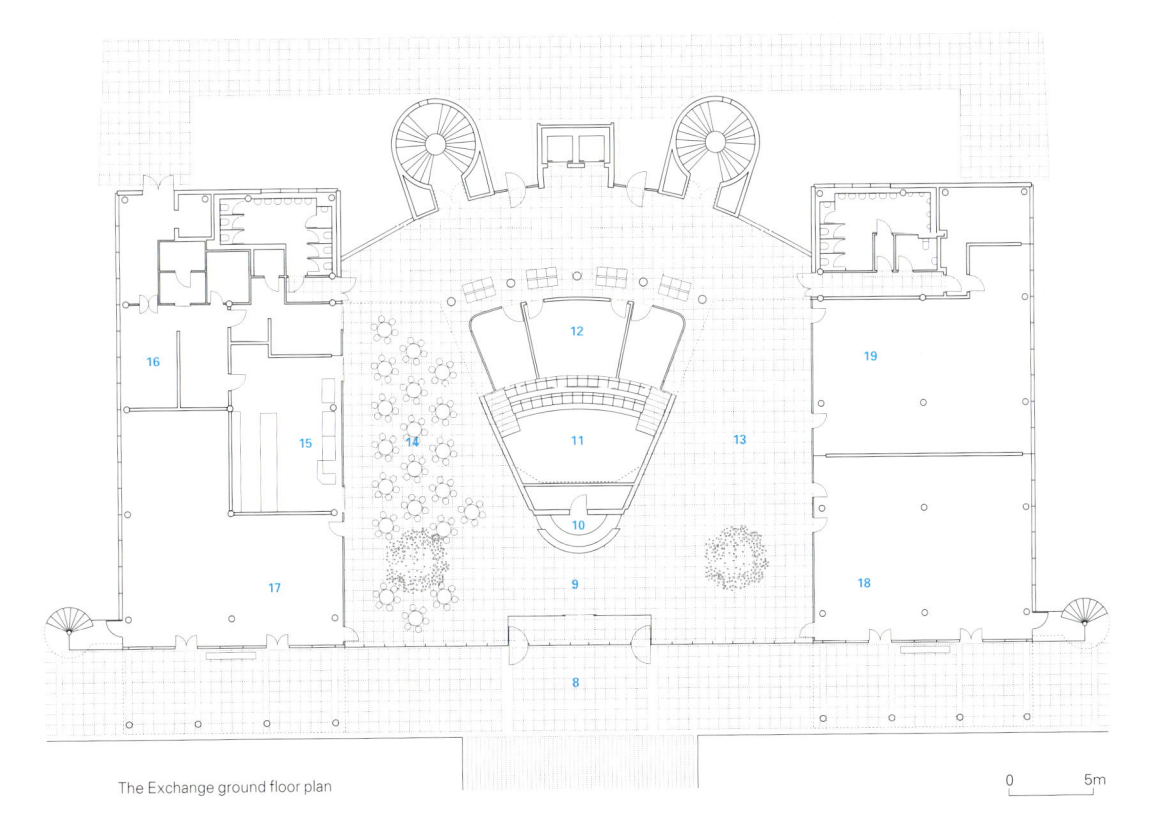

The Exchange ground floor plan

1 Lecture Theatre 200
2 video
3 lift lobby
4 atrium void
5 seminar room
6 classroom
7 meeting room
8 promenade
9 main entrance
10 reception
11 Lecture Theatre 100
12 cloakroom
13 atrium
14 dining area
15 servery
16 kitchen
17 union shop
18 retail
19 bank

Jubilee Campus, University of Nottingham

Left: the canteen is housed in a double-width atrium between the School of Computer Science and the School of Education. The deep, laminated timber roof beams are visible at the top of the picture.

Opposite: a standard-sized atrium in the School of Education. The glass roof incorporates photovoltaic cells providing electrical energy for the air handling plant.

Jubilee Campus, University of Nottingham

1 round back stair
2 WCs
3 store
4 lift
5 kitchen
6 labs
7 garden
8 seminar rooms
9 atrium
10 offices
11 spiral escape staircase
12 reception
13 entrance
14 promenade
15 bridge to island
16 lake

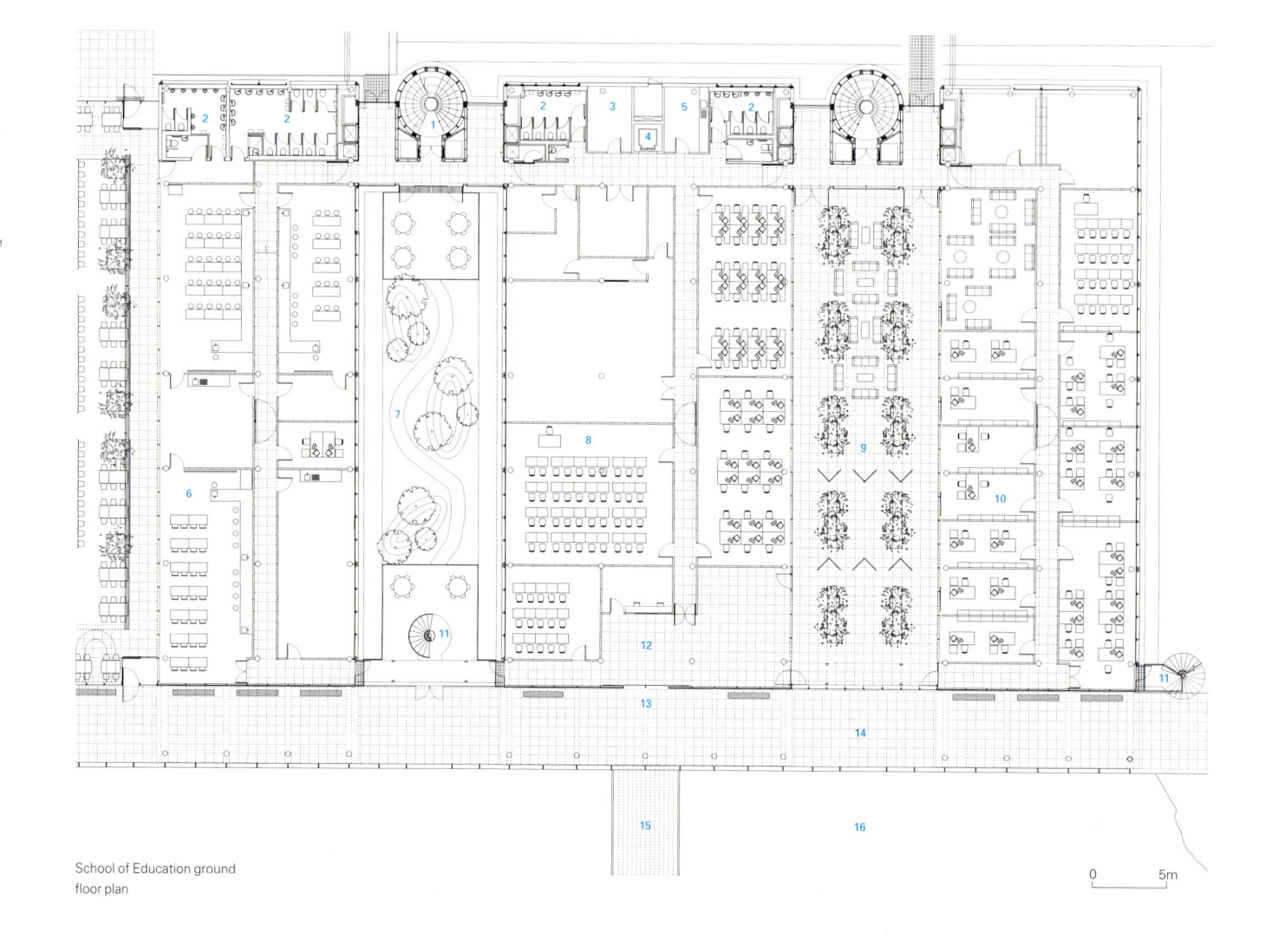

School of Education ground floor plan

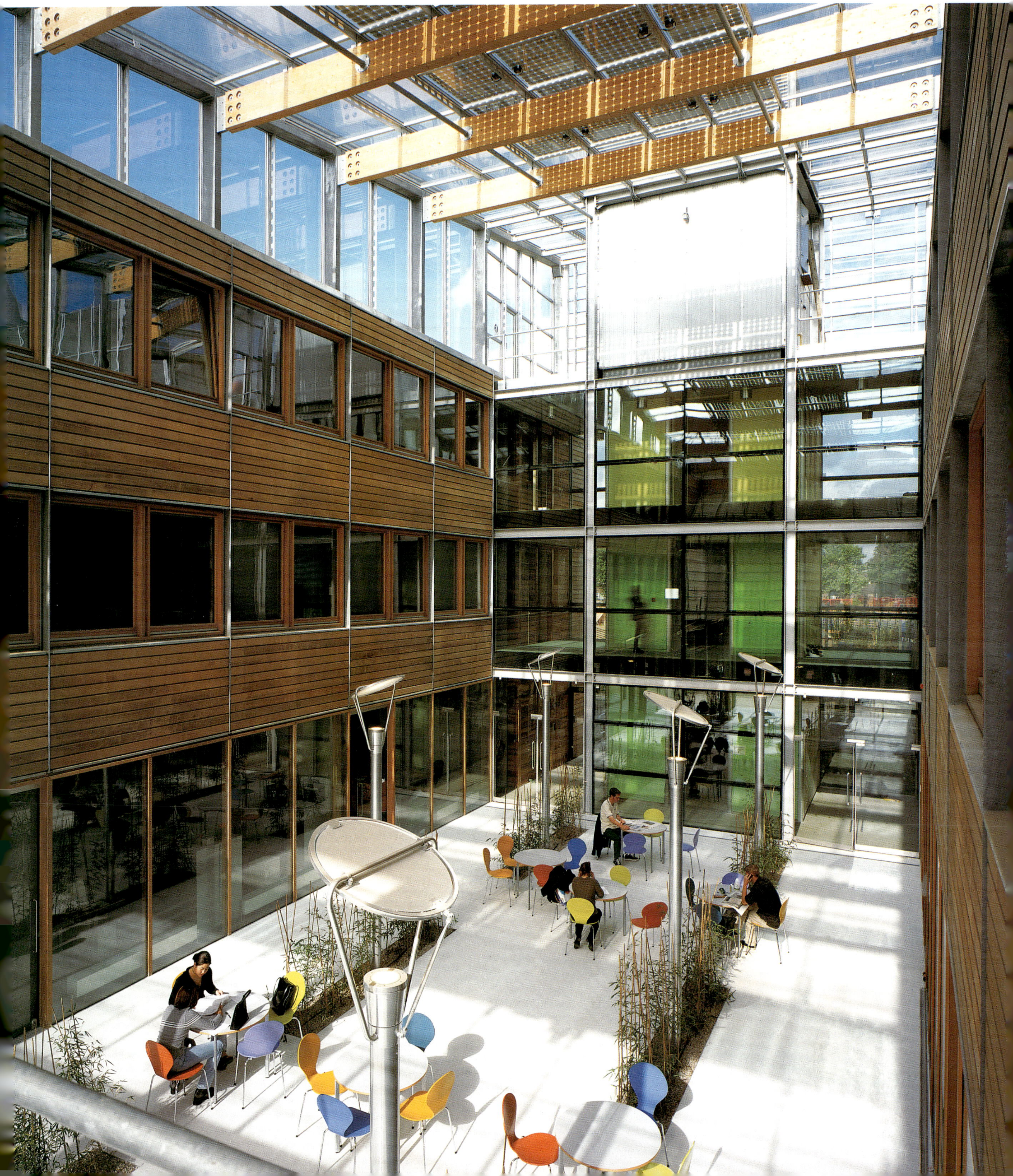

Left: photovoltaic cells within the atrium glazing are sized to match the energy demands of the ventilation fans.

Below: tracking wind-vanes position the air exhaust such that it is always under natural suction.

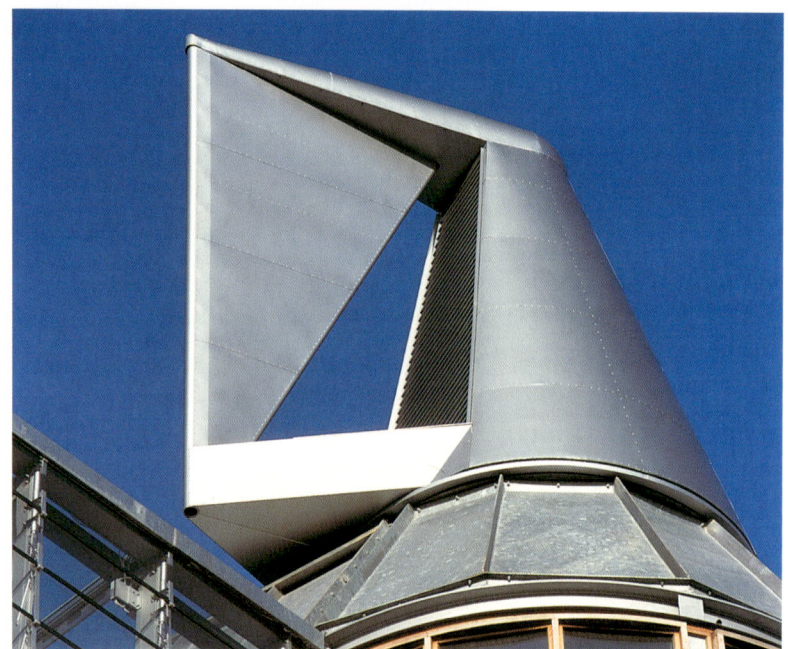

Jubilee Campus, University of Nottingham

Below: principles of ventilation system:
Winter: cool incoming fresh air to air-handling unit is warmed by exhaust air through thermal wheel.

Mid-season: manually operated windows provide natural ventilation. Natural buoyancy of warm outgoing air is ventilated direct to outside through thermal cowl. Thermal mass of slab evens out troughs and peaks of internal room temperature ranges.

Summer day: warm incoming air is cooled by cool outgoing air through the thermal wheel. Photovoltaics within the atrium glazing provide energy for the super-efficient low-pressure drop ventilation system.

Summer night: building is purged of daytime warm air. Incoming cool air cools thermal mass of concrete frame of building. Radiant cooling slabs cause reduction of temperature in air circulated throughout the building.

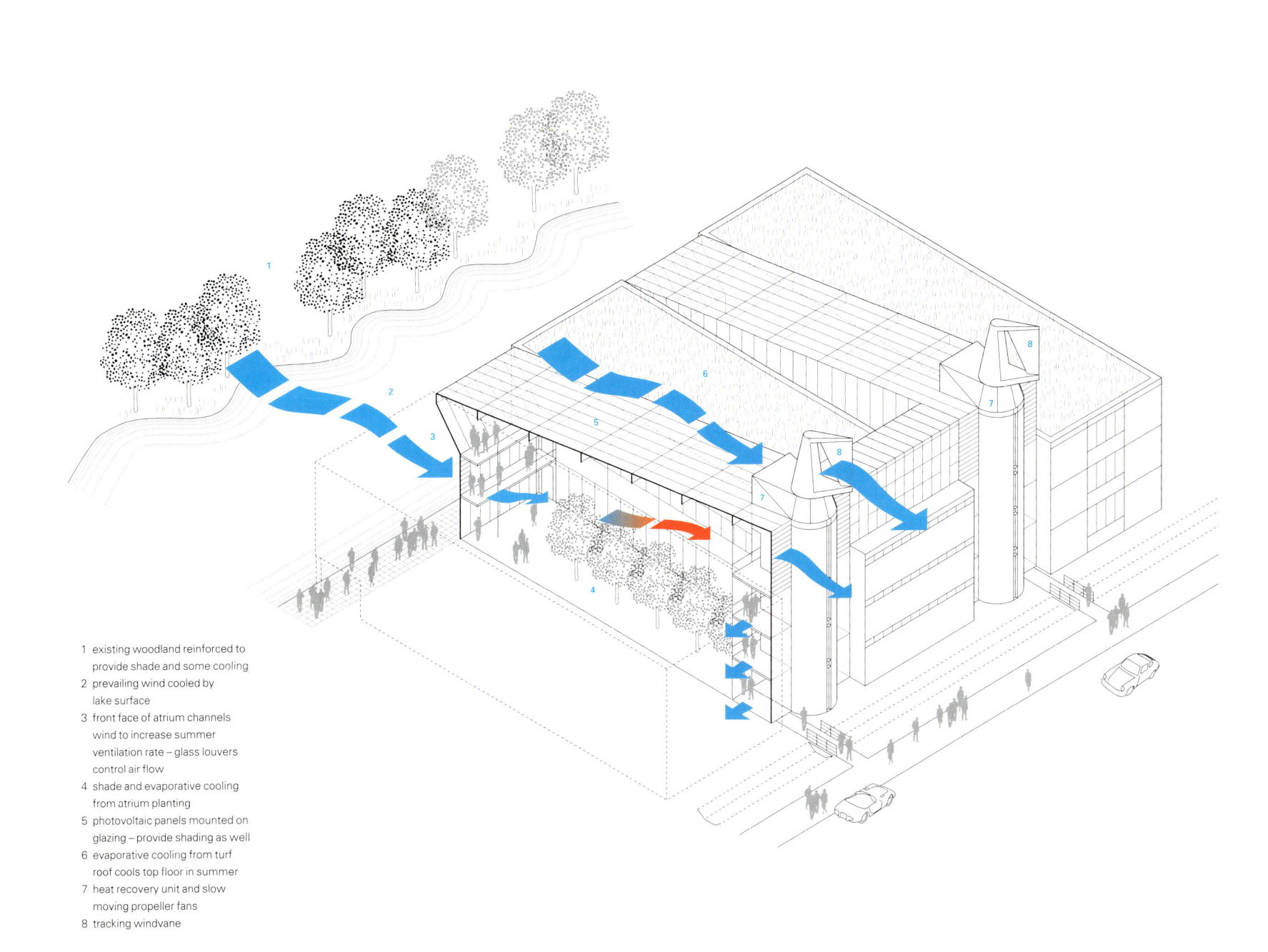

1 existing woodland reinforced to provide shade and some cooling
2 prevailing wind cooled by lake surface
3 front face of atrium channels wind to increase summer ventilation rate – glass louvers control air flow
4 shade and evaporative cooling from atrium planting
5 photovoltaic panels mounted on glazing – provide shading as well
6 evaporative cooling from turf roof cools top floor in summer
7 heat recovery unit and slow moving propeller fans
8 tracking windvane

The Pilkington Laboratories, Sherborne School 1995–2000

Sherborne School occupies a diverse collection of nineteenth- and twentieth-century buildings to the north of the Medieval Abbey Church of St Mary in the centre of the small Dorset town. The school's original intention was to redevelop the western part of the site, between Abbey Lane and Acreman Street; Michael Hopkins, who is an old boy of the school, was asked to draw up a masterplan. Phase one of the plan envisaged the refurbishment of the existing Carrington Building, the demolition of a block of fives courts and the building of a new teaching block with a circular lecture theatre. On the basis of this scheme, the school launched a fund-raising appeal, and applied for grants from the Arts Council and the Sports Council. The grant applications were unsuccessful, however, and only £1 million was raised, well short of the £3.5 million target. A more modest scheme was therefore produced for a new science building on the site of an old swimming pool, between the fives courts and Acreman Street.

A simple two-storey, rectangular block houses physics and electronics laboratories on the ground floor, and chemistry laboratories on the first floor. An unusual feature of the plan is the absence of any internal staircase or lift. This economy was made possible by an almost storey-height level difference across the site. Two flights of external steps lead down to ground-floor entrances at either end of a central corridor. The first-floor laboratories are entered from an open colonnade along the back of the building, which is reached via two short ramps next to the flights of steps.

In townscape terms, the Acreman Street frontage was especially sensitive. The building fills the gap between a row of cottages to the south and a handsome, two-storey house to the north, maintaining the domestic scale and rhythm of the street. A pitched, slate-covered roof was practically obligatory, but in order to reduce the height and bulk of the building, the roof is double-pitched on either side of a central line of rooflights. Louvered chimneys at ridge level serve as outlets for fume cupboards in the chemistry laboratories. External walls are of loadbearing white brickwork, faced with local uncoursed Ham stone to match the neighbouring buildings. Chimneys at the gable ends are supported by ashlar stone corbels, and the regular, repetitive, four-light windows are framed and mullioned in reconstructed stone. The first-floor colonnade is also framed in reconstructed stone, like a continuous ribbon version of the windows. An insulated, timber-framed wall separates the colonnade from the chemistry laboratories. The ground floor is an in-situ concrete slab, but the first floor is of precast planks, with a modular raised floor for services distribution and an exposed soffit.

Although the scale of this building is domestic, there is no attempt to prettify the exterior, which has the plain, practical character of a medieval college or a nineteenth-century workshop.

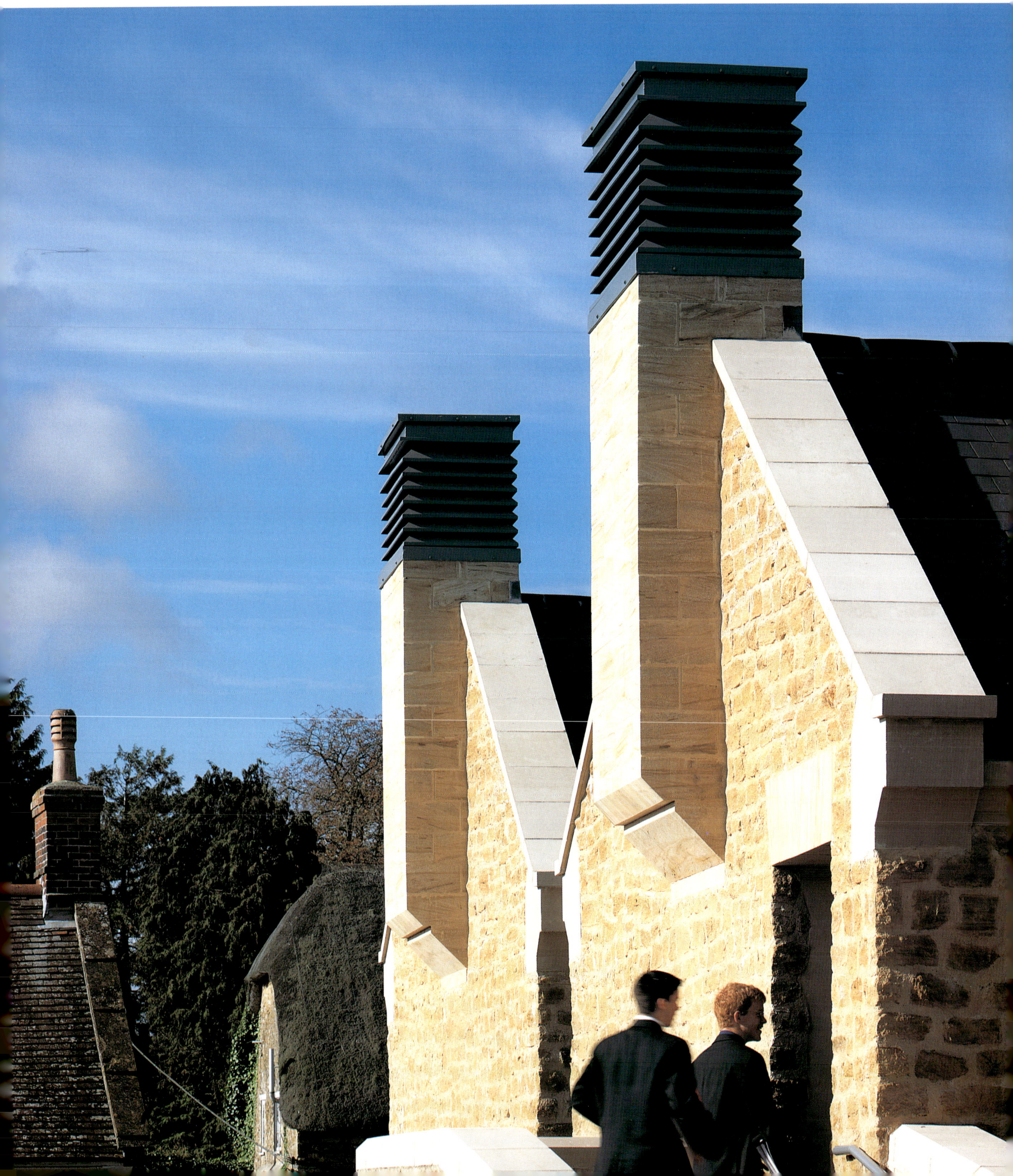

Previous page: external walls are faced with uncoursed Ham stone to match the neighbouring buildings. Corbelled chimneys on the gable ends are outlets for fume cupboards in the chemistry laboratories.

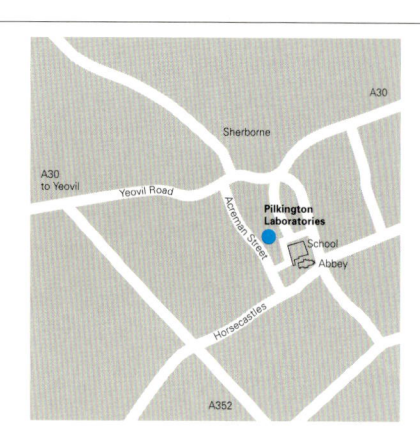

1 chemistry classroom
2 chemistry laboratory
3 physics laboratory
4 preparation room
5 office
6 store
7 plant

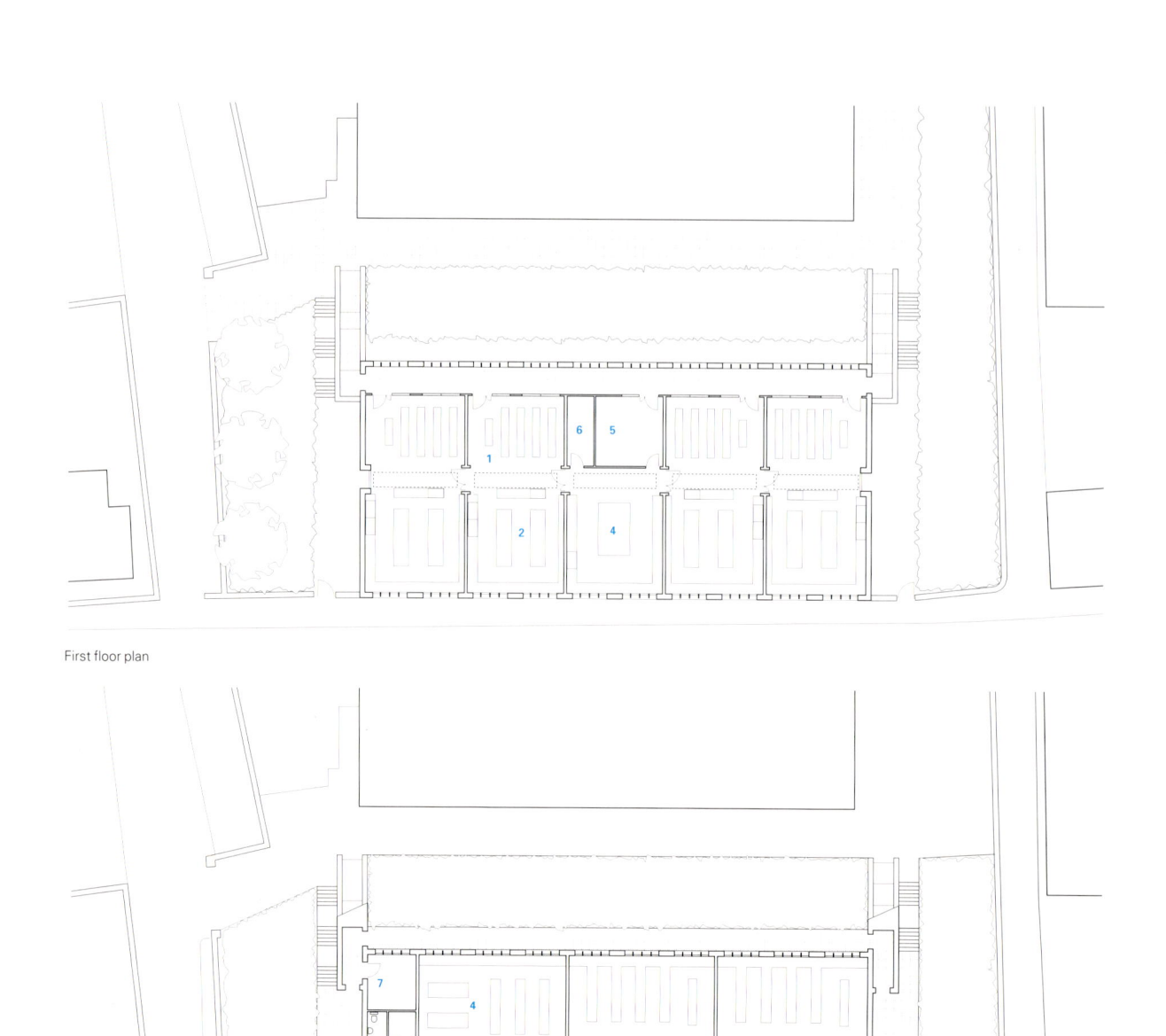

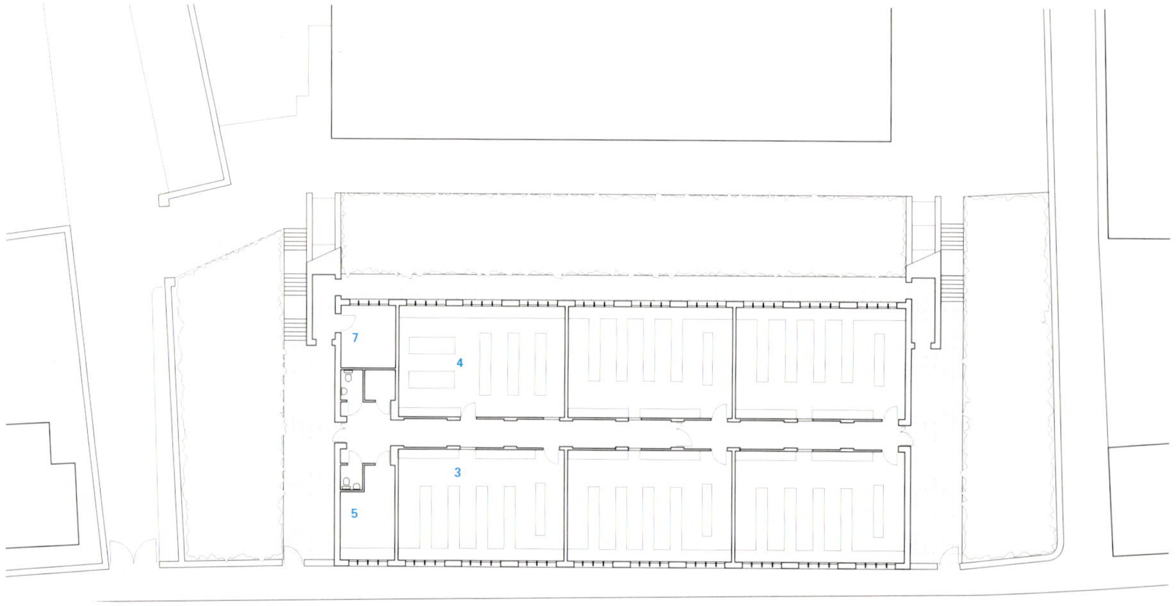

First floor plan

Ground floor plan

Acreman Street

Sherborne School

Left: the first floor is accessible via a pair of external ramps leading to a colonnade along the full length of the east side of the building. There is no internal staircase.

Below: the west elevation continues the line of a row of cottages to the south, maintaining the domestic scale and rhythm of Acreman Street.

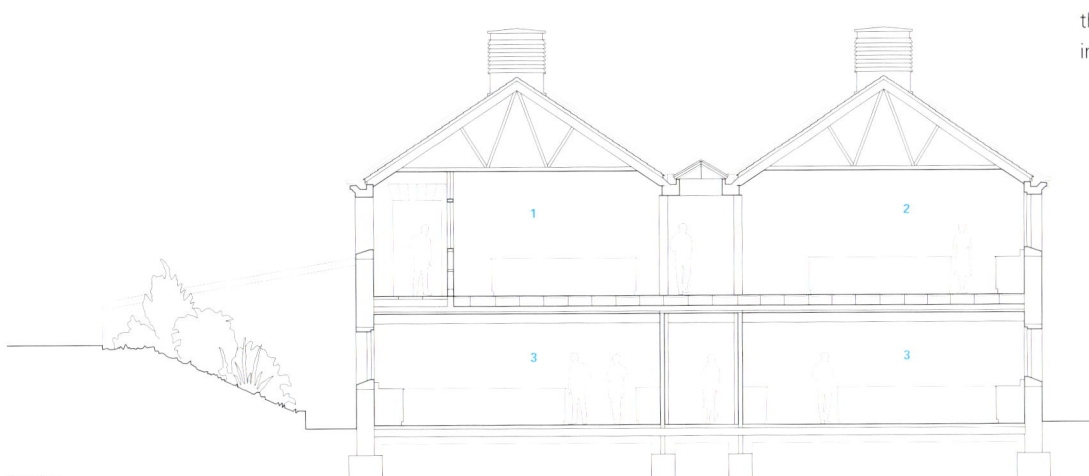

Section

Left: the two parallel pitched roofs are separated by a line of rooflights which define the main circulation route at first-floor level.
Below: each bay can be closed off and is separately accessible from the colonnade.

Opposite: windows have stone mullions, like those of a medieval college, but they merge together to form the first floor colonnade, which is reminiscent of a nineteenth-century workshop.

Sherborne School

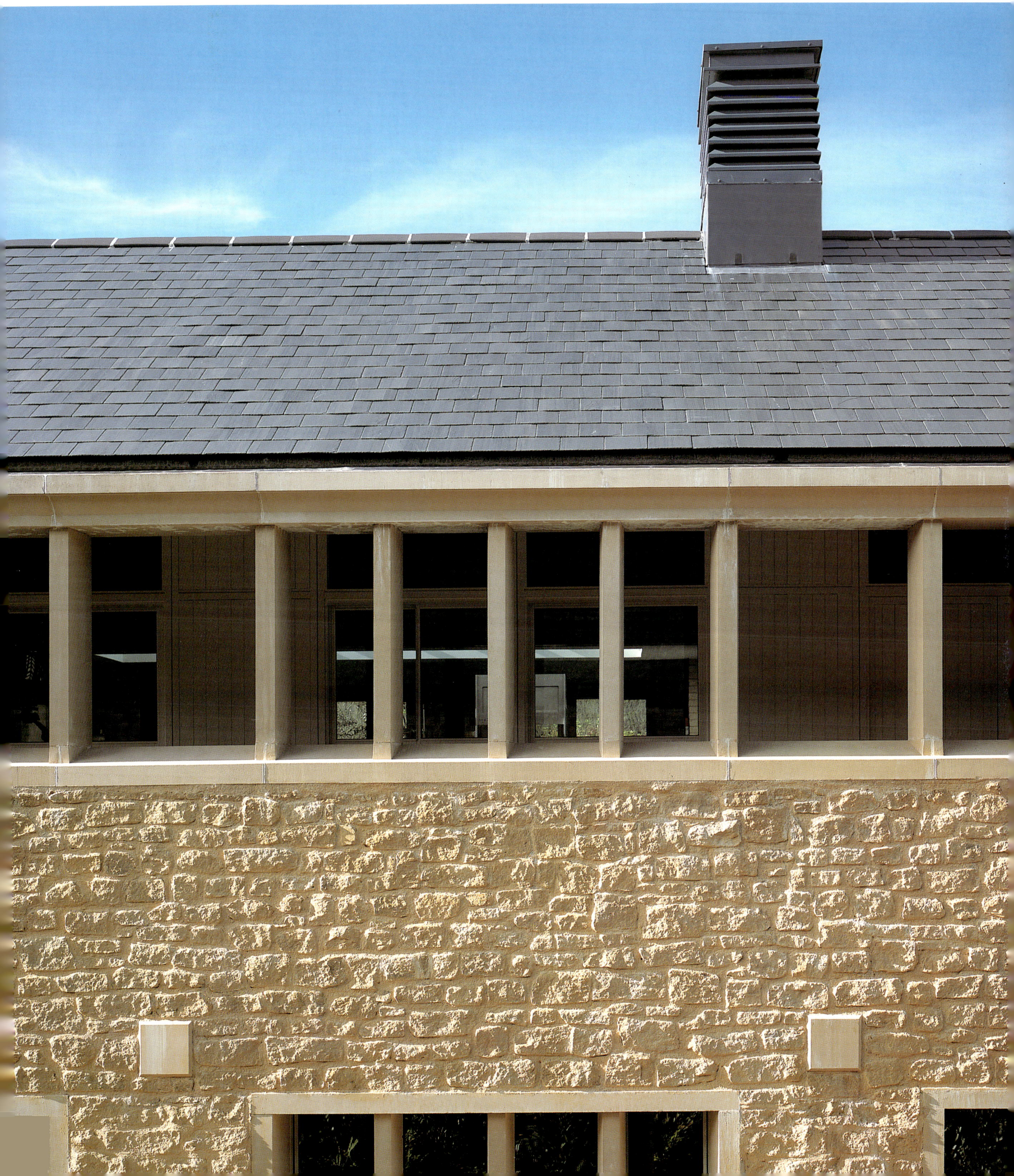

Wildscreen at Bristol
1995–2000

The BBC's Natural History Unit, based in Bristol, produces a third of the world's output of wildlife programmes. Wildscreen is its museum counterpart, combining an IMAX cinema, an electronic zoo and a tropical house. Its triangular site is part of a new leisure quarter, Bristol Harbourside, developed with the help of the Millennium Commission, on a former railway and docklands close to Bristol's city centre. Neighbouring buildings include the famous Watershed arts centre, a science museum and a 500-space car park under a new public square. At the apex of the triangle sits the massive brick drum of the IMAX cinema, clearly visible from the busy traffic intersection to the north, known locally as The Centre. From this hinge point, the building widens out and steps down to the south-west until it meets a two-storey, nineteenth-century leadworks, extended and converted into a cafe and shop with offices on the first floor. Between the drum and the leadworks, the accommodation is organized in parallel strips, each with its own specific architectural character. First, a narrow, glazed atrium separates the cinema from the rest of the building, preserving the geometrical purity of the drum. Next comes a five-storey, vertical circulation zone, containing lifts, lobbies and a pair of spiral staircases. This is attached to a four-storey, loadbearing brick 'black box' containing the interactive, multimedia exhibits of the electronic zoo on two floors, with education rooms above and a fabric-canopied roof terrace on top. At this point, solidity and enclosure give way abruptly to lightness and openness. The next strip is the tropical house, which takes the form of a transparent tent suspended from a pair of raking steel masts. Finally, another, smaller, fabric structure fills the irregular gap between the tropical house and the converted leadworks to form a foyer with entrances at both ends. One entrance faces a small public square to the south of the leadworks, the other faces the foot of Trinity Steps, which climb up the hill to the cathedral.

Circulation routes in the building generally cut across or weave between the parallel strips. Customers for the IMAX cinema do not necessarily want to enter the zoo or the tropical house, so a direct route through the building from foyer to cinema had to be preserved. This is achieved by means of a very unusual architectural device. The concrete floor of the tropical house is lifted, like a carpet, to form a cone-shaped, cave-like passageway, which continues through the divided ground floor of the zoo to emerge in the atrium, opposite the bar in the base of the brick drum. The cinema auditorium is actually a rectilinear box, accessible via a pair of staircases rising from either side of the bar in the space between box and drum. Visitors to the zoo and tropical house follow a prescribed route which begins on one side of the passageway. From here, it winds through both spaces, using the 'hill' above the cave as the link between ground and first floors.

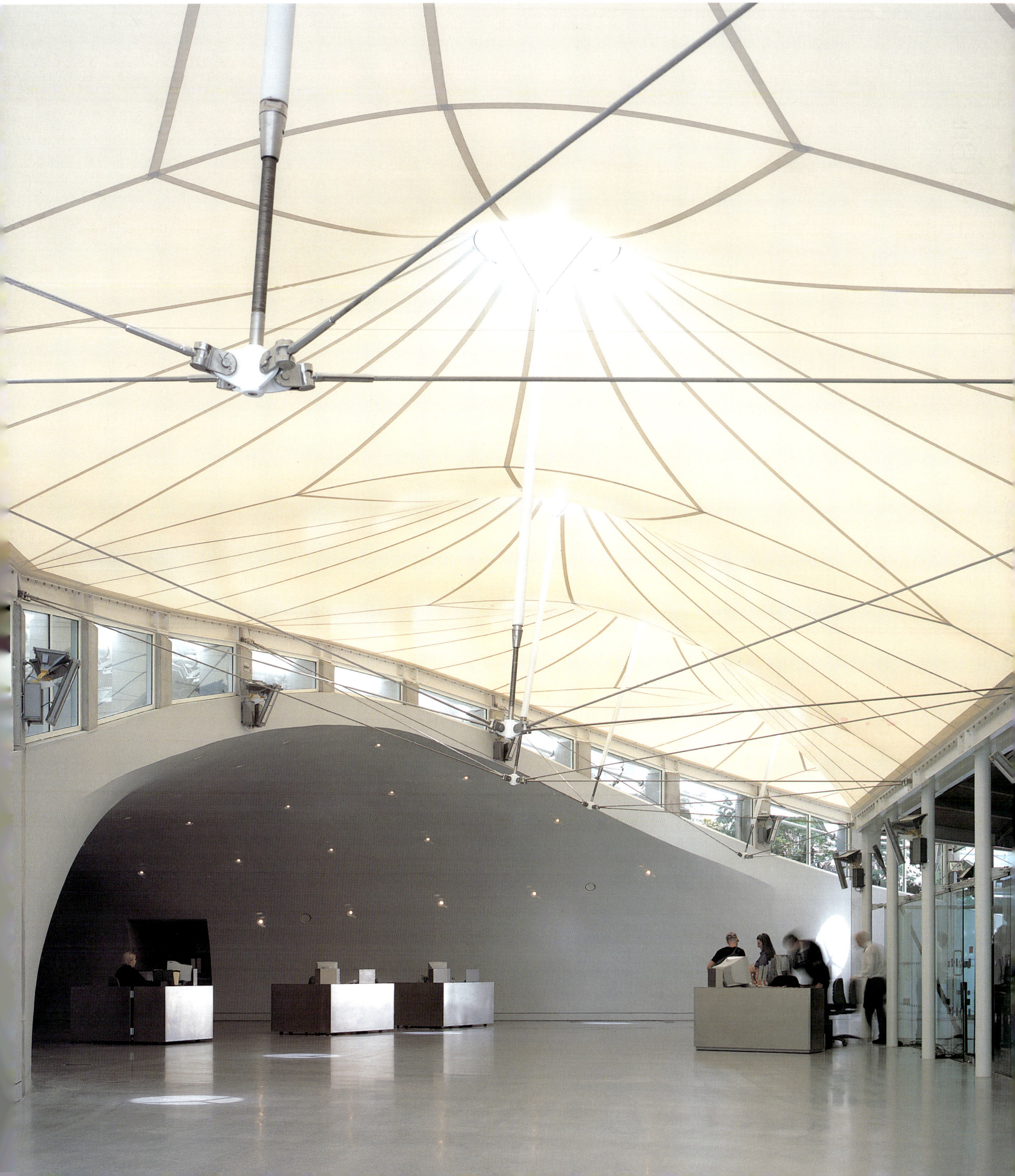

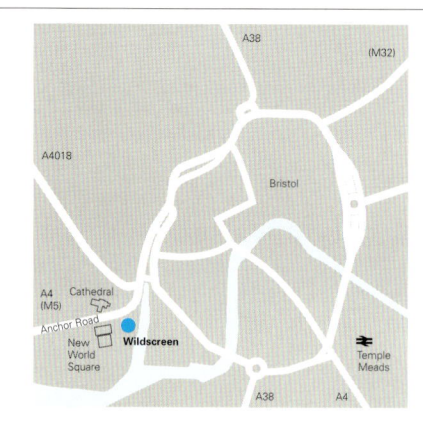

Previous page: curved forms in contrasting materials. The entrance foyer, covered by a fabric roof, reveals a tunnel of sprayed concrete leading to the IMAX cinema.

Differing forms of construction are logical responses to differing functional and environmental demands. The heavy, windowless, loadbearing brick structures housing the cinema and the zoo provide good sound insulation and a high thermal capacity to moderate the internal temperature and reduce the air-conditioning load. In other words, they act as an energy store. The tropical house tent, on the other hand, is an energy receiver, admitting the maximum amount of daylight and using the sun as a heat source. The internal environment is controlled by adjusting the balance between these opposing forces. For example, the heavy south-facing wall of the zoo absorbs heat during the day and reradiates it to the Tropical House at night. Water from the nearby dock is used to cool the air for the mechanically ventilated cinema, reducing the load on the chilling plant.

In early versions of the scheme, a conventional glass-and-steel greenhouse was proposed for the tropical house. This was progressively refined. First, the glass panels were replaced by inflated ETFE (ethyltetrafluorethene) cushions, combining extreme lightness, high light transmittance, good thermal insulation and a self-cleaning surface. Unlike glass, the ETFE panels are flexible and can be warped in two directions, which meant that the rigid steel frame could be replaced by a much lighter, tensioned-cable net structure. A primary ridge cable, running right across the building from corner to corner, is suspended from the raking steel masts. Shorter cables connect the ridge to the brick wall of the zoo on one side and a row of concrete columns on the other. For the end walls of the tent, the structure reverts to a more conventional steel frame with banana-shaped eaves beams supporting vertical trussed mullions infilled with glass.

The structure of the passageway under the tropical house went through a similar process of development and an equally innovative solution was found. First, prefabricated ferro-cement panels were proposed, but were found to be too expensive because the complex geometry of the cave meant that almost every panel would be different. Simplifying the geometry to suit the technology would have meant sacrificing the dynamic, flowing form. Tunnelling technology came to the rescue. Concrete was sprayed in situ onto a mesh of steel reinforcement, allowing generous tolerances. A constellation of small lights are recessed into the roof of the cave. In the small extension to the leadworks, an elegant timber, lean-to roof, supported by slender steel columns, accommodates the shop. The new roof geometry rationalizes the rear face of the existing building, so that the new canopy can be clearly brought up to it. At the same time, it forms lateral restraint to resist the forces imposed on it from the canopy.

This is a building of contrasting spaces and structural forms, sewn together by a complicated but legible circulation system to form a compact plan on a restricted site.

Below: the glass end wall of the Tropical House, left, is supported by a banana-shaped eaves beam and vertical trussed mullions. The converted lead works is on the right, beyond the fabric-roofed entrance foyer.

118

Opposite: interior of the tropical house. The tented roof, formed from air-filled ETFE cushions, is suspended from two raking steel masts. The brick wall on the right absorbs solar heat during the day and re-radiates it at night.

Right: a narrow atrium on two levels separates the IMAX cinema from the electronic zoo. The entrance tunnel is on the left.
Far right: upper level of the atrium.

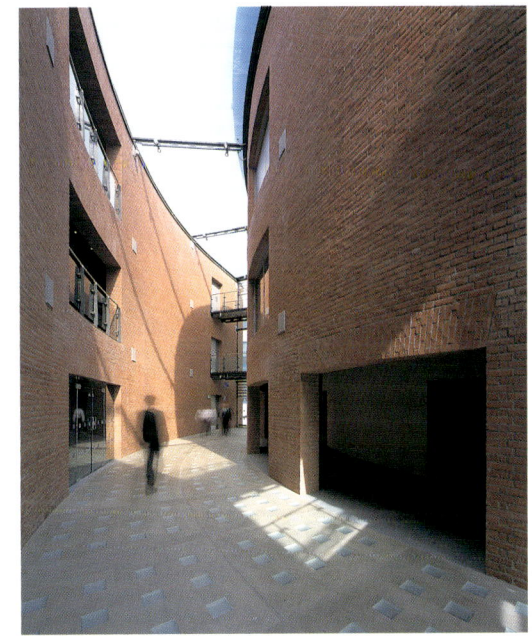

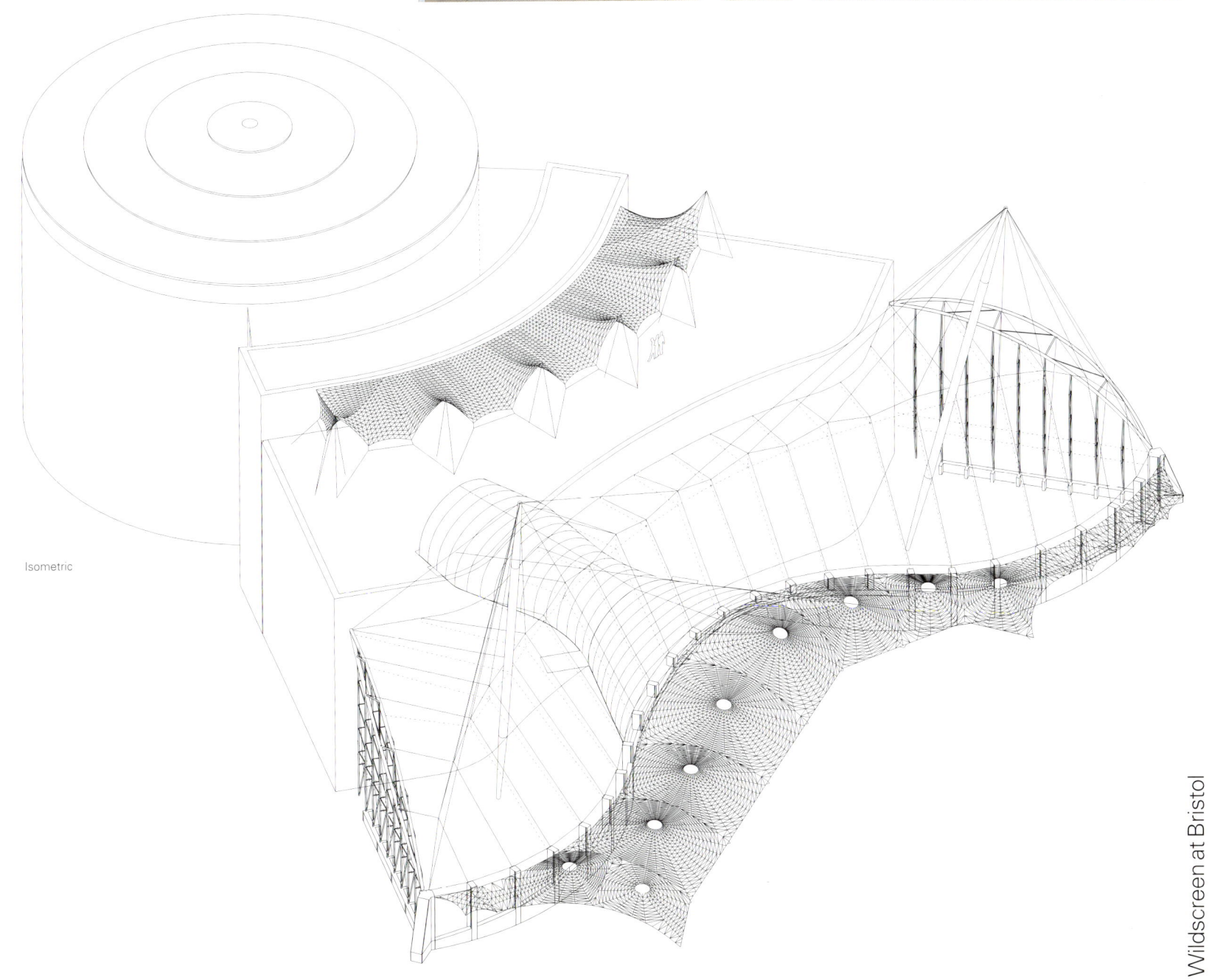

Isometric

Wildscreen at Bristol

Section

1 IMAX Theatre
2 link
3 bar
4 vault
5 tropical house
6 foyer
7 shop
8 café
9 offices
10 Electronic Zoo exhibition
11 exhibition back up
12 education
13 terrace

Anchor Square

Ground floor plan

Fourth floor plan

Wildscreen at Bristol

Left: Interior of the IMAX cinema, with the giant screen on the left. The cinema is a box within a drum. The space between is occupied by plant and circulation.
Far left: The interactive multimedia exhibits of the Electronic Zoo are contained in the 'black box' exhibition space.

Below: The sprayed concrete entrance tunnel burrows under the artifical hill of the tropical house, connecting the foyer with the cinema bar, visible at the far end.

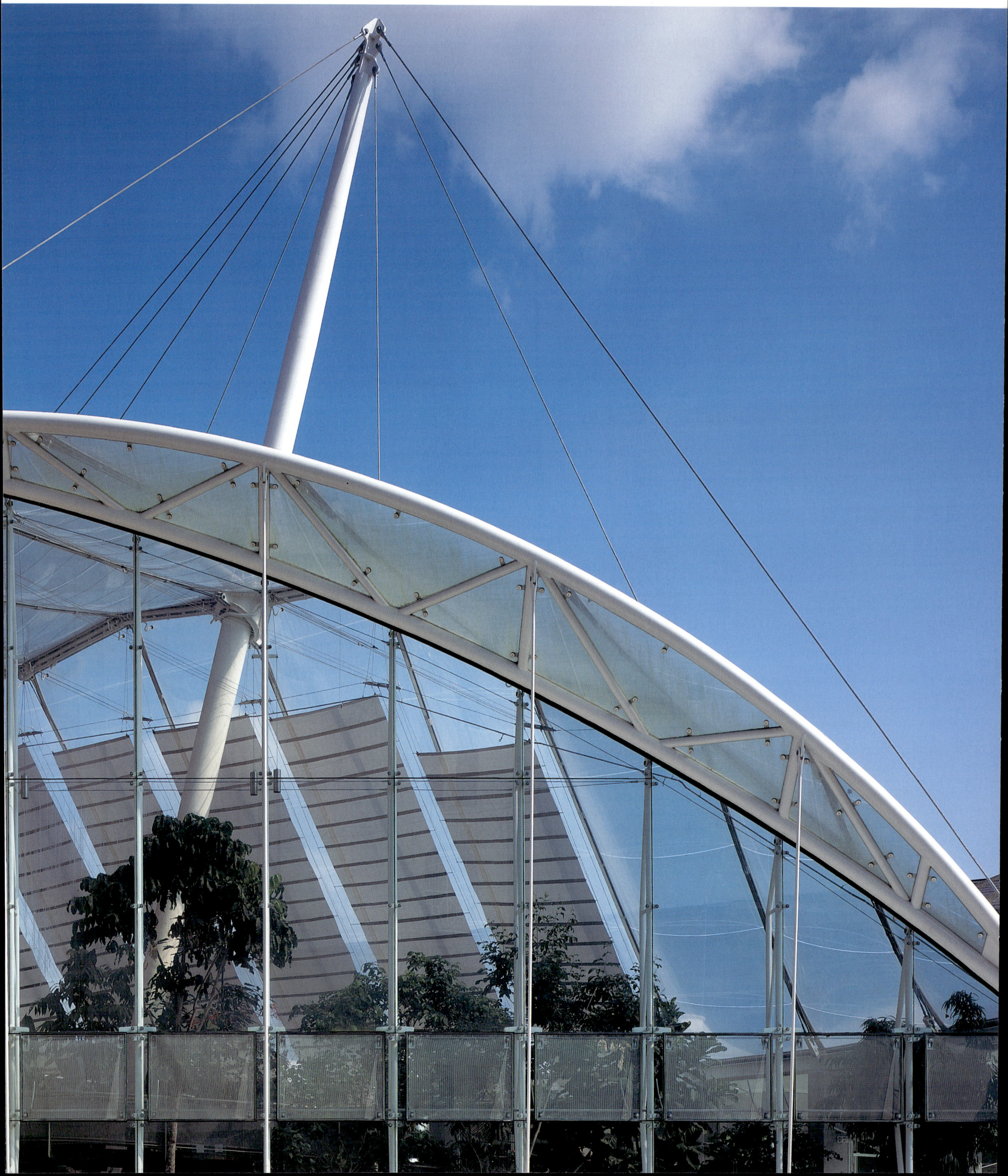

Opposite: one of the pair of raking masts from which the tented roof of the tropical house is suspended. The adjustable fabric blinds that regulate the solar heat gain are visible through the glass end wall.

Right and below: the roof of the tropical house is not a conventional tent structure but a tensioned cable net, seen here under construction, infilled with ETFE cushions.

Wildscreen at Bristol

Sheltered Housing, Charterhouse 1994–2000

Charterhouse, in the City of London, takes its name from the Carthusian priory that occupied the site from 1371 until the Dissolution of the Monasteries in the late 1530s. The priory was replaced by an aristocratic mansion which was later converted into an almshouse and a school. The school moved to Godalming, Surrey in 1872, but the almshouse, known as Sutton Hospital, remained. It now provides sheltered accommodation for elderly men, known as Brothers. A diverse collection of buildings, of various dates spanning 500 years, forms a sequence of quiet, collegiate courts.

Preacher's Court mainly dates from the 1820s. The west side suffered bomb damage during the Second World War and was demolished exposing the tall untidy backs of the buildings in St Johns Street behind a high zig-zag wall. The new development consists of two freestanding buildings which hide the wall and together define the south-west corner of the court, restoring a sense of enclosure. A small, two-storey block, square on plan, contains two flats on the first floor and a tiny library on the ground floor, completely surrounded by an arcade or cloister. Its rectangular, three-storey neighbour contains twelve flats arranged around two lift and staircase cores. It, too, is arcaded but only on the side facing the court. The zig-zag wall cuts into its plan slightly at the back where first-floor flats have the benefit of small external terraces.

Although plain and simple in form and elevational treatment, these buildings are extremely refined in their proportions, dimensional co-ordination and detailing. Red brickwork is the dominant material. Walls are solid and loadbearing, a brick and a half thick, in English bond with real flat arches forming the cloisters and window openings. Parapets with flush stone copings hide shallow-pitched, lead-covered roofs. On the upper floors, the windows are mostly of uniform height, but vary in width and profile from narrow, frameless slits to generous projecting bays made from cast aluminium and large enough to sit in. Cloister-sheltered external walls on the ground floor are non-loadbearing, softwood-framed and oak-panelled – a detail inherited from previous Hopkins buildings such as the Queen's Building at Emmanuel College and the Pilkington Laboratories at Sherborne School.

The interiors are as refined as the exteriors. Living rooms and bedrooms are all oak-panelled, and kitchens and bathrooms are fitted out to a high standard. Lift and stair cores are lit by glass rooflights and treated like exterior spaces, with fair-face brick walls and steel-framed lift shafts infilled with stack-bonded brickwork. The staircase in the library block is not enclosed, and rises from the cloister like an Oxford or Cambridge college.

The opportunity has been taken to improve the external landscaping. Pavements around the new buildings are of York stone and vehicle routes, extending into the neighbouring entrance and Pensioners' Courts, have been resurfaced in bonded gravel. The whole development combines modest, austere forms with high-quality materials, finely crafted.

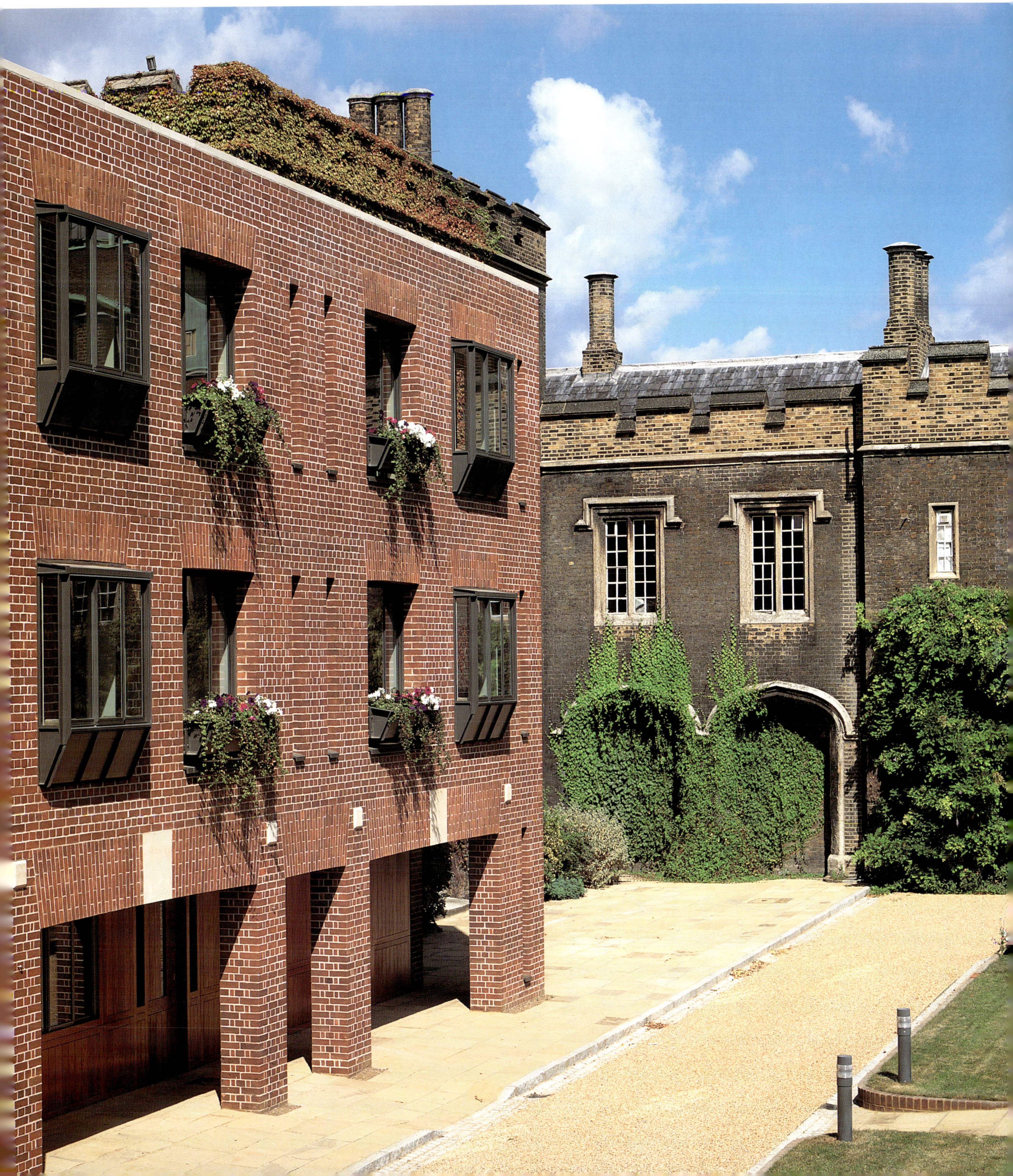

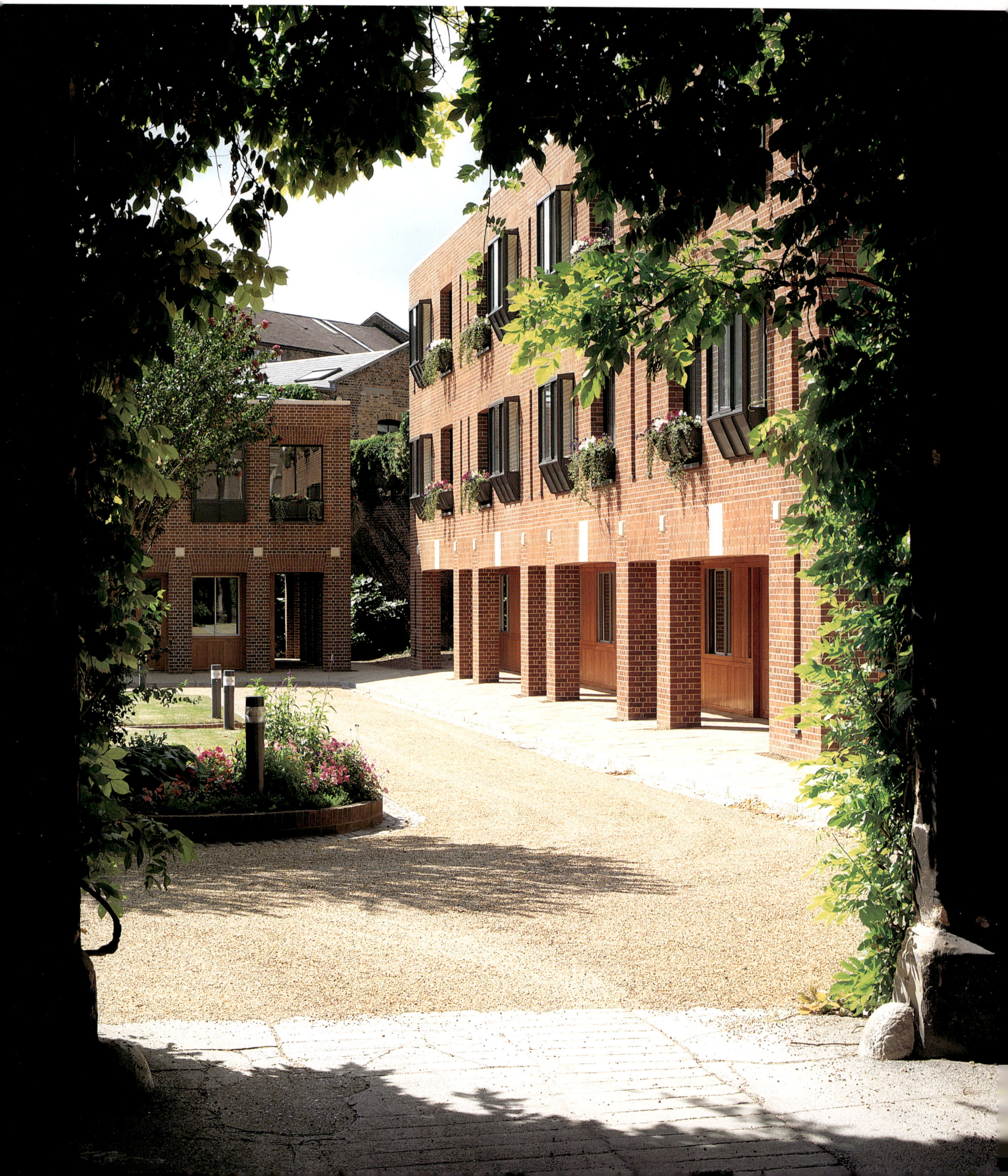

Previous page: the main three-storey block, left, contains twelve sheltered flats for the 'Brothers' and provides Preacher's Court with a handsome new cloister.

Opposite: the two new buildings define the south-west corner of Preacher's Court and hide the untidy back of neighbouring St John Street. The landscaping of the court is improved by a York stone pavement and a bonded-gravel road.

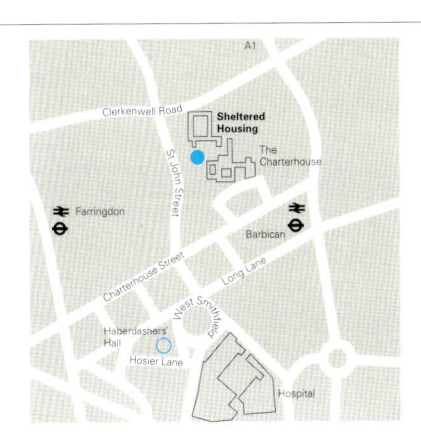

Left: the smaller, two-storey South Building is completely surrounded by a cloister. The staircase rises straight from the cloister in the manner of an Oxford or Cambridge college.

Site plan

1. The Admiral Ashmore Sheltered Housing
2. Preacher's Court
3. Pensioner's Court
4. Master's Court
5. Wash-house Court
6. entrance
7. Charterhouse Square

Sheltered Housing, Charterhouse

Left: kitchens and shower rooms are also very refined, with high-quality finishes and fittings carefully detailed for use by the infirm residents.

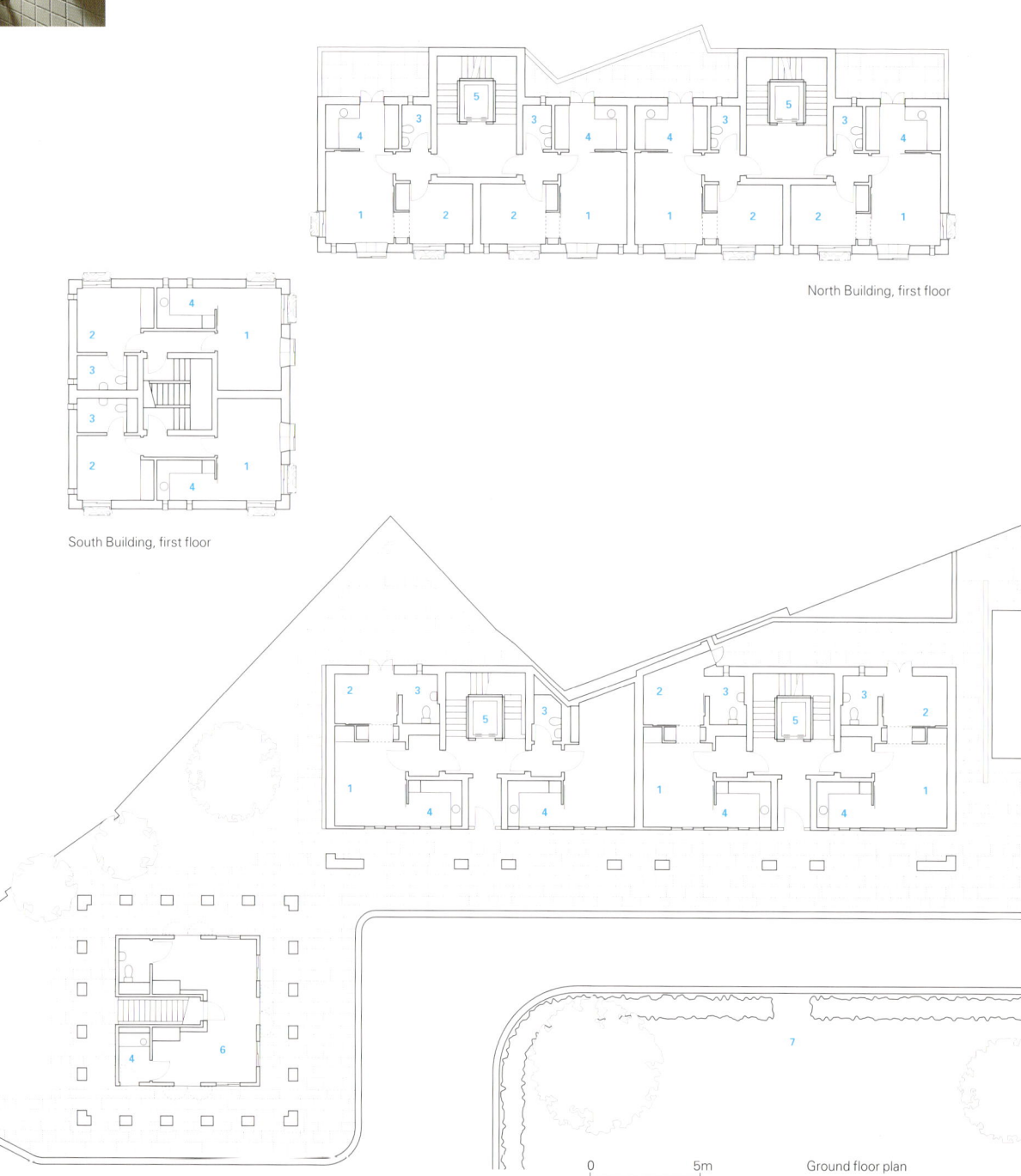

North Building, first floor

South Building, first floor

Ground floor plan

Sheltered Housing, Charterhouse

1 living room
2 bedroom
3 shower room
4 kitchen
5 lift
6 library/common room
7 Preachers Court

Below: the flat interiors are fitted out to a luxury standard. Windows vary from narrow slits to generous projecting bays with leather-cushioned seats.

North Building section 0 2m

Westminster Underground Station 1990–1999

The old Westminster underground station served only the shallow, 'cut and cover' District and Circle Lines. The arrival of the much deeper Jubilee Line extension, and the construction of the New Parliamentary Building, presented the opportunity for a complete redesign. The new station is a much bigger, more complex interchange.

It was considered essential to the open, accessible character of the New Parliamentary Building that its ground floor should be just that – a ground floor at street level, not a raised podium. This, however, created a headroom problem for the District and Circle Lines: the railway lines were therefore lowered by 300 millimetres so that two full storeys could be inserted between platform level and street level. The upper storey contains the ticket hall, accessible from the Bridge Street colonnade of the New Parliamentary Building, and the lower storey contains the platforms. The railway lines cut across the site at an almost 45 degree angle and this has influenced both the plan and the structure of this part of the station. Elements such as dividing walls, escalators and ticket barriers follow either the diagonal grid of the railway line or the orthogonal grid of the building above. Round concrete columns have cruciform capitals which are linked together to form a slightly skewed pattern of rectangular and lozenge-shaped ceiling coffers. The frame is relatively light since it does not have to bear the weight of the building above, which has its own above-ground transfer structure.

Below the District and Circle Lines station lies the 30-metre deep 'escalator box' which provides access to the Jubilee Line platforms. Like most of the other new stations on the line, this is essentially a single volume and therefore quite different from the tangled warren of passageways characteristic of older Underground stations. The concrete diaphragm walls of the box were cast in deep trenchers before the pit was dug. The longer walls, which are unbraced by floors or walls, are stiffened by a vertical grid of beams and buttresses constructed from the top down as excavation proceeded. Further stiffening is provided by horizontal flying shores of solid steel, 600 millimetres in diameter, which connect the buttress walls to a row of concrete columns in the middle of the box. These shores form the supporting structure for the escalators, which are treated as distinct objects within the box, preserving the unity of the space. Travelling up and down the escalators reveals unexpected long views, up, down and sideways and the Piranesian effect is heightened by the finishes, or rather the lack of them. The rough concrete of the box wall remains visible, though framed by the massive grid of the beams and buttresses, and the flying shores are almost brutally simple. Even the finned outer casings of the escalators have an almost military toughness.

The railway tunnels themselves pass to one side of the box, one above the other to keep them as far away as possible from the foundations of the tower of Big Ben.

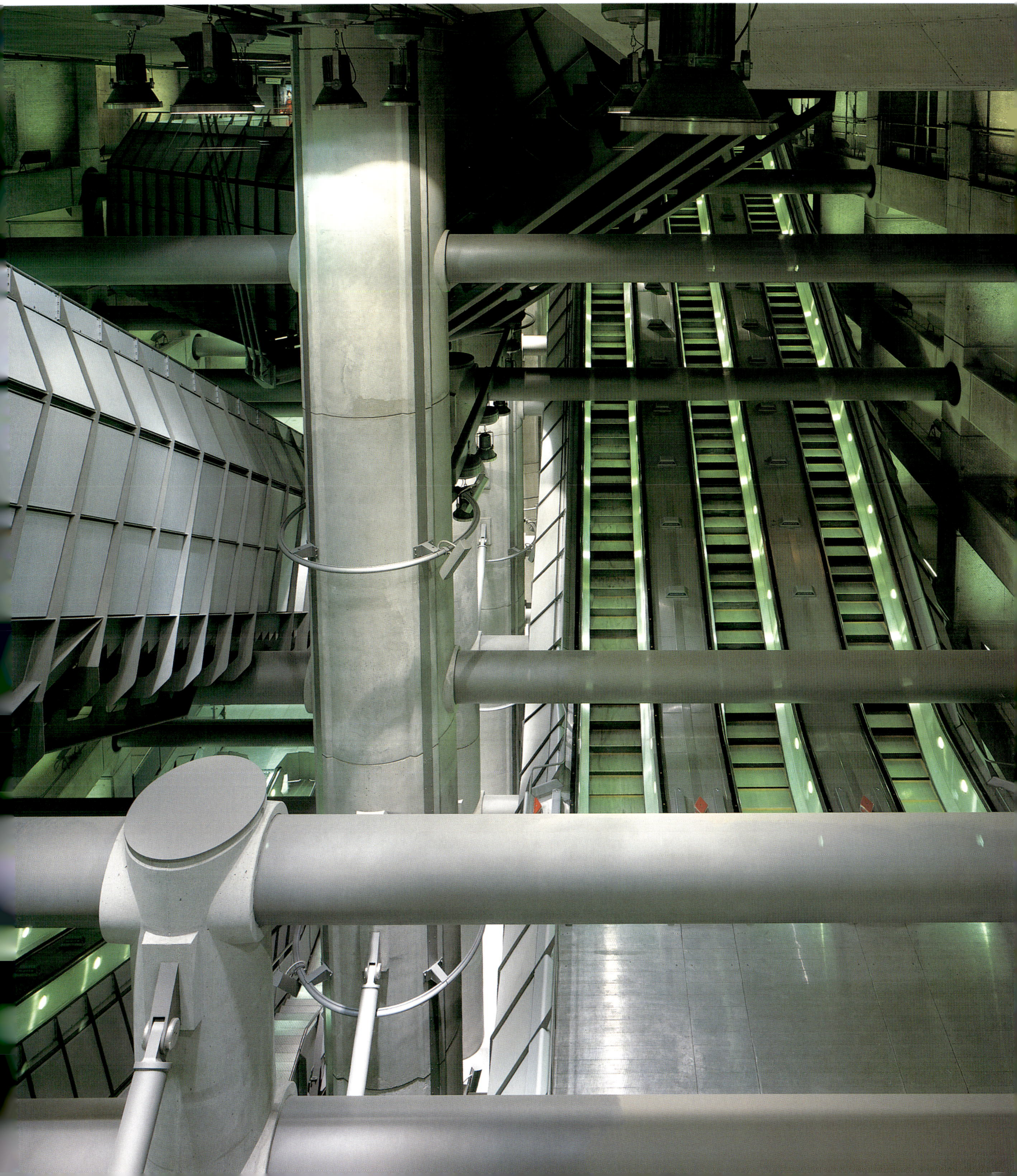

Previous page: the Piranesian interior of the underground 'escalator box'. Solid steel, horizontal flying shores brace the diaphragm walls of the box and also support the escalators.

Below: the ticket hall beneath the ground floor of the New Parliamentary Building. Columns have cruciform capitals linked together by beams to form rectangular and lozenge-shaped ceiling coffers.

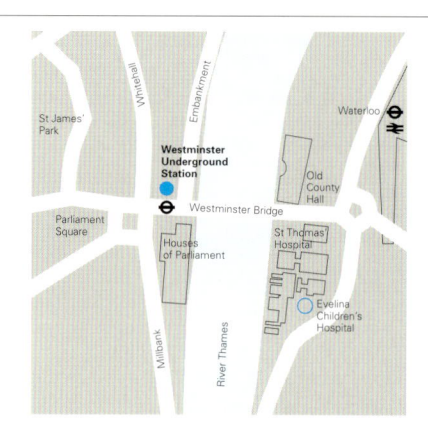

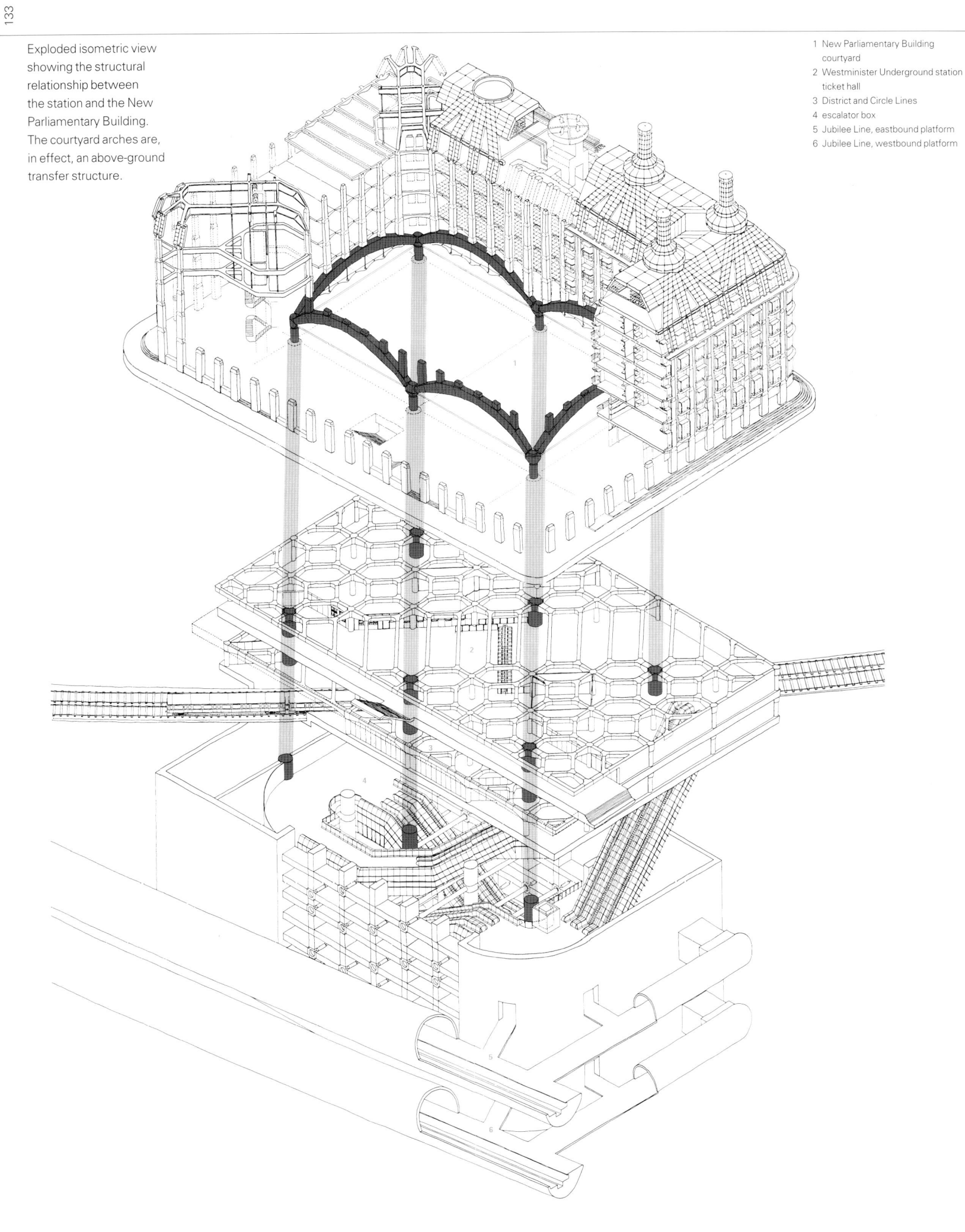

Exploded isometric view showing the structural relationship between the station and the New Parliamentary Building. The courtyard arches are, in effect, an above-ground transfer structure.

1 New Parliamentary Building courtyard
2 Westminster Underground station ticket hall
3 District and Circle Lines
4 escalator box
5 Jubilee Line, eastbound platform
6 Jubilee Line, westbound platform

Westminster Underground Station

Below and opposite: plans showing the relationship between the ticket hall and the escalator box. The circulation routes adapt to the angle of the District and Circle Lines.

Right: District and Circle Line platform.

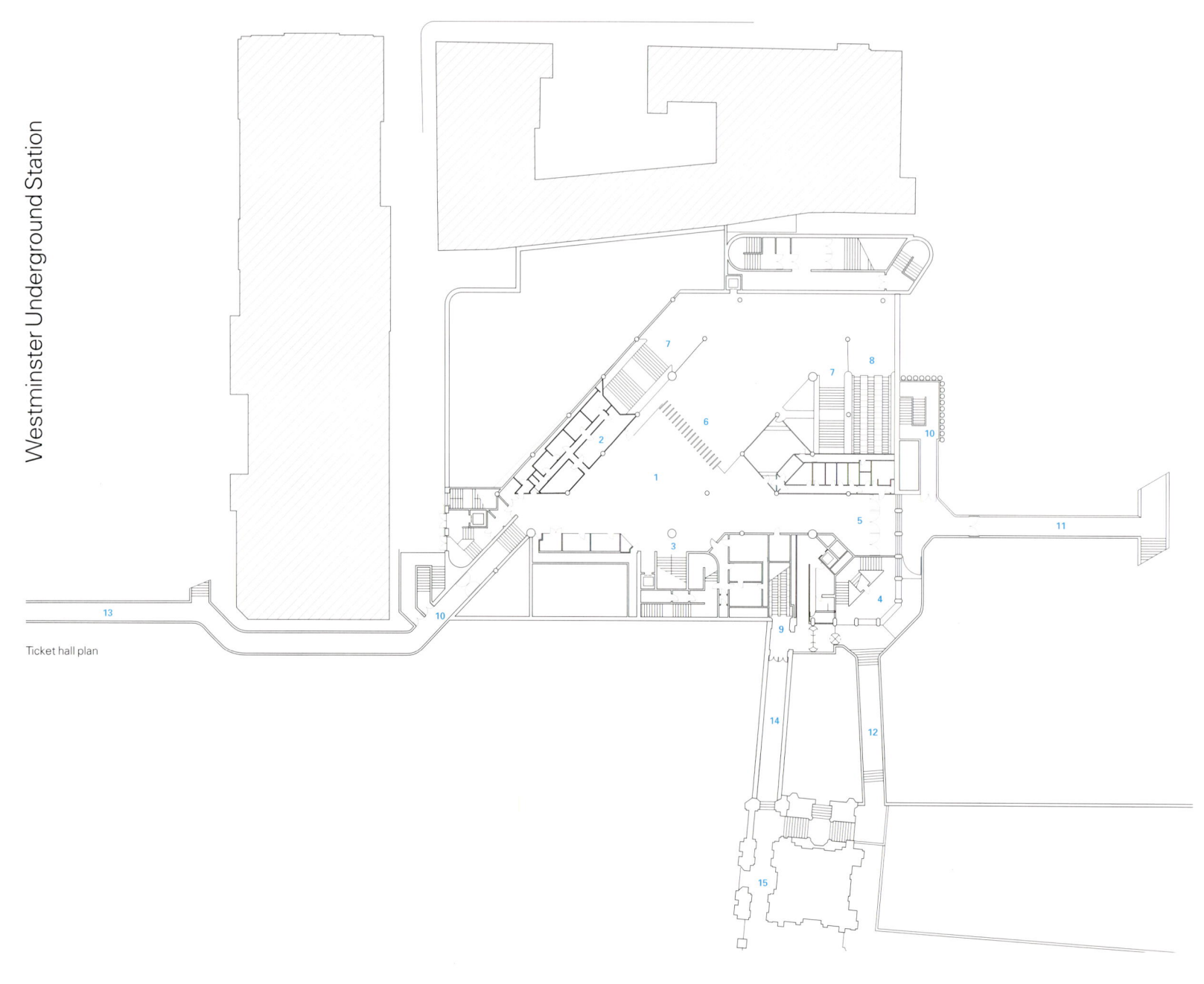

Westminster Underground Station

Ticket hall plan

1 ticket hall level concourse
2 ticket offices
3 main station entrance stairs
4 side entrance station stairs
5 entrance from subways
6 ticket turnstiles
7 stairs to District & Circle Line level
8 escalators to
   main interchange level
9 escalators to New
   Parliamentary Building
10 escape stairs
11 Victoria Embankment subway
12 Bridge Street subway
13 Victoria Street subway
14 tunnel under Bridge Street to
   Palace of Westminster
15 colonnade to New Palace Yard
16 escalators from ticket hall level
17 escalators from
   District & Circle Line
18 escalators to Jubilee Line
   eastbound
19 escalators to District & Circle Line
20 plant
21 Jubilee Line tunnel
   ventilation shaft
22 escape stairs from Jubilee Line
23 services duct
24 void
25 diaphragm wall
26 Jubilee Line eastbound concourse
27 eastbound platform
28 escalators to
   main interchange level
29 escalators to Jubilee Line
   westbound concourse
30 lift

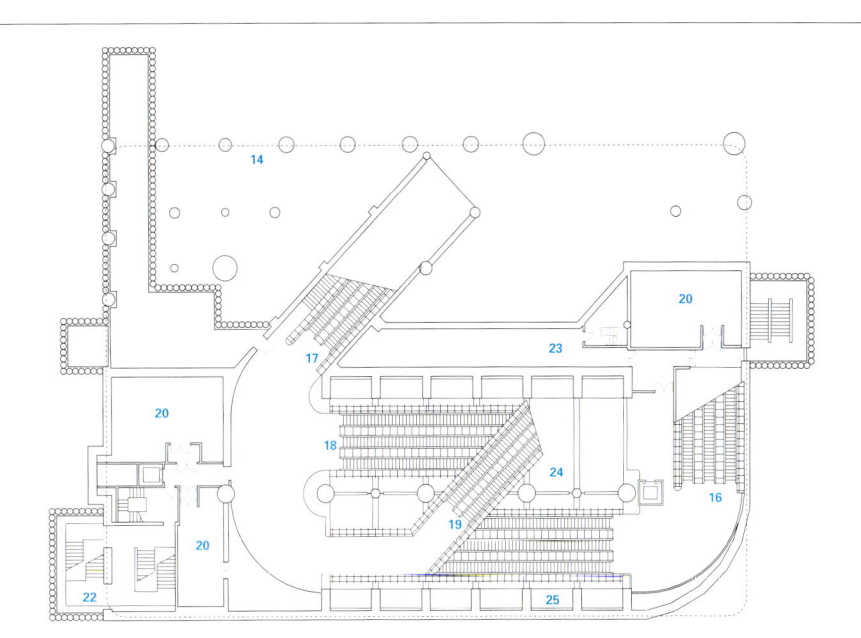

Intermediate level plan

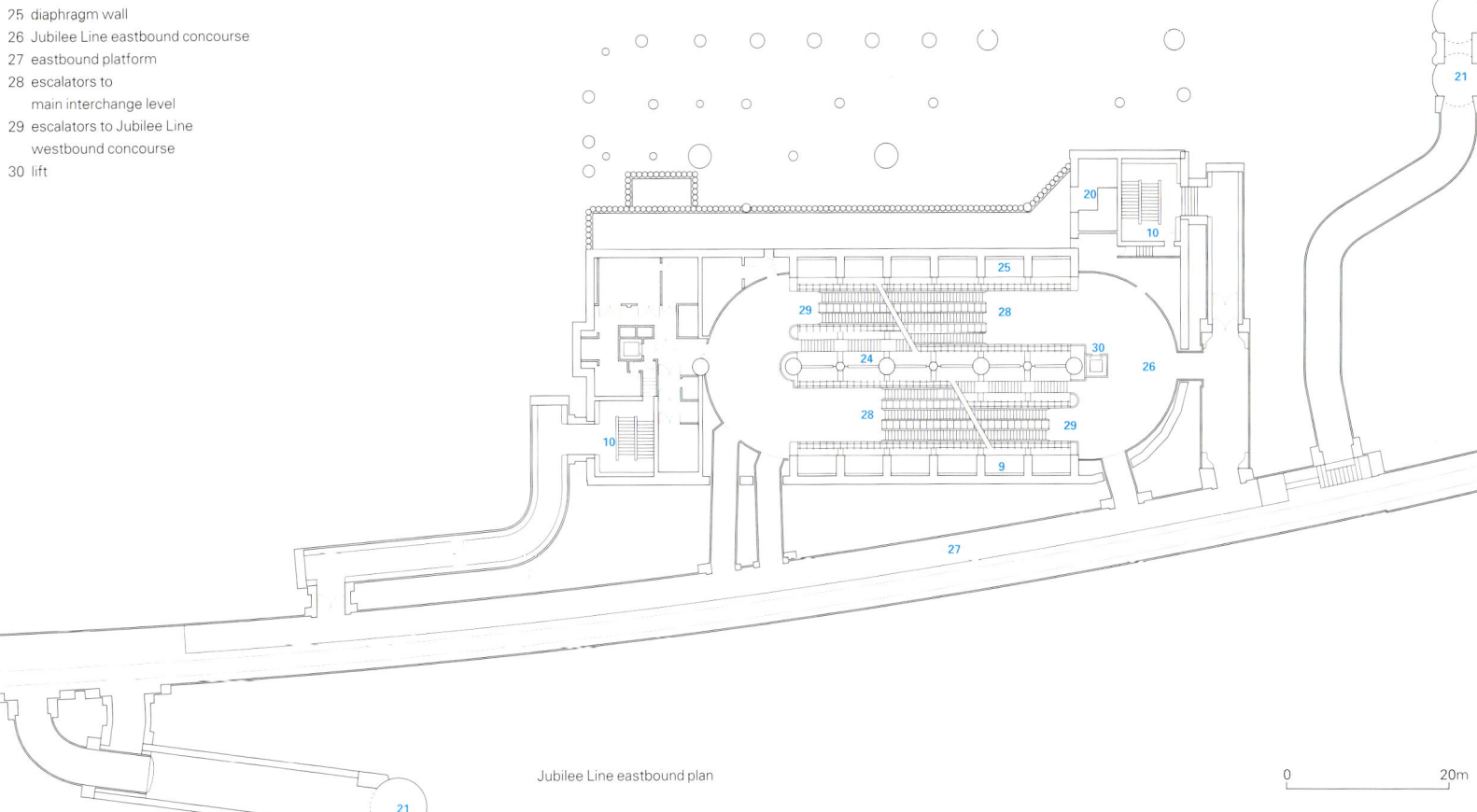

Jubilee Line eastbound plan

0   20m

New Parliamentary Building 1989–2000

A space audit of the whole parliamentary estate, carried out in the late 1980s, revealed an urgent need for more than 200 MP's offices and a new suite of select committee rooms. Earlier Hopkins schemes incorporated listed nineteenth-century buildings on Bridge Street and Victoria Embankment but after the passing of the London Underground Bill it became clear that it would be necessary to clear the whole corner site in order to build the new Jubilee Line station. This opened up the possibility of a substantial new, free-standing building and the creation of a secure Parliamentary Campus extending as far as Parliament Street and Richmond Terrace.

The new building has a simple, rectangular, courtyard plan. Seven storeys high, including two attic storeys, its external profile is similar to that of the neighbouring Norman Shaw Building. At ground level, an open arcade extends along the two street frontages, sheltering the entrance to the tube station, a row of shops on Bridge Street, and the main public entrance on Victoria Embankment. The courtyard is covered by a glass roof at second floor level and surrounded by a two-storey cloister. The upper level of the cloister serves the committee rooms and is accessible to the public via a glazed staircase projecting into the courtyard from the main entrance hall. Two restaurants and a library open onto the courtyard itself, which, though clearly visible from the entrance hall, is mainly for use of MPs and serves as the social focus for the whole parliamentary campus north of Bridge Street. A secure underpass links the courtyard to the Palace of Westminster. On the upper floors, cellular offices for MPs and their support staff are double-banked along continuous corridors, with lifts, staircases and toilets in the corners.

The building was designed in conjunction with the seven-storey high underground chamber of the new tube station. This imposed severe constraints on the structural form. The option of introducing a transfer structure in the form of a thick slab was rejected because it would have meant raising the ground floor and destroying the easy relationship with the surrounding streets. A continuous substructure was available round the perimeter of the site to support the outer walls, but the inner walls round the courtyard had to be supported on only six columns, arranged like the spots on a domino. Shallow, asymmetrical concrete arches braced by steel tension members span between these columns at the level of the first-floor cloister, forming what is effectively an above-ground transfer structure. Loadbearing sandstone piers, prefabricated and prestressed, form the basic structure of the external walls. 'Gullwing' precast concrete floor units span the full 13.5 metres between inner and outer walls, bearing on concrete 'kneeling blocks' in the piers. Because of the limitations imposed by the substructure, lifts and staircases are suspended from complex frame structures spanning diagonally across the corners of the building.

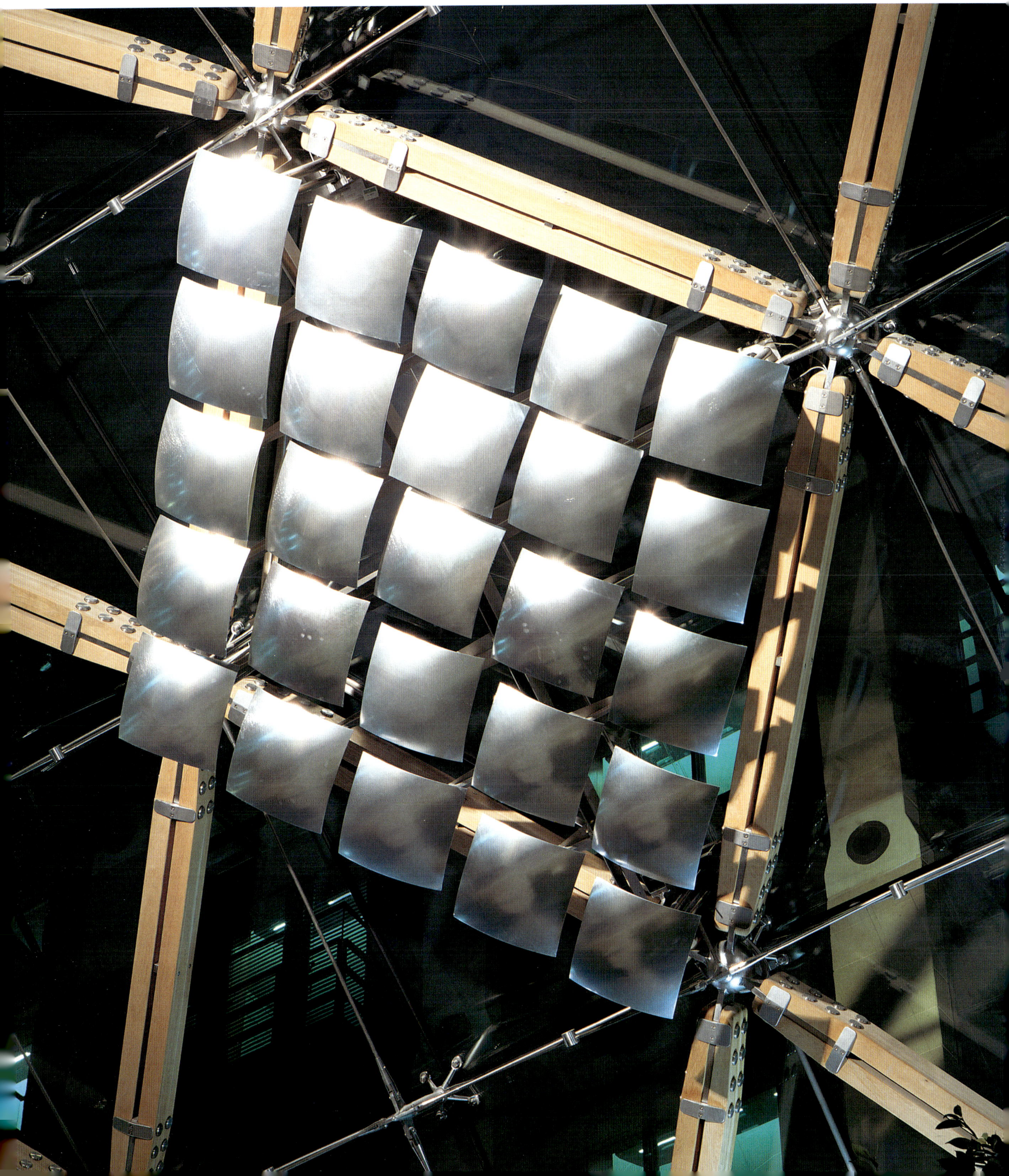

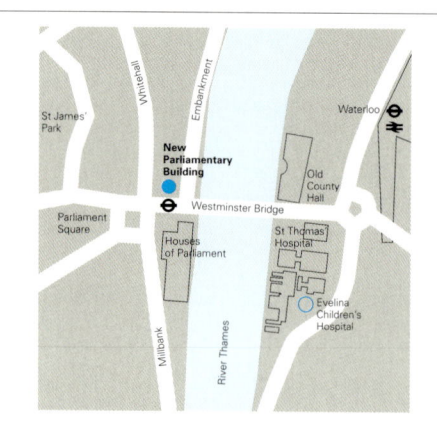

The two-storey attic has a completely different kind of structure, though it, too, has to span clear between inner and outer walls. Welded bronze and steel box girders, doubling as air ducts, form spider-like frames standing on the tops of the sandstone piers. Each spider is topped by a chimney. Saddle-shaped roofs span between the spiders to complete the enclosure. The top floor of the building is mainly taken up by mechanical plant, with only six isolated office areas, but the lower attic floor contains a full complement of MPs' offices, their sometimes curiously shaped windows peeping out between the spiders' legs. Early designs for the courtyard roof proposed an arched steel lattice springing from the capitals of the six 'domino' columns like a Gothic fan vault. The final design has a simpler geometry and the structural material has changed from steel to laminated timber. A flat glass roof around the perimeter is propped off the columns by raking timber struts. This forms a level base for a domed diagrid of straight timber members with stainless-steel joints. The frameless glass skin is supported on a delicate secondary web of steel struts and tension members laced through the timber framework.

It was a requirement of the brief that the building should set an example in energy saving and this has had a profound effect on its form and physiognomy. All offices, regardless of orientation, are equipped with projecting 'light shelves' over the windows. These improve the quality of daylight in the rooms by reducing glare and reflecting light onto the ceiling. They also shade the windows from direct sunlight, preventing excessive solar heat gain. Outward facing windows, some projecting as bays, are sealed against noise and air pollution, but windows facing the courtyard open onto small balconies. This is a heavy building with a high thermal capacity. Sandstone piers, concrete ceilings and suspended concrete partitions between the offices act together like a 'thermal flywheel', evening out the temperature fluctuations in the building. But it is the ventilation system that makes the biggest visual impact. Fourteen tall, bronze chimneys crown the ridge line, echoing the chimneys of the Norman Shaw building and the pinnacles (which are also chimneys) of the Palace of Westminster. They are not just decorative embellishments however, but the terminals of a vertical duct system that embraces the whole building. Each sandstone pier is flanked by bronze clad ducts which expand upwards in proportion to the tapering of the pier and connect at cornice level with the spider's legs of the roof structure. Fresh air introduced at the bases of the chimneys travels down the supply ducts into plenums beneath the raised floors. Exhaust air enters the return ducts through the inward projections of the light shelves.

Solid oak is the dominant material for the interior linings, fittings and furnishings. Corridors borrow light from the adjacent rooms through bay width, frameless glass fanlights between the oak panelled walls and the undulating concrete ceilings.

1 members and plant
2 members and staff
3 committee rooms and conference facilities
4 common areas
5 shops
6 courtyard
7 River Thames
8 Norman Shaw North
9 Norman shaw South
10 No1 Canon Row
11 Canon Row
12 Palace of Westminster
13 Parliament Square
14 Bridge Street
15 Parliament Street
16 Victoria Embankment

Previous page: panel of light reflectors suspended from the glass, timber and stainless steel courtyard roof.
Below: exploded isometric. The building has a simple, rectangular, courtyard plan with five floors of members offices above common and semi-public spaces such as committee rooms and catering facilities.

Above: The New Parliamentary Building is the last in a line of palace-like buildings on the Embankment, which is terminated by Westminster Bridge and the tower of Big Ben.

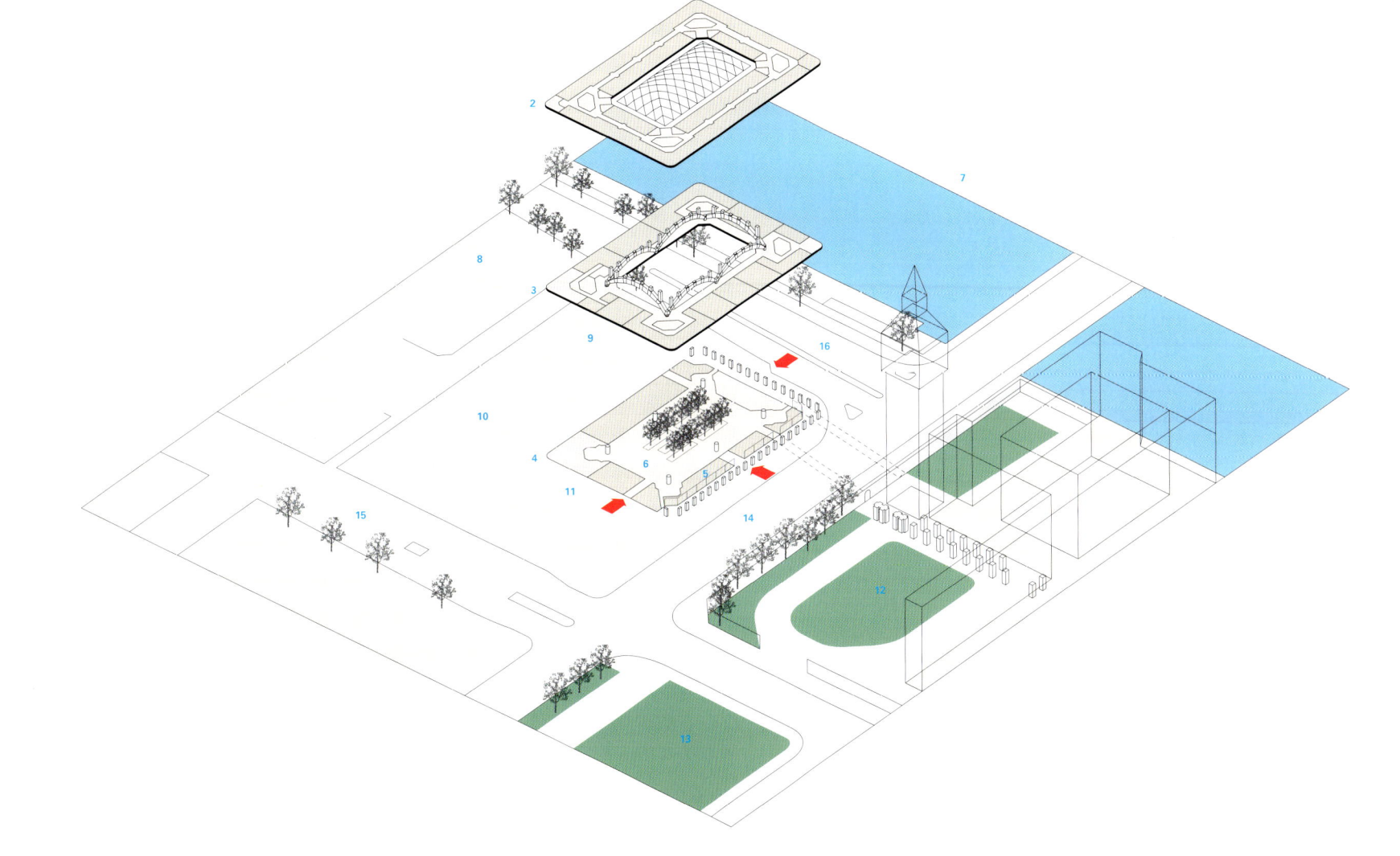

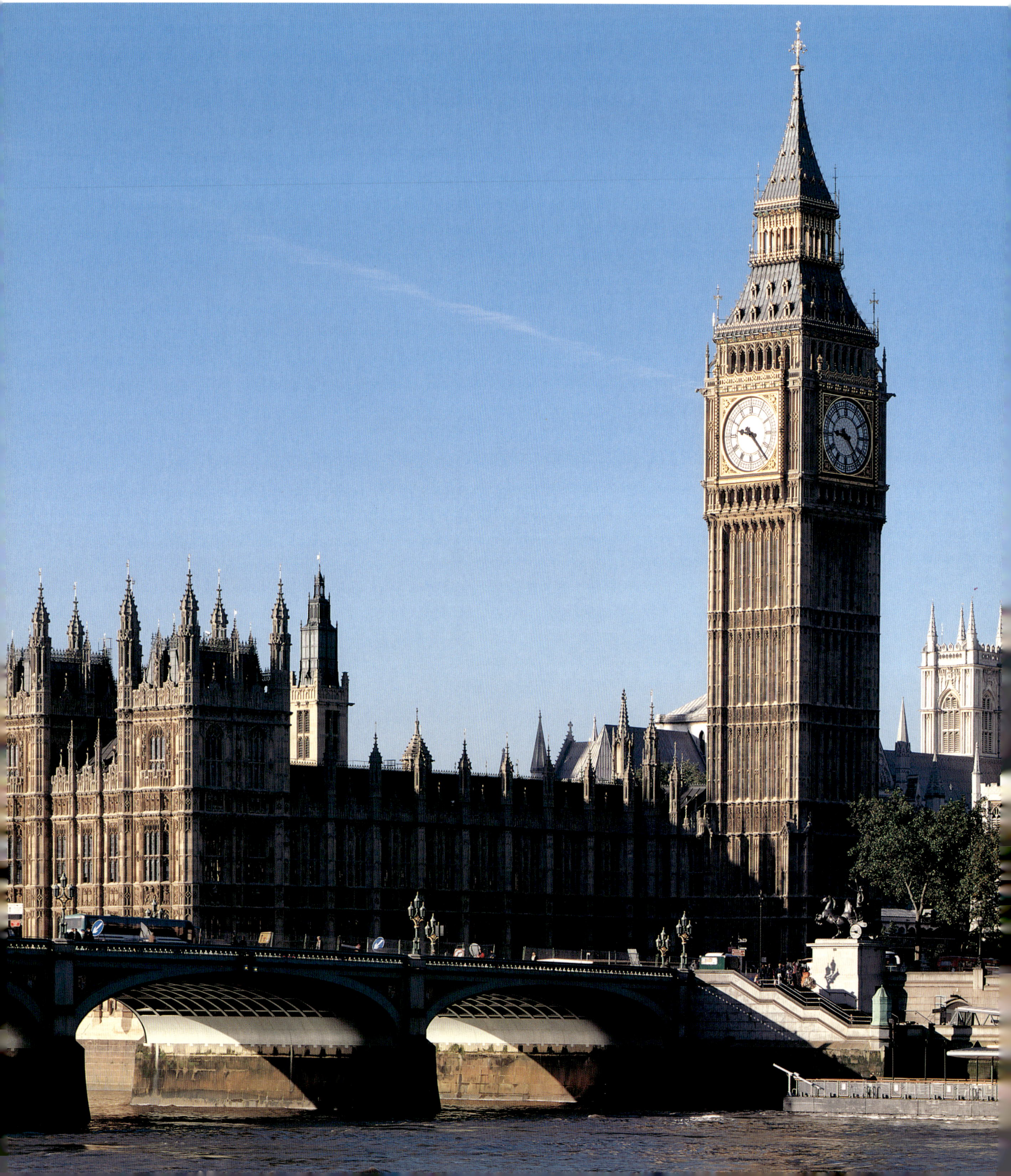

141

Previous page: the building sits comfortably between the Norman Shaw Building and the Palace of Westminster, acknowledging both of its neighbours in its form, materials and detailing. Right: cutaway isometric projection showing the structural relationship between the New Parliamentary Building and the underground station. Shallow arches transfer the weight of the inner, courtyard walls to only six columns.

Below: section through the Parliamentary Campus, showing the continuous secure pedestrian link between the Commons Chamber (right) and the courtyard of the new building. Opposite: viewed from Parliament Square, the crown of bronze chimneys echoes the Gothic pinnacles of the Palace of Westminster, which were also designed to function as chimneys.

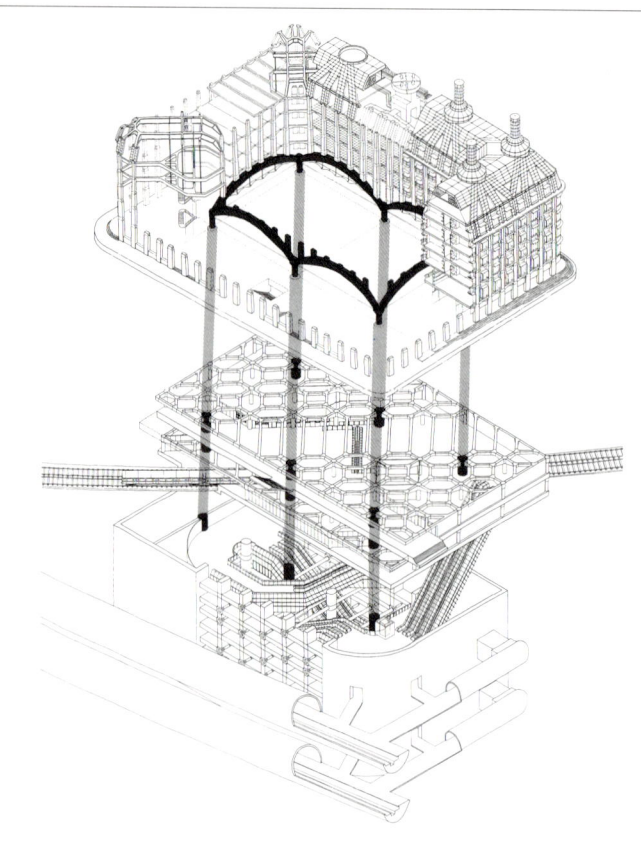

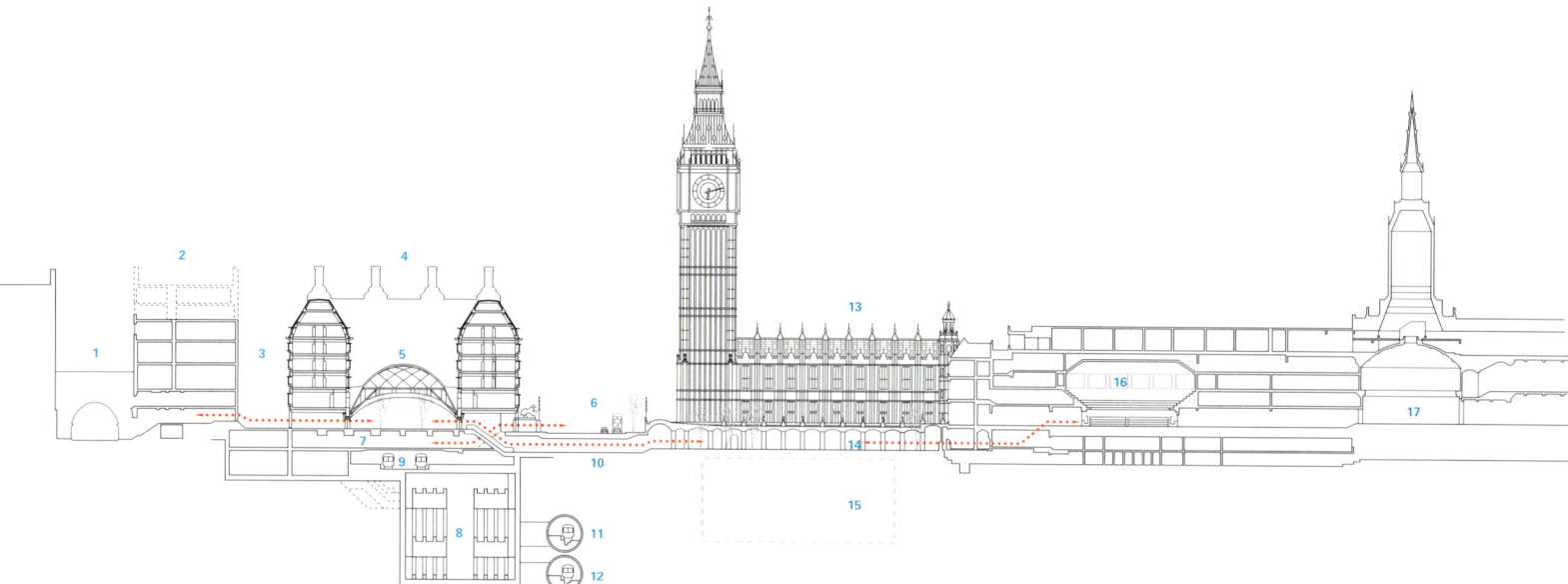

1 Derby Gate
2 Norman Shaw South
3 Terrace
4 New Parliamentary Building
5 courtyard
6 Bridge Street
7 ticket hall
8 escalators
9 District and Circle lines
10 members' subway
11 Jubilee line eastbound
12 Jubilee line westbound
13 Palace of Westminster
14 colonnade
15 House of Commons car park
16 commons chamber
17 central lobby

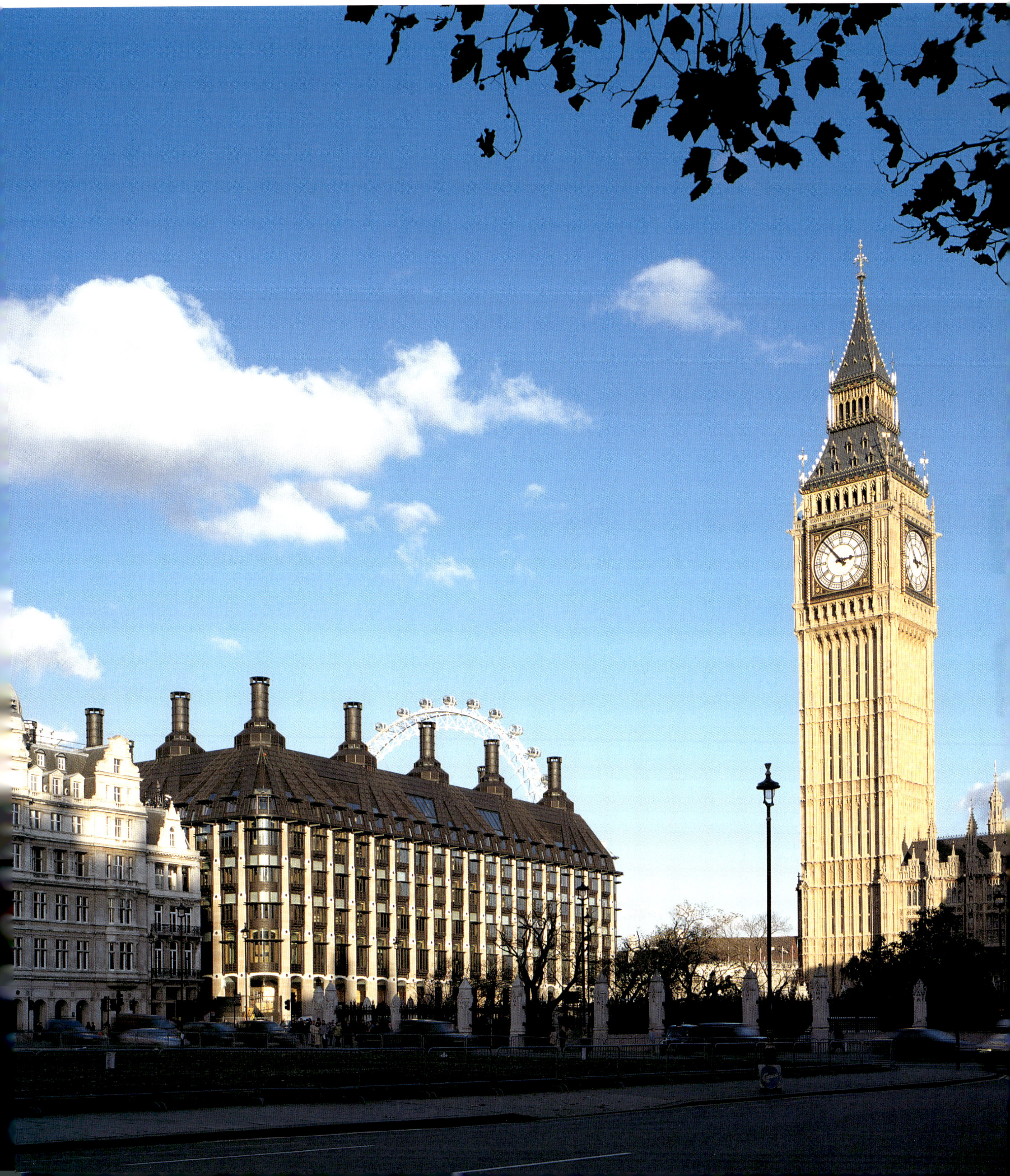

Below: section showing the relation of the building to the courtyard, its glass roof like a bubble in the centre. Office balconies overlook the courtyard.

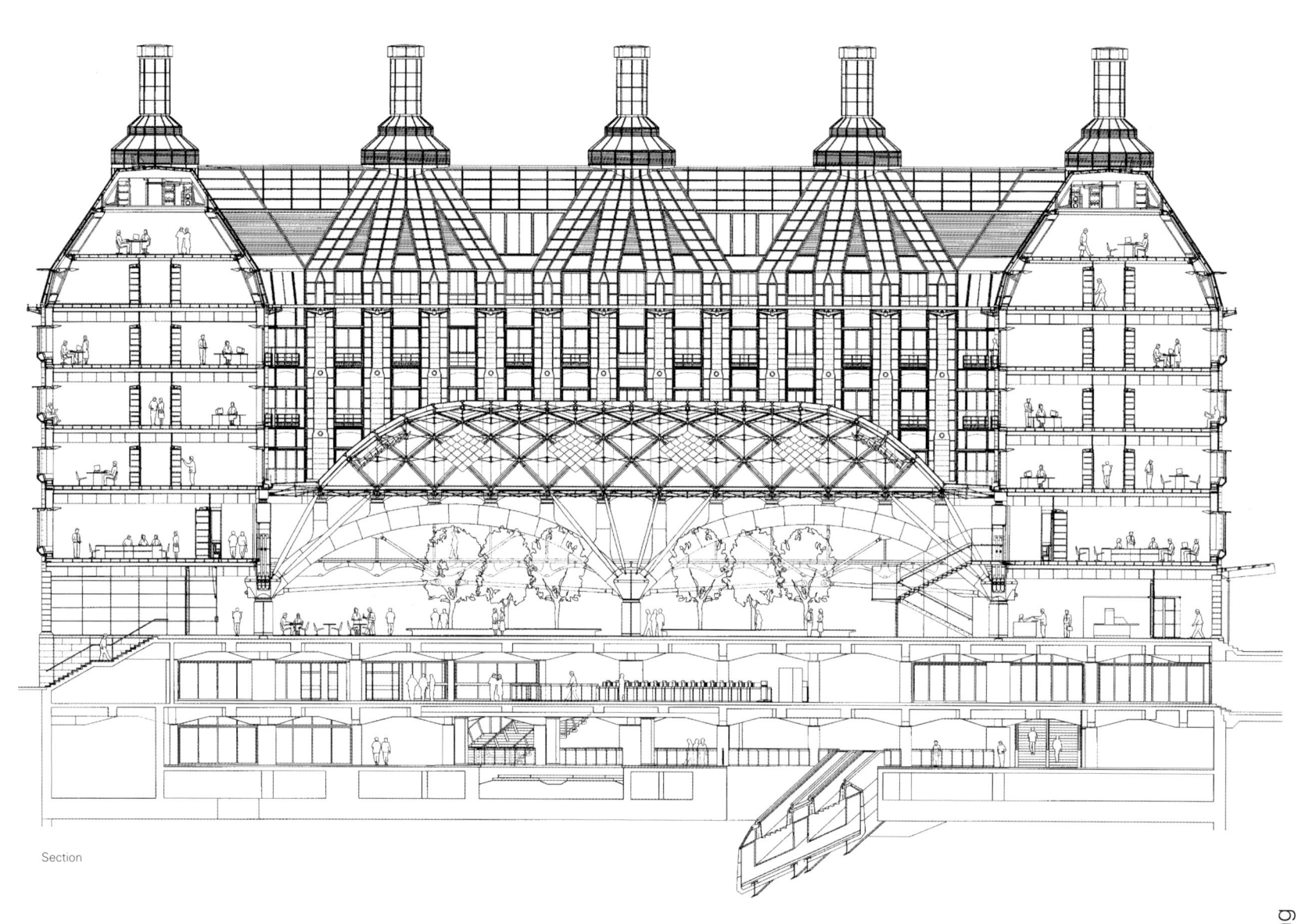

Section

1 clock tower
2 New Palace Yard
3 No 1 Parliament Street
4 No 1 Canon Row
5 Norman Shaw South
6 Parliament Street subway
7 subway link from Palace
8 Embankment subway
9 main entrance
10 stairs to committee rooms
11 courtyard with glazed roof
12 waiter service restaurant
13 restaurant
14 e-library
15 shops
16 arcade
17 Westminster Station entrance
18 kitchens
19 Select Committee room
20 conference room
21 meeting room
22 upper part of glazed courtyard
23 finishing kitchen
24 bridge link to Norman Shaw
25 member's room
26 staff room
27 bathrooms
28 coffee/reading rooms
29 courtyard roof

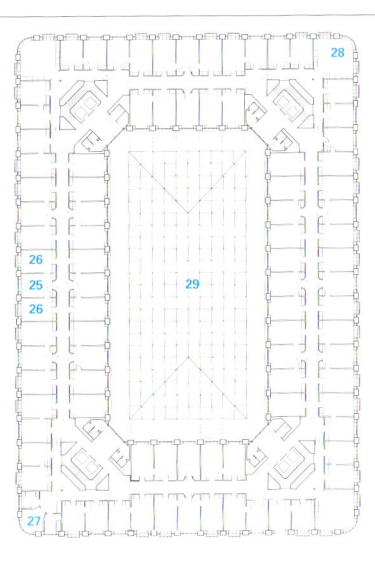

Second to fourth floor

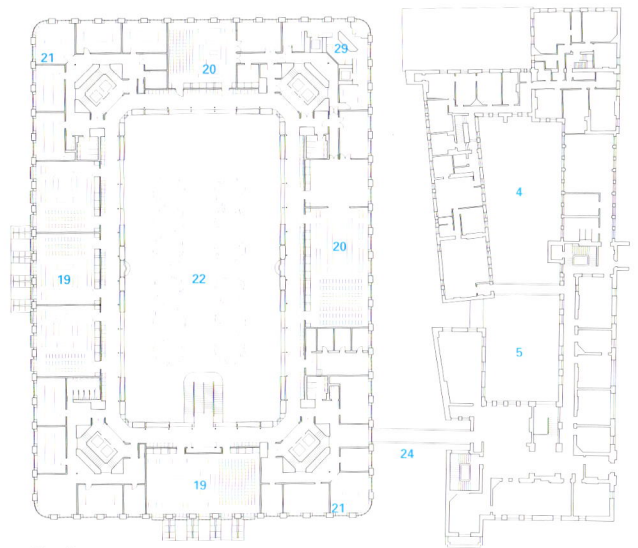

First floor

Ground floor

Bridge Street

Victoria Embankment

February 1998

May 1998

New Parliamentary Building

Top: sequence shows precast concrete floor components and bronze chimney being winched into place by cranes. Prefabrication is an important theme in almost all Hopkins buildings.

Below: prefabrication enabled the superstructure of the building to rise rapidly out of the ground as soon as the substructure of the underground station was complete (from February 1998).

November 1998

April 1999

148

Far left: projecting 'light shelves' on the facade reflect daylight up through high level windows onto the ceilings of the offices, reducing the need for artificial light. Left: a typical member's office. The vaulted ceiling, formed by 'gullwing' concrete panels, makes each office into a separate room rather than just a subdivision of a larger space.

Below: sections showing the environmental strategy. Exposed concrete ceilings and heavy partitions help to even out temperature fluctuations.

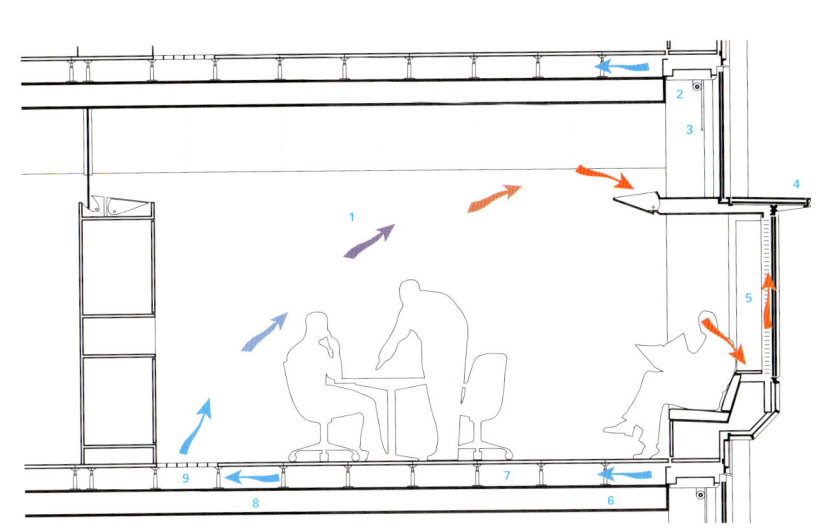

Typical room environmental strategy

1. displacement ventilation
2. extract plenum
3. roller blind
4. light shelf
5. retractable blinds within ventilated cavity
6. concrete floor slab for thermal mass
7. floor plenum
8. cool air slab
9. perforated floor grille
10. exhaust air
11. exhaust air fan
12. fresh air in
13. thermal wheel
14. services distribution rack
15. supply air handling unit
16. facade air shafts

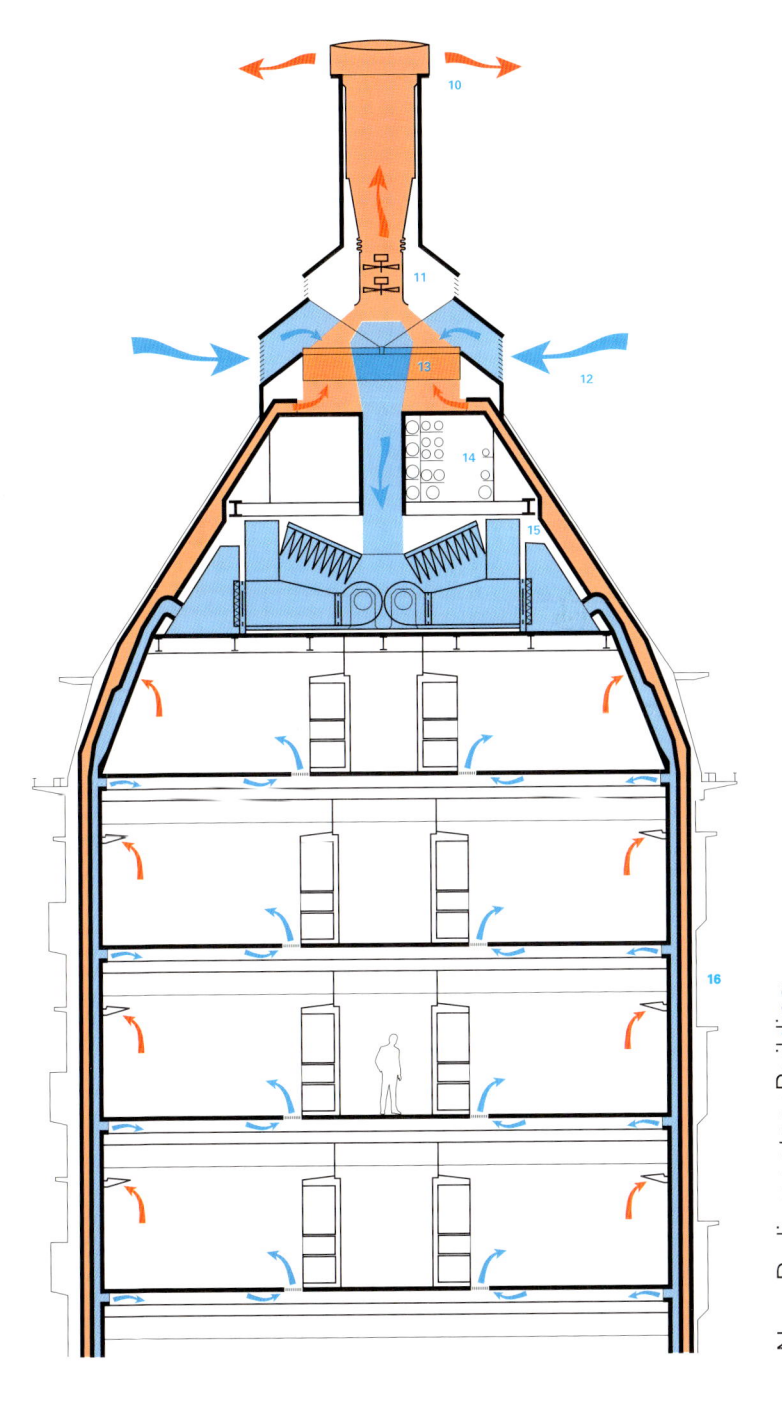

New Parliamentary Building

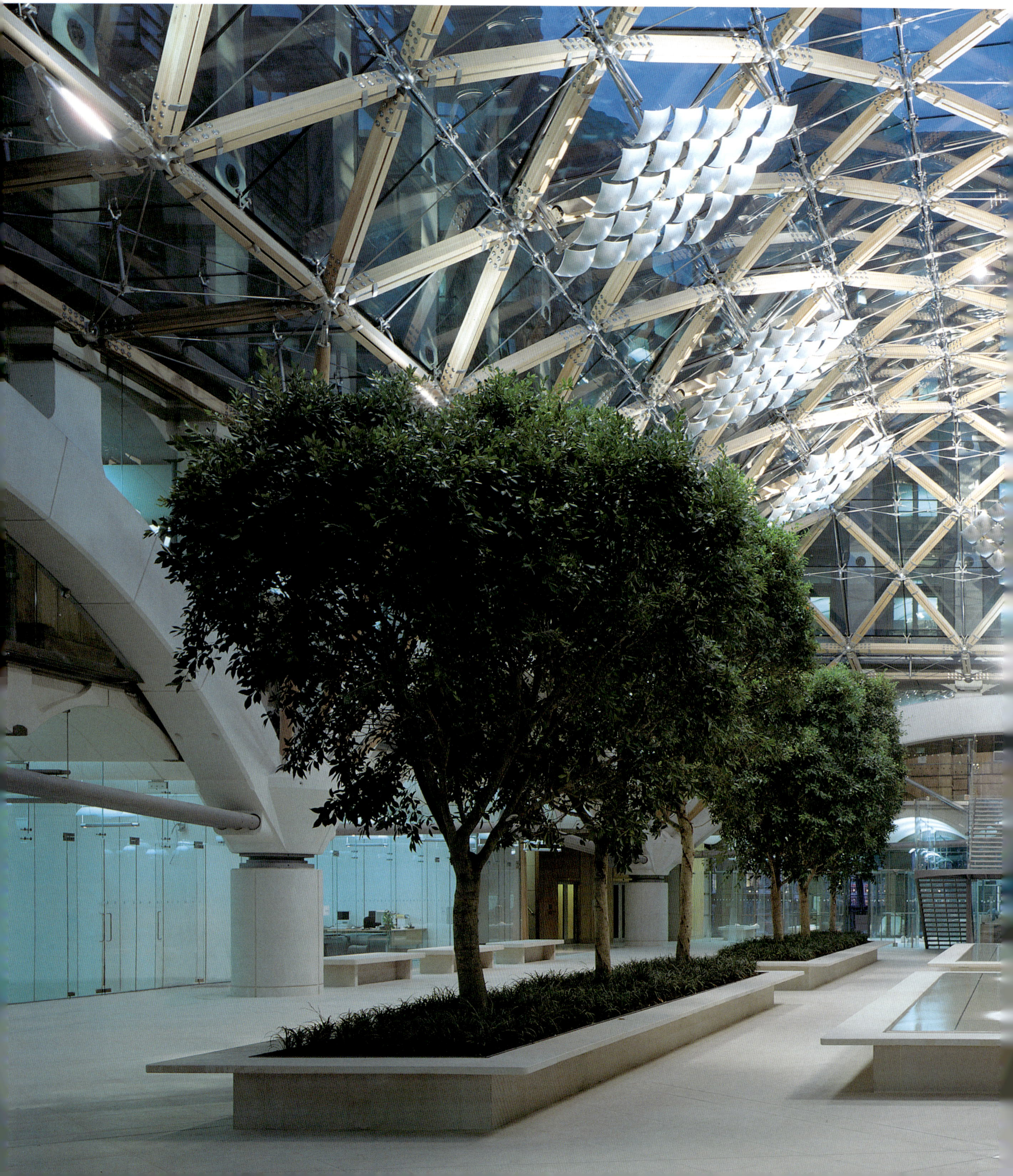

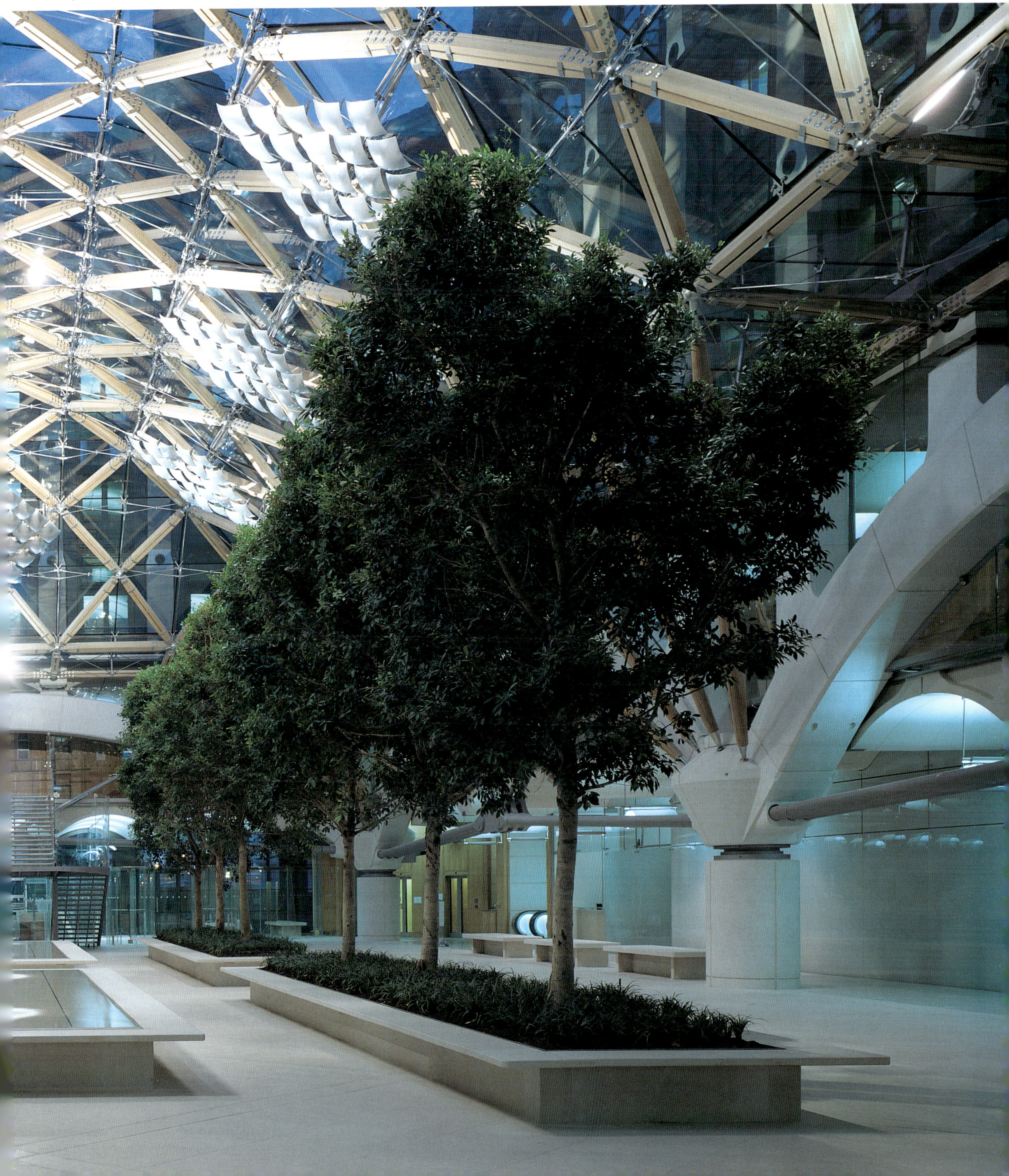

152

Previous page: the courtyard is the social focus of the whole parliamentary campus north of Bridge Street. Though mainly for the use of MPs, it is clearly visible from the main public entrance on The Embankment.
Left: shallow concrete arches on short, round columns support the loadbearing piers of the external walls facing the courtyard as well as the timber-framed roof.
Right: viewed from above, the glass roof swells like a bubble in the courtyard. Offices overlooking the courtyard are provided with balconies.
Below: the glass, timber and stainless steel roof of the courtyard is the modern equivalent of the medieval hammer-beam roof of Westminster Hall.

New Parliamentary Building

Left and below: members of the public reach the first floor committee rooms via a circulation gallery which is open to the courtyard.

Right: the staircase connecting the main entrance with the first floor committee room corridor projects into the courtyard, which is otherwise inaccessible to the public.

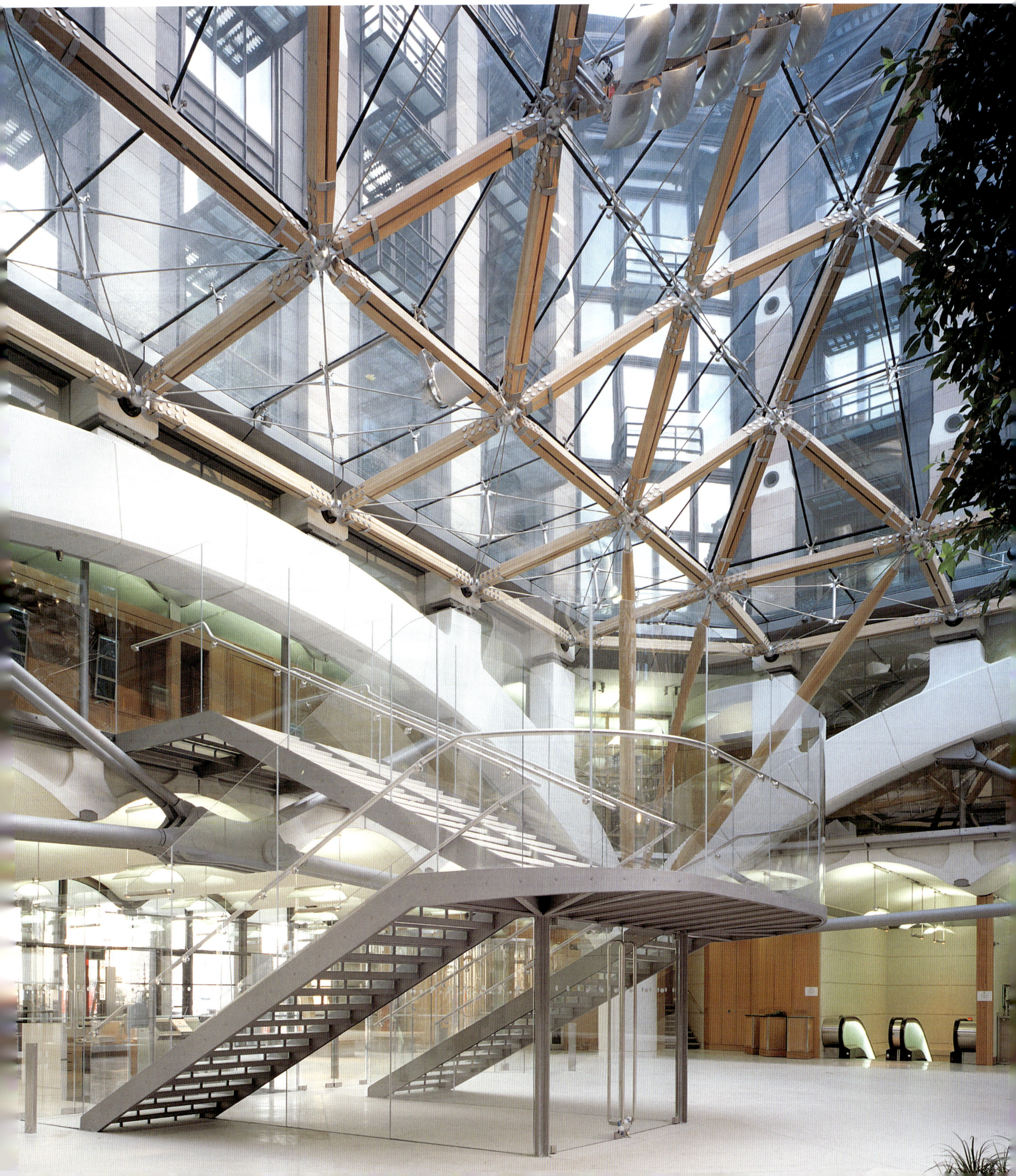

Open House at Westminster: The New Parliamentary Building

Patrick Hodgkinson

'What is the use of a book', thought Alice, 'without pictures or conversations?' as Lewis Carroll wrote in *Alice in Wonderland*. This book has both, but the perceptive may learn more from the pics than the words.

I entered architecture school an aeon ago, but before the end of my studentship it had struck me, first, that much of what we gathered about the Modern Movement was hyperbole that unfortunately *was* taken literally and, second, that it had all come about too fast. A 'heroic period' with too few players of only seven years (1922–9)? What fulfilling architectures of the past had not developed through their periods of transition before settling down to acceptability? Over the years since, my thoughts about these two salient factors have remained.

How was it that so many architects accepted Joseph Paxton's shed, the Crystal Palace, as the progenitor for industrialized architecture while debunking William Lethaby and CFA Voysey, for instance, for lack of progress when both had found constructive ways of building, far removed from revived style, that continue to touch our hearts? What *is* architectural progress? Was even Adolf Loos' homily 'Ornament and Crime', however gripping for those freeing themselves of stale aesthetic slavery, appropriate for our deeper senses? Although 'High-Tech' has given us some remarkable buildings, the problem with the shed, if taken literally, is that its progeny looks too like process unsuited to many conditions of life, while moneyman Paxton himself did not see the Crystal Palace as architecture.

It is almost a century and a half since Charles Barry and AWN Pugin's Palace of Westminster was opened by Queen Victoria – the Victoria Tower and Big Ben were completed later – but until now, although there were a few attempts to build on the Bridge Street site over the last thirty years, little new has been added to the Palace complex. Pugin's *Contrasts* (1836) was published a year after the competition for the building, whose terms had sought a design of Gothic or Elizabethan origin. It is now known that Barry had employed Pugin for the competition and continued to do so until Pugin's death at forty, when the Palace was opened. 'All Grecian, Sir; Tudor details on a classic body', as he had

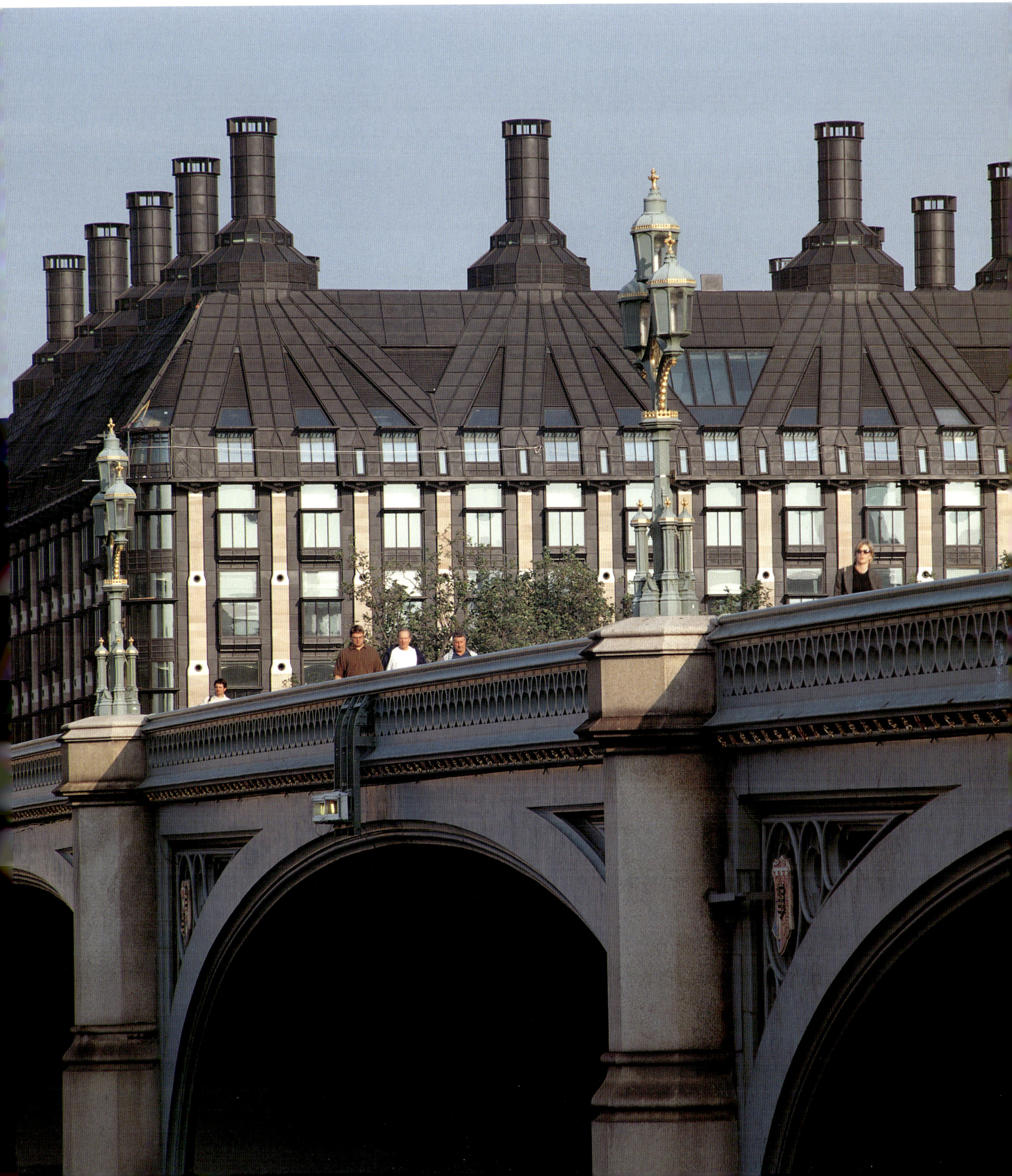

remarked before he died of assumed madness – an architectural dog's breakfast, if ever there was one, to any purist. And yet, seen across the Thames, the Palace remains one of the finest and most romantic images of government in the world. The challenge for Michael Hopkins, in building alongside this superlative facade, who, as a schoolboy, had the distinction of failing O-level Art, was immense.

Ironically, some might argue that Hopkins' resolution of the Parliamentary Building is no less a mixture of opposites than the Palace. A classical palazzo plan with six symmetrical drum columns carries half the load of this colossus – and few politicians are lightweights – past the diagonal of the Circle Line underground tracks beneath it (the Jubilee Line extension tracks run under Bridge Street), while aspects of the facades and roof trappings are reminiscent of Gothic in that they obey apparently freer laws than would the Classic. The real irony for historical theoreticians, though, is that Hopkins has achieved an unlikely, but workable, marriage between these long-term adversaries which makes excellent city sense in an era of sustainability whose technical engineering will become increasingly complex in the future. As a whole, then: brilliance of concept for today.

I class the building alongside Leslie Martin's (with others) Royal Festival Hall (1951) and twenty-five years later, Denys Lasdun's Royal National Theatre, in being part of rational modernism that has a fine genealogy through modern architecture's transitional course; its main difference from those others being Hopkins' lightweight beginnings. Significantly, at first at the David Mellor factory at Hathersage (Derbyshire) and then with the Mound Stand at Lords, Hopkins was the first architect of his declention to marry lightweight construction with traditional mass materials, such as stone and brick. Whether he recalled Kenneth Frampton's quotation of Charles Rennie Mackintosh's statement that 'modern materials, such as iron and glass, "will never worthily take the place of stone because of this defect, the want of mass"', is immaterial. What matters is that the process I have referred to had passed from exclusiveness into a more reasonable rationalism (I use that word in the English, rather than the Italian, sense).

Left: Joseph Paxton, Crystal Palace, London, under construction, 1851.
Above: Leslie Martin, Royal Festival Hall, London, 1951; and Denys Lasdun, Royal National Theatre, London, 1967–76.

Opposite left: CFA Voysey, Broadleys, Windermere, Cumbria, 1898.
Opposite right: William Lethaby, Melsetter House, Hoy, Orkneys, 1900.

The same also applies to Hopkins' wonderful lightweight insertion into Albert Richardson's formerly lugubrious Bracken House and in the essay I wrote about the making of an architectural technology for that building, published in the previous Hopkins volume, I used certain historical references that apply equally to the Westminster building in terms of lines of descent. It is worth remembering them again. In this connection I do not accept the simplification of architecture either as engineering or, alternatively, as art and that is why I have referred to a rational tradition which combines both. Hopkins himself makes it clear that a search for clarity underlay his thinking about Westminster, but in less able hands, clarity can lead to architectural confusion if too much is exposed.

In fact, the formal clarity and three-dimensional transparency of the plans makes the whole layout simple to grasp from the entrance lobby: unusual, but essential for strangers visiting their MPs. At ground level an external arcade wraps around the south and east flanks of the building, the first having shops either side of the entrance to Westminster underground station, where Hopkins' Piranesian structure makes you realize something damned important is happening above; while the second contains the main entrance doors facing the river. The six bold drums mark out the covered courtyard, a general milling space flanked by library, two restaurants and post office with lift and stair towers set back in each corner. On the south side are escalators to a tunnel under Bridge Street connecting to the enclosed arcade which forms the east flank of New Palace Yard and thence to the House itself. Under the glazed roof of the covered courtyard we can see the first-floor gallery access to all the main committee and meeting rooms, which also has a rather beautiful, freestanding dog-leg stair leading up to it. It is at this same level that on the north side a covered bridge leads to Norman Shaw South, which has its own connections to Norman Shaw North and No 1 Cannon Row where further MPs' and staff rooms are located.

The second, third and fourth floors are identical, each containing pairs of MPs' rooms on either side of shared staff rooms and served by wide, central but naturally lit corridors. At the north-east and south-west curved corners are varied MPs' and staff rooms, while the remaining external corners contain either coffee rooms or bathrooms. The fifth floor is similar but its corridor is narrower, for we are now within the mansard roof, and from here separate staircases lead up to exhilarating larger rooms for MPs which have windows on both sides – courtyard and river if you are very lucky – between plant rooms under each major stack. These attic rooms are reminiscent of artists' studios high up above the Seine – just right for discrete partying (but I wasn't thinking of political).

Hopkins has made a highly important stride in the handling of the building's services – and rightly so for a parliamentary building for, as many architects are aware, their clients are often unwilling to meet the high capital costs of real sustainability. Maximum use is made of natural light, reducing the need for electric and saving energy. This is helped considerably by using lightshelves to office windows which deflect high sun but reflect lower daylight to the backs of rooms. Maximum advantage is also taken of the heat storage capacity of the building's structure to assist heating and cooling systems, while the benefits of free cooling from natural ventilation – rather than air conditioning and the unpleasant effects this can have – plus the use of favourable external conditions to help provide an altogether healthier internal environment. One aspect of the sustainability employed (when it was designed it was a London first) is that a bore has been sunk to London's rapidly rising water table so that cool 'grey' (untreated) water is used within the cooling systems, and for wc cisterns, before being shot back into the sewers where more fluid is needed. Mechanical plant for all this is contained mostly up in the mansard, but the air intake ducting leading from there to the floor plenums is hidden. Foul air ducting, on the other hand, plays its part in the complexity of the elevations where Hopkins decided to expose their routes to the fourteen circular stacks at roof level, mounted as they are on polygonal fresh air intakes. The roof itself is a structure of patinated aluminium bronze with certain structural members of mild steel welded to the bronze. The blackness has been criticized, and indeed it could be cleaned off, but I personally prefer it as it is.

In 1967, of course, there was a watershed in what many of us had seen as a natural progression of an all-embracing modern architecture with the appearance of 'High-Tech' and then Robert Venturi's book, *Complexity and Contradiction in Architecture*, advocating 'Post-Modernism'. Both of these were quickly seen by peremptory value judgementalists as *new* styles, rather than variants. More hype, you might say. Neither saw architecture as social craft, but primarily as art. My own background – rare for a Londoner perhaps – had been Parisian in that I had found there amongst the young in the late 1940s an allegiance to existentialism – to being oneself – which spoke to me of the personal freedoms to which a people's architecture should direct itself: humane elegance, essentially. But the Sixties' 'styles' were too limited in scope for such psychological complications although the sexual revolution was then, as it were, in full swing. These were, in fact, merely surface styles lacking depth.

It is largely in the external and courtyard facades at Westminster, as well as in the roof, that new ground has been broken. The facades are comprised of Derbyshire gritstone loadbearing piers which narrow at each floor as they take less weight and which, not unlike the columns of the Smithsons' Economist Building (1964), visually increases their apparent height. They have been pre-tensioned, like those at Hopkins' recent music school for Emmanuel College, Cambridge, the bronze-rimmed circular holes in the shaped concrete loadbearers facilitating tensioning. Next to the piers are the bronze exhaust air ducts which naturally increase their girth at each floor. On the external facades, each MPs' room is given a bay window, whereas those facing into the courtyard have instead a French window and balcony. Above bay or French window are the projecting lightshelves, which appear strange only because they are not traditional to window arrangement. The lightshelves, as unfamiliar elements, are likely to become the focus of unfair criticism. By contrast, the window frames themselves are beautifully simple and are entirely of bronze.

The new building was probably expected by tastemongers to mediate between Pugin's facades and those of Norman Shaw for what had been New Scotland Yard, though both argue with each other somewhat typically of revivalism, where Victorian devilled

Above: Foster and Partners, Hongkong and Shanghai Bank, Hong Kong, 1979–86.

Opposite: New Parliamentary Building.

kidneys were wont to rub shoulders with kedgeree. From the river the new facade, with its rounded external corners and suffering no want of mass, possesses instead its own personality which complements the Palace with insistence. I myself was never too fond of this bit of Shaw's Queen Anne. It was enough for Hopkins to take a lead from Shaw's steep roof and to have moved it into a mansard. How excellent that modern city buildings can have visible roofs once again – and to such purpose! The piers reflect the verticality of Pugin's, albeit wedding-cake, fraudulence against the horizontality of Barry's plan, but Pugin was bright enough to hide the frames of opening windows behind stone so that all we see is a facade simply of highly sculpted stone and flat glass which is the dynamic understatement probably responsible for the particular, and glorious, romanticism of his facade.

Against all that is Hopkins' wish for clarity – a morality that stems from Functionalism – though I've never quite understood why some of us find it necessary to be so clear about construction. As long as a building displays an intent – structural, enclosing, or open – that, to my mind, is all that matters. I would similarly question as to why the rectangular-sectioned exhaust air ducts need exposure? Air ducts are normally rectangular because they are cheap to make that way and are hidden, but, when they are exposed, surely circular tubes would be more expressive of flow: a circle being the most economical shape to surround a given area. They could even have ended up skywards as barley sugar twists instead of plain circular stacks. From across the Thames, though, the roof, with those colossal stacks, is an entirely appropriate exclamation to have put next to the Palace.

Internally, on the upper floors there is an air of quiet sobriety befitting the purpose of the building and singling it out from being just another office block. The first floor committee and meeting rooms have wavy concrete ceilings under the floor plenums with concrete walls or oak-lined where they contain storage. The inner wall of the access gallery overlooking the covered courtyard is also faced in oak. Upstairs, the corridors serving the MP's rooms and staff offices are similarly faced, the rooms and offices each having a single arch of the plenum wave as ceiling. Again the walls are concrete except for the oak-lined rear storage walls. The MPs' rooms are not large, but feel spacious due to immaculate design and that includes the domestic feeling of the windows, especially those with bays. It is here that green leather window seats occur – exactly the same as the benches in the House – perhaps for members to secretly practice their methods of leaping up to intrude upon another speaker. Each MPs' room, although approached through the shared staff room, also has its private door to the corridor so that its occupant can come and go without notice.

Different furniture arrangements can be chosen by occupants, but the furniture itself is all standardized, either Charles Eames or designed by the architects. Whilst it is all in the very best of taste, were I an MP, I would demand to bring in my creaky old bashed-up red leather desk chair to which I am used. With so much standardization in the plans, and for very good reason, surely there should be a let up for those who like to be perverse. Of course, many MPs will do this, so that we can expect a glut of racy, Eames swivel chairs, scarcely used, on the second-hand market.

Both externally and internally, the standard of the fairface concrete everywhere is the finest I have ever seen. I understand this was achieved by precasting off-site in timber moulds and using a Norwegian pale grey marble as aggregate. Some of the individual pieces are very large and therefore great care had to be taken in transporting, craning and protecting them against damage on site. When I first saw the building I did not associate the material with concrete at all: the surface everywhere is so fine I just felt like kissing it. But everywhere, in all finishing materials, is excellence of craftsmanship and that type of quality can only stem from excellence in detailed design thinking, for which Hopkins is a past master.

Of course, the most magnificent original part of the whole Palace is Westminster Hall which, for four hundred and fifty years until 1852, was central to English and British national life: as royal court, as court of law, as parliament and as witness to so many historic occasions. The hall's stonework was the work of Henry Yevele, but its entirely grand, and forever memorable, oaken hammerbeam roof structure – a trick to reduce the outward thrust

Above: New Parliamentary
Building.
Opposite: Westminster
Hall.

of a wide-spanning structure – was by the master carpenter Hugh Herland, completed in 1399. With its 70-feet span it is the largest example of this type of construction and said to be the oldest, stemming from our skills in Gothic building as well as shipbuilding. Over two decades ago I took my friend Leonardo Ricci, the small but fierce Italian architect of several megastructures, into Westminster Hall and he was at first struck dumb by its daring. Then Leo, who thought all Englishmen were liars because they make good diplomats, said that he was amazed that we, of all people, could have produced anything so magical. Foolishly, I walked Leo up Whitehall to see Inigo Jones' Banqueting House, but he refused to enter. Spitting on my shoe he cried: 'Is no banquet 'ouse, is *bank!* Come-a to Italia'.

'Come back to London', I would tell him now, were the venerable Leo still alive, for Michael Hopkins' glass-roofed courtyard is surely one of few really great rooms of our times, a room that certainly reflects the majesty, and the magic, of Westminster Hall – but without its medieval solemnity – though we now have science on our side compared to Herland's dewdropped nose. Its span is the same as that of the Hall. This summer I became tired of architects' glass-roofed atriums and didn't want to see another, but until you've seen Hopkins' you haven't seen an atrium at all. I remember working on Alvar Aalto's top-lit atrium of his Rautatalo building in Helsinki from 1953–4, which probably started the fashion.

At Westminster, the six drum columns take the loads of colossal concrete arches with steel tensioners and thick concrete upstands collecting the loads of the facade piers at second-floor level. It is between these that you see puffing politicians coming and going to committee rooms on the first-floor gallery. The glass roof itself is a diagrid of oak members, vaulted and hipped at each end, with only the slightest of stainless steel ties connecting main joints horizontally. Delicate oak spars transfer the roof's load to shaped concrete pads which also act as springs for the arches atop the drums. The floor of the room, with its raised benches and planters, is Portland stone, the planters containing 7-metre tall fig trees bringing green indoors while other benches surround long troughs of water reflecting patterns from the sky. As it moves around the courtyard, the sun will pour in all day so that light and shade will continually play their essential games with the architecture. I am at once inside and outside. As for artificial light, the method is entirely new for this country. It is achieved by throwing invisible beams of light across the room onto curved, spun aluminium reflectors, suspended in large diamonds under the glass, which happen also to dampen sound, and these simply rain minute particles of light – again beamless – about the whole room: today's chandeliers, shall we say, fantasticating the whole space. During governmental summer recesses, arrangements must somehow be made for the public to see this undeniably great, and sparkling, room. It would do our stiff parliamentary system a power of good.

If you take a look across Parliament Square at the facades of Henry VII's Chapel at the east end of Westminster Abbey, assumed to have been designed by Robert Vertue, you see stonework so excellently crafted, and so English, completed only twenty-four years before the Reformation began. Lethaby described the structure as 'frank and energetic', and we can only mourn the poor quality of so much of the English revivalism that followed, century upon century. Here, instead, is an example *par excellence* of the earlier Gothic architectural technology – the constructional syntax of the meaning of the work, rather than simply a mechanistic recipe – that came to its fruition in England with the Perpendicular. Frank and energetic might equally convey the mood of Hopkins' parliamentary building which, without mimicry, springs also from an equivalent spirit and love of building craft for our own time. While, somewhat cheekily, I have questioned certain details, for myself the building is a masterpiece but, for us here perhaps, it marks the coming of age of modern architecture through its long transition, a fact which separates Hopkins from his peers. But didn't Aesop tell us about a goose-laid golden egg? How absurd!

Instead of Portcullis, Parliament should honour its new members home by renaming it Open House, for that is what its architecture means, and shouldn't that the purpose of the place for every voter?

Sir Michael Hopkins talks to Paul Finch

Paul Finch: When clients employ a well-known architect like yourself, are they are assuming they will get a 'look', which will give them a familiar icon or landmark, or that they will get a particular kind of service?

Michael Hopkins: I wonder? We have produced a range of quite different solutions for different people and for different sites and circumstances, so I don't think they can be coming just for the look. Perhaps they used to come for the steel-and-glass look. But I don't think that anybody has walked through the door and said, 'Please design us a building like this'. I hope they come for the service.

You always have to fight your way through to the front line, through lots of other architects, and in some way get noticed. In the early days, clients used to rely on their instincts more and chose their architects by a visit to their office and the odd building (when they existed). Now there are a series of meetings and presentation of ideas and nearly always a full-blooded competition, sometimes in two stages.

These days, do clients expect to see the master's hand on the conception sketch?

They really believe that one can do something on the back of an envelope, that it doesn't cost anything and it should come very quickly. And just when you think, maybe I'll get this job, they say, well, actually we are just going to talk to half a dozen other architects and ask you all to compete!

There is a common denominator among clients – a building is something that is unique to them. At least this is true once you are outside the realm of commercial developers, who seem to me to have quite a lot of similar objectives. But most clients do have quite independent briefs; things that you have never considered. They ask you to solve problems that you have never come across before in your life, or perhaps you have even avoided – like cricket at school.

With developers, you have brought something very distinctive to the party. New Square near Heathrow, for the developer MEPC, has a bespoke quality even though the brief was to produce a building that was lettable to anybody.

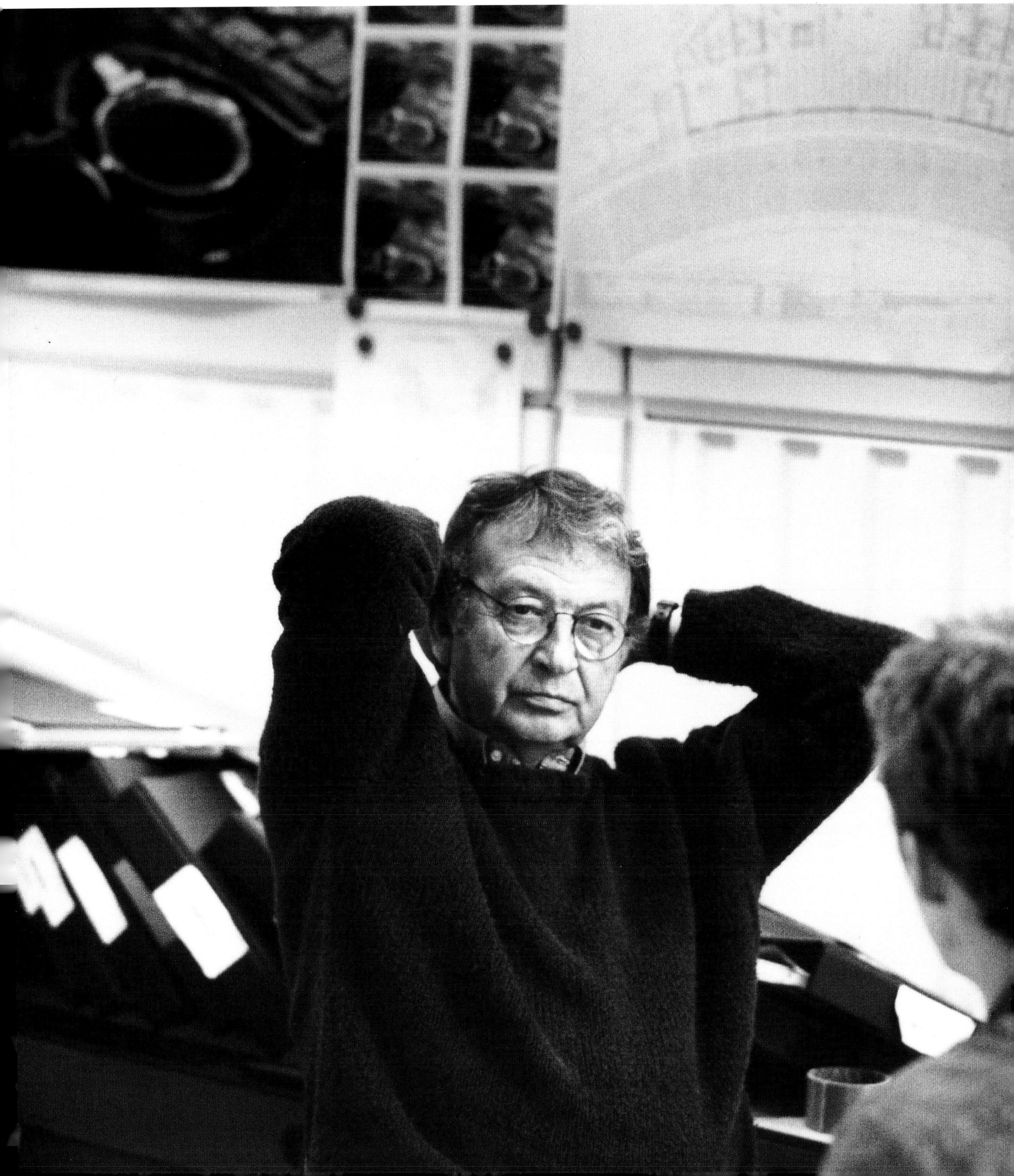

MEPC was the commissioning client and the developer, but they had a pre-let to IBM; IBM had brought the site to MEPC and asked them to develop it on their behalf. But in order to subject themselves to the rigours of the market place, they didn't want to spend more than anybody else did on their offices. I had worked for IBM in the past and, in those days, they paid an extra 10 per cent for architecture but wanted 20 per cent back, as it were. They always wanted decent modern architecture and one responded to that.

Do you find big differences among institutional clients? Are there committees and lots of people making the running, or does it come down to individuals?
You get both. It is easier, in a way, if there is one person and he has got the authority to sort things out within his own organization. The first job we got commercially was through an interview – Greene King (the Suffolk brewery). Why I was on the list, I don't know. I think a building by their Cambridge architects hadn't gone too well, for some reason, so they were looking for a fresh face. They had a very good head brewer, who always listened to our side of the argument; for instance, about whether something would work elegantly as a building, as well as making the brewing functional. He hadn't thought about this sort of thing before, but he knew how to make beer and there were certain things that were important to him, and he understood why some things might be important to us in the making of the building.

You have a very long-term relationship with some clients. What about your MPs scheme at Westminster?
This really has been a long haul, from 1988, I think. When we first heard about the job, it was going to be built by the Department of the Environment. The Parliamentary building came about through a little window of coincidence.

Essentially, there wasn't really a site – just a narrow edge strip around the Westminster District and Circle Line Station. The most important thing that we did for them was to come up with a way of developing the whole site. This was achieved by incorporating the station and lowering the level of the District and Circle lines and the ticket hall forming a new ground level over the whole site. By using some ingenuity, we threaded a structure of six massive support points through the divergent paths of the District and Circle line and the new Jubilee line. This prompted the 'doughnut' building form, with support also picked up at the perimeter.

We were very conscious, as were our client committee, that we were being asked to build a very secure building to last for 120 years, on a major site in London. We were appalled by the working conditions that prevailed for MPs – even worse than for architects.

The new building has a pivotal position in the Parliamentary site. We have made a new link between the existing work places in the Norman Shaw buildings next door and the House. Everybody now passes through the atrium of our building, down the reopened old Conservative Club tunnel under Bridge Street, to answer the Bell to the Chamber. We see the atrium as a meeting place for MPs and their constituents, hence the seats, trees and ponds. It's a nice place to pause as well as scurry through. I believe that the building will fundamentally alter the effectiveness of the MPs' working lives.

What about the underground station? Did working on the Jubilee Line Extension make you feel that you were part of an epoch-making venture, or did it just feel like a difficult one-off isolated job?
I have to say I think our preoccupations were with making the station and the New Parliamentary Building above work together as a sort of organizational synthesis, rather than it being part of the Jubilee line. Our scheme was also dependent on the District and Circle lines agreeing to have the station altered; but without the Jubilee Line Extension happening, I don't think anybody would have redeveloped Westminster Station.

Do you find a difference between public sector and private sector clients, for example, between the JLE and Glyndebourne?
Chalk and cheese. In the JLE, and the whole of the London Underground procurement system, there are layers and layers of organisations and ways of doing things. It's a miracle anything happens. Whereas with the Glyndebourne Opera house, you have

the owner, George Christie, whose idea the project was and who was going to see it through. He provided one key point of reference all the way – he would see all the problems before we did. The building grew on his land, like a crop. There was an extremely smooth handover – it was his already.

Maybe the two sectors are not always chalk and cheese. In the end it is always the individuals one deals with who make or break the process. At Nottingham University, we designed and built a complex new campus for 4,000 students in a record two years. It wouldn't have happened without the clarity of purpose and drive of the Vice Chancellor, Colin Campbell and the Estates Officer Chris Jagger.

When you see prospective clients, are there particular jobs you show them, or a narrative of your work?

When you start in practice, you may have only one tiny little building to show, from which you then have to persuade your client to imagine everything else flowing, so you put enormous emphasis on it. Now, we can show buildings from which they can interpret the way we work, but of course there was a time when we hadn't done a cricket stand, or an opera house, or a parliamentary building, or a cutlery factory, or whatever it may be; never even thought about it before – certainly not a brewery. In a way, that's the enjoyment. If you have a cutlery factory to design, you sit down and think about how you make knives and forks, what makes the client tick, and so on. When a prospective client comes along, you show them all the relevant things, but you also sometimes deliberately show them something that is nothing to do with them at all, but demonstrates the way in which a particular problem is solved. If we can solve a problem for one guy, it shows that we can maybe do the same for another.

I remember a long time ago doing some presentation boards for the V&A Museum when they were interviewing for a masterplanner. We'd never done any museum or gallery work then, so we showed them our early industrial buildings, trying to draw out relevance. They thought this was very funny, but they got the point – and we got the job!

Do you find that clients sometimes have a skewed idea of what they want? I am thinking of the Inland Revenue where, instead of analysing what they told you they wanted, you analysed what they either feared was going to happen, or what they hadn't even dared to ask themselves – for instance, that the relocation would not happen and the development would have to be sold on.

I don't know if we did that consciously – our first preoccupation was to find an architectural form for the client's brief on the site. I looked at residential parts of Nottingham, where the cars were parked in the streets and the streets had trees – there was a happy balance between cars, people and buildings. I think the Inland Revenue had assumed that there would be an underground or multistorey carpark or some complex piece of parking; but we did a series of individual buildings with parking in the streets. Then, because we had just done Glyndebourne, we were thinking quite seriously about bricks. Nottingham has a completely different brick environment – very big tough buildings – which set us thinking of a way to prefabricate brickwork and how to give them a distinctive character. That would have endeared us, if that's not too hopeful a word, to Nottingham planners.

Do you think you were chosen because, by splitting the buildings up, you made it very phaseable, you could stop after one building or at any point; that if the client's brief changed suddenly, it gave them maximum flexibility.

I would say that our design offered them the flexibility to sell a building off, if everyone started paying less income tax or something like that. I'm sure that was one of the reasons we were chosen. Happily, from our perspective the right people were in charge at the Inland Revenue; they were prepared to accept it as a non-standard government site – this one actually had a public street on which you pushed prams to get to the supermarket. They liked all those sorts of things.

One of the noticeable things about the practice's work over the last decade has been the increasing concern with people moving through sites and through the buildings: a more public architecture.

That is perhaps a function of being asked to do larger schemes. Schlumberger had a very particular client, who thought endlessly about the relationships between his work groups and who should be near who, etc. Easy contact for the exchange of ideas was an integral part of their working process, but the building was in the middle of a field; it had a drive down to it, but had no relationship with any other buildings, and so it had no public outside.

On the other hand, the Jubilee Campus at Nottingham sets out from the start to make a new public place in the City from a worn out industrial site. With the simple idea of building a linear lake and a promenade alongside connecting all the teaching facilities and support buildings, it has a very clear dynamic.

Schlumberger has a good relationship with the public because millions of people have seen it from the motorway – many more than have seen most Cambridge colleges…
Perhaps they think that all of Cambridge is like that! As a child of my generation at the Architectural Association, we were immensely preoccupied with how people grouped together, and how architecture could be made out of these groupings, or how plans and sections could be made out of them. Schlumberger was a case in point: how you persuaded people, who wanted to just sit in their own little room, to talk to mathematicians over here and engineers, or scientists over there. These are people who wouldn't traditionally talk to each other; you needed a building (this is the director speaking) which would actually make them communicate with each other, which would then lead to ideas, which would then make money. You are dealing with a little closed community – 120 people – whereas at Nottingham University you are dealing with a community of 4,000 people.

How has the size of your office changed over the last decade?
It gets bigger all the time. There are about 100 people now, double what it was ten years ago; it went up and then came down a bit during the recession – it's been incremental. When we started off, because I had been in practice before, I was used to biggish clients, like IBM or Willis Faber. We grew new buildings from small; but always, at the same time, we had fit-out jobs for companies like IBM, Financial Times and Willis Faber, and these were useful bread and butter jobs. It wasn't really exciting architecturally, but you could do a good job then put all your spirit into two or three nice little buildings at the same time.

Do you notice differences in the people who want to come to work for you now? Are there people who come in for an interview who are attracted to this particular kind of public interface, or is it just that they like architecture?
I don't do interviews anymore – I should do; they probably just want a job. The difference now is that a large proportion are young and comparatively new – more and more are female or foreign. Under our directors, we now have a strong 35 to 40 age group, who are capable of dealing with a client when we're not there and of getting things designed and built.

All the big architects have a sort of diaspora, people who have worked for Richard, Norman and you, who have then gone on to do their own thing. When John [Pringle] and Ian [Sharratt] left, it was done with pretty good grace. In a way, perhaps it energized the practice?
When people leave it does give new opportunities. Bill Taylor has continued as director with Patty and me. Now we have been joined by Andy Barnett, Jim Greaves and David Selby, with Pam Bate heading up our interior work. As a group, they are responsible for all our major projects. Perhaps more significantly, we have grown a group of ten project directors, all of whom have been with us for about a decade and are now coming through strongly, taking on more responsibility.

Thinking about public perceptions, I would guess that knighthoods and gold medals [the Royal Gold Medal for Architecture, awarded by the RIBA to Michael and Patty Hopkins in 1994] have got an up side because there are people who think, this practice must be OK and call up. On the other hand, there may be people who think, oh well, they are the upper stratosphere now and I couldn't afford them.
I suppose there are people that react either way – one never knows.

What was it like being a quasi client on the British Museum?
I would much rather be doing the job myself! That's not because Fosters are not doing it well – they are – but it's a really nice job to do.

Can I ask you about your own houses? You achieve maximum effect with different styles of architecture and very different surroundings.
Our house in Hampstead is a response to doing something very quickly which related to things one was thinking about when the site became available in 1975. At the time, we were doing a low-cost building for IBM in Portsmouth. I was interested in the possibility of using a very small-scale steel structure to modulate space for domestic use. Those thoughts happened to coincide with a time when property prices were rising, and all the money went on the site with not much left for the building. There was also an admiration for Eames; not in doing what Eames did, but doing something more repetitive that might have a slightly wider application.

The repair to the ruined sixteenth-century timber-frame house that we had from student days in Suffolk, which cost £400 in 1962, was the starting point for our whole interest in an architecture which arose out of how things are made.

So your domestic projects outside London are the only ones where really you are not building new. Even things that ostensibly look like refurbishment, upon examination turned out to be nothing of the sort – for instance, the Bracken House building in the City has retained the end pieces, but has a completely new middle. Glyndebourne is a brand new building, it's just that it fits into a historic context. The Mound Stand makes use of existing foundations and brick, but it really is new, the same with the Parliamentary building or the Nottingham campus. But the architectures are very different. You can't say 'Well, if it's the Parliamentary building it will be steel and glass, any more than you can say 'Well, if it was the MEPC building it is bound to be stone'. They are responses in terms of materials and architectural approach which have to do with landscape and other givens, rather than putting a 'Hopkins building' on the site.
If that's what the practice does, then I am well content.

Hampshire County Cricket Club 1994–

Hampshire County Cricket Club was founded in 1863. Since 1885, it has been based at Northlands Road in a residential area of Southampton, but that ground has become cramped, with insufficient car parking and no room for expansion. The Club has therefore aquired the lease on an open site of approximately 150 acres on the outskirts of the city, close to the M27, on which it intends to establish a centre of cricketing excellence for the county, including a new ground with seating for 10,000 spectators, a nursery ground and a range of coaching facilities. The masterplan also includes an indoor bowling green, all-weather sports facilities and a nine-hole golf course.

The heart of the proposed development is the ground itself. The sloping site is cut and filled to form a level, oval table surrounded by an earth bank or berm, the inner slope of which forms the base for a continuous ring of raked seating. Such an intensely focused arena is unique in English cricket, but players appreciate the heightened sense of occasion that it creates for important matches. An avenue of London Plane trees on top of the berm establishes an immediate sense of space and provides shade for a ring of members' car parking. A continuous fence between the carpark and the match ground provides security, controls access and prevents the distraction to the batsmen of sun dazzle on car windscreens. Berm, trees and fence all help to keep out the noise of the nearby motorway. The ground modelling is a piece of architecture in its own right, the solution of a complex equation taking into account orientation, acoustics, economy of cut and fill and the requirement that the twenty pitches should be laid on virgin ground to avoid settlement.

The match ground is dominated by the members' pavilion, a four-storey, steel-framed structure standing at the top of the slope where the berm merges into the hillside. Curved on plan to follow the line of the boundary and covered by a suspended fabric canopy, this building owes an obvious debt to the Mound Stand at Lord's (1987). The canopy shelters a raised terrace of raked seating which sits over a large, flexible dining space known as 'The Long Room'. Hospitality suites below look out over the berm seating. Behind and on axis with the pavilion sits a rectangular, marquee-like structure cut into the slope of the site. This houses the Cricket Academy, a single open space which can be used for six-a-side indoor matches or for net practice in six lanes. Two lower levels accommodate changing rooms, fitness training rooms and three squash courts.

A double-height atrium links the pavilion and the Cricket Academy. It has a transparent tented roof, formed from inflated cushions of ETFE foil. Aligned with the ring of members' parking, the atrium is the circulation hub of the whole complex. Three more tents mark the public entrances to the arena. In future phases, it is envisaged that hospitality tents and future stands will extend out on either side of the pavilion on top of the berm as the ground develops.

Below: computer generated image. The sports complex occupies an open site on the outskirts of Southampton, close to the M27 motorway. The cricket ground takes the form of a level oval, cut into the sloping site.

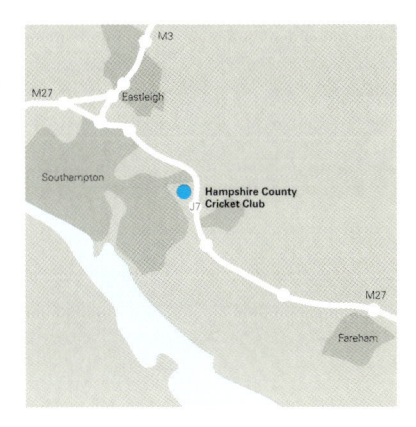

1 void over Long Room
2 main kitchen
3 atrium roof
4 indoor nets
5 external walkway
6 main Pavilion and Cricket Academy
7 main match ground
8 avenue of plane trees

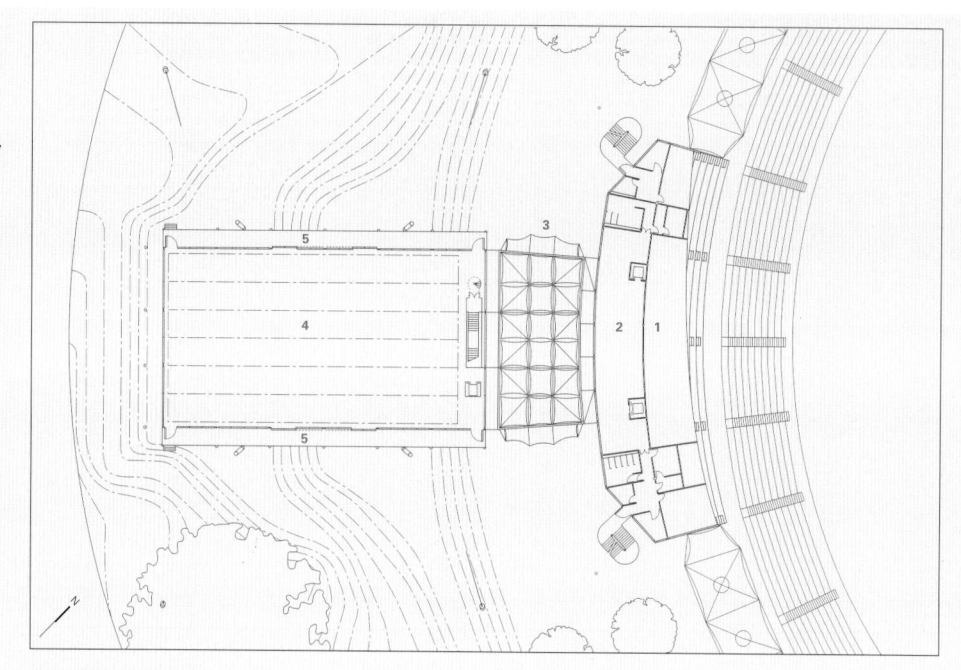

Regional Cricket Academy
and Members' Pavilion,
second floor plan

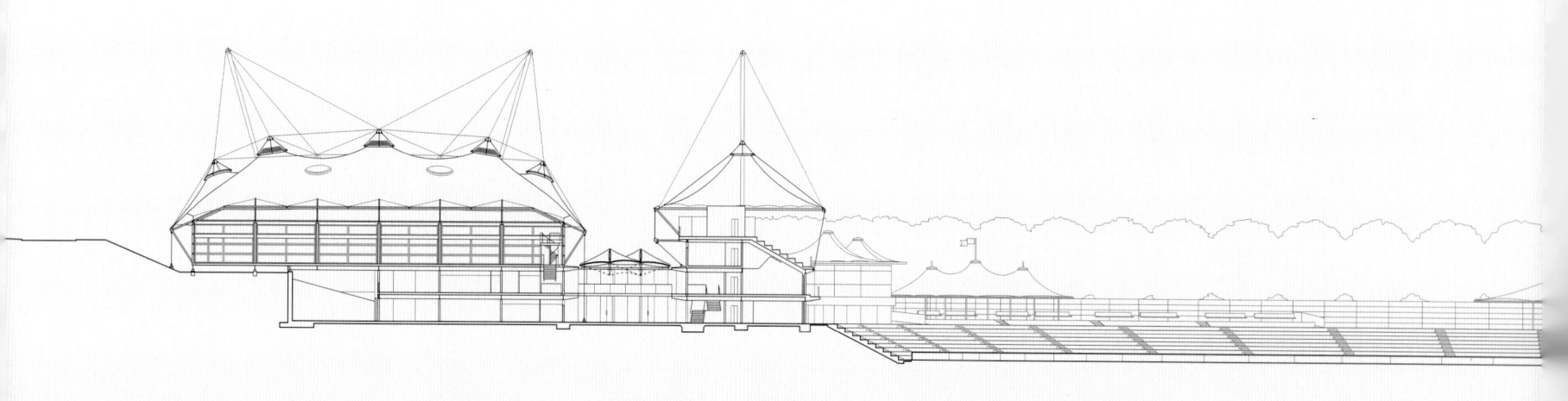

Hampshire County Cricket Club

Section

Opposite: plan showing the relationship between the boundary of the ground, the Pavilion, and the Cricket Academy. The atrium between the Pavilion and the Academy is the circulation hub of the whole complex.

Below: section through the cricket ground showing the slope of the site and the surrounding earth berm. The balance of cut and fill had to ensure that the pitches were laid on virgin ground.

Above: view from the boundary with the tented pavilion in the distance. The perfect arena form is unique among English cricket grounds. Players appreciate the heightened sense of occasion that it creates.

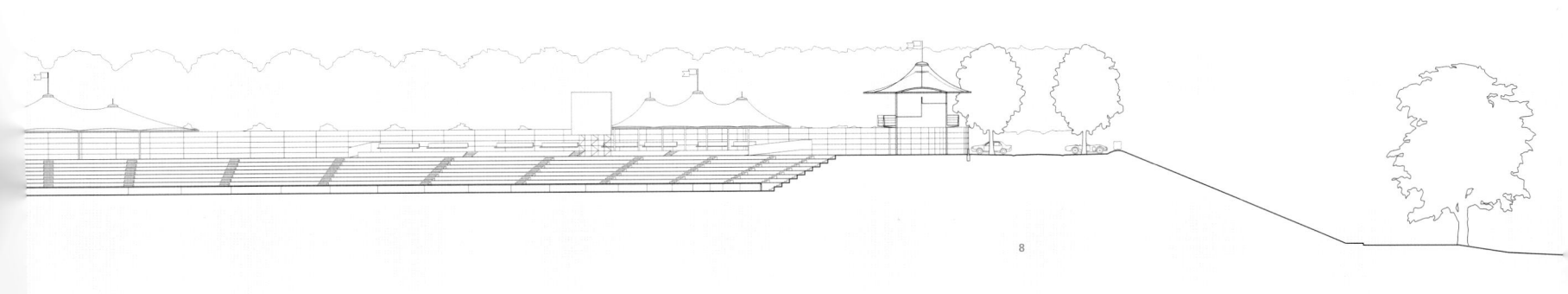

Manchester City
Art Gallery

1994–

The new Manchester City Art Gallery, which will be completed in 2001, unites and extends two early nineteenth-century buildings designed by Sir Charles Barry: the Royal Manchester Institution, built in 1823 in the Greek Revival style, and the Athenaeum, an Italianate gentlemen's club built in 1837. The Institution later became the City Art Gallery, and the Athenaeum was extended after a fire in 1873 by the addition of a baroque theatre in a tall attic storey, giving the building a decidedly top-heavy look. These two buildings occupied a little less than three-quarters of a rectangular urban block in the Georgian grid plan of central Manchester. The fourth corner of the block was left vacant and, until recently, was used as a carpark. An alleyway known as Back George Street bisected the block, passing between the two buildings.

The new art gallery scheme extends the Athenaeum onto the car park in such a way as to create a tripartite composition, mirroring the ABABA symmetry of the old art gallery. A glazed link connects the two buildings across Back George Street on the common axis. The main entrance to this new, unified building is through the Ionic portico of the old gallery. In the full-height entrance hall, a grand staircase leads up to first-floor level where the old top-lit galleries, in strictly symmetrical array, remain mostly undisturbed. A footbridge in the glazed link, slightly sloping to accommodate a difference of floor level, crosses over to a second entrance hall in the new extension. This has its own grand staircase and two freestanding lift towers. Galleries in the new building, incorporating the old Athenaeum, match the scale and symmetrical arrangement of the old galleries. Thus the whole of the first floor becomes a continuous sequence of well-proportioned public rooms.

The ground floor of the old art gallery, raised well above the surrounding streets on a vaulted semi-basement, accommodates important commercial functions, such as shops, a coffee bar and a restaurant, and a special Manchester Gallery for exhibitions about the history of the city. The ground floor of the extended Athenaeum contains classrooms, study areas and loading dock. Basements of both buildings house offices, archives, service functions and a large picture store. Whereas the old art gallery is essentially a two-storey building, the new extension is permitted to rise higher within the limit imposed by the upwardly extended Athenaeum. There are two new open-plan galleries on the second floor and the old baroque theatre, with its arcaded walls and plaster vaulted ceiling, will be used for exhibitions of decorative art.

This is Hopkins' first engagement with monumental classical buildings and the external cladding of the new extension, a rainscreen of stone panels in bronze frames on an abstract tartan grid, is a departure from the usual loadbearing masonry. The underlying structure, however, is typically rational. Precast concrete floor panels with exposed, vaulted soffits are supported on a bolted precast concrete frame.

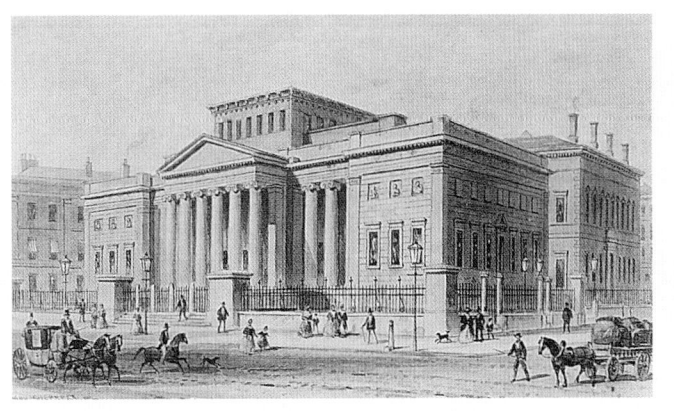

Left: a nineteenth-century print showing the two buildings by Charles Barry which form the basis of the new gallery: the Royal Manchester Institution in the foreground and the Athenaeum behind it to the right.

Below: perspective sketch of the glazed bridge that crosses Back George Street at first-floor level. The wall in the foreground has been cut away to show the entrance hall in the new extension.

Top: the external wall of the new extension is a rainscreen of stone panels in bronze frames on a tartan grid.

Bottom: the new gallery now occupies a whole city block. The new extension, bottom right, infills a corner that for many years was used as a carpark. The Athenaeum is on the left.

Left: the full-height entrance hall of the old Royal Manchester Institution, with its grand staircase, has been restored but otherwise remains largely unaltered.

Right: a mason carves the volute of an Ionic capital for the restored Greek Revival entrance portico.

1 existing entrance hall
2 gallery (existing)
3 shop
4 glazed link
5 atrium
6 galleries (Athenaeum)
7 galleries (new)
8 art lift
9 exhibition gallery (New)
10 loading bay
11 picture store
12 support areas
13 Mosley Street
14 George Street

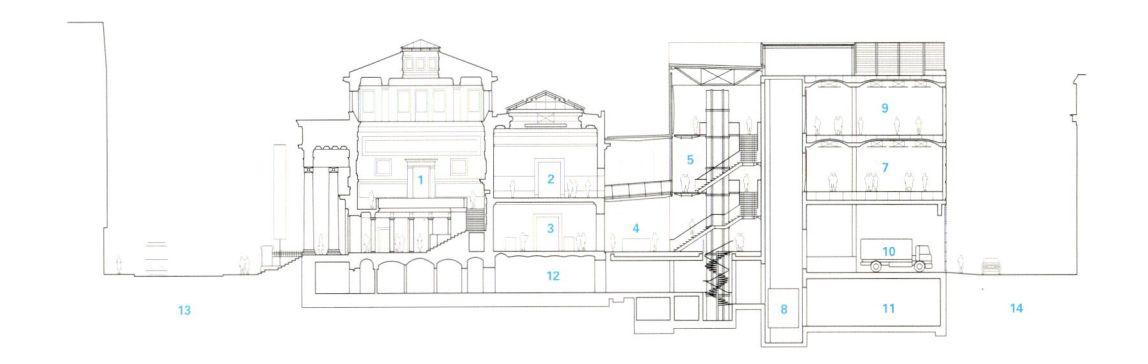

Section

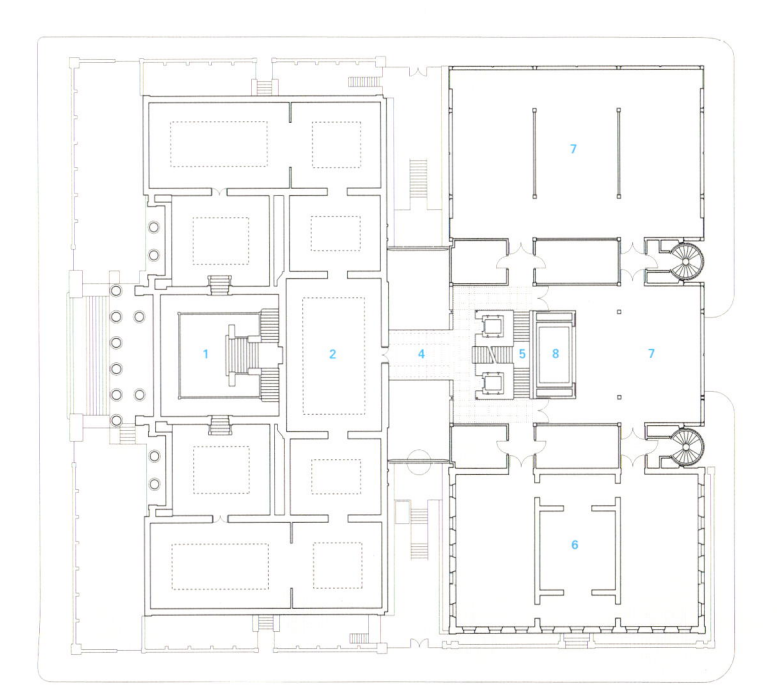

First floor plan

Manchester City Art Gallery

Royal Academy
of Arts   1995–

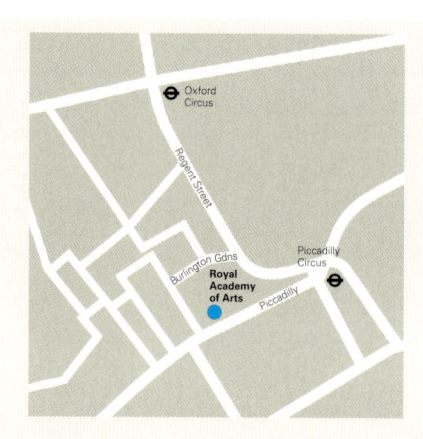

Immediately to the north of the Royal Academy of Arts in Piccadilly, with only a service yard in between, lies 6 Burlington Gardens, a large Victorian institutional building originally designed by Sir James Pennethorne for the University of London. Until recently, it was occupied by the Museum of Mankind, but it is currently being vacated and its availability has been the spur for a comprehensive replanning of the buildings that make up the Royal Academy.

The alterations that have been proposed extend and improve visitor and educational facilities at the Royal Academy, and at the same time bring order and clarity to a fine, although awkwardly disposed, sequence of rooms. The existing main staircase, leading up to the first-floor galleries, retains its original position on the central axis of the entrance hall. The spaces around it, however, have been opened up and expanded into a new gallery, shop and café. From here, visitors can continue along the axis, via a vaulted corridor, to a central atrium housing a foyer and bar in a new link block on the site of the old service yard. The block is three storeys high and extends across the entire width of the building. It contains a lecture theatre on the ground floor, members galleries on the first floor, and sculpture and print-making studios on the top floor. The axial route now continues, via a complex, multi-flight symmetrical stair, through to new front-of-house facilities, including new ticket sales areas and cloakrooms, and the grand entrance hall of the Pennethorne building and finally out into Burlington Gardens. Number 6 Burlington Gardens will be mainly occupied by offices, teaching spaces and function rooms. The attic storey, however, will be replaced as a top-lit home for the RA. The School has its own entrance in the alleyway on the east side of the building and can therefore function as a self-contained unit. One of the major advantages of this particular scheme is that the Royal Academy's chief existing asset – the suite of fine, top-lit first-floor galleries – remains practically untouched except for the removal of the gallery shop.

An important part of the new plan has already been executed: the re-organization and repaving of the entrance court off Piccadilly. Cluttered with parked cars, this potentially fine urban space, with its statue of Joshua Reynolds, had become anything but welcoming. Now the cars have been banned, the levels have been adjusted for better disability access, and the surface has been paved in flags and setts, mainly of grey Cornish granite. When the scheme is complete, the old porch will be demolished and a 'cordonata' or graded ramp, based on Italian precedent, will lead up to the main entrance. The central flagged area of the court, designed for the display of sculpture, incorporates fountains arranged in an apparently random pattern. In fact, they trace the pattern of stars visible on the night of 16th July 1723 – the night that Joshua Reynolds, the founder of the Royal Academy, was born.

Below: the foyer and bar in the new three-storey link block looking north into 6 Burlington Gardens. The entrance to the lecture theatre is on the right.

Right: the facade facing the courtyard has a long and complicated history dating back to the seventeenth century. The Hopkins scheme removes the most recent addition – a porch by Norman Shaw.

Below: model cut away to reveal the first-floor plan, with the courtyard to the top, 6 Burlington Gardens to the bottom and the main galleries in the centre, around the octagon.

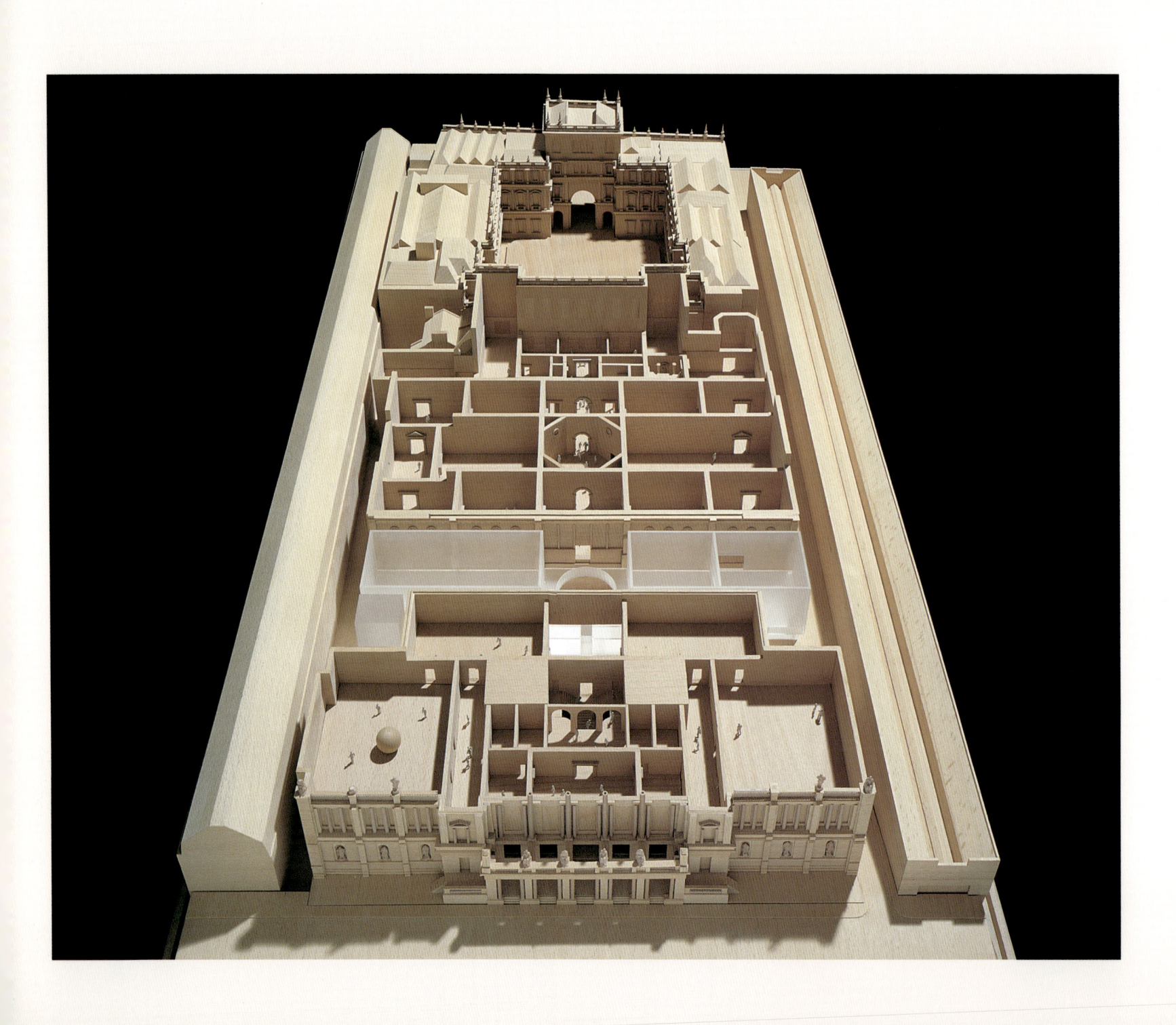

181

1 entrance hall	10 casts corridor	19 coats/toilets
2 ticket office	11 education	20 plant
3 members' room	12 life room	21 atrium and new galleries
4 friends' room	13 loading bay	22 new schools
5 restaurant	14 art handling	23 education/corporate
6 café	15 foyer/bar	24 Royal Academy courtyard
7 shop	16 lecture theatre	25 Burlington Gardens
8 link to Burlington Gardens	17 administration	26 public route
9 collections storage	18 existing galleries	

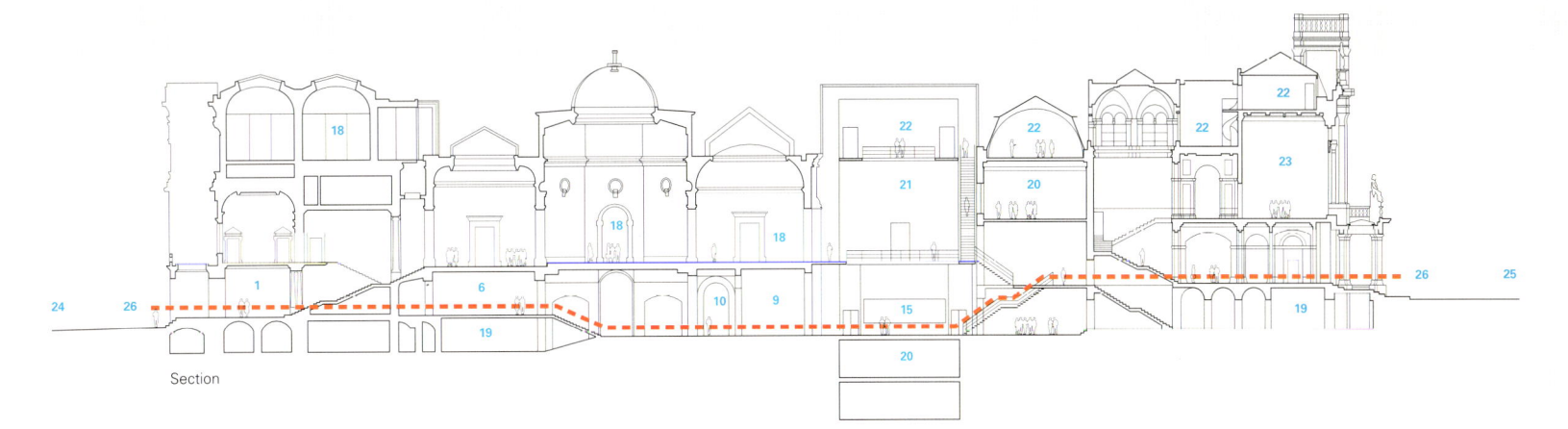

Section

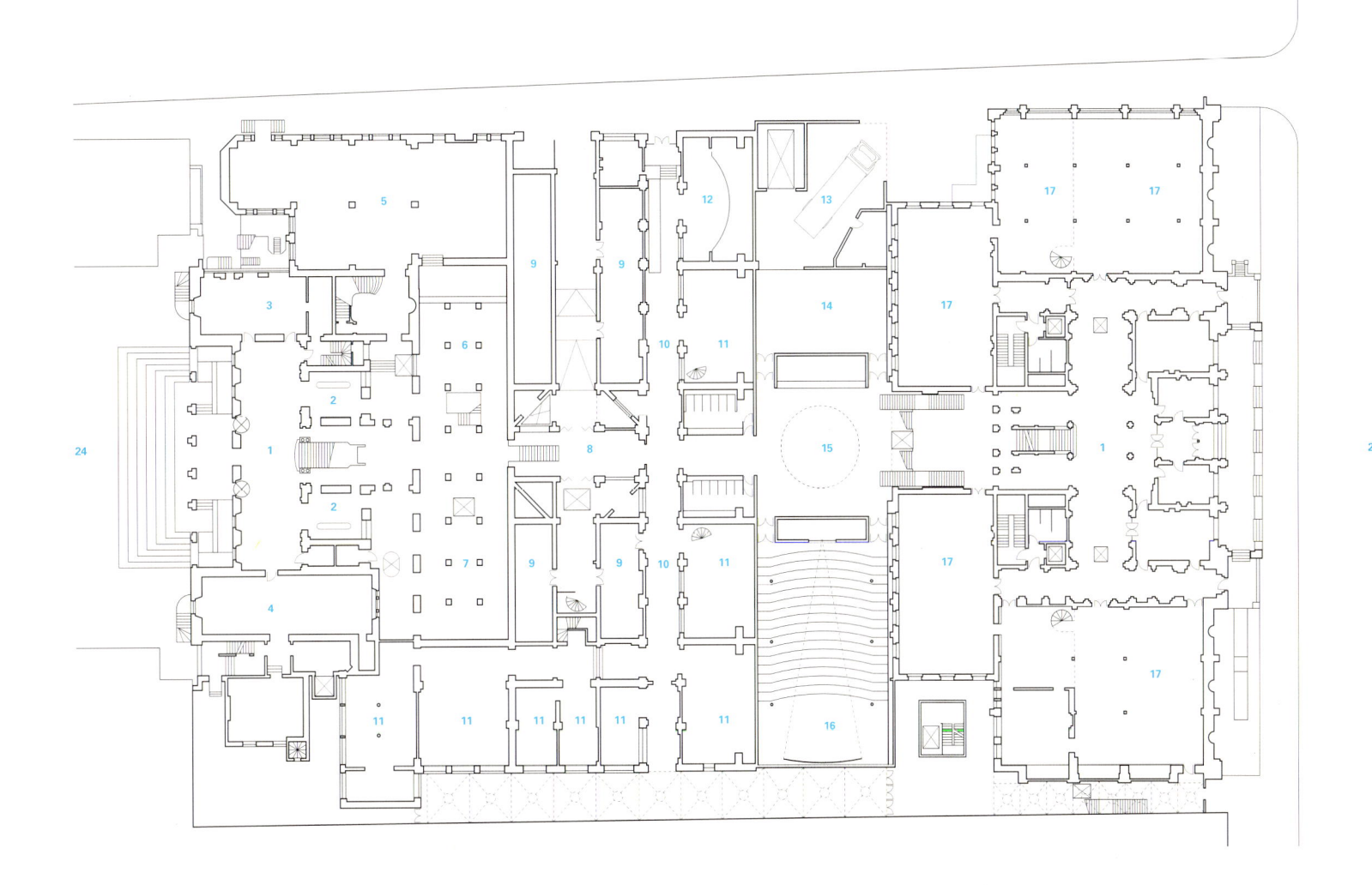

Ground floor plan showing public route

Royal Academy of Arts

Norwich Cathedral Education and Visitors' Centre

1995–

Visitors' centres for ancient buildings usually avoid physical contact with the monuments they serve. At Norwich Cathedral, however, the proposed new hostry and refectory are built right up against the outside walls of the medieval cloister. This is a bold strategy, but the old walls are treated with great respect. Barely touched by new construction, they remain visible in their full height inside the new buildings.

Both new buildings are simple, linear, two-storey structures with pitched roofs. The hostry, on the west side of the cloister, contains a shop and an exhibition space on the ground floor, with meeting rooms on the first floor. It is entered through the pointed arch of a ruined original entrance to the hostry. New stone walls flank the porch, built over the foundations of an old wall, long since demolished. As if to emphasize the respectful relationship with these remains, the new walls are raised off the ground on stub columns and flat arches of steel reinforced stone. Above the walls, the roof is also raised on stub columns. Openings between these various elements are infilled with frameless glass so that, though the main materials are traditional – random limestone for the wall, dressed Clipsham stone for columns, arches and quoins, and cast lead for the roof covering – the overall articulated form is unmistakably modern. Inside the building, the first floor structure is of timber spanning between precast concrete beams and columns. The beams cantilever out towards the old cloister wall, but stop short of it. Timber columns, standing on the ends of the cantilevers, support exposed roof trusses of oak with steel tension members. The new building is connected at one end to the south aisle of the cathedral via the old locutory, the room in which the medieval monks greeted visitors. This now serves as a lobby, allowing wheelchair access to the cathedral through a new door formed by carefully rearranging the existing colonnettes. At the other end of the hostry, the plain gable wall is infilled with oak louvres.

The refectory, on the south side of the cloister, contains a kitchen, toilets and store rooms on the ground floor, with a restaurant and servery on the first floor. The structure is similar to that of the hostry except that here the outer wall is an upward extension of the existing refectory garden wall, and the ground-floor accommodation is enclosed by a lightweight structure, effectively a building within a building. Timber columns rise from the ground floor through the double height volume to support the roof trusses on the cloister side. At the east end of the refectory, the ruins of a medieval house have been extended and reroofed to accommodate the main entrance to the refurbished library in the upper level of the cloister. Windows in the south wall of the library overlook the interior of the refectory.

By daring to engage with the old buildings directly, rather than keeping its distance from them, the new visitors' centre continues a centuries-long process of gradual extension and alteration to the cathedral complex.

183

Below: view from the southwest, with the new Education and Visitors' Centre behind the trees in the foreground. The main entrance is through the pointed arch of a ruined medieval porch.

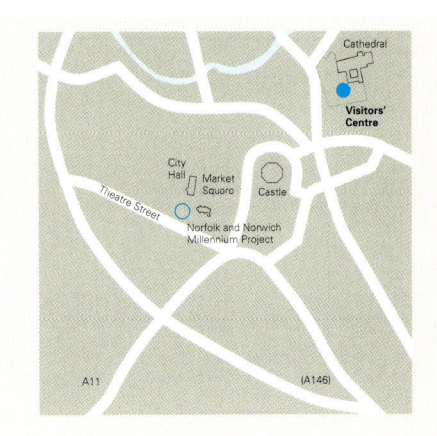

1 locutory
2 exhibition
3 reception
4 shop
5 offices
6 kitchen
7 toilets
8 upper close

Below: plan of the nave and cloister. The two new buildings are built against the south and west walls of the cloister, daring to engage directly with the medieval structures.

Opposite: west elevation. The walls of the hostry are raised on stub columns and flat stone arches. The lead-covered roof is also raised on stub columns and the gaps are infilled with frameless glass.

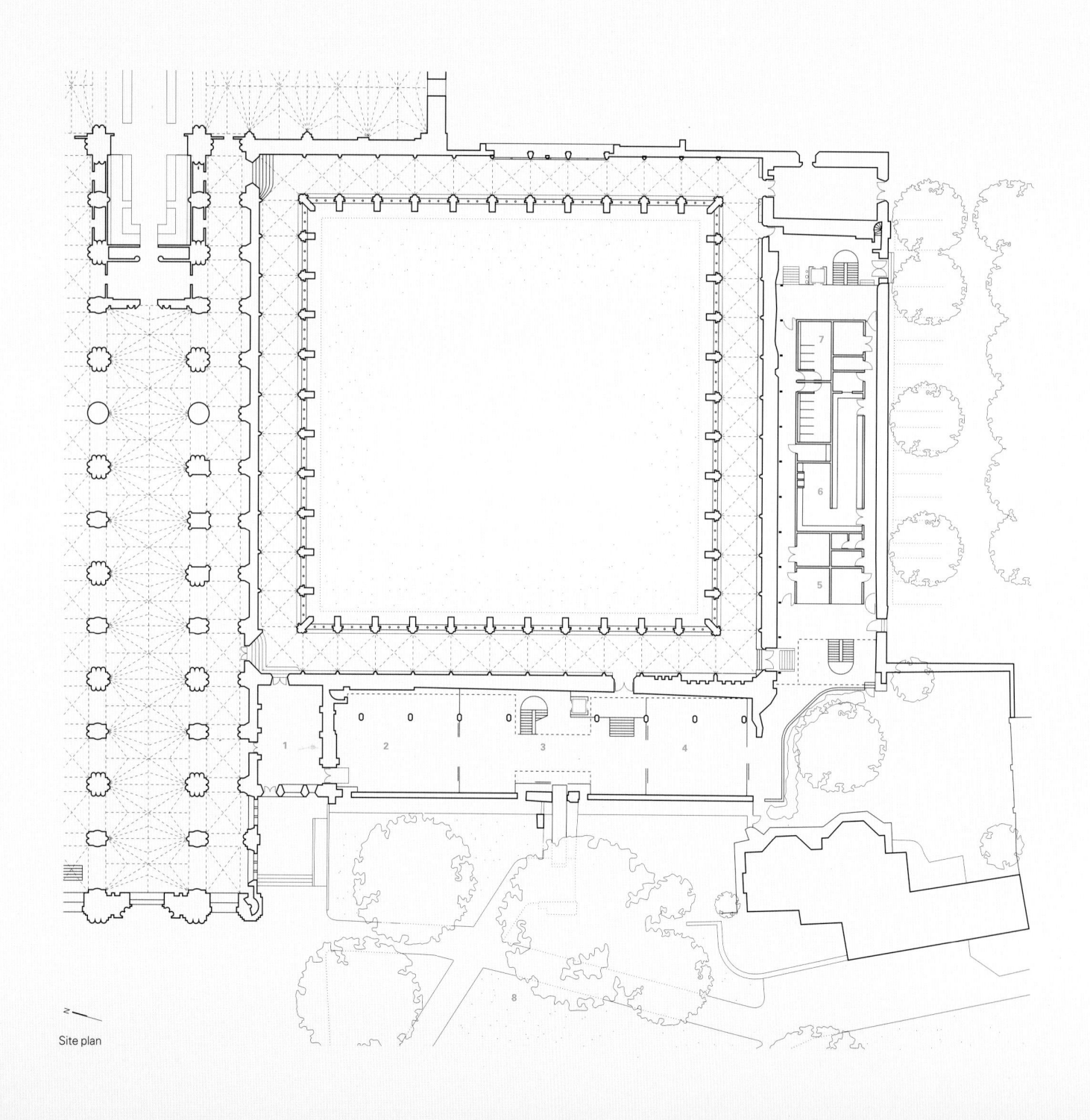

Norwich Cathedral Education and Visitors' Centre

Site plan

Right: model showing the relationship between the new building on the right and the old cloister on the left. The outer surface of the old wall is exposed in the new building.

West elevation

Norfolk and Norwich Millennium Project
1996–

When the central library in Norwich was destroyed by fire in 1994, the City and County Councils of Norfolk and Norwich decided to join forces, and, with the aid of National Lottery funding provided by the Millennium Commission, build a major new knowledge and information hub for the whole region. The old library site was combined with the adjacent carpark to form a complete city block surrounded by some of the most important buildings in Norwich: the City Hall, the Theatre Royal, the Assembly House and the church of St Peter Mancroft.

The new building, due to be completed in 2001, is a unified three-storey block, horseshoe-shaped on plan, opening its arms to the Gothic tower of the church to the east. The space between the arms is roofed over and enclosed at the east end by a recessed glass curtain wall to create an atrium, known as the Forum. An almost storey-height level difference across the site is accommodated by raising the ground floor on a flat plinth with a wide double flight of steps at the northeast corner. Publicly accessible parts of the library occupy the semi-circular west end, including the D-shaped apse of the atrium on both ground and first floors. This creates a raised platform, open to the main volume of the atrium, with a 2-metre high glass screen along the edge. Bookcases and study bays are arranged radially in a traditional 'panopticon' plan. This may be the main reason for the rounded end of the building, although it is a favourite Hopkins form inherited from buildings like Glyndebourne Opera House and the Queen's Building at Emmanuel College.

At ground- and first-floor levels, the arms of the horseshoe contain cafés, shops and a tourist information centre; these overlook the Forum, with a continuous balcony at first-floor level. At second-floor level, the arms accommodate more private uses: the library book stack in the north arm, and a business centre in the south arm. One other major public function breaks the symmetry of the horseshoe form. On the south side of the building, on the first floor, a second, smaller apse contains a 200-seat multimedia theatre. A basement under the theatre is designed to house a 'Heritage Visitor Attraction'.

The structure of the building is mainly in-situ reinforced concrete, built over a two-level, basement car park. Most mechanical plant is contained in an attic storey, set back behind a parapet. The main enclosing elements are reinterpretations of familiar Hopkins devices. The external wall is of semi-loadbearing brick, punctuated by a regular rhythm of plain window openings. Typically, the bricks are specially made and are 19mm longer than a standard brick, to suit both straight and curved bays, and in response to the scale of the building and that of the bricks used on the nearby City Hall. The Forum roof is supported by tubular steel bow-string trusses, forming pointed ellipses, infilled with glass or zinc-covered metal decking. Although not a tent, the roof nevertheless bears a marked family resemblance to the fabric roof of the Saga pavilion at Folkestone.

Below: site model viewed from the southeast. The building opens its arms to the church of St Peter Mancroft to the east. The semicircular extension on the south side of the horseshoe contains a 200-seat multimedia theatre.

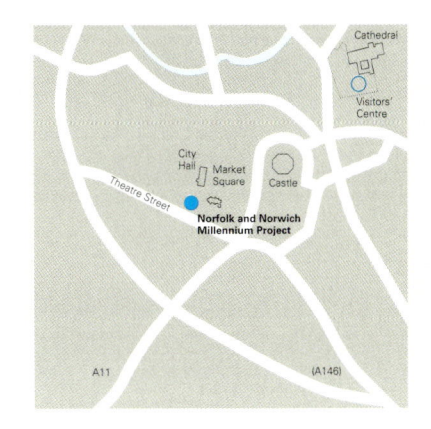

1 library
2 forum
3 visitor centre
4 catering and retail
5 auditorium
6 square
7 void over forum
8 offices

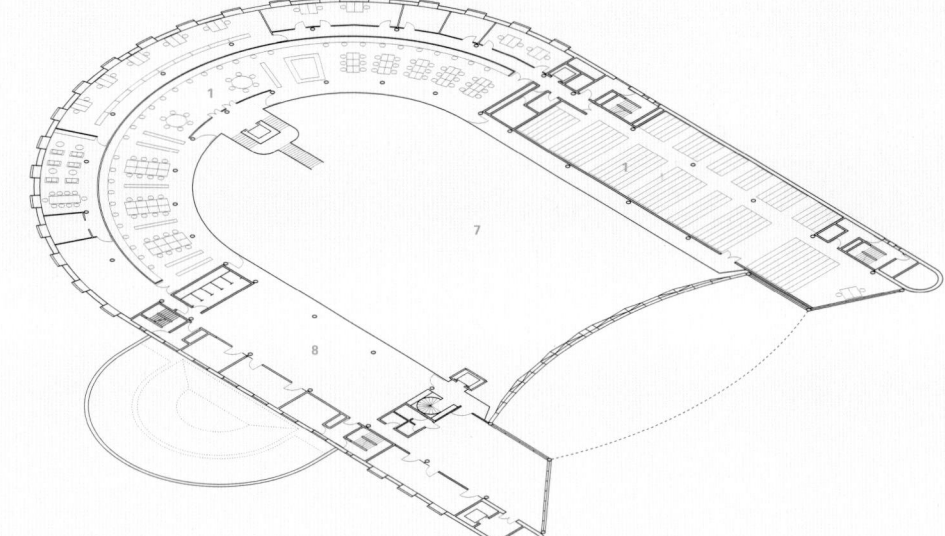

Second floor plan

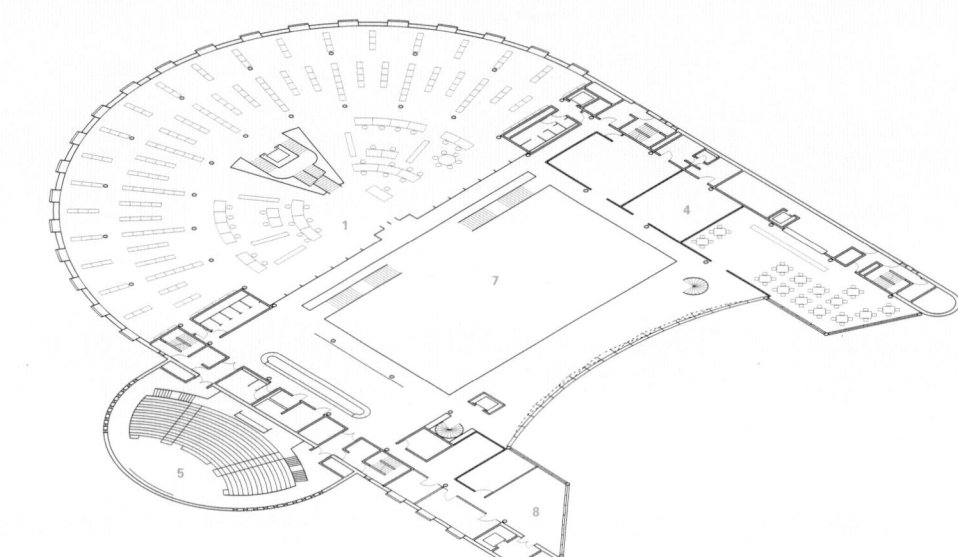

First floor plan

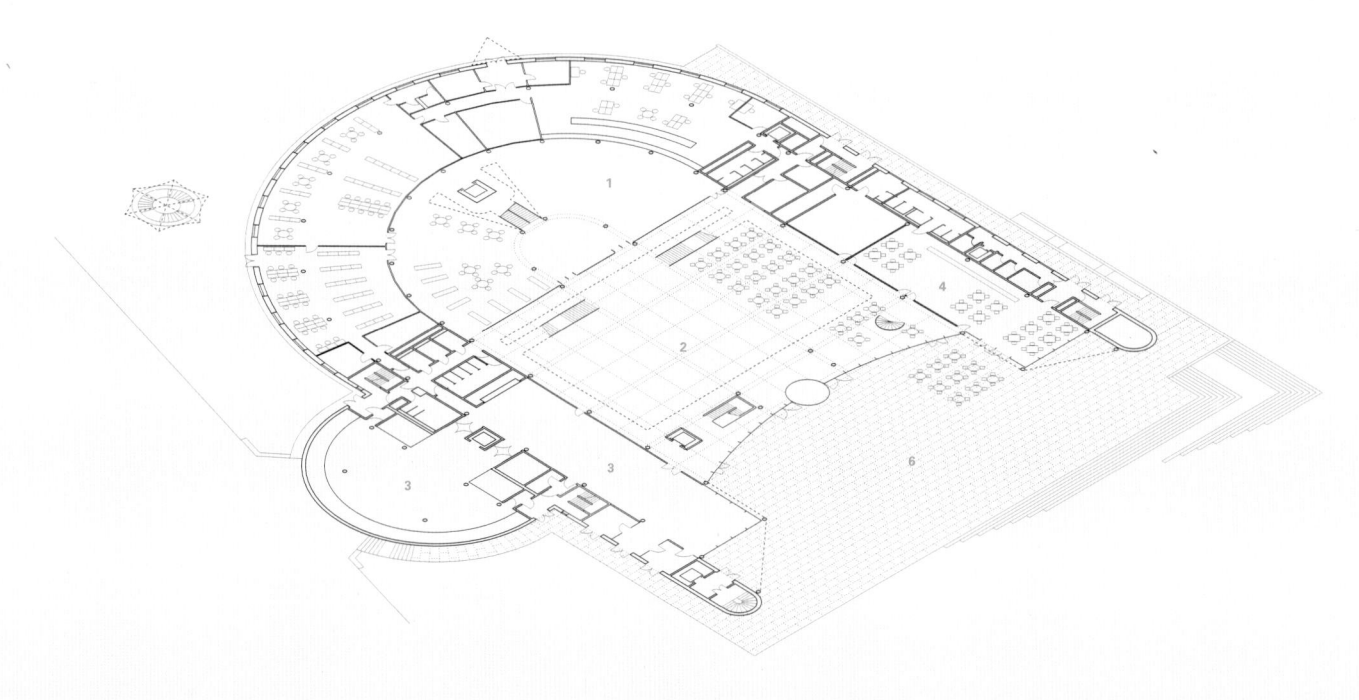

Norfolk and Norwich Millennium Project

Ground floor plan

Opposite: exploded isometric showing the general arrangement of spaces on the three main levels. The library mainly occupies the apse-shaped west end of the building with book stacks on the top floor of the northern arm of the horseshoe.

Below: the building viewed from the south, under construction, with the church of St Peter Mancroft on the right and the tower of City Hall in the distance.
Right: computer generated image of interior looking out towards St Peter Mancroft.

Haberdashers' Hall

1996–

The Worshipful Company of Haberdashers is one of the the 'Great Twelve' livery companies in the City of London. Its proposed new headquarters, designed to last at least 125 years, is a two-storey building on a completely landlocked site in the middle of a city block. Its interiors are lavish, though restrained. The only visible external walls are those surrounding the perfect square of a central courtyard, where they form a cloister of loadbearing brick piers and flat arches somewhat reminiscent of the exterior of Glyndebourne Opera House.

The main entrance, a discrete passageway through an imposing warehouse building now converted into loft apartments, leads to a generous loggia extending across the width of the courtyard. This is the first in a sequence of classically proportioned, axially planned spaces through which members and guests progress on their way to the major ceremonial rooms on the first floor. A square lobby, occupying the corner of the cloister at the right hand end of the loggia, offers a choice of two routes. To the left, a plain opening leads to cloakrooms and toilets via a second loggia, almost identical to the first but this time glazed in. Known as the Orangery, it maintains a quasi-external character, with York stone paving and brick walls. Straight on from the lobby, at the end of the axis, lies the main staircase – a big spiral in a top-lit brick drum. At first floor level a Reception Gallery to the right, over the Orangery, forms the foyer of the theatre-like, apsidal Courtroom, which is flanked symmetrically by the Luncheon Room and the Committee Room. At the far end of the Reception Gallery, another square corner lobby opens into the culminating room of the sequence – the 20 by 10 metre Livery Hall.

Each of these first floor ceremonial rooms is a contained, centred space, expanding upwards into a hipped roof. In the triad of meeting rooms, the ceilings are of plastered concrete with lantern lights, but in the Livery Hall, used mainly for formal dinners, the ceiling is a diagonal grid of laminated timber beams connected by cruciform stainless steel shoes and infilled with acoustic slatted wood panels. A delicate cat's cradle of stainless-steel tie rods and push-up struts braces the structure. This is a modern version of a medieval hall roof, but conceived as a three-dimensional, spaceframe structure rather than a linear sequence of heavy trusses or hammer beams. Walls are oak-panelled from floor to ceiling, but again this is an austere modern version of a traditional form – flush and grooved rather than carved and gilded. Tall sash windows look back across the courtyard to a drawing room and library suite over the entrance loggia.

The remainder of the building contains secondary, supporting functions: offices, staff rooms and kitchens on the ground floor, and flats for the Master and the Beadle at first floor level on the fourth side of the courtyard. Finally, a basement extends under the whole building, accommodating a car park, storage spaces, plant rooms and a very large wine cellar.

Below: on this completely landlocked site, the only external walls are those of the courtyard, which is a perfect square surrounded by a cloister.

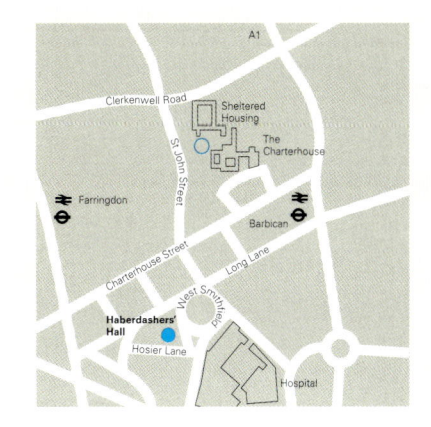

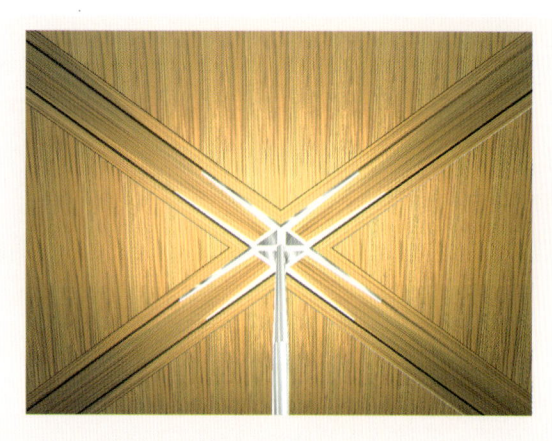

Left: computer generated image showing detail of the ceiling of the Livery Hall. A diagonal grid of laminated timber beams with stainless steel cruciform connectors is infilled with acoustic slatted wood panels.

Below: the Livery Hall, which is used mainly for formal dinners, is a modern version of a medieval hall, complete with minstrels' gallery. The walls are oak-panelled from floor to ceiling.

Haberdashers' Hall

1	reception gallery	15	porter's lodge
2	livery hall	16	loggia
3	luncheon room	17	courtyard
4	court room	18	colonnade
5	committee room	19	orangery
6	main stair	20	cloaks
7	display room	21	members' facilities
8	drawing room	22	offices
9	library	23	kitchen
10	master's flat	24	staff area
11	beadle's flat	25	loading bay
12	servery	26	refuse
13	wine bin	27	flats
14	entrance hall	28	residential carpark

Section

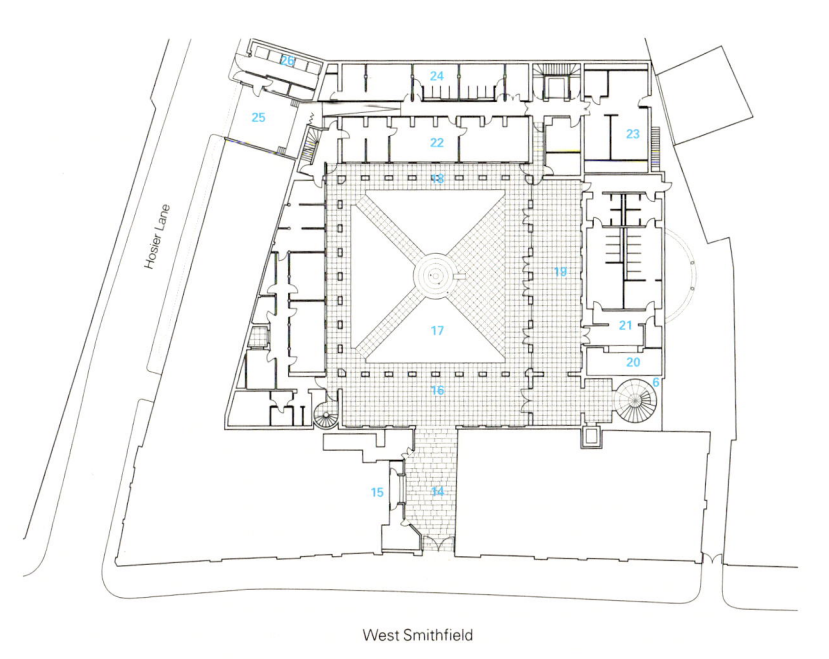

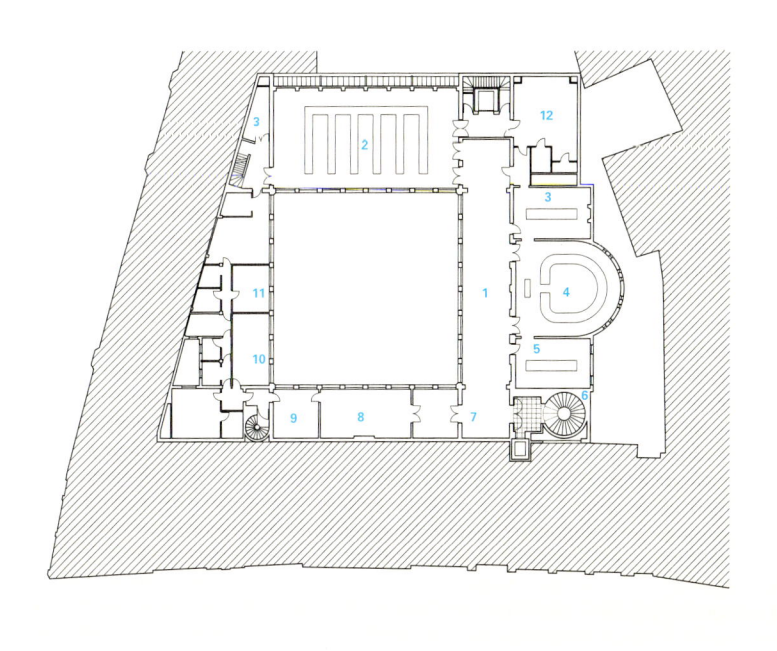

Ground floor plan

First floor plan

Goodwood Racecourse 1997–

Goodwood Racecourse is part of Goodwood Estate which includes the famous motor racing circuit; it is also home to the Dukes of Richmond. Set among the undulating countryside of the South Downs, it has remarkable views to Chichester and across the sea to the Isle of Wight. Facing increasing competition from other sports and cultural events for a share of the corporate entertainment market, Goodwood decided to improve the quality of the racegoing experience by upgrading its facilities. Attention focused on the parade ring, winner's enclosure and weighing-in building behind the main grandstand. The axial relationship between these three elements worked well, but the weighing-in building was an awkward obstacle in the promenade between parade ring and grandstand. In the new scheme, the slope of the site is terraced so that the winners' enclosure and parade ring are a full storey height below the promenade.

A new weighing-in building forms part of the retaining structure, with its roof at the level of the promenade and a fully glazed wall facing the winners' enclosure. It is a simple, in-situ concrete structure, with a flat roof slab supported on round columns. Jockeys' changing rooms are at the back of the building against the retaining wall, with offices for stewards and a room for the BBC at the front. Stepped spectator stands, of reconstructed stone with flint risers, extend from the flank walls of the weighing-in building and wrap round the parade ring. This leaves the promenade free to be remodelled as a boulevard, defined by mature trees. At its west end, the boulevard curves southwards, crosses the horsewalk that links the parade ring to the racecourse, and meets the other major new intervention, a tree-lined main entrance road with a turning circle and drop-off point. Entrance road and boulevard therefore form a clearly legible circulation spine through the whole site.

Having adjusted the ground form and circulation, the next step was to re-introduce the all-important catering and hospitality facilities. These are mainly accommodated in three marquee-like structures, in use for approximately 22 days every summer, between the boulevard and parade ring, with the central tent standing on the roof of the weighing-in building. Each tent has a central servery island surrounded by space for tables. A PVC membrane is supported by a pair of steel masts with outriggers. The 'garden party' effect is enhanced by timber boarded floors and the apparent absence of any enclosing walls, though the outer two tents are fitted with freestanding glass screens to provide shelter from occasional strong southerly winds. A fourth tent straddles the main entrance at the drop-off point, sheltering a pair of small timber cabins containing a ticket office and a meeting room. Moving the main entrance created a vacant site to the west of the main stand. A new seafood restaurant and champagne bar, similar in form and structure to the new weighing-in building, takes advantage of this prime location, overlooking the members' lawn with a clear view of the horsewalk.

Below: site model viewed along the axis of the parade ground, the winners' enclosure and the weighing-in building, with the back of the grandstand beyond. Three tent structures accommodate catering and hospitality facilities.

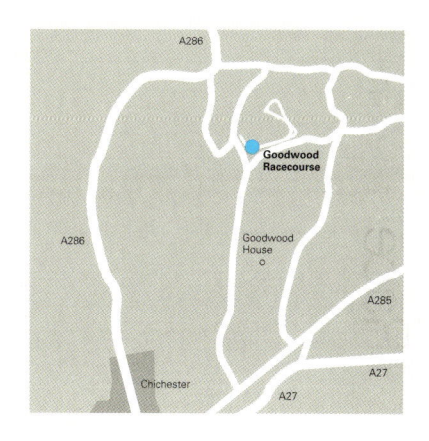

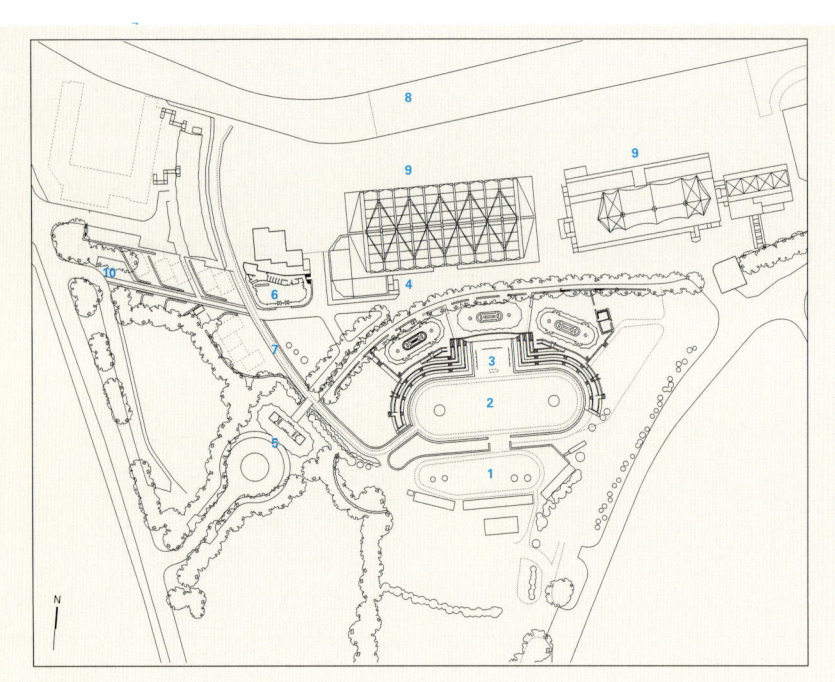

Site plan

1. pre-parade ring and stables
2. parade ring
3. winners' enclosure
4. concourse
5. west entrance pavilion
6. restaurant
7. horsewalk to racecourse
8. racecourse and finish line
9. grandstand
10. old west entrance

Goodwood Racecourse

Below: the parade ground and the winners' enclosure are a full storey height below the promenade at the back of the grandstand. Stepped spectator stands form a partial amphitheatre.

The Cakehouse, St James' Park
1998–

John Nash designed St James' Park in the Picturesque style, with grassy swards, winding paths, informal clumps of trees and a lake. The previous Cakehouse – a white, pointed structure, like a concrete and glass bell tent – was designed to contrast with this pseudo-natural landscape. But Nash never envisaged such an obviously man-made intrusion on the scene, and the proposed new Cakehouse takes the opposite approach. This building is conceived as a fold in the ground, a mound and a cave, with a curving plan derived from the geometry of the adjacent paths. Landscape and building merge into one another. A covered external terrace forms an intermediate territory between the lakeside Broadwalk and the restaurant interior. The park benches that line the Broadwalk here attach themselves to the raised edge of the terrace, which in turn merges into the restaurant interior through a wall of full-height sliding glass doors. The back wall of the restaurant, which incorporates the serving counter, is the continuation of a gradual S-curve that peels away from the line of the path several yards south of the building. A new path follows this curve, mounts a flight of wooden steps above a vertically planted wall, then veers off onto the roof of the terrace where there is a promenade with more fixed benches and an uninterrupted view of the lake. The rest of the roof is covered with earth and grass, falling gently away to the west.

In both use and construction, this is really two separate buildings that meet along the line of the S-curve like pieces in a free-form jigsaw. One contains the kitchen, toilets, storage and staff areas, arranged in a straightforward cellular plan and contained in a submerged reinforced concrete box – an underground bunker, with a covered service yard at the north end. Plan and section have been carefully manipulated to avoid disturbing the bank of trees immediately to the rear, and to connect to existing underground rooms inherited from the original building. The other building is a completely different kind of structure in which the open, flowing spaces of the restaurant and terrace are defined by a timber-framed roof. Laminated beams are connected to round columns by specially designed galvanized steel nodes. Floors, walls and ceilings are clad in timber, mainly European Larch, and the terrace is a timber-boarded deck with open joints over a drainage channel. Though a lightweight structure, the building, with its earth-sheltered roof, has a high thermal capacity, keeping it warm in winter and, more importantly, cool in summer. Further protection against solar heat gain in the restaurant is provided by the overhanging roof and an array of vertical wooden slatted panels mounted between the columns. There is no air conditioning, only a mechanical extract system in the kitchen to remove food smells and draw fresh, cool air from the lake through the restaurant.

The organic symmetry of this pavilion is unusual among Hopkins' designs. In Nash's terms, it is a grotto rather than a temple, a part of the landscape rather than an object on display.

Below: model viewed from the southwest. The building is both a mound and a cave, a part of the landscape rather than a freestanding object.

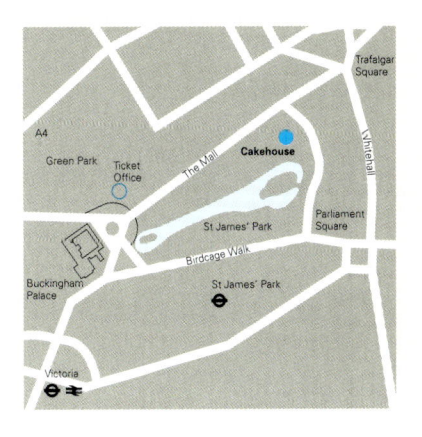

Below: the curving plan of the building is derived from the geometry of the surrounding paths laid out by John Nash. The grassed roof provides an elevated terrace from which to view the lake.

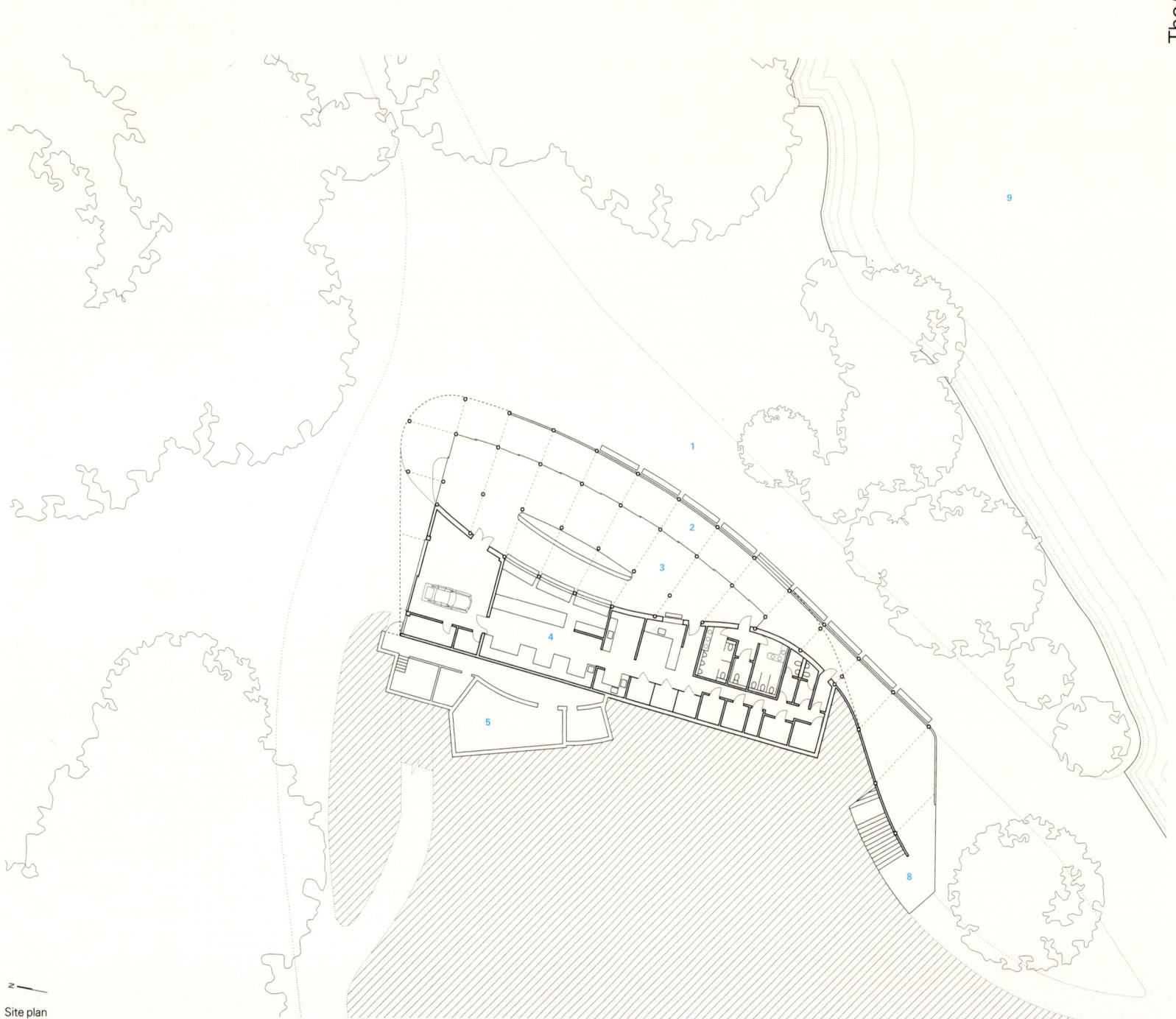

The Cakehouse, St James' Park

N
Site plan

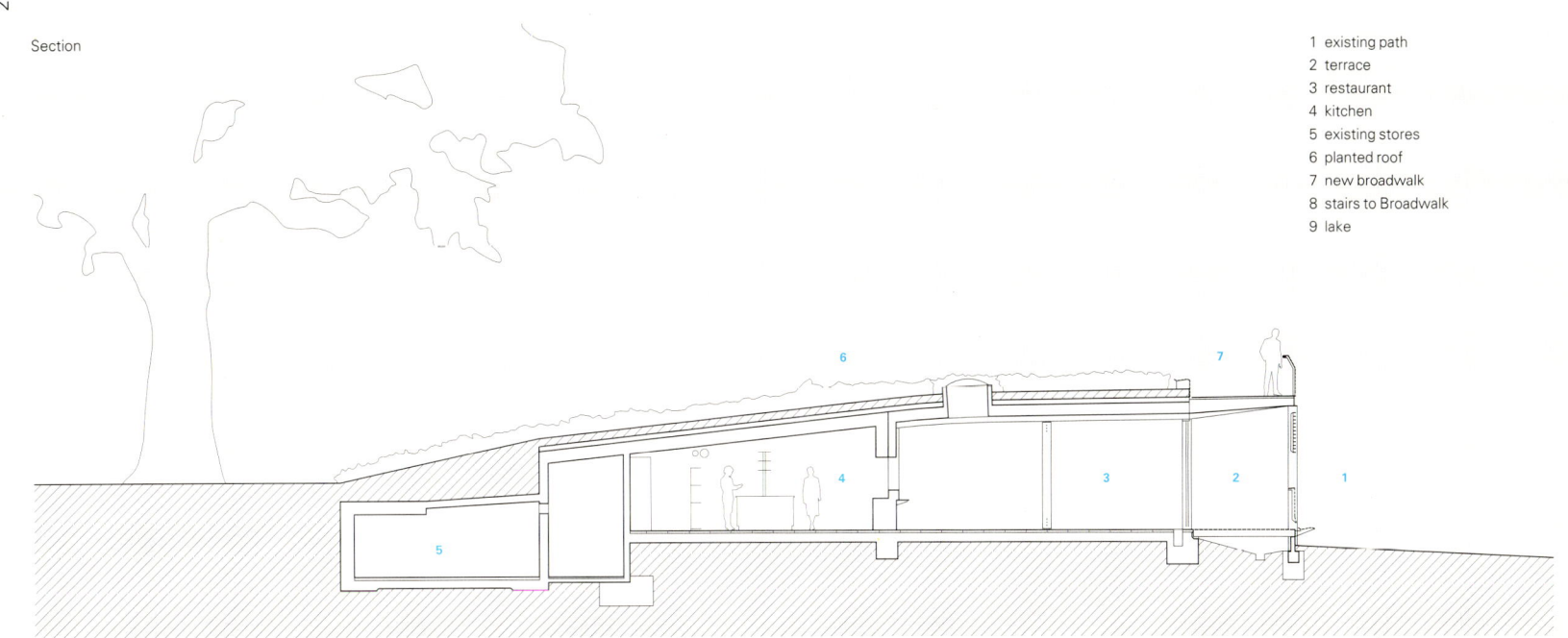

Section

1 existing path
2 terrace
3 restaurant
4 kitchen
5 existing stores
6 planted roof
7 new broadwalk
8 stairs to Broadwalk
9 lake

King Fahad National Library, Saudi Arabia
1999–

The competition scheme for a new national library in Riyadh uses a basic formal matrix of 84 concrete and terracotta 'parasols', arranged in 14 by 6 rectangles. The building sits between a large walled garden and a public plaza, beside a road of motorway proportions. The plaza and the ground floor of the building are on one level, slightly higher than the road, with two layers of car parking under the plaza. The garden, however, is a full storey height lower, taking advantage of the natural slope of the site. The building is divided vertically into two main zones: base and superstructure. Closed book stacks and staff offices are housed in the basement plinth, while the visiting public mainly occupy the flowing spaces under the concrete and terracotta parasols at ground-floor level. The main public areas are divided into four zones: the men's library; the women's library; a shared information and exhibition area; and an entrance court called King Fahad Plaza, which is open-sided but shaded by the canopy of linked parasols. The towers of the parasols support the ground floor 'table-top' slab, but in certain bays they also support bridge-like structures at both first- and second-floor level containing open-access book shelves. Vertical circulation is mainly via spiral staircases which are inside the towers.

The parasols are the key elements of the building's design, both structurally and environmentally. Each consists of a 16-metre diameter canopy supported by a 4-metre diameter tower. The hollow towers are made of reinforced concrete at basement level and reinforced terracotta masonry above the ground-floor slab. The canopies are also hollow, composite structures. A shallow cone of concrete and terracotta, sculpted into a wavy or wrinkled profile to give it integral strength, spans between a compression ring on the top of the tower and tension ring around the circumference. A second inverted concrete cone sits on top of the tension ring, rising to a tapered, cylindrical chimney. As well as providing the main means of vertical circulation within the building, the towers also serve as plant rooms and ventilation ducts. Cool air from the basement is drawn up through perforations in the walls of the towers and distributed at low level into the main public areas. Warm air from the top of the space is drawn out through the cones of the parasols by the suction effect of the chimneys. Mechanical air-handling plant is housed in some of the towers to assist the cooling process, for example by drawing cool night air in through the chimneys and down the main shafts of the towers to the basement.

Though its urban context is unremarkable, the building responds in subtle ways to its cultural context, notably in its use of traditional materials. The serpentine external walls, for example, are made of reinforced mud brick on a base of local limestone. And the simplicity of the repetitive, modular plan is perhaps intended to be reminiscent of the great mosques of the early Islamic period.

Below: model showing the rectangle of 84 parasols in the sunken, walled garden, with the motorway and plaza in the foreground. There are two layers of car parking beneath the plaza.

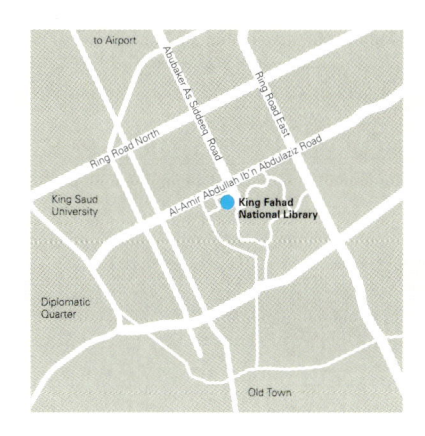

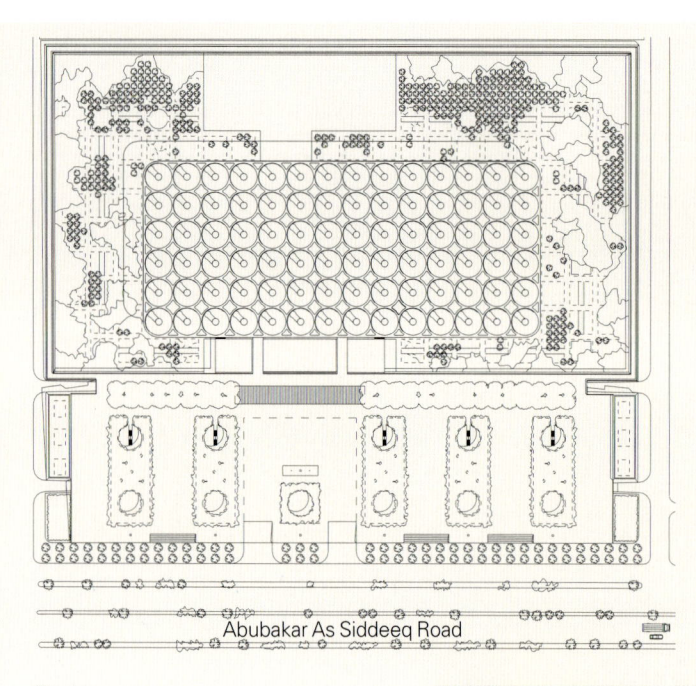

Below: composite reflected ceiling plan, showing the structure of the main ground-floor slab, the interlocking parasols and the serpentine external wall with the first- and second-floor bridges shaded.

Bottom: section. The main book stack, accessible via a regular grid of corridors, is housed in the plinth below ground floor level. Staircases are accommodated in the hollow towers.

Site plan

King Fahad National Library

1 Administrative Services department
2 Books and Periodicals Collection department
3 Special Collections department
4 Archives department
5 Childrens Library
6 Women's Library
7 Cultural Activities department
8 Kingdom Information Centre
9 Saudi Librarian Association
10 bridge
11 courtyard
12 foyer
13 prayer area
14 reflecting pool

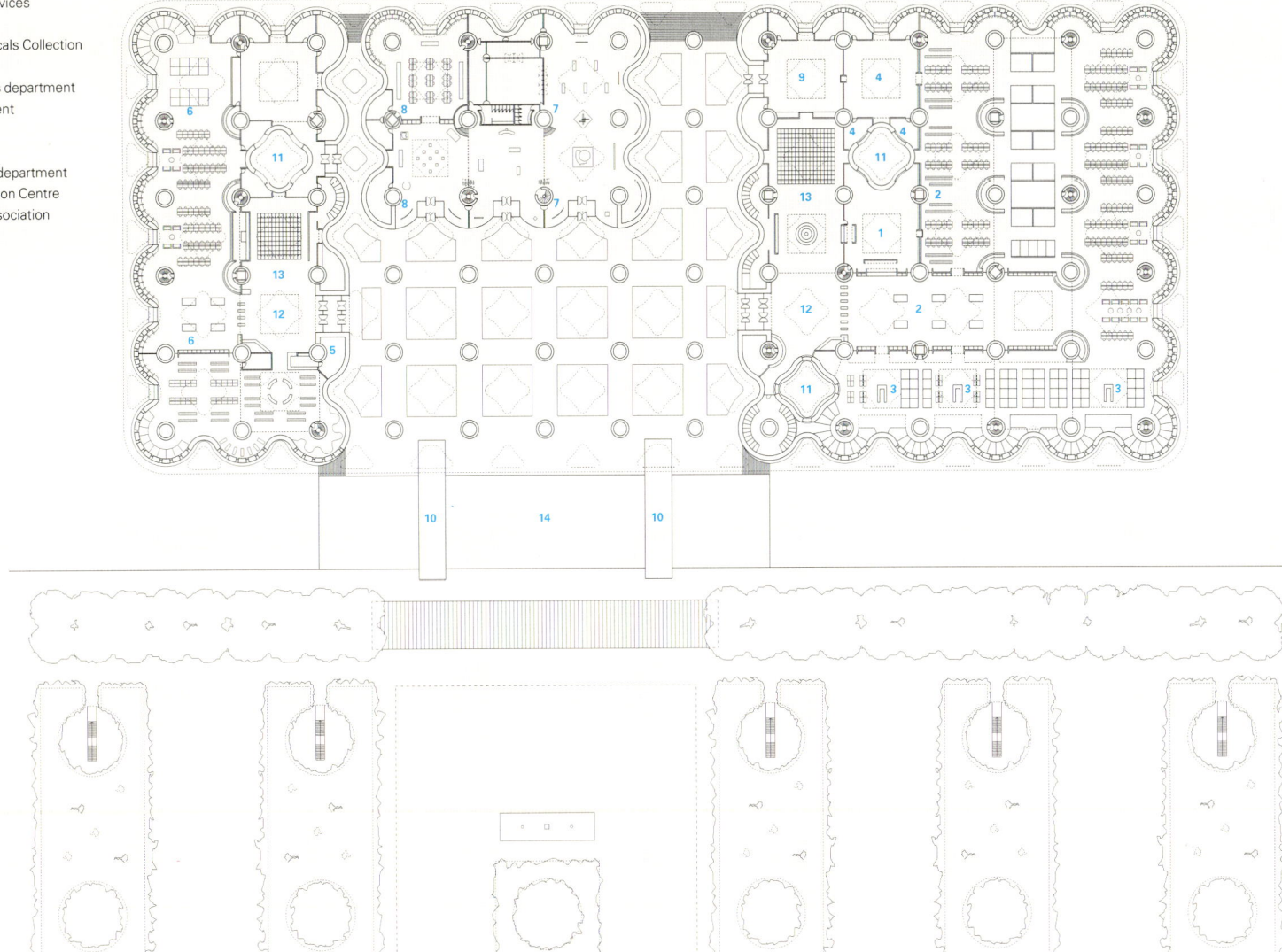

Ground floor plan

The Wellcome Trust
1999–

The Wellcome Trust is the world's largest medical research charity and the main funder of the Human Genome Project. At present its 600 staff are spread over five different sites in the Euston area of London. The proposed reorganization will consolidate the accommodation in a new building on Euston Road, between the original 1930s neo-classical Wellcome Building and the corner of Gower Street. The original building will be converted to house the Trust's library and museum collections, making them more accessible to the public.

The massing of the new building responds sensitively to the surrounding streets and neighbouring buildings. Office space is divided between two parallel blocks, one ten storeys high facing north across the busy traffic corridor of Euston Road, and one five storeys high facing south across the quiet back street of Gower Place. A big curved metal and glass roof unites the blocks, bridging over a narrow internal atrium. Great care has been taken to minimize the visual impact of the new building on the early nineteenth-century courtyard of nearby University College. On the Gower Street corner, the otherwise symmetrical plan is cut back to improve access to Euston Square Underground station.

In the north block, a typical floor plan consists of five column-free bays, each 12 metres by 18 metres, separated by double-height 'mini atriums' and service elements such as lifts, toilets and vertical ducts. This arrangement is reflected in the Euston Road elevation which is recessed between the bays. The outer recesses form niches for rounded staircase towers clad in glass blocks, and the inner recesses accommodate exposed, cross-braced steel frames to provide east-west lateral stability. North-south lateral stability is provided by stiffened steel-plate fin walls flanking the recesses. The main office bays are clad in floor-to-ceiling triple-glazed glass panels. As in most Hopkins' designs, therefore, the facade clearly expresses the spatial and structural logic of the building. Its strongly modelled, articulated form gives the building a vertical posture to match the scale and rhythm of the old Wellcome Building next door. The basic classical configuration of base, column and attic is also echoed in the new building which has recessed display windows on the ground floor and a set back top floor subsumed into the curved roof.

The lower, south block has a similarly modelled and articulated facade, though its floor plans are simpler and shallower, without the intervening mini atriums. A staff restaurant occupies what would be its roof were it not sheltered by the frameless glass membrane of the roof proper and takes advantage of rooftop views across Bloomsbury. Open bridges span across the atrium up to the fifth floor to link the two blocks.

The structural frame of the building is of steel, with concrete-filled round columns, I beams and in-situ concrete floors. The tempering function of exposed concrete is taken over by chilled suspended ceilings which act like negative radiators.

Below: computer montage showing the completed building in its Euston Road setting. The original Wellcome Building is in the foreground on the left.

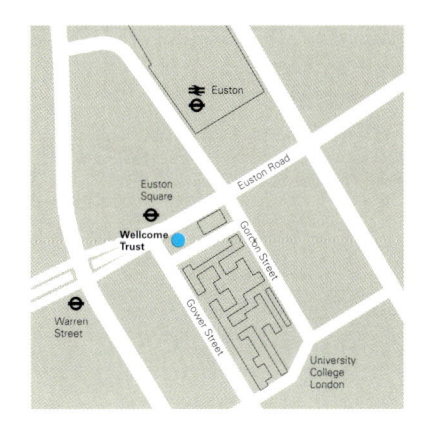

Below: cross section showing how the building steps down to match the scale of Gower Place, but is contained within the curved envelope of the roof. A full-height atrium separates the north and south blocks.

Right: the building is cut back at the Gower Street corner to improve access from the south to Euston Square underground station.

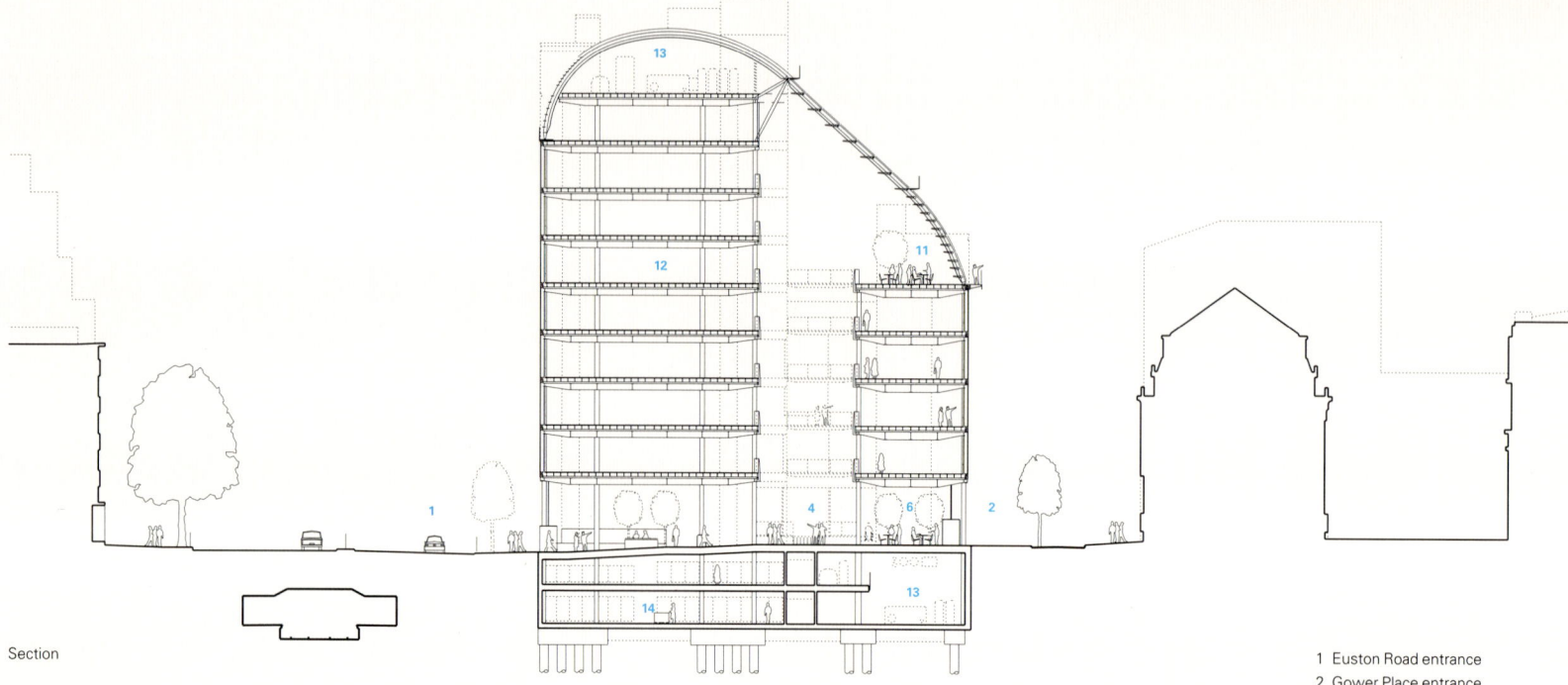

Section

1 Euston Road entrance
2 Gower Place entrance
3 reception
4 atrium
5 mini atria
6 café
7 stair tower
8 lifts
9 goods lift
10 WCs
11 restaurant
12 offices
13 plant
14 book storage
15 existing Wellcome Building
16 link to existing Wellcome Building
17 Euston Square underground Station

The Wellcome Trust

Below: typical floor plan showing the relationship of the new and existing buildings, the long atrium between the north and south blocks, and the 'mini atria' in the north block.

Bottom: ground floor plan. New and old buildings together occupy the whole city block between Euston Road and Gower Place.

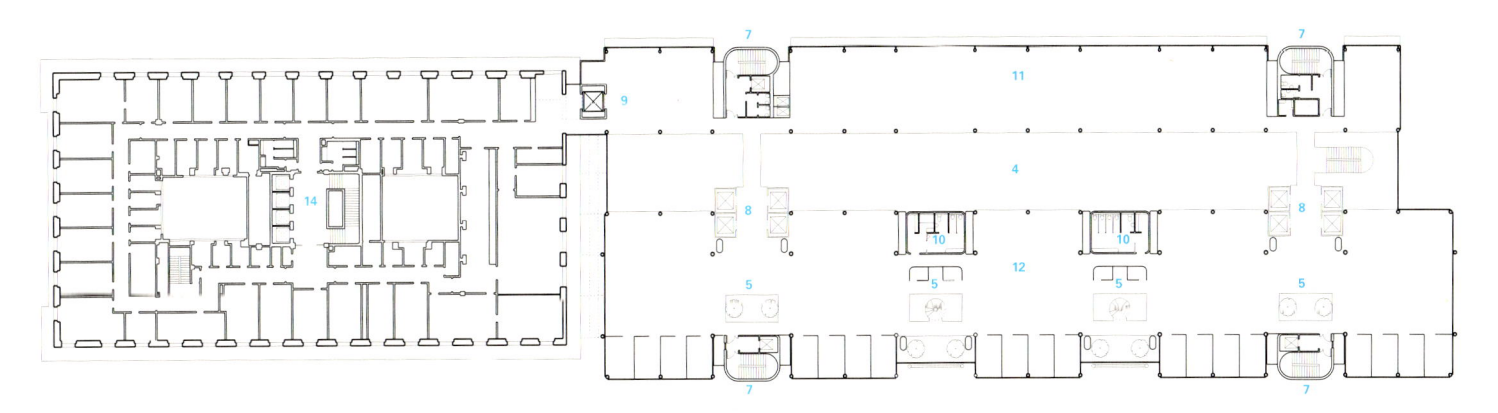

Fifth floor plan

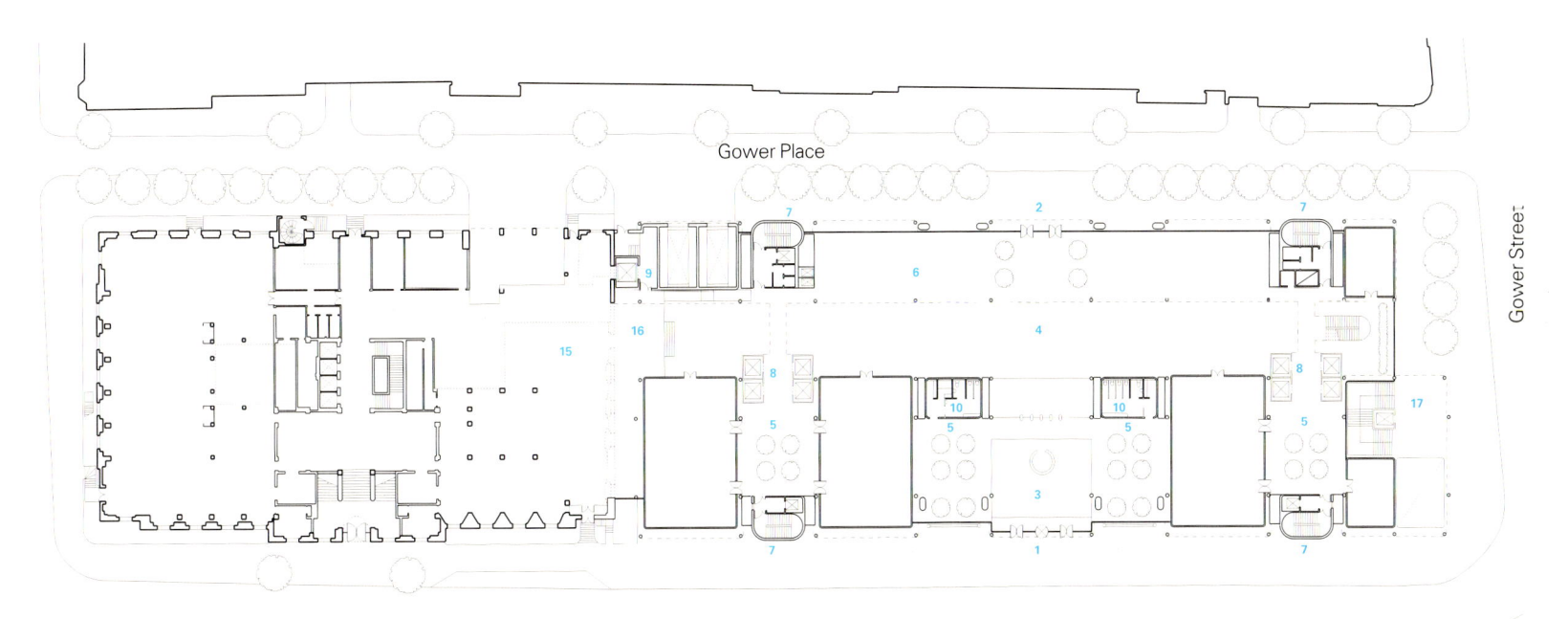

Gower Place

Gower Street

Euston Road

Ground floor plan

Evelina Children's Hospital
1999–

This was the first time that Michael Hopkins and Partners had approached hospital design, and as such, they preferred to think in terms of other building types – in particular offices and hotels – in order to break away from the norm of endless corridors and dull, airless wards. The most important space in the proposed Evelina Children's Hospital at St Thomas's is a four-storey high, glass-walled conservatory. This is the social heart of the building, which has been deliberately designed to be flexible so that it can accommodate a number of different activities. There is a café and waiting area, but the remainder of the space is adaptable for play sessions, classes, exhibitions, a library and even small theatrical productions. Set at third-floor level, where it can take advantage of views over the gardens of Lambeth Palace to the south and east, the conservatory is overlooked on the north side by three floors of wards and a top floor of staff offices. The 18-metre wide, air-conditioned ward floors are divided longitudinally into three zones: single bedrooms are situated on the north side, open wards and day spaces are on the conservatory side and service spaces, such as nurses' stations and utility rooms, are in between. An open-sided circulation route takes the place of the usual straight corridor.

More specialized medical functions, such as outpatient clinics, therapy rooms and operating theatres, occupy the three-storey (plus basement) podium below atrium level. The compact, 36-metre deep floor plans are made legible and given breathing space by a wide concourse at each level, pierced by generous light wells through which the conservatory above can be glimpsed. The main public entrance to the building, off Lambeth Palace Road, is at the east end of the ground floor concourse and there is a secondary entrance at the west end, off the main hospital street. Like the conservatory, the ground floor concourse is big enough to accommodate performance spaces and play structures as well as the main reception area. Two 'wall climber rocket' lifts rise through the light wells into the conservatory and continue upwards to serve the ward floors.

Flexibility is the keynote of the structural and services design. The structure is precast concrete, on a 9 by 7.2 metre column grid, largely dictated by the optimum width for a ward. Raised floors were ruled out on maintenance and hygiene grounds so horizontal services are distributed above suspended ceilings. Standard floor slabs have cast-in slots for local service connections. Highly serviced rooms such as kitchens and toilets will be made as pre-fabricated pods which can be repositioned if and when the building is replanned. Visually, the most important element of the building is the wrap-around conservatory wall and roof with its steel diagrid structure and frameless glass skin. In winter, it will act as a passive solar collector and in summer, natural, stack effect ventilation will prevent excessive heat gain.

Below: site model, showing the relationship between the new building and the existing hospital complex. Lambeth Palace Road is on the right and the River Thames is on the left.

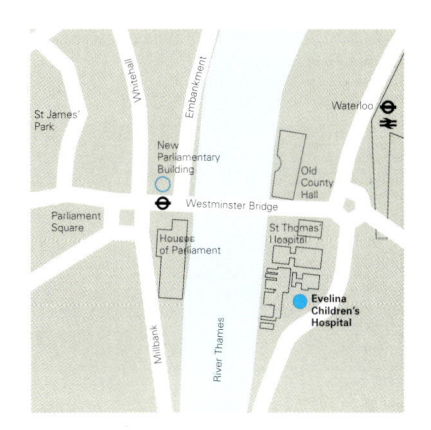

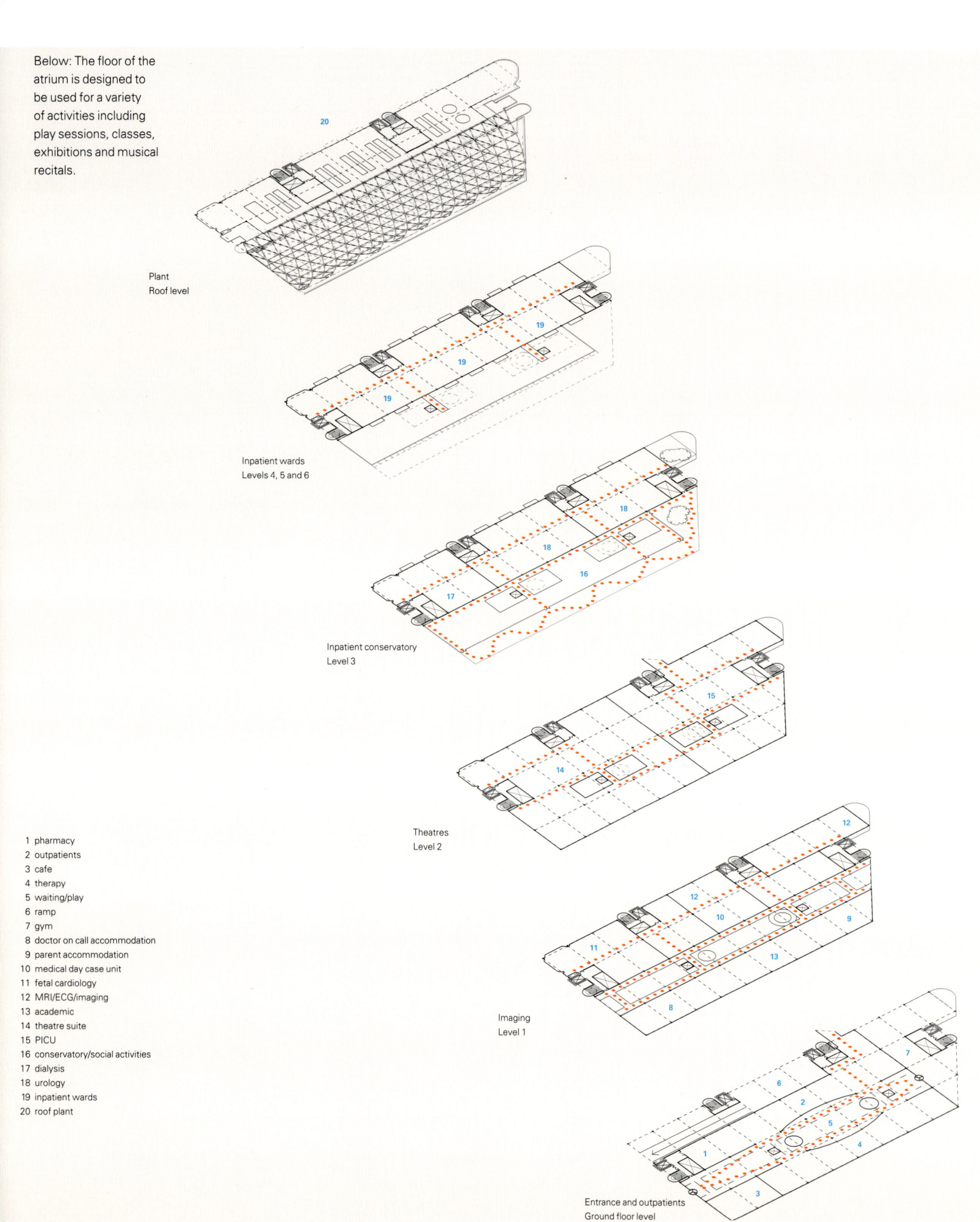

Below: The floor of the atrium is designed to be used for a variety of activities including play sessions, classes, exhibitions and musical recitals.

Plant
Roof level

Inpatient wards
Levels 4, 5 and 6

Inpatient conservatory
Level 3

Theatres
Level 2

Imaging
Level 1

Entrance and outpatients
Ground floor level

1 pharmacy
2 outpatients
3 cafe
4 therapy
5 waiting/play
6 ramp
7 gym
8 doctor on call accommodation
9 parent accommodation
10 medical day case unit
11 fetal cardiology
12 MRI/ECG/imaging
13 academic
14 theatre suite
15 PICU
16 conservatory/social activities
17 dialysis
18 urology
19 inpatient wards
20 roof plant

Left: the four-storey high conservatory is set at third-floor level, where it enjoys views over the Gardens of Lambeth Palace and the public park, from which this view is taken.

Below: cross section. All wards overlook the conservatory, the social heart of the building, with its café, its aerodynamic curved roof and its 'wall climber rocket' lifts.

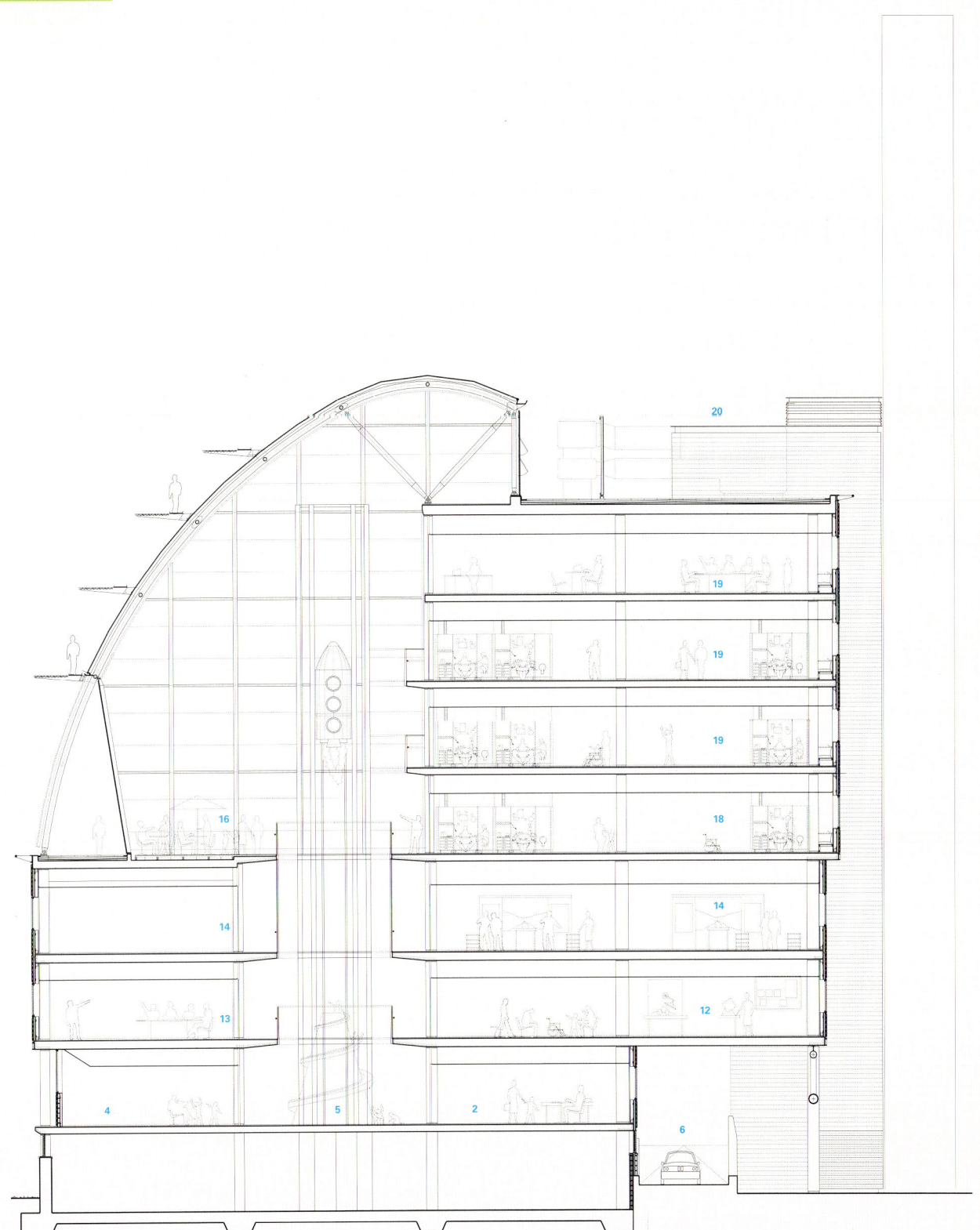

Evelina Children's Hospital

National College of School Leadership
2000–

The proposed National College for School Leadership is essentially a residential conference centre offering short courses for head teachers and their deputies. The site is close to Nottingham University's new Jubilee Campus, also designed by Michael Hopkins and Partners. The new building terminates a southward extension of the existing lake, with its main entrance on the south side, across a water pond. In scale, structure, materials and spatial arrangement, the building bears a marked family resemblance to the neighbouring campus buildings. Like them, it alternates simple, three-storey blocks with full-height glazed atria. The three-storey blocks have in-situ concrete frames with round columns on an economical 6-metre square grid, and their upper storeys are clad in timber boarding. The glass roofs of the three atria slope down towards the lake and are supported on laminated timber beams spanning the full width between the blocks. All these features are inherited from the campus buildings. There are, however, some important differences between them. The line of existing campus buildings follows the curve of the lake, but each individual building remains strictly rectilinear. The NCSL building, however, is curved, wrapping slightly around the end of the lake as if to contain it. The alternating rhythm of block and atrium is made the more complex by the introduction of two large single-storey spaces to accommodate the auditorium and the dining room. It is these wedge-shaped spaces that create the apparent curve of the building. They are surrounded by the three-storey blocks and their roofs are landscaped to create courtyards at first-floor level. Another important difference between the NCSL and the earlier buildings, is that the blocks of the NCSL have very shallow plans, most are only one structural bay deep. The first and second floors are given over entirely to hotel-style bedrooms with en-suite bathrooms. Most of these rooms are accessed via single-loaded corridors which become open galleries around the atria.

Teaching and social spaces are all located on the ground floor. The landscaped atria serve as informal lounging, meeting and relaxation spaces, opening onto a lakeside promenade. They also provide circulation between the ground-floor rooms, which are fitted out as seminar rooms, meeting rooms, computer suites and staff offices. The meeting rooms flanking the central atrium are enclosed by sliding/folding partitions, so that the atrium can be opened up, linking the auditorium on one side and the dining room on the other. Each atrium contains a large spiral staircase giving direct access to the hotel corridors and galleries. The central atrium contains a second free-standing object – an egg-like structure, hovering at first-floor level on the axis of the main entrance. The space under this object is shared by the main reception desk and a bar. The egg is an open-access computer room, which is no doubt intended to be as much symbolic as functional.

1 National College of School Leadership
2 lake
3 academic departments
4 Central teaching facility
5 Learning Resource Centre

Site plan

Below: model showing the new building viewed across the lake at night. Atria open onto a lakeside promenade.

Below: longitudinal section through the whole building, showing the alternation of narrow three-storey blocks with generous landscaped atria and single-storey enclosures housing the refectory and the auditorium.

Bottom: model showing the gentle curve of the building, like a dam terminating the broad expanse of the lake. The main entrance is on the far side.

1 central atrium
2 east atrium
3 west atrium
4 dining hall
5 auditorium
6 study room
7 seminar room/office
8 grass roof
9 open courtyard
10 solar water heaters

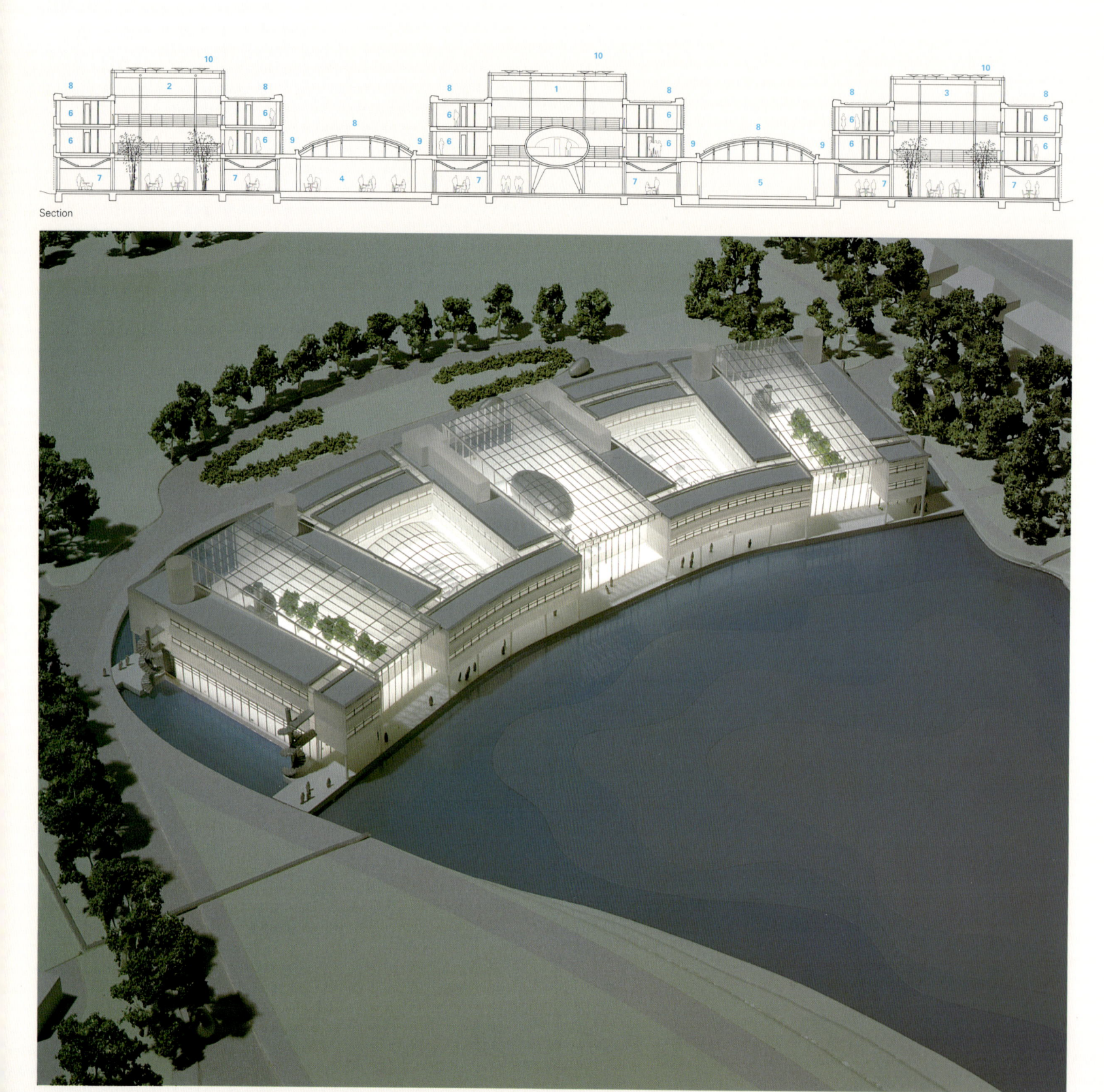

Section

Left: computer generated image showing the central atrium dominated by the hanging structure of the open-access computer room. Bedroom corridors take the form of open galleries overlooking the atrium.

Below: computer generated image. The atria, like those of the faculty buildings on the university campus, have sloping glazed roofs supported by laminated timber beams.

University College Suffolk
1998–

University College Suffolk was designated as such in 1996 and is affiliated to the University of East Anglia. Michael Hopkins and Partners was commissioned to prepare a scheme, or 'vision', for a possible extension of the college on land between the existing campus, to the east of Ipswich city centre, and the so-called Wet Dock to the south. The outline brief called for teaching and administration buildings, laboratories for the Department of Health and Applied Science, a refectory, a learning resources centre and a library. In addition to these higher education facilities, the brief also called for buildings of a more public character, including a conference centre, a performing arts centre and an exhibition gallery. The vision was required to reflect the college's ambition to become a 'televersity', using the latest teaching and learning technology for the efficient delivery of its courses. Any future development would also play an important part in the regeneration of Ipswich docks.

The site is currently divided into two unequal parts by Fore Street but there are plans to incorporate this street into a semi-pedestrianized green route'. A more serious constraint on development is the proposed new major road which cuts diagonally across the site between the existing campus and Fore Street. The Hopkins scheme diverts this road slightly in order to create a generous, roughly rectangular site for the main higher education buildings. A linear teaching and administrative block, stepped in profile and angled at the corner, defines the north and east boundaries of this site.

A learning resources centre, with a refectory on the ground floor, defines the western boundary and a library and telematics centre, housed in a typical Hopkins tent, completes the enclosure on the south side. A new sheltered garden is therefore created in the centre of the site and this is linked to the existing campus via a diagonal pedestrian route. The laboratories for the Department of Health and Applied Science are accommodated in a separate block on the neighbouring site to the west.

The second, slightly smaller site between Fore Street and the West Dock has a more public character. Some existing buildings are retained, but the waterfront is completely transformed by two big new public buildings: the conference centre and the performing arts centre. These are connected by another tent structure, housing the foyer spaces and the exhibition gallery, set back behind a wide dockside plaza. The wedge-shaped auditorium of the performing arts centre creates a triangular plan. At the apex of the triangle, on the edge of the dock, a high, round tower gives character and definition to the dockside plaza.

The scheme is little more than a feasibility study and one of its main functions is to help the college's fund-raising activities. It is, however, made plausible by the many precedents for these building types in the work of the practice: the Jubilee Campus, for example, or the IBM headquarters at Bedfont Lakes, not to mention tent structures at Inland Revenue, Saga and Dynamic Earth.

Below: site model showing the two sites on either side of Fore Street: the main teaching buildings to the left and the public buildings facing the Wet Dock to the right.

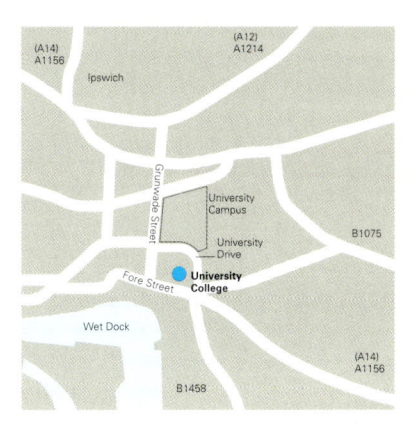

Below: sketch perspective of the interior of the library and telematics centre, housed in a trademark Hopkins tent.

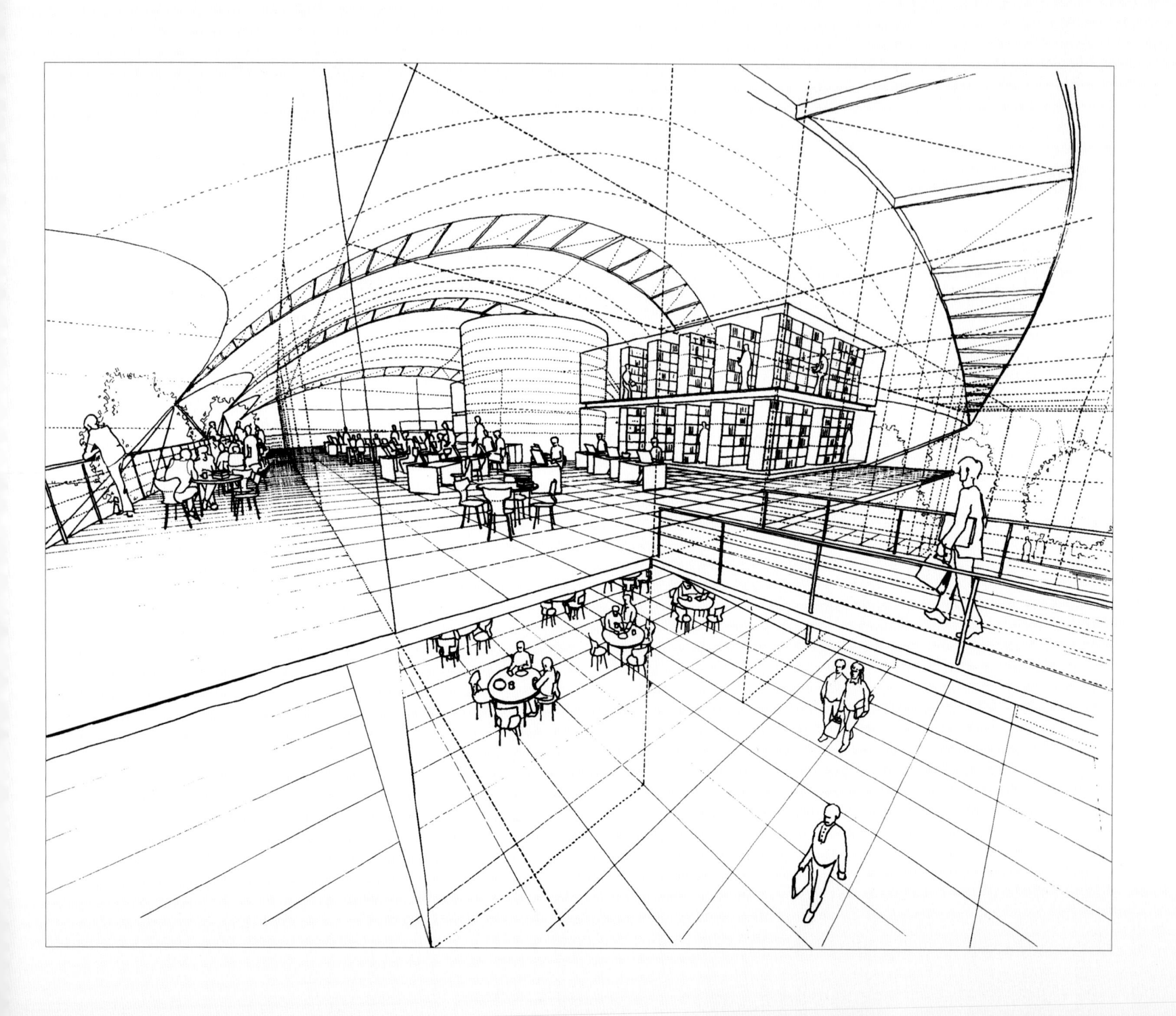

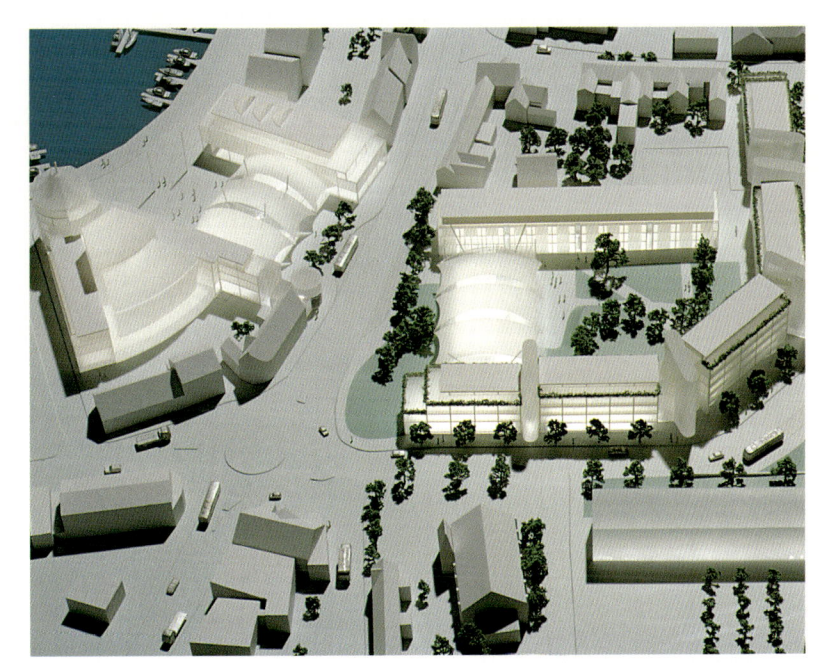

Left: site model viewed from the east. A diagonal path links the existing campus, out of the picture to the right, with the Wet Dock, visible top left.

Below: the dockside complex is dominated by a high, round tower on one corner of the triangular performing arts building, right.

University College Suffolk

Hopkins Gravitas

Charles Jencks

Style Worry and Trans-Style Once, while poring over drawings of the 1920s Los Angeles Stock Exchange with its architect, a man of venerable bearing, I committed a notorious faux-pas: 'What style', I asked of his Art Deco Classical monument, 'is your building?' He looked at me with that smile teachers reserve for their dimmest students and, with an air of utter conviction, answered, 'timeless'. Architects, like politicians, do not ordinarily like to discuss issues of classification or, when pinned down, like Margaret Thatcher, they respond with the sobriquet 'universal'. From Christopher Alexander to Mies van der Rohe, Auguste Choisy to Buckminster Fuller, theorists and architects have been claiming the timeless way of building, ultimate truth, and universality. Perhaps they have good reason to do so – there *are* universals of architecture – but their style and form vary at every moment in space-time, which is why historians can date their buildings.

Only electrons and other ultimate particles are truly interchangeable; every other piece of matter keeps some record of the contingent buried within its universal shape. The particular style and grammatical form an architect adopts is as original as a fingerprint and much more subject to choice. Art historians, as much as the general public, often question these matters of free choice, whereas architects, knowing they are contentious issues, and wishing to believe their work has an objective necessity, tend to deflect the question sideways. Style and form either follow function, or its first cousins, economics, ecology, construction or building code. *Anything* but something arbitrary or personal.

The blood spilt recently over style wars in Britain, or the disdain with which High-Tech architects dismissed the notion of High-Tech style, show that style worry, that nineteenth-century anxiety, is still with us. Histories of Modernism, such as Nikolaus Pevsner's, also show the attempts to explain away the problem. In his 1936 book *Pioneers of the Modern Movement* he justified the white International Style as the 'true' and only 'universal' style of the twentieth century, indeed the only 'moral' one, and so convinced was he of these truths that he ended up calling it (positively) 'totalitarian'. Needless to say the word was changed, in later editions, to 'universal'.

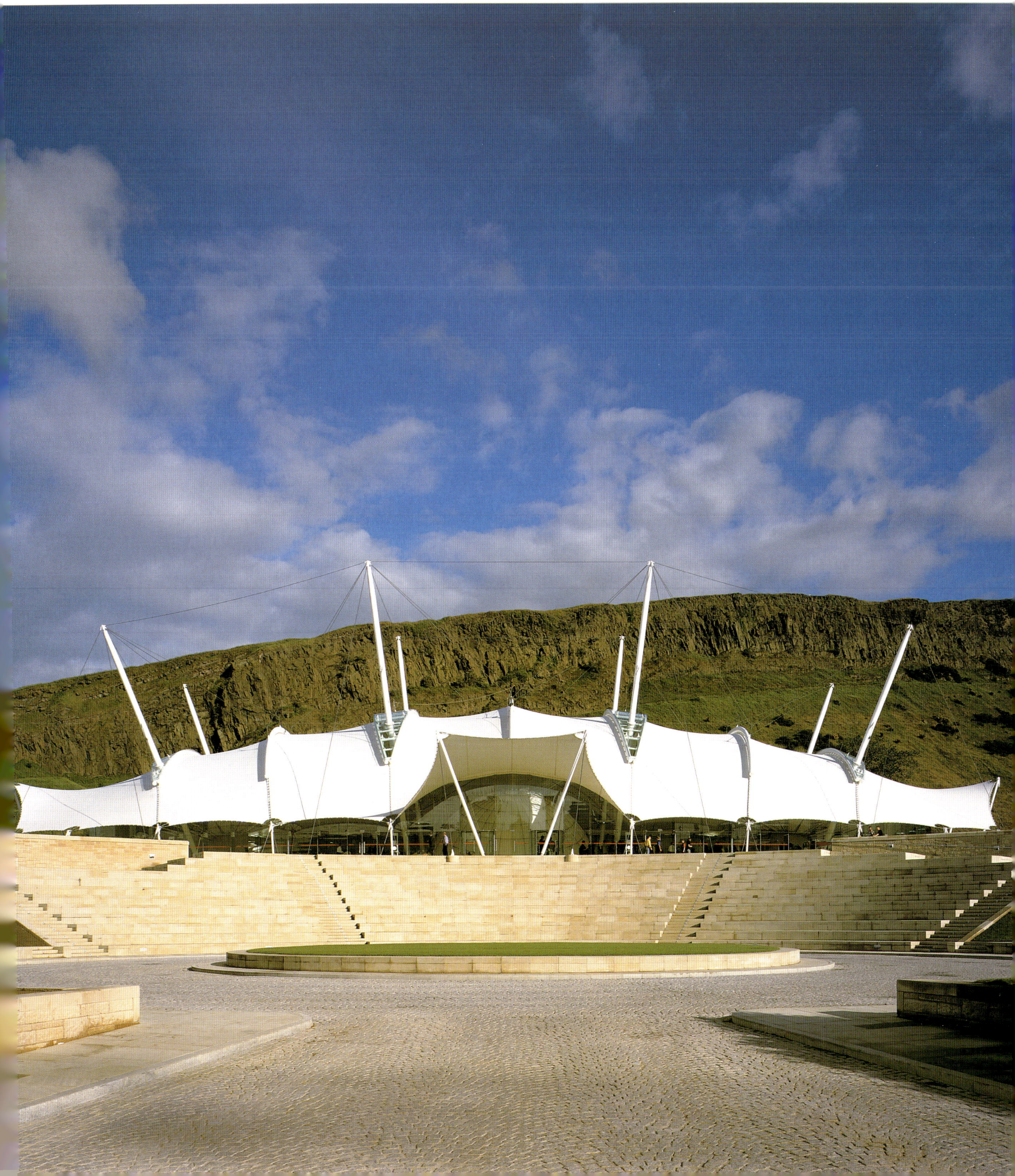

His slip of the adjective is just as revealing as that of the Los Angeles Stock Exchange designer. Classicists, Modernists, product designers, airplane and ship builders all aim at being universal – truthful, honest, as close to the bone as possible. Getting near to efficient form will take the engineer towards universal structural forms. If these forms are inevitably beautiful, as Plato and so many classicists assumed, then designed objects will end up looking either like nature's forms, or nature's laws. At least that was the Modernist hope. These assumptions, or something like them, have always echoed around the functionalist tradition, and were also prevalent in the Architectural Association in the late 1950s when Michael and Patty Hopkins were students there. However, in the sophisticated intellectual climate of this school, subject to the criss-cross of international debate, a simple version of this doctrine could not be held very easily. The student had to check his opinions against critics such as Alan Colquhoun and Robert Maxwell, architects such as the Smithsons, and characters such as Cedric Price and Sam Stevens. The simple formula, 'truth is beauty' could not withstand arguments initiated by Le Corbusier who showed that a beautiful wicker basket became, when more efficiently stuffed with too much paper, ugly. Beauty, style, good form needed a more robust and complex defence.

The work of Michael Hopkins and Partners evolved within such a climate of debate – they were at the AA then – and evolved consistently, starting from the position of the functionalist. Michael Hopkins, as a young man and the son of a builder from Bournemouth, enjoyed the practical activity of boat building, and reconstructing basic structures such as timber-framed houses. His affinities, in taste and background, were in effect close to Mies van der Rohe, who was trained both as a builder and in the classical school of philosophy at Aachen. There, since the thirteenth century, circulated the idealist arguments of Thomas Aquinas, and even his famous epithets that 'God is in the details', 'truth leads to beauty' and 'less is more'. Adapted in the nineteenth century by Flaubert, they were so often repeated by Modernists that amnesia set in. It was soon presumed that Mies coined them – amnesiacs always credit him today – but they can probably be traced back to the Egyptians – or the Greeks at least.

Followed rigorously, they may lead to a certain language of architecture, the style for which I would like to use the trans-stylistic term of *gravitas*. When applied to architecture, it not only implies a high seriousness and stern demeanour, but something taut, impersonal, complete – a system willing to proclaim itself with finality. One does not argue with the *gravitas* of the Parthenon any more than that of the Apollo space shuttle, or the Alps. Awe and submission to the facts of nature are the normal response, even when one knows they are not facts, and that nature is partly a human construct.

The method that produces an architecture of *gravitas* sometimes starts design with a certain constructional unit. A detail, a column, an arch, a bay window generates a system, and then the architect attempts to manipulate it to see if everything the building needs might be made with it. The game is in the cleverness and repetition of the unit; and the winning of the game is when the system works as a whole and there is nothing extraneous, nothing more to be

Bay Rhythms compared: Hopkins House, 1975–6 (left): A, A, A, A, A, A. From the side, Schlumberger Cambridge Research Centre, 1982–92 (above): a, B, a, B, a, B, a. Lord's Cricket Ground, 1984–91 (opposite left), from the street the tent's rhythm above steel, glass, brick arches: a, B, etc.

Bracken House: 1987–92 (opposite centre): A, b etc. New Parliamentary Building, 1989–2000 (opposite right): A, b, A, b, A, b, etc. Opposed to a classical closure at the ends, several of Hopkins' facades imply an infinite extension, as if the bay had no beginning or end.

added or subtracted. The result is a perfect architectural proposition, a logical proof in three dimensions. Something like this is what Lutyens meant by the High Game of Architecture, or Reyner Banham by *le secret professionnel* of this, the second oldest profession. The Greek temple is its icon, and Hopkins' favourite exemplar, Paxton's Crystal Palace, is one of its offspring.

Essentializing the bay – Greek terror Consider the development of Hopkins' work over twenty-five years. It has changed in several important respects – famously from being the internally referenced High-Tech product to the contextually related hybrid that even Prince Charles (mistakenly) admired as the acceptable face of Modernism (a point to which I shall return). But throughout such changes were even deeper continuities: rooting design in the constructional unit, above all the repetitive bay. It is this commitment that gives Hopkins work its classical *gravitas*, makes it comparable to Greek, Gothic and Renaissance architecture and very different from the atectonic work of mud huts, Le Corbusier's church at Ronchamp and Frank Gehry's new museum at Bilbao.

The Hopkins House of 1975–6 starts the evolution. It is a five- by six-bay solution whose perfect classical repetition is only broken by two off-centre doors and one off-centre staircase – otherwise Palladio could have designed the plan. Other of his High-Tech buildings of the early eighties have symmetrical blank sides and regular open bay fronts – just like Greek temples, except for the ultra-thin details and lack of a metaphorical Order. His soaring tents for the Schlumberger scientists at Cambridge are laid out as symmetrical pavilions between two arms, just like a chateau sets its central hall and salon on a symmetrical axis that opens onto the countryside. 'Just like', apart from the slender proportions and a host of details that make the comparison rather ludicrous. But these classical comparisons, even if far-fetched in some respects, bring out a truth that is not sufficiently acknowledged. His planning, his bay rhythms and conceptual clarity are all within the classical tradition, even more than that work of Mies which recently has been understood to be classical.

We can follow the development of the bay rhythm as Hopkins' work becomes larger and more complicated. At first his bay articulation is pure repetition, like the Greek temple, all bays are the same A, A, A, A, A, A. By 1982 and Schlumberger, the side elevation of the tents have the Renaissance syncopation that Raphael used: a, B, a, B, a, B, a. By 1984 and the Lord's Cricket Ground, the tents themselves follow these up and down rhythms, like the pistons of an engine. By 1987 and Bracken House, where Hopkins had to accommodate a pre-existing classical structure, the bays turn into proper bay windows and, squeezed tightly into a curve, they pulsate frenetically in alternation – void, solid: A, b – like the rat-a-tat-tat of a machine-gun. Every thin bronze barrel pulls in or pushes out with such constrained energy the building positively explodes with glass and metal. The most recent New Parliamentary Building called, appropriately for my argument, Portcullis House, carries the military metaphor even further. Here, on the long side, twenty stone barrels taper and shoot upwards, their fusillade is answered by twenty black barrels shooting the other way, and these are supported by five giant canons – the exhaust stacks for ventilation.

Yet, the military precision is subtly countered by the reverse taperings that fit into each other so beautifully and so sensibly. Is it the High Game of Architecture, *le secret professionnel*? Absolutely. The tapers are even equivalent to the entasis on a Greek temple. That is, they are a visual refinement, an ecological invention and a structural truth all in one. But, and this is the real point, they are carried through without any inflexion. Inevitability and necessity reign, impersonality and function, public sobriety and solemnity – in other words, *gravitas*.

Here lies another unexpected association. An expert on classical architecture, John Onions, once confided in me that, having written several books on Greek architecture, some of its overtones started to bother him, especially after Muammar Gaddafi brought him to Libya to lecture on the subject. Gaddafi wished to become another Caesar of the grand Mediterranean style, and it was this insight that made Onions aware of the relation of the Greek temple to the unit of the Greek army, the phalanx. They were both beautifully and rigidly organized as rectangles of repetitive bays – a proportion of

8 by 17 – as tight, efficient instruments that allowed no variation from the system. It is this quality that adds to the positive feelings of fear that the Greek temple evokes. Le Corbusier, as often, is the expert on such implicit meanings. After spending six weeks on the Acropolis he characterized the classical temples as 'domineering killing machines', as 'tragic carcasses' which recalled 'the conquered treasures' of the Greek nation. He sees the guttae and mutules looking like 'armour' and 'rivets'. And, with imagination possibly enflamed by reading the *Iliad*, he saw all this military energy as the ultimate in truth and heroism. After thirty years of rereading his reaction to the Parthenon, I am still troubled and moved by his insight:

'See what confirms the rectitude of temples, the savagery of the site, their impeccable structure. The spirit of power triumphs. The herald, so terribly lucid, draws to the lips a brazen trumpet and proffers a strident blast. The entablature with a cruel rigidity breaks and terrorizes. The sentiment of an extra human fatality seizes you. The Parthenon, terrible machine, pulverizes and dominates [everything for miles around].'

'Cruel entablature', 'terrible machine'. Fear modulates architectural beauty, the sense of power heightens the experience, because they are connected by the savagery of the monumental site with cosmic truth. Public architecture in the West often aspired to this equation of truth, beauty and terror. Indeed, over the last twenty years, the poet Ian Hamilton Finlay has made a garden art from the equation, and brought the paradox to our attention through his writings. His investigations into the French Revolution, his elision of the Temple of Apollo with the Apollo missile, his celebration of the aircraft carrier, tank, machine-gun and classicism reveal connections many people find disturbing. They are meant to be disturbed, because as Onions has also discovered, in classical architecture public power and virtue were born together.

The beauty of dialectics I am not suggesting Michael Hopkins set out to make the equivalent of Le Corbusier's Parthenon or Ian Hamilton Finlay's revolutionary classicism. Anyone acquainted with his personality would find the idea perverse, because his manner

Noyon Cathedral 1170–1185

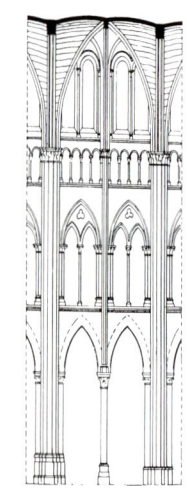

Laon Cathedral after 1170

Rheims Cathedral begun 1211

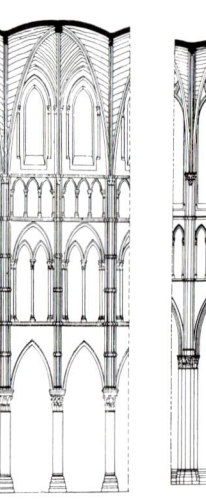

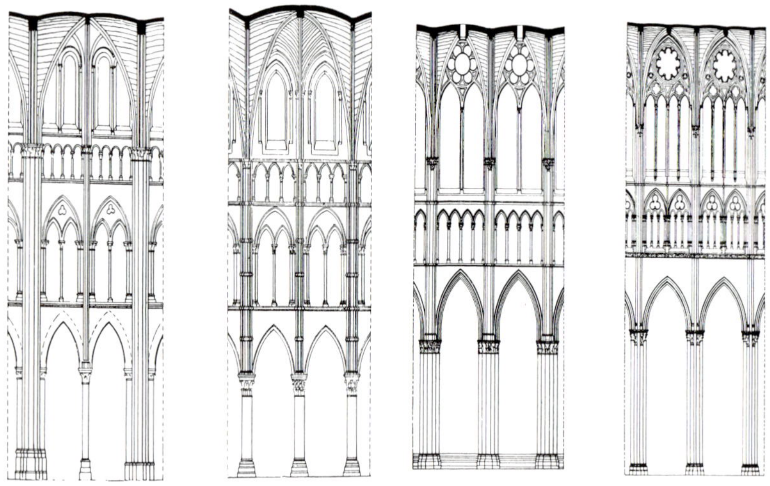

Amiens Cathedral begun 1220

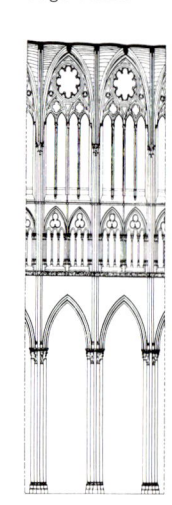

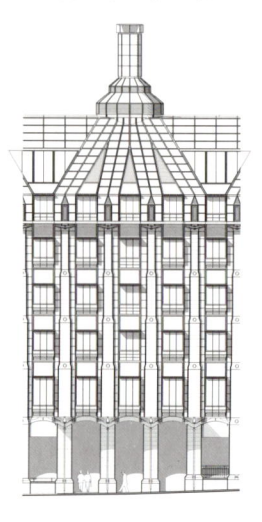

Above: Gothic nave dialectics. Early emphasis on the horizontality of the bay, with its sexpartite vault, evolves towards a greater resolution of horizontal and vertical forces as the wall is dematerialized. The dialectic may have been pushed by a desire for lighter construction and more glass, as well as the scholastic habit of thought. In any case, the Order was meant to be logically consistent and manifest its parts so that one could read the top ribs at the base – parts were all logically deducible at the end of the evolution: a perfected Order.
Left: elevation detail of New Parliamentary Building.
Right: New Parliamentary Building from courtyard. Both the wooden/steel canopy and the stone/concrete arch mix tensile and compressive forces in a hybrid manner, separating them out, manifesting each force and turning them into well-constructed details. The impersonality and perfection of the Orders is both Gothic and Miesian, but the hybridization is Post-Modern, a reminiscence of Viollet-le-Duc.

is affable and warm, not confrontational. Unlike Le Corbusier, he seeks to reconcile opposite periods of architecture, stitch together historical periods, listen attentively to the client and resolve conflicts in a gentle manner. Moreover, he does to classicism what the Gothic architect did: he lightens its mass, breaks it up with light and ultra-thin structural members. Indeed, if one follows the evolution of the interior of the Gothic cathedral, one finds parallels with the development of his bay systems, and it is worth elaborating the comparison because it shows Hopkins in another light.

Over time, Gothic development and Hopkins' work both tend towards increasing lightness and tautness of oppositional visual forces – as if the horizontal and vertical members were in some kind of expressive competition, each trying to claim priority until the wall surface dissolves away in a shimmering filigree of light. The evolution of the Gothic cathedral towards dematerialization has several explanations, some materialistic, some empirical and – the most tantalizing – that of Erwin Panofsky, cultural.

In his *Gothic Architecture and Scholasticism*, 1951, Panofsky argues the point that the cathedral evolved with the same habit of mind – scholasticism – that philosophers and logicians applied to thought. In writing their treatises, their *Summa Theologiae*, they sought to resolve the dictates of reason and faith by applying a systematic dialectical method. First this was the *Sic et Non* method of Abelard, then it became a tripartite argument: *videtur quod, sed contra, respondeo dicendum* – basically what we would call today: thesis, antithesis and synthesis. Since scripture, like architecture, was full of contradictions, none of which could be easily dismissed, the treatises had to be divided up into smaller and smaller propositions where resolution was possible. If a rib were necessary for centring and visual continuity, for instance, then it had to be resolved all the way up and down the elevation, through clerestorey, triforium, gallery and arcade. This was the High Game of architecture in the thirteenth century, and it made a cathedral progressively more articulate and consistent until it reached the end game at Amiens and Beauvais. Here all possible *sics* are set against all possible *nons*, horizontal and vertical forces achieve maximum resolution, the interior nave elevation is stretched taut, and the wall has dematerialized. In the accompanying illustration, I have extended the argument of Panofsky by summarising the forces in two dimensions: one can see the visual effects of the horizontal string course and triforium set against the vertical effects of the colonnettes and bay space.

Refinements of this dialectic were crucial to the architect. Just as entasis was important to the Greeks, just as thin tension members matter to the High-Tech architect, the Gothic architect sweated over such distinctions, and it is equally hard to see them – unless one makes a great effort. For instance, we know, from the thirteenth-century drawings of Villard de Honnecourt that the central triforium colonnette at Reims is slightly larger than those to either side. The drawing here does not reveal this, but the tiny vertical emphasis *is* there, and it leads to the next step, at Amiens, where the colonnette is joined up right through to the clerestory. The distinction, then, *did* matter to the architect, just as the resolution of faith and reason mattered to the scholastic.

It is arguable that while such refinements are only understood by an elite, they are intuited by everyone. We feel the rightness and balance of these contending forces even if we cannot see them; we feel the perfection of a system pushed to its limits even if we have no idea how it is done. *Le secret professionnel*.

Hopkins often reduces structural members to thin colonnettes that continue logically from top to bottom, and he also reduces the wall to the minimum required by structure and services. Turning to the interior of Portcullis House – one almost wants to call it 'the internal nave elevation' – one can find many of the same taut qualities as at Amiens. On the top four storeys the bay is repeated A,b – Void, solid – implying endless extension. But then, at the bottom, the system suddenly breaks apart into an entirely different game and something rather unexpected. In order to support the loads at only six points, so that they can be taken into the underground station deep below, and to provide a covered courtyard for the MPs, a new move is made in wood and steel. The resultant structure is hybrid, in fact doubly so, something that extends Hopkins' approach far from the Modernist approach of structural simplicity, and also from the Greek or Gothic consistency. We are in new territory, a page has turned.

The Mies van der Rohe of Post-Modernism The interesting truth of Michael Hopkins' position in British architecture is that, while stemming from both the Modernists and High-Tech architects, and their commitment to a simple, honest expression of structure and materials, he has nevertheless accepted a more complex position. Since his work at Lords Cricket Grounds and Bracken House, he has allowed himself quotes from the past and a reproduction of past details – arches, stone imposts and references to Guarino Guarini's Palazzo Carignano most conspicuously where that made sense. For instance, at Hopkins' reinvention of Bracken House near St. Paul's Cathedral a previous building on the site used a curved front adapted from Guarini, because this solution fit the context so well. Hopkins, granting this truth, saw no reason to come up with something entirely different just for the sake of being novel. Characteristically, he does not feel compelled to reinvent the wheel. This relaxed and inclusive attitude towards the past, and the present, context was a value fought for by Post-Modernists in the 1970s, but Hopkins carries it through with a difference. He, more than others, is committed to presenting the integrity of each constructional element, accentuating its 'thisness' to borrow a term from literary criticism ('this bronze collonnette', 'this hanger', 'this stone arch'). The elements thus have the quality that Mies and Carl Andre gave the brick, and Mies gave the I-beam. They become perfected Platonic forms shown in their abstract generality, not idiosyncratic variations from a norm as with most Post-Modernists.

Prince Charles was wrong: Hopkins is the acceptable face of *Post*-Modernists, because he has shown that the open-minded pluralism extended to urbanism, function and society could also be extended towards structural honesty. If a building 'demands' a mixed structure, as does the Portcullis House courtyard, then give up the simple-minded commitment, amounting to Modernist dogma, of a unitary system and mix wood, stone, steel and concrete. The wood relates the courtyard to the famous hammer-beam structure across the street, the late-Medieval Palace of Westminster, and shows how the twenty-first century can make an equivalent tour-de-force with a thin filigree of 'flitch' connections (here again is the High-Tech injunction 'make it thinner', but now applied to a cultural task). The struts of this roof and more particularly, the contrasts between struts, arches and tensile members of the interior wall recall the hybrid structures of the French rationalist Viollet-le-Duc.

Viollet, learning from the Gothic its lessons of dematrialization and experiment, put forward a functional and expressive attitude towards structure. His rationalism – and Hopkins follows him in this – was creative and non-dogmatic: structures could be taken from all possible sources and the best ones combined for their particular qualities. Thus for a Hall design for a large audience of 3,000 people, Viollet chooses a heavy stone structure for its insulation properties (as Hopkins was to do), a modified Gothic ribbed structure for decreasing the weight of the dome, and a cast-iron strut structure for its thinness, compressive and tensile strength and cantilevers. The *ad hoc* mixture of Romanesque, Gothic, Pantheon and nineteenth-century engineering, John Summerson condemns as 'somehow just not quite the thing'. For the Classicist *and* Modernist Summerson, adhocism is impure and ugly though, he admits, Viollet's approach was right, and his '*respect absolu pour le vrai*' commendable.

The paradox for Summerson is that Viollet had a great 'flair for style in everything – in women, in cats (for whom he had a profound respect), in objects of everyday use. And he could sense style in a locomotive or a gun'. Furthermore, Viollet-le-Duc was not a simplistic functionalist who believed utility automatically produced beauty. As he wrote: 'Everything has a positive reason, and if our instinct finds a line repellent, it is because the line is not really right, nor are we acting rationally in making it'. In others words: the designer should follow reason but let the instinct, or intuition, be its judge.

This seems an eminently sensible method, an undogmatic rationalism that will produce hybrid and complex designs more fitting than those allowed by the classical and modern canons of beauty restricted, as they are, to simple notions of consistency. Of course this raises the question 'how much simplicity or

Left: Viollet-le-Duc's design for a Concert Hall, from *Entretiens sur l'Architecture*. A hybrid of stone, iron, brick and a style that mixes Romanesque, Gothic, the Pantheon, and nineteenth-century engineering.

Above: Bracken House. The street elevation is both simple in form, from afar, and complex in detail, up close, responding to contrary pressures of urban propriety and constructional articulation.

complexity is right for a building? – something to be addressed again with every new project. Let me look at two Hopkins buildings I have recently revisited.

Bracken House, next to the City of London and viewing St Paul's Cathedral, is, because of its site and history, at the simple end of the spectrum when it comes to its overall figure, but it is very complex in its details. From afar it is sober in its classical massing, but up close it is riotous in its window struts and entrance canopy. This pleasing opposition means one is drawn in slowly to discover greater and greater surprise. The curved front is a sympathetic reinterpretation of the previous building, that is, Albert Richardson's reinterpretation of Guarino Guarini's reinterpretation of a Baroque Roman palazzo.

Post-Modernism, as Umberto Eco defined it, is how to deal with the 'already said' in an age of lost innocence, when one must utter the well-known words 'I love you'. His solution, to have a character say 'As Barbara Cartland would have said: I love you madly' is one method that allows the lovers to acknowledge that each other is aware that it is a cliché, but one that can be uttered as long as it is recognized by ironic quotation marks.

Bracken House is not just a series of quotes, as my example may imply, but a highly integral completion of a game started long ago. Richardson designed the pink *Financial Times* building in 1955, in an industrial Classical Baroque manner incorporating the slight curves of the eighteenth-century Palazzo Carignano by Guarini. Heavy, blocky, chunky it was, but massiveness broken by champhered corners and an even bay rhythm. Hopkins takes up the curves in a giant central atrium, and then swells them outwards as Guarini did – but mixes the grammar of cast iron, glass wall and bronze, the materials Richardson used. An interesting bay rhythm is created which is repeated on the large scale, but varied in curve and articulated up close.

The cornice line, heights and basic tripartition of the older decorations are kept, and – the point of Post-Modernism – transformed. The 'Order' of cast iron and bronze has a repetitive sobriety, again a *gravitas* that is almost heroic. But, in the end because of its modest role as an office building, it is understated.

Above: Dynamic Earth seen from Holyrood Road with Salisbury Crags and Arthur's Seat as a backdrop (top), and (bottom) mock Gothic versus tensile sails. Double coding framing the crags. Dissonant angles; violent contrasts, classicism and anti-classicism in juxtaposition.

If Hopkins were given a significant public building with a monumental and expressive role, he could produce today's equivalent of the Doric or Gothic Order, that is an expressive system related in its constructional parts.

As the Dynamic Earth Pavilion shows, constructed for the Millennium in Edinburgh, the result might mix genres and structural types. This building has an appropriate image that celebrates the content of the exhibitions on the inside, the explosive earth. As well as looking like a welcoming tent, it has other overtones that lift the spirits that strike off interesting associations. The spikes and segmental forms resemble trilobites and other ancient creatures simulated within the building and, if the new Scottish Parliament is finally built directly opposite, the white sails and upturned boat hull of Hopkins will complement the nautical imagery of Enric Miralles' ship of state.

Architecturally, there is one obvious precedent for Hopkins' solution. The sails of the tent fly over a massive ground plane, the way the shells of the Sydney Opera House hover on a raised landform. The contrasts are also heightened here in a particularly post-modern way. High-Tech struts are played against heavy, ancient forms to accentuate the qualities of each. On the front, a circular entrance court, a *cour d'honneur* lacking its statue of Louis XIV, the drop-off point in contemporary bus-speak, leads to, and becomes, a Greek amphitheatre, lacking only its stage. This theatre, with its very simple rhythmical steps, is a veritable Epidaurus in carefully sculpted stone. Its severe beauty has a *gravitas* that is almost heroic; it certainly stands up to the other great landmarks in this proverbial Athens of the North. Around the back, the masonry platform melds with the previous structure on the site, the old Scottish and Newcastle Brewery, and manages to turn its mock Gothic turrets and crenelations to something positive: a terrace framing the vista of the great crags.

No other city in the world has a great geological event right in its belly and, at least here, is a suitable celebration of it. Indeed, one can say that Hopkins does for the crags what the Sydney Opera House does for the harbour of that city; celebrate nature through spectacular contrast. The image of delicate white sails set against huge black rocks is one that people will recall when they think about Dynamic Earth, and in that sense the building is likely to become another icon for the city. Edinburgh already has several temples contrasting with a heroic landscape, the classical opposition that the Greeks turned into a striking formula: man against nature, or the tragic opposition between human culture and an indifferent cosmos. With Hopkins the contrasts are not austere, but playful – indeed very much like sailboats tossing around on a windy day. But they prove again an old point which many people are surprised is true: if you have a very beautiful landscape then a good contrasting building can make it even better.

Over the last fifteen years, Michael Hopkins has made a virtue of working both with and against the sites he has been given. It is this double-coding, done with understatement and fine detailing, that makes him the 'Mies van der Rohe of Post-Modernism'. His Glyndebourne Opera House additions, his extension at Lord's Cricket Ground, his transformation of Bracken House next to St Paul's, all fit into the past fabric, yet make subtle oppositions to it. Here in Edinburgh his double-coding is more extreme, the contrasts more tense. Fully glazed walls and fins smash right into the ground; cables, masts and white fabric curves are juxtaposed with the masonry crenelations. While the Edinburgh classicism of circle, axis, symmetry and monumentality is carried forward, these ancient moves are countered with contemporary ones: a slash of light follows giant ribs down to an anti-classical support. Most dissonant are the masts and entrance spikes that are rammed into the oh-so-tasteful surface, Punk jewellery meant to draw blood.

That Hopkins has thought about this, and turned it into a theme, there can be no doubt. In comments recorded for the opening of the building, he identifies urban contrast as a defining quality of the city: 'Edinburgh's much-admired urban character comes from a balance between nature and artifice…' His artifice strikes just the right note of *gravitas* and celebration, civic propriety and cosmic pleasure. Along his avenue of expressive structural inquiry, he sets a challenge of new Orders for our time and in this respect becomes the standard, the architect to surpass.

Michael Hopkins and Partners

Directors

- **Michael Hopkins**
  CBE, RA, AADipl, RIBA
  Born 1935
  Founded Practice in 1976
- **Patricia Hopkins** AADipl
  Born 1942
  Co-founded Practice in 1976
- **William Taylor**
  MA DipArch RIBA
  Born 1957
  Joined Practice in 1982
  Partner in 1987
- **David Selby** BA(Hons) DipArch RIBA
  Born 1954
  Joined Practice in 1984
  Director 1999
- **James Greaves**
  BA(Hons) DipArch RIBA
  Born 1957
  Joined Practice in 1987
  Director 1999
- **Andrew Barnett**
  MA DipArch RIBA
  Born 1960
  Joined Practice in 1984
  Director 1999
- **Pamela Bate** MA BA(Hons) Arch
  Born 1955
  Joined Practice in 1989
  Director 1999

Financial Director 1999
Henry Buxton ACA

Project Directors 1999
Ernest Fasayna
BA(Hons)DipArch RIBA
Patrick Nee BSc(Hons)
BArch RIBA
Simon Fraser BArch(Hons) MArch RIBA
Michael Taylor BA(Hons) DipArch RIBA
Chris Bannister BA(Hons) BArch RIBA
Annabel Hollick BSc(Hons)MA(RCA)RIBA
Edward Williams MA DipArch RIBA
Jonathan Knight BA(Hons) DipArch(Cantab) RIBA
Arif Mehmood BA(Hons) DipArch MScArch RIBA

Past Directors
Peter Romaniuk BSc BArch RIBA
1980–2000
John Pringle AADipl RIBA
1979–1997
Ian Sharratt MA (RCA)
1976–1997

Past Associates
Bill Dunster MA (Hons) RIBA 1985–1999
Stephen Macbean BSc (Hons) DipArch RIBA
1990–1997
Brendan Phelan BA (Hons) BArch RIBA 1989–2000
Robin Snell MA DipArch RIBA1983–1993

Michael Hopkins and Partners
27 Broadley Terrace
London NW1 6LG
Tel: +44 (0)20 7724 1751
Fax: +44 (0)20 7723 0932
Email: mail@hopkins.co.uk
www.hopkins.co.uk

Chronology: 1989–2000

1989–1994
Glyndebourne Opera House
Lewes, East Sussex

1989–2000
New Parliamentary Building
Westminster, London

1990–1999
Dynamic Earth
Holyrood Road, Edinburgh

1990–1999
Westminster Underground Station
Westminster, London

1992–1995
Inland Revenue Centre
Castle Meadow, Nottingham

1993–1995
Queen's Building, Emmanuel College
Cambridge

1993–1996
Jewish Care
Finchley, London

1994–1995
Buckingham Palace Ticket Office
Green Park, London

1994–1996
Fleet Infants School
Music and Drama Room
Hampshire

1994–2000
Sheltered Housing, Charterhouse, London

1994–
Hampshire County Cricket Club
Southampton, Hampshire

1994–
Manchester City Art Gallery
Manchester

1995–2000
Wildscreen at Bristol
Harbourside, Bristol

1995–2000
The Pilkington Laboratories, Sherborne School
Sherborne, Dorset

1995–
Norwich Cathedral Education and Visitors Centre
Norwich, Norfolk

1995–
Royal Academy of Arts, Courtyard
Piccadilly, London

1995–
Royal Academy of Arts, 6 Burlington Gardens
Piccadilly, London

1996–1999
Jubilee Campus, University of Nottingham
Nottingham

1996–1999
Saga Group Headquarters
Folkestone, Kent

1996–
DSS Offices
Newcastle

1996–
Haberdashers' Hall
City of London

1996–
Norfolk and Norwich Millennium Project
Norwich, Norfolk

1996–
Wigmore Hall Feasibility Study
Westminster, London

1997–
Goodwood Racecourse
Goodwood, Sussex

1998–
The Cakehouse
St James' Park, London

1998–
University College Suffolk
Ipswich

1999–1999
King Fahad National Library
Riyadh, Saudi Arabia

1999–
Evelina Children's Hospital
Westminster, London

1999–
Hosier Lane
City of London

1999–
The Wellcome Trust
Euston Road, London

2000–
Glyndebourne Rehearsal Stage
Lewes, East Sussex

2000–
National College for School Leadership, University of Nottingham
Nottingham

2000–
Northgate Development
Chester, Cheshire

2000–
StadsFeestzaal Restoration
Antwerp

2000–
Two Millharbour, Millennium Quarter for Fidelity Investments
Docklands, London

Credits: Buildings

Glyndebourne Opera House
Glyndebourne, Lewes, East Sussex
1989–1994
Client: Glyndebourne Productions Ltd
MHP Directors: Michael Hopkins, Patricia Hopkins,
MHP Associates: Andrew Barnett, Pamela Bate, Robin Snell
MHP Design team: Edward Williams, Arif Mehmood, Justin Bere, Tommasomo del Buono, Peter Cartwright, Nigel Curry, Jim Dunster, Alison Fisher, Loretta Gentilini, Julie Hamilton, Lucy Lavers, Margaret Mitchell, Emma Nsugbe, Kevin O'Sullivan, Martin Pease, Claire Tarbard, Mark Turkel, Andrew Wells
Engineer: Ove Arup and Partners
Main contractor: Bovis Construction
Quantity surveyor: Gardiner & Theobald
● Awards: 1994 British Construction Industry, 1994 Concrete Society, 1994 RFAC, 1994 RIBA, 1994 Supreme Brick, 1995 Carpenters, 1995 Civic Trust, 1995 Financial Times, 1996 USITT

Inland Revenue Centre
Castle Meadow, Nottingham
1992–1995
Client: Inland Revenue
MHP Directors: Michael Hopkins, William Taylor, Ian Sharratt
MHP Associates: Pamela Bate, Peter Romaniuk, Brendan Phelan, Bill Dunster, Stephen Macbean
MHP Design team: Ernest Fasanya, Simon Fraser, Jonathan Knight, Lynn Bacher, Nathan Barr, Russell Baylis, Jason Cooper, Max Connop, Paul Cutler, Alison Fisher, Lydia Haack, Alan James, Amanda Lanchbery, Catherine Martin, Carol Painter, Brian Reynolds, Guni Suri, Claire Tarbard, Charles Walker
Engineer: Ove Arup and Partners
Main contractor: Laing Management Ltd
Quantity surveyor: Turner and Townsend
● Awards: 1995 Brick Association, 1995 Textile Architecture, 1996 Concrete, 1996 Green Building, 1997 Civic Trust, 1999 IOC/IAKS

Queen's Building, Emmanuel College
Cambridge
1993–1995
Client: Emmanuel College
MHP Directors: Michael Hopkins, Patricia Hopkins,
MHP Senior Associate: James Greaves
MHP Design team: Michael Taylor, Buddy Haward, Mark Turkel, Alex Mowatte, Alison Fisher
Engineer: Buro Happold
Main contractor: Sir Robert McAlpine
Quantity surveyor: Davis Langdon & Everest
● Awards: 1996 RFAC, 1996 RIBA, 1996 RIBA Education, 1997 Carpenters, 1997 Natural Stone

Buckingham Palace Ticket Office
Green Park, London, SW1
1994–1995
Client: Royal Collection Enterprises
MHP Directors: Michael Hopkins, William Taylor
MHP Design team: Jonathan Knight, Annabel Judd, Susan Cox, Alison Fisher, Andrew Jordan, Jenny Stevens
Structural engineer: Ove Arup and Partners
Main contractor: Holloway White Allom
Construction manager: Laing Management Ltd

Jewish Care
Colney Hatch Lane, Finchley, London, N11
1993–1996
Client: Community Trading Ltd
MHP Directors: Michael Hopkins, Patricia Hopkins
MHP Associates: Andrew Barnett, Pamela Bate
MHP Design team: Edward Williams, Arif Mehmood, Jim Dunster, Alison Fisher, Steve Harris, Ken Hood, Abigail Hopkins, Lucy Lavers, Yale Melameade, Ian Milne, Andy Wells, Jane Willoughby
Structural engineer: Jampel Davison & Bell
Main contractor: Try Build Ltd
Quantity surveyor: Basil Cohen

Saga Group Headquarters
Sandgate, Folkestone, Kent
1996–1999
Client: Saga Group Ltd
MHP Directors: Michael Hopkins, William Taylor, Ian Sharratt
MHP Senior Associate: Pamela Bate, Brendan Phelan
MHP Project director: Michael Taylor
MHP Design team: Buddy Haward, Abigail Hopkins, Stephen Jones, Andrew Jordan, Annabel Judd, Sophy Twohig, Paul Cutler, Simon French, Matthew Driscoll, Alan Jones, Lydia Haack, Taro Tsuruta, Jon Buck, Amanda Lanchbery, Martyn Corner, Alison Fisher, Chris Gray
Engineer: Ove Arup and Partners
Main contractor: Schal
Project manager: Davis Langdon Management
Quantity surveyor: Davis Langdon & Everest

Dynamic Earth
Holyrood Road, Edinburgh
1990–1999
Client: The Dynamic Earth Charitable Trust
MHP Directors: Michael Hopkins, Patricia Hopkins, James Greaves, Ian Sharratt
MHP Project director: Annabel Hollick
MHP Design team: Gerard Page, Ben Cousins, Daniel Fugenschuh, Sarah Thomson, Andrew Morrison, Meriel Blackburn, Martyn Corner, Alison Fisher, Andrew Stanway, Jane Willoughby, Andrew Young
Engineer: Ove Arup and Partners
Main contractor: Laing Management (Scotland) Ltd
Project manager: Leel, Kier Project Management
Quantity surveyor: Gardiner & Theobald
● Awards: 2000 Civic Trust

Jubilee Campus, University of Nottingham
University Park, Nottingham
1996–1999
Client: University of Nottingham
MHP Directors: Michael Hopkins, William Taylor, Pamela Bate
MHP Associate: Bill Dunster
MHP Project director: Simon Fraser
MHP Design team: Jan Mackie, Matthew Hoad, Martyn Corner, Alison Fisher, Steve Harris, Toki Hoshino, Steve Mason, Uli Moeller, Gina Raimi, Rachel Sayers, Jenny Stevens, Eric Svenkerud, Alex Sykes, Alexis Trumpf
Engineer: Ove Arup and Partners
Main contractor: Bovis Construction Ltd
Project manager: MACE
Quantity surveyor: Gardiner & Theobald
● Awards: 2000 British Construction Industry, 2000 HotDip Galvanising, 2000 Lord Mayor's Special

The Pilkington Laboratories, Sherborne School
Acreman Street, Sherborne, Dorset
1995–2000
Client: Sherborne School
MHP Directors: Michael

Hopkins, Patricia Hopkins, James Greaves
MHP Design team: Andrew Morrison, Jane Greaves, Sarah Thomson, Alison Fisher, Andrew Stanway, Therese Wendland
Engineer: Anthony Ward Partnership
Main contractor: Woodpecker Properties Ltd
Quantity surveyor: Davis Langdon & Everest

Wildscreen at Bristol
Harbourside, Bristol
1995–2000
Client: At Bristol Ltd
MHP Directors: Michael Hopkins, Patricia Hopkins, Andrew Barnett, James Greaves
MHP Project director: Edward Williams
MHP Design team: Julie Gaulter, Tom Holdom, Martyn Corner, Gary Clark, Natasha Cox, Alison Fisher, Claire Fleetwood, Caroline Hislop, Martin Knight, Henry Kong, Aikiri Paing, Jenny Stevens, Tim Whiteley
Engineer: Buro Happold
Main contractor: Bovis Construction Ltd
Project manager: Symonds
Quantity surveyor: Davis Langdon & Everest

Sheltered Housing Charterhouse
Charterhouse Square, London, EC1
1994–2000
Client: The Governors of Suttons Hospital in Charterhouse
MHP Directors: Michael Hopkins, Patricia Hopkins, James Greaves
MHP Associates: Brendan Phelan, Arif Mehmood
MHP Design team: Buddy Haward, Martyn Corner, Alison Fisher, Chris Gray, Simon French, Sarah Thomson, Sophy Twohig
Engineers: Buro Happold
Main contractor: Eve Construction
Quantity surveyor: David Langdon & Everest

Westminster Underground Station
Bridge Street, Westminster, London, SW1
1990–1999
Client: London Underground Ltd
MHP Directors: Michael Hopkins, John Pringle, David Selby
MHP Project directors: Patrick Nee, Arif Mehmood
MHP Design team: Annabel Hollick, Margaret Leong, Emma Adams, Rebecca Chipchase, Georgina Hall, Gail Halvorsen, Neils Jonkhans, Ian Milne, Gina Raimi, Amir Sanei, Alexandra Small, Sabrina Suma, Taro Tsuruta, Geoff Whittaker, Hannah Wooler
Engineer: G Maunsell & Partners
Main contractor: Balfour Beatty: Amec
Quantity surveyor: Gardiner & Theobald
● Awards: 2000 RFAC Trust Millennium Building of the Year, 2000 Civic Trust, 2000 British Construction Industry

New Parliamentary Building
Victoria Embankment, Westminster, London, SW1
1989–2000
Client: Parliamentary Works Directorate
MHP Directors: Michael Hopkins, Patricia Hopkins, John Pringle, David Selby, Pamela Bate, Peter Romaniuk
MHP Associates: Patrick Nee, Bill Dunster, Brendan Phelan, Stephen Macbean, Robin Snell
MHP Design team: Chris Bannister, Simon Fraser, Michael Taylor, Gary Collins, Neil Eaton, Amir Sanei, Steve Harris, Angus Waddington, Alexandra Small, Emma Adams, Susie Bach, Toby Birtwistle, Robert Bishop, Rebecca Chipchase, Martyn Corner, Paul Cutler, Alison Fisher, Julian Gitsham, Mark Greene, Gail Halvorsen, Buddy Haward, Andrew Jordan, Margaret Leong, Phillip Metternich-Sandor, Vanitie Mossman, Toki Nakae, Anna Radcliffe, Gina Raimi, Mark Robinson, Jenny Stevens, Tom Stevens, Alex Sykes, Taro Tsuruta, Peter Ungar, Tony White, Hannah Wooler, Andrew Young
Engineer: Ove Arup and Partners
Construction manager: Laing Management Ltd
Project manager: Schal
Quantity surveyor: Gardiner & Theobald
● Awards: 2001 Institute of Structural Engineers David Alsop Award

Hampshire County Cricket Club
Northlands Road, Eastleigh, Southampton, Hampshire
1994–
Client: Hampshire County Cricket Club
MHP Directors: Michael Hopkins, William Taylor, Peter Romaniuk
MHP Project director: Ernest Fasanya
MHP Design team: Tim Sloan, Rud Sawers, Paul Vick, Spencer Guy, Jan Mackie, Stefanie Arnold, Kate Ashurst, Stuart Blower, Susan Cox, Alison Fisher, Stephen Fletcher, David Fox, Matthew Hoad, Andrew Jordan, Tobias Lossing, Stephen Macbean, Kristi Roger, Arifa Salim, Jenny Stevens
Engineer: Buro Happold
Main contractor: P Trant Ltd
Quantity surveyor: Denley King & Partners

Manchester City Art Gallery
Mosley/Princess Street, Manchester
1994–
Client: Manchester City Council
MHP Directors: Michael Hopkins, Patricia Hopkins, William Taylor, David Selby
MHP Project directors: Jonathan Knight,

Credits: Projects

Arif Mehmood
MHP Design team:
Robert Gregory, Tim Sloan, Alexandra Small, Kate Ashurst, Shahid Chaudry, Martyn Corner, Alison Fisher, Alex Franz, Spencer Guy, Caroline Hislop, Lydia Kan, Stephen Luxford, David Merllie, Gina Raimi, Paul Segers, Gabby Shawcross, Jenny Stevens, Sonja Stoffels, Sophie Ungerer, Andrew Wood
Engineer:
Ove Arup and Partners
Main contractor:
Bovis Construction
Quantity surveyor:
Gardiner & Theobald

Royal Academy of Arts, Courtyard
Piccadilly, London, W1
1996–
Client: Royal Academy of Arts
MHP Directors: Michael Hopkins, Patricia Hopkins, David Selby
MHP Project directors:
Arif Mehmood,
Michael Taylor
MHP Design team:
Catherine Outram, Neil Eaton, Carsten Kling, David Marks, Hannah Wooler
Engineer: Harris and Sutherland
Main contractor:
Poultney Gallagher
Mechanical engineer:
Peter Deer and Associates
Electrical engineer: Acton Design Partnership
Quantity surveyor: Davis Langdon & Everest

Royal Academy of Arts, 6 Burlington Gardens
Piccadilly, London, W1
1995–
Client: Royal Academy of Arts
MHP Directors: Michael Hopkins, Patricia Hopkins, David Selby
MHP Project directors:
Arif Mehmood,
Michael Taylor
MHP Design team:
Margaret Leong, Catherine Outram, Jamie Brown, Martyn Corner, Alison Fisher, Chris Gray, Andrew Jordan, Carsten Kling, Maria Kramer, James O'Leary, David Marks, Hannah Wooler
Engineer: Alan Baxter Associates
Quantity surveyor:
Northcroft

Norwich Cathedral Education and Visitors Centre
12 The Close, Norwich, Norfolk
1995–
Client: Norwich Cathedral
MHP Directors: Michael Hopkins, Andrew Barnett
MHP Design team: Bruce Fisher, Martyn Corner, Stephen Jones, Henry Kong, Steve Mason, Tim Whiteley
Engineer: Buro Happold
Quantity surveyor:
Davis Langdon & Everest

Norfolk and Norwich Millennium Project
1 Theatre Street, Norwich, Norfolk
1996–
Client: Norfolk and Norwich Millennium Co. Ltd
MHP Directors: Michael Hopkins, William Taylor, David Selby
MHP Project director:
Michael Taylor
MHP Design team:
Abigail Hopkins, Gary Clark, Laura Carrara-Cagni, Sophy Twohig, Will Kavanagh, Jonathan Knight, Bruce Fisher, Stuart Blower, Barbara Campbell-Lange, Martyn Corner, Dan Dorell, Alison Fisher, Claire Fleetwood, Chris Gray, Spencer Guy, Mark Hatter, Martin Kaefer, Martin Knight, Ken McAndrew, Arifa Salim, Jenny Stevens, Alexis Trumpf, John Vine
Engineer: Whitby Bird & Partners
Main contractors:
Oscar Faber Group Ltd, R G Carter Ltd
Quantity surveyor:
Turner and Townsend

Haberdashers' Hall
West Smithfield, City of London, EC1
1996–
Client: The Haberdashers' Company
MHP Directors: Michael Hopkins, Patricia Hopkins, James Greaves
MHP Design team:
Amir Sanei, Tony White, Andrew Morrison, Sarah Thomson, Jack Hosea, Meriel Blackburn, Chris Gray, Andrew Stanway, Therese Wendland
Engineer:
Ove Arup and Partners
Main contractor:
Holloway White Allom
Quantity surveyor:
Robinson Low Francis

Goodwood Racecourse
Goodwood, Chichester, West Sussex
1997–
Client: Goodwood Racecourse Ltd
MHP Directors: Michael Hopkins, James Greaves
MHP Project director:
Edward Williams
MHP Design team: John Ridgett, James Reader, Caroline Hislop, Ashu Chathley, Martyn Corner, Chris Gray, Andrew Stanway, Therese Wendland
Engineer:
Ove Arup and Partners
Main contractor: John Mowlem & Company plc
Quantity surveyor:
Gardiner & Theobald

The Cakehouse
St James' Park, London, SW1
1998–
Client: Hudson Rowe Parks Ltd/The Royal Parks
MHP Directors: Michael Hopkins, Andrew Barnett, Pamela Bate
MHP Design team:
Gary Clark, Stephen Jones, Wilson Au-Yeung, Martyn Corner, Andy Shaw, Tim Whiteley
Engineer:
Ove Arup and Partners
Quantity surveyor:
Gardiner & Theobald

DSS Offices
Newcastle
1996
Client: AMEC Capital Projects Ltd – Construction Division
MHP Directors: Michael Hopkins, William Taylor, Peter Romanuik, Pamela Bate
MHP Design Team:
Peter Mouncey, David Fox, Andrew Harrison, Ken Hood, Stephen Macbean, Rud Sawers, Matt Williams, Angus Waddington, Craig Babe, Alex Gino, Spencer Guy, Rory Campbell-Lange, Jon Buck, Stephen Luxford, Rachel Carsley, Inderjit Kaur, Peter Richardson, Jenny Stevens, Jacqui Kytle, Melanie Ehlers, Nicole Weiner.
Cartwright Pickard Architects:
Peter Cartwright, James Pickard, Steve Durn, Steve Coyle, Bridan Reynolds, Yasmeen Shami, Ian Wright
Structural engineers:
Fairhurst & Partners, Mouchal International Consultants
M&E Services engineer:
Hoare Lee & Partners
Quantity surveyors:
Bucknall Austin, Summers & Partners

King Fahad National Library
Riyadh, Saudi Arabia
1999
MHP Directors: Michael Hopkins, William Taylor
MHP Project director:
Chris Bannister
MHP Design team: Kate Ashurst, Ashu Chathley, Martyn Corner, Ben Cousins, Niels Jonkhans, Stephen Luxford, Steve Mason, Jenny Stevens, Tom Stevens, Taro Tsuruta
Consultant engineers:
Buro Happold

The Wellcome Trust
210 Euston Road, London, NW1

1999–
Client: The Wellcome Trust
MHP Directors: Michael Hopkins, William Taylor, Andrew Barnett, Pamela Bate
MHP Project directors: Annabel Hollick, Michael Taylor, Simon Fraser
MHP Design team: Wilson Au-Yeung, Martyn Corner, Julie Gaulter, Alex Gino, Chris Gray, Steve Harris, Caroline Hislop, Tom Holdom, Henry Kong, Nils Langer, Aurelie Lethu, Steve Mason, Emma Nsugbe, Aikari Paing, Andy Shaw, Alex Sykes, Angus Waddington, Tim Whiteley
Structural engineer: WSP Consulting engineer
Construction/Project manager: MACE
Services engineer: Cundall Johnston & Partners
Quantity surveyor: Turner and Townsend

Evelina Children's Hospital
Lambeth Palace Road, Westminster, London, SE1
1999–
Client: Guy's and St Thomas' Hospital NHS Trust
MHP Directors: Michael Hopkins, William Taylor, Andrew Barnett, Pamela Bate, Peter Romaniuk
MHP Project director: Patrick Nee
MHP Design team: Andrew Harrison, Ken Hood, Doron Meinhard, Gary Collins, Matt Williams, Alexandra Small, Namit Agarwal, Sam Aldred, Jeannine Baker, Elizabeth Bartlett, Rory Campbell-Lange, Martyn Corner, Simon Goode, Chris Gray, Phu Hoang, Aidan Hoggard, Steve Mason, Jenny Stevens, Tom Stevens, Sonja Stoffels
Engineer: Buro Happold
Main contractor:
Quantity surveyor: Davis Langdon & Everest

National College of School Leadership, University of Nottingham
University Park, Nottingham
2000–
Client: University of Nottingham
MHP Directors: Michael Hopkins, William Taylor
MHP Project director: Simon Fraser
MHP Design team: Jan Mackie, Matthew Hoad, Andrew Ardill, Martyn Corner, Sophie Histon, Stephen Luxford, Steve Mason, Arifa Salim, Pascale Schulte
Engineer: Ove Arup and Partners
Main contractor: Laing Management Ltd
Quantity surveyor: Gardiner & Theobald

University College Suffolk
Ipswich, Suffolk
1998–
Client: Suffolk College
MHP Directors: Michael Hopkins, David Selby
MHP Design team: Neils Jonkhans, Catherine Outram, Jenny Stevens, Taro Tsuruta, Martyn Corner
Engineer: Harris and Sutherland
Quantity surveyor: Davis, Langdon & Everest

Select bibliography

General
- *Architectural Review*, 'Hopkins' Rules', Colin Davies, May 1984
- *Country Life*, 'Beyond High-tech', Ken Powell, 17.11.1988
- *The Independent*, 'The Acceptable Face of Modernism', Roger Berthoud, 8.11.1989
- *British Architecture Today*, 'Six Protagonists', British Pavilion; 5th Int. Biennale of Arch. Venice 1991
- *The Times*, 'New designs on National Treasures', Marcus Binney, 4.3.1992
- *RSA Journal*, 'Technology Comes to Town – MH', 1.5.1992
- *Hopkins: The Work of Michael Hopkins and Partners*, Colin Davies, Phaidon Press, 1993
- *The Independent*, 'Architects honour husband and wife team', Jonathan Glancey, 17.2.1994
- *The Times*, 'Husband and wife win architecture medal', 17.2.1994
- *World Architecture no 30*, 'An English Eccentric in Power', Martin Pawley, 1.7.1994
- *Architects' Journal*, 'New Year's Honours', 12.1.1995
- *The Telegraph*, 'Architect's practical preaching', Rowan Moore, 15.2.1995
- *Country Life*, 'The Country Life Interview – Patty Hopkins',13.3.1997
- *Architectural Review Supplement*, 'Buro Happold: An appreciation', Susan Dawson, November 1999

Glyndebourne Opera House
- Thames and Hudson, *Glyndebourne – Building a Vision*, Marcus Binney & Rosy Runciman, 1994
- *Architecture Today*, 'Arcadian Overtures', Mark Swenarton, 1.5.1994
- *Architectural Review*, 'Glyndebourne', Colin Davies, June 1994
- *Architects' Journal*, 'A Day in the Life of Glyndebourne', Kenneth Powell, 13.10.1994
- *Building*, 'New musical hall express', Denise Chevin, 10.12.1999

Inland Revenue Centre
- *Architects' Journal*, 'Prefabricating the superstructure', Barrie Evans, 16.6.1993
- *Architecture Today no 56*, 'Building Tax Haven: MHP at Nottingham', 1.3.1995
- *Arups Journal*,

'New Inland Revenue Centre' John Berry, John Thornton, 1.4.1995
- *Architectural Review*, 'Raising the Revenue', Peter Davey, May 1995
- *Architectural Review*, 'Building the Revenue', Alistair Gardner, May 1995

Queen's Building, Emmanuel College
- *Building Design*, 'Perfectly Mannered', Clare Melhuish, 26.5.1995
- *Architects' Journal*, 'A House in the Country – Reinventing Structural Stone in Cambridge', Marcus Field, 1.6.1995
- *Architectural Review*, 'Cambridge Credo', Colin Davies, February 1996

Buckingham Palace Ticket Office
- *Architects' Journal*, 'Summer themes welcome visitors to the Palace', Deborah Singmaster, 8.9.1994
- *Architectural Review*, 'Nautical but Nice', Penny McGuire, December 1994

Saga Group Headquarters
- *Architects' Journal*, 'Seaside Saga: Hopkins' double bill', Isabel Allen, 8.7.1999
- *RIBA Journal*, 'A Family Affair', Jeremy Melvin, 1.12.1999

Dynamic Earth
- *Architecture Today*, 'Holyrood Renaissance', Brian Edwards, 1.2.2000
- *Architectural Review*, 'Under Arthur's Seat', April 2000
- *Architectural Design*, 'The Dynamic, Castrophic, Melodramatic, Noisy, Beautiful (and Kitsch) Earth', Charles Jencks, 22.5.2000

Jubilee Campus, University of Nottingham
- *Architectural Review*, 'Campus Arcadia', February 2000
- *Architecture Today EcoTech Supplement*, 'Green Agenda: Hopkins & Partners at Nottingham', 1.3.2000

Wildscreen at Bristol
- *Architectural Review*, 'Wildscreen At Bristol', April 2000
- *Bristol's Twentieth-Century Buildings*, 'Millennium Landmarks', Tony Aldous, 2000
- *Architects' Journal*, 'Call of the Wild', Jeremy Melvin, 13.11.2000

Westminster Underground Station
- *Architects' Journal*, 'Going Underground', Martin Pawley, 3.2.2000
- *Architectural Review*, 'Underneath the Politics', Penny Mcguire, June 2000
- *The Jubilee Line Extension*, 'Westminster Station', Kenneth Powell, October 2000

New Parliamentary Building
- *ECO*, 'Mother Nature', 1.6.1997
- *Architecture Today*, 'Heart of Oak: Timber Engineering at Portcullis House', Mark Swenarton, 1.6.1999
- *The Times*, 'A Sister for the Mother of all Parliaments' Marcus Binney, 21.3.2000
- *Building Design*, 'Happy Campus', Katherine Bateson, 9.6.2000
- *The Sunday Times*, 'The House Next Door', Hugh Pearman, 6.8.2000
- *The Evening Standard*, 'A Triumph at Westminster', Simon Jenkins, 19.10.2000
- *The Structural Engineer*, 'The New Parliamentary Building: Portcullis House', John Thornton et al, 19.9.2000
- *Architectural Review*, 'Commons Sense', Peter Davey, February 2001

Page numbers in italic refer to illustrations

Aachen 224
Aalto, Alvar
  Rautatalo building, Helsinki 163
Alexander, Christopher 222
Amiens Cathedral *226*, 227
Andre, Carl 228
Aquinas, Thomas 224
Architectural Association (AA) 11, 168, 224
art galleries
  Manchester City Art Gallery 174, *175–7*
  Royal Academy of Arts, London 178, *179–81*
Arts Council 108
Athens 226
atria
  Hampshire County Cricket Club 169
  Jubilee Campus, University of Nottingham 90, 92, *102*, *105*
  National College of School Leadership 214, *217*
  Norfolk and Norwich Millennium Project 186
  Royal Academy of Arts 178
  Saga Group Headquarters 74, *78*
  see also courtyards
auditoria
  Emmanuel College, Cambridge 52, *54*, *57–8*
  Glyndebourne Opera House, 22–4, *23*, *28*, *35*
  Jubilee Campus, University of Nottingham 92, *96*, *98*
  National College of School Leadership 214
  University College Suffolk 218
Banham, Peter Reyner 11, 225
Barnett, Andrew 19, 168
Barry, Sir Charles
  Athenaeum, Manchester 174, *175*
  Palace of Westminster, London 156, 161
  Royal Manchester Institution 174, *175*, *177*
Bate, Pamela 19, 168
bay rhythm *224–6*, 225–6, 227
BBC 194
  Natural History Unit 114
Beauvais Cathedral 227
Bedfont Lakes *12*, 13, 218
Bracken House, London 8, *18*, 19, 159, 169, *225*, 225, 228, *229*, 230, 231
brickwork 13, 16–19
  Charterhouse 124
  Glyndebourne Opera House 24, *29–31*
  Inland Revenue Centre 36, 38, *44*, 167
  Jewish Care 66
  Norfolk and Norwich Millennium Project 186
Bristol 114
British Museum, London 169
Brown, Neave 11
Buckingham Palace Ticket Office, London 11, 60, *61–5*, 194

Index

The Cakehouse, St James'
    Park, London 198,
    199–201
Cambridge 168
Cambridge University 52,
    53–9
Campbell, Colin 167
Canary Wharf, London *9*
cathedrals *226*, 227
Charles, Prince of Wales
    225, 228
Charterhouse, London 9,
    14, 124, *125–9*
chimneys
    New Parliamentary
        Building 138, *143*, *146–9*
    Pilkington Laboratories
        108, *109*
Choisy, Auguste 222
Christie, George 167
cinema, Wildscreen 114,
    116, *119–21*
classicism 13, 227
cloisters
    Charterhouse 124, *125*,
        127
    Haberdashers' Hall 190,
        191
    Jewish Care *69*
    New Parliamentary
        Building 136
Colquhoun, Alan 11, 224
courtyards
    Charterhouse 124
    Haberdashers' Hall 190,
        191
    Jewish Care 66, *70*
    Jubilee Campus,
        University of Nottingham
        100
    New Parliamentary
        Building 136, *150–5*,
        163, 166

see also atria
David Mellor Cutlery
    Factory, Hathersage 8, *11*,
    158
David Mellor Offices and
    Showroom 8, *10*
de Mare, Eric 8–9
Department of the
    Environment 166
District and Circle Line,
    London 130, 166
Dunster, Bill 19
Dynamic Earth, Edinburgh
    14, 15, 16, *16*, 72, 82,
    83–9, 218, *230*, 231
Eames, Charles 13, 14,
    161, 169
Eco, Umberto 230
Edinburgh 82, 231
Emmanuel College,
    Cambridge 9–11, *11*, 19,
    52, *53–9*, 124, 160, 186
energy conservation 16
    Inland Revenue Centre
        36–8
    Jubilee Campus,
        University of Nottingham
        90–2, *106–7*
    New Parliamentary
        Building 138, 159
    Wildscreen 116
European Union 16
Evelina Children's
    Hospital, London 16,
    210, *211–13*
Financial Times 168, 230
Finlay, Ian Hamilton 226
flats, Charterhouse 124,
    128–9
Flaubert, Gustave 224
Folkestone 72
Foster, Norman 6, 168,
    169

Hong Kong and Shanghai
    Bank *160*
Frampton, Kenneth 158
Fuller, Buckminster 8, 222
Functionalism 161
Furneaux Jordan, Robert
    11
Gaddafi, Muammar 225
Gehry, Frank
Guggenheim Museum,
    Bilbao 225
Glyndebourne Opera
    House, Sussex 8, 11, 13,
    13, 14, 16, 22–4, *23–35*,
    52, 166–7, 169, 186,
    190, 231
Goodwood racecourse 11,
    15, 194, *195–7*
Gothic architecture 138,
    156, 158, 163, *226*, 227
Greaves, James 19, 168
Greek architecture 225–6,
    231
Greene King Brewery,
    Bury St Edmonds 6, 166
Grimshaw, Nicolas 6
Guarini, Guarino
    Palazzo Carignano 228,
    230
Haberdashers' Hall,
    London 11, 14, 190,
    191–3
Hampshire County Cricket
    Club 11, 15, 170, *171–3*
Herland, Hugh 163
High-Tech style 6, 8, 11,
    13, 15–16, 156, 222,
    225, 228
Honnecourt, Villard de 227
Hopkins' House,
    Hampstead 6, *7*, 169,
    224, 225
hospital

Evelina Children's
    Hospital, London 210,
    211–13
Hutton, James 82
IBM 13, 166, 168, 169, 218
IMAX cinema, Wildscreen
    114, *119–21*
Inland Revenue Centre,
    Nottingham 8, 13, 14,
    15, 16, 19, *19*, 36–8,
    37–51, 72, 74, 167, 218
International Style 222
Ipswich 218
Jagger, Chris 167
Jewish Care, London 14,
    66, *67–71*
Jones, Inigo
    Banqueting House,
        London 163
Jubilee Campus,
    University of Nottingham
    15, 16, 19, *19–21*, 90–2,
    91–107, 167, 168, 169,
    214, 218
Jubilee Line extension
    (JLE) 130, *131–5*, 136,
    158, 166
Kahn, Louis 14–15
    Phillips Exeter Academy,
        New Hampshire 14, *14*
King Fahad National
    Library, Saudi Arabia 202,
    203–5
laboratories
    Pilkington Laboratories,
        Sherborne School 108,
        109–13
    University College
        Suffolk 218
Laon Cathedral *226*
Lasdun, Denys
    Royal National Theatre,
        London 158, *158*

Le Corbusier 11–13, 224,
    226, 227
Ronchamp 225
Lethaby, William 156, *159*,
    163
libraries
    King Fahad National
        Library, Saudi Arabia 202,
        203–5
    Norfolk and Norwich
        Millennium Project 186
    University College
        Suffolk *220*
Libya 225–6
lighting
    Inland Revenue Centre
        36
    Jewish Care 66
    New Parliamentary
        Building 138, *149*, 159,
        160, 163
London Underground 130,
    136, 166
Loos, Adolf 156
Lord's Cricket Ground 8, *8*,
    11, 13, 158, 169, 170,
    225, *225*, 228, 231
Los Angeles Stock
    Exchange 222, 224
Lutyens, Edwin 11, 225
Mackintosh, Charles
    Rennie 158
Manchester City Art
    Gallery 174, *175–7*
Martin, Leslie
    Royal Festival Hall,
        London 158, *158*
masonry structures 13
materials 16–19
Maxwell, Robert 224
MEPC 164–6, 169
Mies van der Rohe,
    Ludwig 13, 14, 222, 224,

225, 228
Illinois Institute of
    Technology 13
Seagram Building, New
    York 13
Millennium Commission
    82, 114, 186
Miralles, Enric
    Scottish Parliament 231
Modernism 156, 222–4,
    225, 228
Mound Stand, Lord's
    Cricket Ground 8, *8*, 11,
    13, 158, 169, 170, 225,
    225, 228, 231
Nash, John
    St James' Park, London
        198, 200
National College of School
    Leadership 214, *215–17*
New Parliamentary
    Building, London 8, 11,
    13, 14, 15, *15*, 16, 19,
    130, *133*, 136–8,
    137–55, 156–63, *157*,
    161, *162*, 166, 169, 225,
    225–7, 227, 228
New Square Development,
    Bedfont Lakes *12*, 13,
    164–6
Norfolk and Norwich
    Millennium Project 11,
    186, *187–9*
Norman Shaw House,
    London 136, 138, 159,
    160–1, 166
Norwich Cathedral
    Education and Visitors'
    Centre 11, 14, 182,
    183–5
Nottingham 36, 167
Noyon Cathedral *226*
offices

Inland Revenue Centre, Nottingham 36–8, *37–51*
New Parliamentary Building 136–8, *137–55*, 161
Saga Group Headquarters, Folkestone 72–4, *73–81*
Wellcome Trust 206, *207–9*
Onions, John 225–6
Palace of Westminster, London 136, 138, *140, 142*, 156–8, 161–3, 228
Palladio, Andrea 225
Panofsky, Erwin 227
Parliament *see* New Parliamentary Building, London
Parthenon, Athens 226
Patera Building System 6, *9*, 13
Paxton, Joseph
  Crystal Palace, London 156, *158*, 225
Pennethorne, Sir James 178
Pevsner, Nikolaus 222–4
photovoltaic cells 92, *106*
Pilkington Laboratories, Sherborne School 6, *9*, 108, *109–13*, 124
planetarium
  Dynamic Earth 82, *85, 89*
Plato 224
Portcullis House, London *see* New Parliamentary Building
Portsmouth 169
Post-Modernism 228, 230
prefabrication 19

Price, Cedric 224
Pringle, John 19, 168
Prouvé, Jean 13, 14
Pugin, AWN
  Palace of Westminster, London 156–8, 160, 161
Queen's Building, Emmanuel College, Cambridge 11, *11*, 13, 14, 19, 52, *53–9*, 124, 160, 186
Raphael 225
Reims Cathedral *226*, 227
Renaissance 225
Reynolds, Joshua 178
RIBA 168
Ricci, Leonardo 163
Richardson, Albert 11, 159
Financial Times building 19, 230
Riyadh 202
Rogers, Richard 6, 168
Romaniuk, Peter 19
Royal Academy of Arts, London 11, 178, *179–81*
Saga Group Headquarters, Folkestone 13, 14, 15, 16, *16*, 38, 72–4, *73–81*, 186, 218
St James' Park, London 198
St Thomas's Hospital, 210
Saudi Arabia 202
Schinkel, Karl Friedrich 13
Schlumberger Research Centre, Cambridge 6, 13, 15, 16, *17*, 38, 72, 168, *224*, 225
Selby, David 19, 168
Shankland, Graham 11
Sharratt, Ian 19, 168
Shaw, Norman 160–1, 179

sheltered housing
  Charterhouse, London 124, *125–9*
Sherborne School 6, *9*, 14, 108, *109–13*, 124
Smithson, Peter and Alison 224
  Economist Building, London 160
Sports Council 108
stations
  Westminster Underground Station 130, *131–5*, 136, 166
Stevens, Sam 224
Stirling, James 11
stonework
  Dynamic Earth 82
  Emmanuel College 52
  Pilkington Laboratories 108, *109*
structural rationalism 13, 16
Suffolk 169
Summerson, John 11, 228
Sydney Opera House 231
symmetry 14–15
Taylor, William 19, 168
tents 15–16
  Buckingham Palace Ticket Office 60, *61, 63–5*
  Dynamic Earth 82, *83–9*
  Glyndebourne Opera House *31*
  Goodwood Racecourse 194
  Hampshire County Cricket Club 169
  Inland Revenue Centre 38, *41, 46, 50–1*
  Saga Group Headquarters 72, *73, 80–1*

University College Suffolk 218, *220*
Wildscreen *115*, 116, *118–19, 122–3*
Teulon, SS 72
Thatcher, Margaret 222
theatres
  Dynamic Earth 82, *88*, 231
  Glyndebourne Opera House 22–4, *23–35*
  Norfolk and Norwich Millennium Project 186
Tropical House, Wildscreen 114, 116, *117–19, 122–3*
University College Suffolk 218, *219–21*
University of East Anglia 218
University of Nottingham 19, *19–21*, 90–2, *91–107*, 167, 168, 169, 214
V&A Museum, London 167
ventilation
  Buckingham Palace Ticket Office 60
  The Cakehouse, St James' Park 198
  Glyndebourne Opera House 24
  Inland Revenue Centre 36–8, *42–3*
  Jubilee Campus, University of Nottingham 90–2, *101, 106–7*
  King Fahad National Library 202
  New Parliamentary

Building 138, *149*, 159, 161
Saga Group Headquarters 72, 74
Venturi, Robert 160
Verity, Frank 8
Vertue, Robert 163
Viollet-le-Duc, Eugène 226, 228, *228*
Voysey, CFA 156, *159*
Wellcome Trust 206, *207–9*
Westminster Abbey, London 163
Westminster Hall, London 161–3, *163*
Westminster Underground Station, London 130, *131–5*, 136, 159, 166
Wildscreen at Bristol 15, 16, 38, 114–16, *115–23*
Willis Faber 168
windows
  Charterhouse 124, *129*
  Inland Revenue Centre 36
  Jewish Care 66
  New Parliamentary Building 138, *149*, 159, 160, 161
  Pilkington Laboratories *113*
woodwork
  Buckingham Palace Ticket Office 60, *61*
  Glyndebourne Opera House 22
  Haberdashers' Hall 190, *192*
  Jubilee Campus, University of Nottingham 90

Woollen Mill, Stonehouse 9
Wren, Christopher 52
Wright, Frank Lloyd
  Guggenheim Museum, New York 92, 96
Yevele, Henry 161

Photography credits

(l) left, (r) right, (t) top, (c) centre, (b) bottom

© Dave Bower p8(bl)
©Martin Charles p10, p13, p26/7, p29, p30, p31(cl), p32, p45, p159(bl,bc), p225(bl,bc)
©Chorley Handford p39
©Gus Christie p31(tr)
©Sean Corrigan p185(tr), p211
Hayes Davidson p75(bl)
©Richard Davies cover, p8(br), p15, p23, p25, p28, p43(tl), p121(tl), p137, p139(tr), p140/1, p143, p146(tl,tc,tr,cl,cr), p147(tc,tr,cl,cr), p148, p149(tl,tc), p150/1, p152, p153(tr,c), p154(tl,c), p155, p157, p161, p162, p165, p169, p180, p193(b), p195(b), p199(b), p201(b), p215(b), p216, p219(b), p221(tl,c), p225(br), p227
Alan Delaney p229
©Dynamic Earth p85(r)
©Mark Fiennes p11(bl)
©Chris Gascoigne/VIEW p67
©Dennis Gilbert/VIEW p9(cl), p11(bc), p16(bc), p17, p19(bc), p37, p40/1, p42, p47, p48, p51, p53, p55, p56, p57(cr), p58tl, p59, p68(b), p69(cr), p70(t,b), p73, p75(tr), p76/7, p78, p80(tr), p81, p99, p103(cr), p109, p111(b), p112(tl,c), p113, p115, p117, p118, p119(tc), p121(tc,b), p122, p131, p132, p134(tr), 224(cr)
GMJ Design p207(b), p208(tr)
©Len Grant p176(tl), p177(tl,tc)
©Martine Hamilton Knight p20/21, p44(tl), p94/5, p97, p100, p102, p105
©Mike Hoban p34(tl), p35
Patrick Hodgkinson p163(bl)
Tom Holdom p123(c,tr)
©Keith Hunter p16(bl), p83, p84(bl), p89, p223, p230(tr)
©Ahrend-Michael Jones p44(cr)
Jonathan Knight p44tc, p50(tl,c)
Ian Lambot p160
Sir Denys Lasdun p158(c)
Ian Lawson p91, p101(tr), p104, p106(tl,c)
©Peter MacKinven/Ove Arup & Partners p19(bl)
©Peter MacKinven/VIEW p86/7, p230(cr)
©Manchester City Art Gallery p175(tc), p176 (b)
Melon Studio Ltd p171(b), p216/7
©Tom Miller p187(b), p203(b), p179
©James Mortimer p7
©University of Nottingham p93(tl)
Ianthe Ruthven p125, p126, p127(c), p128(tl), p129(b)
Amir Sanei p192(tl)
©Timothy Soar p12, p18, p61, p62(b), p63(cr), p64/5
South Bank Board Press Office p158(c)
Michael Taylor p189
©Morley Von Sternberg p9(tl), p34(c)
©Matthew Weinreb p224(bl)
Adam Wilson p119(tr)

Acknowledgements

Michael Hopkins and Partners would like to thank Rebecca Chipchase, Nicky Dewe, Chris Gray and Jenny Stevens for their assistance, as well as the IT department, finance team, library and administration department of Michael Hopkins and Partners. Thanks are also extended to Colin Davies, Patrick Hodgkinson, Charles Jencks and Paul Finch for their texts, and to John Hewitt for his contribution to this book.